On 31 January 1968, three days after the beginning of the Tet holidays, mortar and rocket fire began pouring into our compound. It sounded like the Fourth of July, except louder. The Communist 122mm rocket was particularly menacing. It weighed 112 pounds and had a range of ten miles. Carrying an immense warhead of forty-two pounds, each one sounded like a low jet fighter ripping through the sky overhead. They made thunderous explosions, which shook the ground. Although extremely inaccurate, they scattered huge chunks of jagged metal, which tore through anyone and anything in its kill radius.

Rushing into the bunkers, we stumbled and fell on top of one another like the Keystone Kops. Explosions continued, jolting the ground around us. The bunker was a four-foot-deep, four-foot-wide trench, protected by a steel culvert and a few layers of sandbags. It probably could not have withstood a direct hit, especially from one of the rockets. . . .

PATHFINDER

First in, Last Out

Richard R. Burns

BALLANTINE BOOKS • NEW YORK

A Ballantine Book
Published by The Ballantine Publishing Group
Copyright © 2002 by Cathy Burns
Introduction copyright © 2002 by Gary A. Linderer

www.ballantinebooks.com

ISBN 0-8041-1602-4

Manufactured in the United States of America

First Edition: March 2002

10 9 8 7 6 5 4 3 2 1

Introduction

It is a signal honor to write this introduction to *Pathfinder*. I am one among many who have been honored to call Richie Burns my friend. Our ties go back to 1968, in Vietnam, where we crossed paths in the 101st Airborne Division at Camp Eagle. He and some of his fellow Pathfinders used to come over to the LRP compound and visit. Two of Richie's mates, Buz Harding and Ron Reynolds, extended six months to serve with the LRPs; Richie returned to the states. Ron was killed while serving on a long range patrol mission in the A Shau Valley in May, 1969; Buz made it home.

When Richie and I reconnected in 1991, he was working as a therapist in the psych program at the Veterans Administration hospital in Gainesville, Florida. It was then that I discovered that Richie had decided to stay in the army, returning to Vietnam to serve an extended tour as a Pathfinder and an adviser to the South Vietnamese Airborne. After completing this tour, Richie joined Special Forces and served the remainder of his twenty-year military career with 10th Group, retiring with the rank of E-8. I guess I can claim some responsibility for Richie becoming a writer. I conned him into writing a column for *Behind The Lines,* a military special-operations magazine that I published. His column, called *Burns' Ointment,* educated veterans on the causes and effects of PTSD. Richie's insight on that topic was both unique and innovative, and his advice to troubled vets proved more effective than the ineffective pap coming from VA psychologists and psychiatrists around the country. It wasn't long before the column became highly popular among our subscribers, many of whom contacted him to seek help. Generously, Richie gave it.

He never considered himself a writer; his communications skills were apparent to all but him. He graciously agreed to be the guest speaker at two LRP/Ranger reunions that I attended and proved to be the highlight of the entire reunion.

I tried for years to get Richie to write a book about his experiences in Vietnam, but his humility would not allow him to tell his story when so many others had yet to be told. It was about this time that Richie was diagnosed with colon cancer. I still remember the day he told me that he had beaten the cancer after a successful operation and had decided to take my advice and start writing his book.

Richie's cancer returned a year later, this time with a vengeance. He started a long battle to defeat the horrible disease that had attacked him in the prime of his life, as it was to so many other Vietnam vets. Richie made up his mind that this insidious disease would not defeat him, nor would it keep him from completing his book. He told me that he had too much to live for and too much to do to let cancer get the best of him. He had a lovely wife and two fine children to support him.

Well, he finished the book. He wouldn't let anyone read it until it was done. Ballantine editor Chris Evans sent me the completed book proof when he asked me to write the introduction. I've had my share of honors during my life. Writing the intro for *Pathfinder* ranks as one of the greatest. This story of a young man's combat tour as a Pathfinder with the elite 101st Airborne Division in Vietnam is a lesson in duty, courage, brotherhood, and love. The role of the Pathfinders in the Vietnam war is a well-kept secret. I know of no other book that has told their story. These small detachments of dedicated professionals quietly went about their business, developing their trade and improving their skills in a war that became more and more reliant on helicopters. No one will ever know how many American and allied lives they saved by their dedicated performance under fire. When you read this book you will understand what I mean. Richard Burns has done a great service to his fellow Pathfinders, sharing his and their stories with the rest of us. No longer will their valor and achievement go unrecognized. He has brought them to the light where legends are made.

Richie lost his final battle with cancer on October 19, 2001. He died just a few months before he could see the birth of his first grandchild or witness his book in print. He died as he lived—a loving husband and father, a man, a soldier, and a brother to his brothers. This book is his legacy. We will miss him, but we know that he has gone on ahead, preparing the LZ—always the Pathfinder.

Gary A. Linderer
F Company, 58th Inf. (LRP)
101st Airborne Division

A scholarship fund has been set up in honor of Richard Burns at Florida State University. Anyone wishing to make a donation should make their checks out to:

FSU Foundation—The Richard Burns Scholarship Fund

Mail to:

The Florida State University
School of Social Work
Tallahassee, Florida 32306-2570 Attention: Patricia Handschy

Donor Name _____

Address _____

_____

Phone number _____

Donation amount _____

Pledge amount (yearly)_____for ____years

Donations are tax deductible.

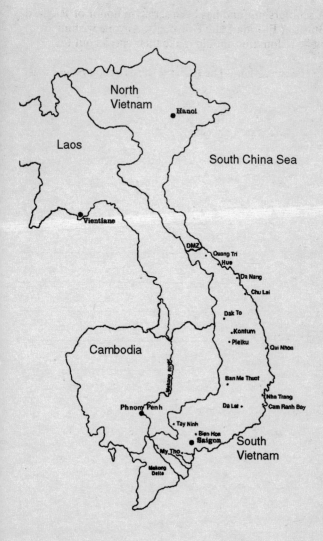

Chapter One

The C-119 cargo plane sat on the airstrip at Fort Benning, its engines whining. The smell of the aircraft's exhaust filled my nostrils. It looked like a large rectangular box with curved corners and two long tails protruding toward the rear. Now I understood why it was nicknamed the "flying boxcar." I wondered how the hell something configured in that shape could possibly fly. It was my first parachute jump, and I was mentally rehashing all of the jump procedures that had been taught over the past two weeks.

The jumpmaster screamed out, "Roster number sixty-seven!"

I responded automatically, "Here, Sergeant!"

He pointed his finger at the ground. "This is your position in the stick."

I quickly placed myself in line and snapped to attention as best I could while wearing the parachute. "Clear, Sergeant. Airborne!"

I couldn't believe my luck. I was positioned as third from the last man to jump. What a relief! All weekend I had dreaded being the first man in the door. I was afraid of heights and didn't want to stand in the door and look down at the ground for any length of time. I had flown in a plane only once in my life, and that had scared the hell out of me.

After a few moments, my stick boarded the left side of the aircraft and we took our seats. The cabin held forty-two jumpers, so we were packed like sardines. In no time I felt the perspiration building inside the sweatband of my helmet and on my hands.

1

The plane raced down the runway, its engines shriek-ing. I could barely hear myself speak to the guy sitting next to me. Jolting forward, the aircraft quickly increased speed. The rapid acceleration thrust my upper torso to-ward the rear. We were airborne in a matter of seconds. Everyone on board was solemn.

The plane repeatedly vaulted and swayed, making the flight to the drop zone especially rough. During a previous class, one of the instructors had said he was more afraid of riding in a C-119 than of jumping out of one. As the plane continued to bounce and weave about the sky, I began to understand the significance of his comment.

The jumpmaster opened the door, releasing a deafen-ing roar of wind. I was overwhelmed by the sound of the blast; it was much louder than I had imagined it would be. A brilliant light from the outside invaded the cabin.

The jumpmaster rendered the six-minute warning. Moments later, he thrust both his palms straight out in our direction and shouted the first jump command, "Get ready!" We had rehearsed the jump commands so many times, the response was instantaneous. Everyone slapped their hands to their knees and placed one foot forward. Although I couldn't hear his next command, I could see the jumpmaster rotate his arms into the air, gesturing the second command, "Stand up!"

I was somewhat surprised by the feebleness in my legs as I rose to my feet. As the jumpmaster continued the jump-command sequence, the time it took us to carry out his in-structions seemed much faster than when in training. I thought, this is it, the moment we've all trained so hard for.

In no time I heard the command I had eagerly awaited but also dreaded: "Go!"

The first student left the plane. The rest of us started shuffling toward the door. I heard the snap hooks scraping and banging against the anchor-line cable and the jump-master repeatedly yelling "Go!" My mouth was dry, my lips sticking together. Now only three students were left in front of me. As the light at the door rapidly approached, I gaped at the brightness. The man in front of me leaped into the open space. I stared in amazement as his body was momentarily suspended in the air, then violently swept away.

It was my turn; my heart was pounding. Determined to jump on command, I hurriedly positioned myself in the door. The moment I'd imagined for so long was about to occur. I stared into the blue sky and clouds and awaited the tap that would send me leaping into the air. Suddenly the jumpmaster waved his hand in front of my face.

"Hold it!"

Stunned and confused, I wondered if I had done something wrong. He shouted in my ear, "Ran out of drop zone, gonna have to make another go-around. Just relax and stay where you are."

In any other setting I would have laughed over the irony of the situation. Here I was, on my first parachute jump, afraid of heights, standing in the door, 1,250 feet in the air, and this guy is telling me to relax and not to go anywhere. I stared out to the horizon and tried not to look down. That proved impossible as the plane banked on my side, causing me to face the earth horizontally. I wondered why I wasn't falling out and concluded that centrifugal force must be holding me in place, the way it did on amusement park rides. Then I wondered why I was even worried about falling out, since I had a parachute on anyway. I let out a sigh of relief as the plane leveled again. The jumpmaster must have sensed my nervousness. "Are you scared, trooper?"

"Yes, Sergeant."

"Good. As long as you're scared, you won't screw up."

The plane banked again, then leveled off. The jumpmaster pointed to a patch sewn on the left pocket of his field jacket. It was a large, colorful patch, backgrounded in black, with a yellow winged torch and a bright red flame streaking across it. "Do you know what this is?"

"No, Sergeant!"

"This is a Pathfinder badge."

It was a beautiful patch. As a matter of fact, it was the

most colorful patch I had ever seen in the army. At that
precise moment, however, I really didn't care. Didn't he realize that in a few minutes I could be dead? I peeked down
at the ground and saw how small the trees appeared; I immediately stared back at the horizon again. He pointed to
the ground below. "Do you see those trees?"

"Yes, Sergeant!" My eyes were watering from the wind,
but hoping he might relate something of importance I
would need to know, I strained to take a long look.

"That's where Pathfinders jump, in the trees. If you're
lucky enough, someday you might be a Pathfinder."

"Yes, Sergeant!" I yelled in a soldierly manner. I
thought to myself, Are you kidding? I'll be lucky just to
make it through the next few minutes.

I felt the jumpmaster's tap as he yelled, "Go!"

Unhesitatingly, I leaped out the door. My body reacted unconsciously as a result of endless hours of jump-
school indoctrination.

"One thousand . . ." I heard myself counting above
the roar of the wind. The blast threw my legs up above
me; I felt my body swirl through the sky. On the count of
"four thousand," I came to an abrupt stop as the canopy
snapped open. I glanced upward, observing the plane
streaking away a few hundred feet above me. God, what
a sight! I checked the canopy for tears or holes, then
viewed the drop zone below. It was very quiet; everything
seemed peaceful and serene. I felt like I was on top of the
world, and I didn't want to come down. It was an exhilarating feeling. At that moment, I knew I wanted to continue jumping, maybe even for the rest of my life.

Our second parachute jump was that afternoon.
Everyone was swapping jump stories as we trucked to the
barracks. Crescendos of laughter followed each tale, and
they became more extravagant as time went on. I was beginning to understand the deep camaraderie I'd heard
existed among Airborne soldiers. I felt I had finally discovered my niche in life.

On the third jump I hit the ground really hard. The

winds were high, and I came smashing in to the rear. I didn't have my chin tucked in tight, as I'd been instructed; therefore, my head slammed into the ground. I stood up, fixed in a daze until a medical jeep arrived. The medics asked me simple questions, but I couldn't remember anything. It immediately became apparent that I had sustained a concussion along with some form of amnesia.

A medevac (ambulance helicopter) flew me off the drop zone to Martin Army Hospital. I had been there a few hours awaiting X rays when an injured sergeant arrived. He appeared to have a broken leg. There was something strangely familiar about him. I continued to stare at him, trying to remember where I had seen him before. In minutes my mind cleared. I recognized him as one of my classmates. Instantly, my memory returned. I pleaded with the doctor to release me. The last thing I needed was to be recycled and not graduate with my class. The doctor tried to persuade me to stay, but I guess he felt sorry for me, because he let me go. I had a hell of a headache, but I made damn sure I had my chin tucked in on the following two jumps.

Graduation day came at the end of Jump Week. Of the one thousand students beginning Class 27, a little over five hundred made it to graduation. Someone barked loudly over the intercom that all students were to fall out of the barracks and load up on the trucks for transport to Infantry Hall for the graduation ceremony. Everyone looked very sharp in their dress greens, showing off glider patches and spit-shined jump boots.

I was climbing onto the truck when I heard my name called. I was ordered to report to the 43d Company orderly room to the first sergeant. I had never reported to a first sergeant before and felt anxious as I stood at attention in front of his desk. First Sergeant Donovan then proceeded to render me a royal ass-chewing for having gotten hurt on his drop zone. After he was finished, he instructed me to get the hell out of his office at a double time if I wanted to graduate. I ran through the doorway before he had a chance to change his mind. As I was fleeing, I detected a slight grin on the first sergeant's face. When I got outside, I had no problem climbing onto the bed of the truck, since I was ten pounds lighter in my fourth point of contact.

The days that followed consisted of two or three formations a day, during which one of the cadre would yell out assignments. After the roll call, those who had orders threw their duffel bags onto trucks and were driven to an out-processing facility.

It was early March 1967, and the majority of assignments were to Vietnam with the 173d Airborne Brigade or the 1st Brigade, 101st Airborne Division. By the end of the second day, most of my classmates had shipped out. I was becoming increasingly concerned that I might not be sent to Vietnam. Although I had graduated from high school and completed basic, infantry, and airborne training, I had not yet reached my eighteenth birthday. I thought that my age had somehow held me back from receiving a combat assignment.

On the morning of the third day, the TAC (teach, access, and counseling) sergeant called off twelve names; mine was among them.

"You cherries be back here in one hour wearing clean fatigues and spit-shined boots. You shitbirds are going to be interviewed for an assignment right here at Fort Benning."

I couldn't believe it. I was getting screwed out of going to Vietnam. But why? It couldn't be just because I was seventeen; the rest of the guys standing with me were all eighteen or over. I stared at each one of them, trying to determine what we might all have in common. Damned if I knew. I'd figure something out. I didn't join the paratroops to sit out the war at Fort Benning, Georgia.

An hour later we marched a mile down the road to a wooden World War II vintage building. Above the front door was a large scroll that read: 187 PATHFINDER DET. I immediately became apprehensive. First of all, I didn't want to be stationed Stateside and miss out on the war. Second, I didn't want to spend the rest of my time parachuting into trees and clearing paths with a machete. I thought I would decline the interview but I was afraid that if I voiced my opinion, I'd piss off the TAC sergeant. So I thought, What the hell? I'll go along for the ride. Besides, I won't get selected anyway.

I didn't have to wait long; I was picked first to report inside. I stepped into the room. Behind a long table sat a lieutenant, a staff sergeant, and two buck sergeants. I was struck by the age of the lieutenant. At first I thought I'd read his rank wrong. He was much older than the others.

"Private Burns reports as ordered, sir."

The lieutenant addressed me. "Have a seat, Private. Do you know why you are here?"

I tried not to appear nervous as I answered, "Not really, sir!"

"Well, six of our men have received orders for Vietnam, and we need replacements. We have decided to interview you based on your aptitude scores. Do you know what kind of unit we are?"

I was pretty sure it was a Pathfinder unit because of the scroll over the front door, and each person on the panel had a Pathfinder badge on his left breast pocket. I was confused, however, since each had a black baseball hat with airborne wings attached. I thought only the jump instructors wore black hats. I took a guess. "I believe you're a Pathfinder unit, sir."

"That's correct. Do you know what Pathfinders do?"

Now I took advantage of the opportunity to impress him with my vast knowledge. I remembered the words of the jumpmaster on my first jump. "Well, sir, I do know that you jump into trees."

A roar of spontaneous laughter erupted among the panel members. I certainly didn't know what was so hilarious. The staff sergeant said something to the lieutenant like, "I don't believe it!" After they regained their composure, the lieutenant, still chuckling, responded, "Well, unfortunately, I have to admit you're right; we do have a tendency to land in the trees at times."

The staff sergeant grinned at the lieutenant. He then stared back at me, his expression suddenly becoming serious. "I'll tell you what Pathfinders do. Pathfinders are the first in and the last out. That's the Pathfinder motto!"

"We work in two- or three-man teams, sometimes even alone. We either parachute, rappel, or helicopter into an area to guide the rest of the forces into the drop or landing zone." He pointed to the flaming torch embroidered on his Pathfinder badge. "That's what this torch symbolizes. We light the way for the rest of the Airborne."

There was a slight pause, then he continued. "We also have to be experts in communications, air-traffic control, call for fire, and a hundred other skills." He glanced back at the lieutenant. "And yes, in this detachment, some of us do hit the trees, but we usually leave that to the lower enlisted or the officers."

There was another roar of laughter, then the lieutenant muttered, "I don't know about that. I landed in my share of trees as an NCO [see Glossary for explanation of this and other military terms]."

I was too confused to understand what they were joking about. I thought the sergeant had said something unfavorable about officers, but the lieutenant was laughing. I was also surprised by the familiarity they displayed toward one another, disregarding rank. They all seemed very comfortable together.

The lieutenant went on to explain that all of them seated at the table had served in Vietnam with Airborne units and that he was a former Special Forces NCO. I expressed my concern about the possibility of missing out on a chance to fight for my country if selected. He and the others assured me that the likelihood of my eventually going to Vietnam was fairly good. Moreover, Pathfinder training would only increase my combat skills. Impressed by their experience and manner, I told them that if I was picked for their unit, I would do my best. It was around noontime the next day when the six of us selected received word to report to the 187th Pathfinder Detachment.

A basic Pathfinder detachment consisted of two officers and thirteen enlisted men. Each member had to be a qualified parachutist and either Pathfinder qualified or preparing to attend Pathfinder school. The 187th Pathfinder Detachment was understrength; consequently, it consisted of only one lieutenant, one staff sergeant, two sergeants, and two corporals. Normally, privates were never assigned to the unit out of jump school, but Vietnam was sucking up Airborne NCOs at a fast pace.

The primary mission of the 187th was to provide Pathfinder support and demonstrations of airmobile operations to the infantry school and units assigned to Fort Benning. In the months that followed, we newly assigned privates learned to set up drop zones for personnel and equipment, landing zones for rotor and fixed-winged aircraft, air traffic control, and the rigging and sling loading of equipment. Training was conducted day and night. All classes were taught first in the classroom and then hands-on in the field.

We got plenty of parachute jumps. Besides jumping on missions, we also put on Pathfinder demonstrations every other week for graduating infantry officer candidates to impress upon them the importance and new strategic value of airmobile techniques. Four of us would parachute from an army fixed-wing U-6 Beaver into a small drop zone called Concord DZ. We would then set up a helicopter landing zone for extraction. Concord DZ was so tiny that at least one of us always landed in the tall pine trees that surrounded it.

In early July our detachment received four slots for Pathfinder school. Upon arrival we were escorted to our living quarters, an open bay with bunk beds. As I was making my bunk, a tall private first class from the 101st Airborne Division approached. Pointing to the bed next to mine, he asked, "Is this bunk free?"

I glanced around, "Yeah, I think so. I haven't seen anyone take it yet."

"Good!" He threw his duffel bag down and reached out his hand. "Hi! My name is Ron Reynolds. I'm from the 101st Pathfinders at Fort Campbell. There's a few of us here from my unit, along with our lieutenant."

I shook his hand and said, "Glad to meet you. My name is Richie Burns. I'm stationed here at Benning with the 187th Pathfinders. There's a group of us here from my unit also."

Reynolds chuckled. "You sure do talk funny. Where the hell are you from, New Yawk?"

I was taken aback. *I* talked funny. That guy's drawl was so bad that if he were counting to four on a static-line jump and had a malfunction, he'd bounce before he got to number three. "No, I'm not from New Yaaawk. I'm from Massachusetts, near Boston."

"Oh, Bawston, Massa-tusetts." He smiled. "I could tell you were a damned Yankee."

Now, normally a remark like that would have pissed me off, but the guy had a genuine warmness about him that instantly told me it was all in fun. We both laughed and immediately hit it off. In the weeks that followed, Reynolds proved to be an extremely intelligent individual who exhibited leadership and confidence. His mild manner, personality, and demeanor reminded me of Sheriff Taylor of *The Andy Griffith Show*.

The Pathfinder course was five weeks in duration and proved to be physically and academically demanding. Students learned how to establish and control helicopter and airplane landing zones, drop zones, and the proper use of a variety of navigational aids.

Instructors drilled us in the techniques of air-traffic control, ground-to-air communications, and aircraft guidance procedures. This was especially important when dealing with airplanes. They forced us to memorize a number of formulas vital to calculating time, distance, and the speed of aircraft. Furthermore, we had to consistently commit to memory aircraft tail numbers and their location in traffic at all times. Lack of proper control, not understanding flight patterns, or forgetting where each plane was located in traffic could cause a crash or midair collision.

Pathfinder delivery methods, such as helicopter assault, rappelling, parachuting, and land infiltration, were rehearsed regularly. On a helicopter assault, it was imperative that Pathfinders either precede or accompany the first aircraft into the landing zone (LZ) in order to decide the best direction for approach and departure, plan the number of helicopters that could safely land at one time, check the surface winds and conditions, and provide warning of the enemy situation or of obstacles.

We practiced parachuting, land navigation and patrolling, and rappelling as ways to infiltrate into denied areas. Proficiency in rappelling also proved essential for retrieving downed aircraft in areas with heavy vegetation.

I was fortunate to have received much of this training back at the detachment. However, the Pathfinder school program of instruction was more comprehensive, so I remained consistently on the go. In that kind of training environment, a student had to stay motivated and alert or anything could happen.

An example of the mishaps possible occurred while jumping in on a field-training exercise. Five of us were loaded down with various electronic and visual navigational aids in addition to our individual and combat equipment. Our mission was to parachute into an area at dusk and set up a night, fixed-wing landing strip. The jump aircraft was an army U-1 Otter airplane capable of holding five parachutists with full equipment. The Otter, like the U-6 Beaver, is exited from the sitting position; the height of the door is less than four feet.

All of our equipment was packed in a parachutist adjustable equipment (PAE) bag weighing approximately ninety pounds and attached vertically to the front of each jumper. The bag was secured to the jumper's leg by a retaining strap to prevent it from swaying during the opening of the parachute. Two quick-release straps were rigged to the top of the container, and a twenty-foot lowering line was attached from the bag to the parachute harness. This allowed the jumper to disconnect the bag from his body before landing. It is imperative the jumper pull both releases simultaneously. (On a previous PAE jump, I tried pulling one release at a time. The heavy weight of the bag jammed the second release, and I rode the bag into the ground. Fortunately, I just received a lot of bruises and a bloody nose, but I sure learned my lesson.)

Sergeant Fountain, the Pathfinder instructor, shouted the command, "Stand up!" We secured our seats in the up position and sat on the floor. We proceeded through the normal sequence of jump commands, and when the first man was told, "Sit in the door!" he took his position. Exiting the Otter for the first three jumpers is not too difficult because they are relatively close to the door. Jumpers four and five have it rough, however, because they must slide across the floor from the front of the aircraft to the rear. This is quite a distance to maneuver when loaded down with a PAE bag. Unfortunately for me, I was jumper number five.

The green light came on. Sergeant Fountain yelled "Go!"

The first and second man left the plane. The third was struggling to the door. I yelled to the jumper in front of me, "Start moving forward!"

He was a foreign classmate, from Tunisia, so I thought perhaps he didn't understand me. He looked confused, so I pointed to the door. "Let's go! Move forward!"

Now, all three jumpers in front of us were gone. Damn, it seemed like the door was a football field away. Sliding across the floor was really strenuous. Our legs were restricted by the weight and length of the PAE bag; we couldn't bend our knees.

The Tunisian eventually positioned himself in the door. Sergeant Fountain motioned for him to go, but he didn't move; he just stayed there. Fountain had his hand on the man's shoulder and was screaming "Go!" The Tunisian looked up, terrified. He was either frozen in the door or caught somehow on the aircraft. Fountain got behind him and gave him a shove. I heard the Tunisian yell as he tumbled from the opening.

Too much time had elapsed, and I knew Sergeant Fountain was going to stop me, because we were running out of drop zone. I was too psyched up to wait for a second go-around; I wanted out.

I quickly thrust my legs forward, attempting to grasp the outside of the aircraft. As I strived to get a hold, the wind caught my legs and yanked me outward. I slid down the side of the aircraft, my left shoulder and equipment bouncing off its skin. Damn it! I'm going to be towed! I looked up and saw the plane's tail whoosh over my head. I instantly began rehashing in my mind the procedures a towed jumper was to perform, then I felt the opening shock of the parachute. Whew!

I regained my composure and glanced up to check my canopy. I swear my suspension lines looked as if they were twisted all the way to the skirt of the parachute. Kicking my legs in a bicycle movement, I finally spiraled the lines free. Once unwound, I viewed the landscape below. I could barely see the drop zone. I was going to have a hell of a hump with all the equipment. At least the slower drop speed of the Otter had caused a sluggish deployment of my parachute. I would have drifted even farther away if I'd had a longer time under canopy.

The ground was coming up fast. At approximately one hundred feet I released the PAE bag and felt a hard tug as it reached the end of the lowering line. The wind had picked up and the terrain was speeding under my feet. I prepared to perform a right parachute landing fall (PLF) when I noticed a barbed-wire fence swiftly approaching. I tucked my knees into my chest and just skimmed over it. I heard a loud grunt as my body slammed into the earth. The force of the wind kept my chute inflated. It was tugging at me, but I wasn't being dragged. Something had me anchored. My equipment had landed on the other side of the fence and was tangled in the barbed wire! I struggled with the quick releases until I freed the canopy from the parachute harness. I lay there for a moment and let out a sigh of relief.

Eventually I untangled the equipment bag and lowering line from the barbed wire. Boy, some farmer was going to be pissed. I stuffed the parachute in its kit bag, attached the reserve to it, and flung them both over my head. Grasping my weapon, I glanced down at the equipment. How in the hell was I going to carry all that stuff? Scanning the countryside, I spotted a lone figure off in the distance. He was making his way to the assembly point to link up with the rest of the team. He didn't realize that he was one lucky SOB that we were not at war with Tunisia.

One thing I liked about Pathfinder school was the philosophy. A student was allowed to make certain mistakes as long as the student learned from them. The more mistakes made in training and corrected, the less chance that same mistake would be made in combat. The cadre constantly stressed flexibility and placed each student in rapidly changing situations to observe how he would perform under pressure.

My turn came on a graded night exercise. Each student had to individually guide in and land a UH-1D helicopter in the dark, by verbal communication only. The task had to be accomplished in a reasonable amount of time, without the assistance of visual aids. Since it was a graded exercise, under the school's rules, each student had to pass in order to graduate from the course.

Ron Reynolds had just completed his turn and was returning to the waiting area. It was too dark to make out the expression on his face, and I was curious as to how he had performed. "How did you do, Ron?"

Ron said, "I was sweating it at first, but once I got into it, it was a piece of cake."

Just then we heard the Pathfinder instructor bellow, "Pathfinder Burns. Front and center."

Ron must have noticed the worried look on my face. "Don't worry, Rich; you're going to do fine. If I can pass this part, I know you can." Ron's remarks were reassuring.

I walked into the small clearing and the Pathfinder instructor, Sergeant Kuykendall, motioned me to his side. "Okay, Pathfinder Burns, you were briefed earlier on what to do. Once the aircraft contacts you for guidance, I expect you to have it sitting here on the ground in front of me in five minutes. Any questions?"

I pondered for a second. "No, Sergeant!"

Sergeant Kuykendall glanced at his watch. "Begin!"

I examined the radio and performed a frequency and communications check to make sure it was operable and functioning properly. No sweat! I was already beginning to feel confident. Ron was right. This was going to be a piece of cake. Besides, I'd done it many times before back at the detachment. I was just never graded.

The radio handset barked, "Pathfinder Control, this is Flight One. Over."

I sighted the chopper out in the distance about five miles to the north. It was an overcast night, but visibility wasn't too bad.

Sometimes it's difficult to determine the direction an aircraft is flying at night when it is way off in the distance; an illusion occurs where the aircraft seems to change flight paths. However, I'd learned a trick through my experiences in the detachment. A helicopter has a green light in its right side and a red light on its left; therefore, I could always tell the direction of flight by the color of its light. In this case, only the green light of the helicopter was visible, so I knew it was traveling from west to east.

"Flight One, this is Pathfinder Control. Over."

"Pathfinder Control, this is Flight One, approximately five miles to the north. Request landing instructions. Over."

"Roger, Flight One. This is Pathfinder Control. I have you in sight. Steer right and take up a heading of one eight zero. Over."

I watched as the chopper's green light vanished,

replaced by red. A 180-degree heading should have positioned the aircraft toward me with both of its lights in view. Instead, the helicopter was traveling east to west.

"Flight One, are you on a one eight zero heading? Over."

"Roger, Pathfinder Control, one eight zero."

Damn! The bird's instruments had to be screwed up. It figured. Right when I'm getting graded. "Flight One, this is Pathfinder Control. Disregard heading and guide in on my instructions. Over."

"Roger, Pathfinder Control."

"Flight One, steer hard left. Over." A hard left would turn him my way quickly. I would give him the command "on course" when I wanted him to stop turning.

The chopper was steering left and lined up directly toward my position. "Flight One, this is Pathfinder Control. On course. Over."

Although the pilot acknowledged the on-course command, the bird continued to turn left. It was now heading west to east.

"Flight One, steer hard right. Over."

"Roger, steering hard right."

I waited until the chopper was on line again, heading toward me. "On course."

"Roger. On course." The pilot continued to steer right after receiving the on-course command. He was flying in a circle. Now I was pissed. Maybe I had the wrong helicopter. I searched the skies to make sure no other birds were in the area.

Sergeant Kuykendall was scrutinizing me. "What's the matter, Pathfinder? You having a problem?"

Nervously, I answered, "No, Sergeant . . . well, yes, Sergeant. The pilot's not responding to my instructions."

"Well, you better do something quick. Your fellow soldiers are relying on you to bring him in, Pathfinder. Besides, we don't have all night. If you don't hurry up, I'm going to have to dock you on your time."

"Yes, Sergeant!" Great! I come all this way, one bird in the sky, a straight-in approach, and I get stuck with a pilot who has his head up his ass.

I gave the pilot two more steering commands; the results were the same.

"Flight One, this is Pathfinder Control. Do you know what the hell you're doing up there? Over."

I heard the pilot chuckle. "I'm trying to follow your instructions, Pathfinder Control."

Damn. The pilot thought it was funny! I was thoroughly frustrated. I envisioned that winged torch on the Pathfinder badge flying from my grasp as I flunked the Pathfinder course. "Goddammit, Flight One. Listen to my instructions and follow them."

"Pathfinder Burns!" It was Sergeant Kuykendall. He was writing something down. "Improper radio procedures."

I was at a loss. I held the handset and just stared at it. I didn't know what else to do. Just when I thought I was going to scream over the horn, someone stepped out of the dark and put a hand on my shoulder. It was SFC Robert Itzoe, the student class senior NCO. Sergeant Itzoe was also an instructor on the Ranger committee, and therefore had a certain amount of influence with the Pathfinder cadre.

"Relax, Burns; they're screwing with you," Sergeant Itzoe stated calmly. "They just want to see how you perform under pressure, that's all. When you find yourself under pressure like that, just calm down and take a few moments to think; you'll know what to do."

I had a great deal of confidence in Itzoe, and his presence had a calming effect upon me. I pondered a moment and brought the handset back to my mouth. "Flight One, this is Pathfinder Control. Over."

"Pathfinder Control, Flight One."

"Roger, Flight One. If you do not want to follow my instructions, come in on your own. Over."

Sergeant Kuykendall was smiling as he reached for the

handset. "That won't be necessary, Flight One. Follow the student's instructions. Over."

"Flight One. Roger."

Itzoe was right. It was a setup. Once Kuykendall talked to the pilot, he followed my instructions and the bird was on the ground in a matter of minutes. After the helicopter left, Kuykendall turned to me. "Sorry about that, Burns. The fellas back at your detachment were afraid you might be a little cocky, so they told us to put a little pressure on you. Keep you on your toes. Don't worry, though, you passed. You did a good job."

I shut down the radio and let out a sigh of relief. "Damn, Sergeant, you guys had me worried."

I thanked Sergeant Itzoe for his help and walked back to the tree line. I learned a valuable lesson about performing under pressure that night and never forgot Itzoe's advice to take a moment and think. I didn't know that in the very near future, I would find out what it is like to perform under real pressure.

On 10 August 1967, thirty-three of our original class graduated from Pathfinder school. Sergeant Itzoe was designated Honor Graduate, and rightfully so. He was an experienced NCO who always made himself available to the rest of us by offering advice and assistance. At that time I never dreamed it would be the last time I would ever see him. Sergeant First Class Itzoe was killed in action less than a year later while serving with the 101st Airborne Division in Vietnam. I'm sure it was a sad day for many people; I know it was for me. The army lost a fine leader on that day.

When I said farewell to the guys from the 101st Pathfinders, their detachment commander, Lieutenant Wilberding, approached me. "PFC Burns, I enjoyed being a fellow student with you through the course. If you ever get tired of the 187th, look me up. I'd be glad to have you as a member of my detachment."

I thanked Lieutenant Wilberding for his offer; Reynolds and I promised to keep in touch.

The four of us from the 187th couldn't wait to get to the tailor shop to have the Pathfinder badges sewn on our uniforms, especially on our greens. On the dress uniform, the Pathfinder badge was sewn on the left sleeve, approximately four inches up, and really looked sharp. It was very prestigious. Pathfinder-qualified personnel were rare; qualified privates first class were even more scarce. Even though we were still privates first class, since we were Pathfinder qualified, we could now perform missions on our own.

When reporting back to the detachment, we discovered a new shortage of personnel; the two corporals were leaving the service, and one of our group from jump school received a hardship discharge. Consequently, with an increased emphasis on airmobility at the Infantry School, we stayed excessively busy in the weeks that followed, conducting Pathfinder operations around the clock. The upsurge in deployments forced those of us who were newly qualified to gain a lot of experience and confidence in our abilities. However, our occupation was not without its dangers.

On one occasion I was aboard a helicopter that experienced mechanical failure. We were lucky enough to bounce into a small clearing, narrowly avoiding the trees. Another time I was landing a flight of five helicopters at night. The lead chopper bounded forward, right over my position. I rolled away from the skid just in time, but it smashed the hell out of the radio.

Hazards aside, I loved being a Pathfinder. It was never boring, since each new mission was challenging or different in some way.

I went home on leave for a couple of weeks in October. When I returned to the barracks, I was met on the stairs by one of my fellow detachment members, Randy McConnell. Randy was a large, muscular soldier who had played football for Michigan State before he dropped out of college and was drafted. He was nicknamed Stump because of his husky size.

"Stump, what's happening?"

Stump had a big smile on his face. "I hope you enjoyed your leave, Richie!"

"Yeah, it was okay." Now Stump was snickering and had an "I know something you don't" look on his face. Obviously something was up. "Why, what's going on?"

He seemed real excited, like a kid opening a Christmas present. "We all came down on orders."

"Orders! What are you talking about? Who? Orders for where?"

"All of us. While you were on leave, we all got assigned to Fort Campbell." Stump was snickering again. "You might as well leave your bags packed."

I was in shock. At first I thought he was kidding. What possible motive would the army have for assigning us to Fort Campbell when our own unit was shorthanded? However, I knew by Stump's expression that he was telling the truth. "What do you mean, Fort Campbell? What the hell's at Fort Campbell for us?"

His voice became more serious. "We're being assigned to the 101st Airborne Division. Rumor has it that the whole division is going to Nam. Hell, the detachment sergeant said that half of Fort Benning is on orders for the 101st."

My head was swimming. "You got to be shitting me."

He slapped me on the back, almost knocking me over. "I am not shitting you, ole buddy."

He held up some papers rolled in his hand. "These are my orders. I'm outta here tonight. Everyone else has already left. Brad, Ed, John, they're all gone."

I had a thousand questions but didn't know where to begin. "Stump, do our orders have us assigned to the 101st Pathfinders?"

Stump shrugged his shoulders; he seemed hurried. I could tell he was eager to get on leave. "Nah, but that doesn't mean anything! As far as I know, nobody on orders is assigned to a particular unit in the division. We'll probably be assigned to the 101st Pathfinder Detachment when we get there."

Stump was turning the papers in his hand and fidgeting. "I gotta finish clearing, Richie. Listen, the detachment sergeant wants to see you right away to turn in your gear, flight jacket, and get your clearing papers. If I don't see you again, I'll see you at Campbell."

We shook hands, and I went to report to the detachment sergeant.

I turned in my equipment and picked up my orders and clearing papers. Since the unit had completed most of the clearing stations for me, I was instructed to depart the following evening. I had the whole barracks to myself that night. It sure seemed strange to see all of the mattresses bare, everything stacked away and empty. A desolate, absolute silence filled the room.

I lay in my bunk and pondered the day's events. I guess I really was heading for Vietnam. Why else would so many paratroopers get orders at the same time for the 101st unless it was departing for Vietnam? I felt a mixture of fear and excitement. Wow! What luck! I'd be going to Vietnam with an Airborne unit, but not just any Airborne unit; I'd be going into combat as a member of the 101st Screaming Eagles.

Chapter Two

Strolling through the airport in Louisville, Kentucky, was like watching the invasion of Normandy; there were paratroopers everywhere. Every other person I encountered was Airborne. Anyone en route to Fort Campbell usually changed planes there. Soldiers had to travel in uniform and all were brandishing newly sewn Screaming Eagle patches on their left shoulders, denoting their assignment to the 101st Airborne Division. One couldn't help but notice the bewilderment on the faces of the civilian onlookers.

Upon arrival in Clarksville, Tennessee, outside Fort Campbell, a group of us got together and shared a taxi to the 101st Replacement Company. The driver parked near an open field to one side of the replacement company building. We stared at each other in awe. Tables placed along the side of the building were crammed with clerks busily shuffling forms and pecking on typewriters. Six long lines, each containing literally hundreds of paratroopers, protruded from the tables. The lines seemed to stretch endlessly across the open field.

We paid the taxi driver and unloaded our gear. I moved to the line marked "A thru E." For the rest of the day I sat on my duffel bag in the hot sun, wearing dress greens, inching forward every few minutes.

After what seemed an eternity, my turn arrived at the table. I handed the clerk my assignment instructions and filled out a few forms while he searched through a folder.

"Okay, Burns! Here's your unit assignment orders within the division."

I read the orders. "There must be some mistake, Specialist."

The clerk appeared annoyed. "What do you mean?"

"Well, it says here I'm assigned to the 2d Battalion, 17th Cavalry as a scout, MOS 11 Delta. I'm an 11 Bravo. Besides, I'm a Pathfinder." I pointed to the Y skill identifier on my MOS that designated Pathfinder qualification. "I should be assigned to the 101st Pathfinder Detachment."

"Sorry, man, I don't make the orders; I just hand them out. You're gonna have to try and get them changed when you get to your new unit."

Frustrated, I spoke up. "Listen, is there anyone here I can talk to about squaring this away?"

The clerk let out a sigh. "Look, man, there's a hundred guys behind you waiting to process in. A lot of them are probably not going to be happy with their assignments either."

I realized at this point my plight was futile. I asked the clerk where the 17th Cavalry was located, and he pointed me in the general direction.

It was late in the evening when I finally reported to B Troop, 2/17 Cavalry barracks. The NCO on duty assigned me a bunk, footlocker, and wall locker. Feeling discouraged, I began to unpack my duffel bag when someone tapped me on the shoulder. It was Louis "Brad" Bradford, one of my fellow Pathfinders from the 187th.

Brad had a big smile plastered across his face. "What's going on, Richie?"

Instantly my spirits lifted. "I don't believe it. Are you assigned here, too?"

"Yeah! We're even in the same platoon."

What luck! I immediately felt better knowing Brad was in the same situation I was in. Perhaps we could work together on getting transferred to the Pathfinders.

Brad motioned for me to follow him. "Come on, Richie, I want to show you something."

Leaving our platoon area, we walked down a long

hallway connected to another open bay. A group of soldiers lingered around their bunks. Brad yelled to a couple of guys over in the corner. "Hey, guess who I found?"

Two men headed toward us, Stump and Ed Brown, two more Pathfinders from the 187th. I sure was feeling a lot better about my assignment.

All four of us had been assigned as scouts. Discussing our situation, we determined that some REMF in personnel figured Pathfinders and scouts sounded similar, and that's how we got assigned to the unit.

Very little training was accomplished in the weeks that followed. We conducted a few ambushes and some reconnaissance missions, but most of the time was taken up performing maintenance on vehicles or packing and loading equipment for transport to Vietnam.

Stump and Ed liked the platoon they were assigned. They had a good platoon sergeant and platoon leader. Both were promised leadership positions and possible promotions. Brad and I, on the other hand, were placed in a platoon without a platoon sergeant or platoon leader. Consequently, there was a total lack of leadership and communication. Every day was one of utter confusion. No one was really to blame. The division was attempting to muster forty-five hundred troops to bring it up to strength for deployment. Hence, every unit within the division was short on personnel. I really missed the responsibility and excitement of being a Pathfinder. It seemed as if all my training and experience were being wasted.

On my first day in the unit, I inquired about a transfer to the Pathfinders. I was informed that any action regarding enlisted soldiers had to go through the first sergeant. I requested to see the first sergeant and was granted an audience about a week later.

First Sergeant Saul was a short, stocky, hard-faced soldier who talked with a European accent. He wasn't known for his interpersonal skills. The day of my appointment, I made damn sure I was squared away. As I stood in the hallway outside the first sergeant's door, I glanced down to make sure my boots hadn't been scuffed. I straightened my "gig line" (pants seam), took a deep breath, and knocked.

A voice bellowed, "Come in!"

I stepped into his office and snapped to parade rest about two paces in front of his desk. "First Sergeant, PFC Burns reports!"

First Sergeant Saul put his pen down and glared up at me. "At ease, soldier. What's on your mind?"

Shit! I better be careful how I approach this. The last time I stood in front of a first sergeant's desk, I received a royal ass-chewing. "Well, First Sergeant, I'd like to talk to you about a possible transfer to the division Pathfinders."

Saul remained expressionless as he spoke. "What's the matter, don't you like my unit?"

Damn! This was not going well. "Oh no, First Sergeant! It's not that. It's just that . . . well . . . you see . . . I was a Pathfinder at my last duty station, and . . . uh, I'm also Pathfinder qualified."

Saul glanced at the open folder on his desk. "We got you down here as a scout. You don't like being a scout?"

I cleared the lump from my throat. "Oh no, First Sergeant. I like being a scout." Well, it was half true anyway. Although I didn't like mechanized infantry, I enjoyed reconnaissance missions and small-unit tactics. "It's just that I feel I would be more of an asset to the division as a Pathfinder, since I have that experience and training."

"Well, I'll allow you to put a 1049 requesting a transfer, but I can tell you right now, I can't approve it. We're short bodies, and that's all there is to it."

I guess I looked disappointed, because First Sergeant Saul stood up and walked around to the front of his desk. He actually became pleasant. "Listen, you've got a high clerical score on your records, and I can use a clerk. If you want, I can give you a job working in the orderly room."

His offer hit me by surprise. I didn't like being a scout all that much, but I'd like being a clerk even less. Don't get me wrong! An orderly room clerk could make or break a unit. I just couldn't picture myself as a "Remington raider." "Oh no, First Sergeant. I appreciate the offer, but I'd like to stay in the platoon. I'd still like to put in that transfer, though."

Saul stiffened a little and walked back behind his desk. "Go tell the specialist next door you want a 1049 typed up."

"Yes, First Sergeant. Thank you, First Sergeant." I left his office with a sigh of relief. The first sergeant didn't seem that bad a guy after all.

When Brad found out that I had filled out a request for transfer, he followed suit. Stump and Ed wanted to stay with the 17th Cav. I decided to telephone Lieutenant Wilberding, the 101st Pathfinder Detachment commander, to inform him that Brad and I were at Fort Campbell and had requested reassignment to his unit. Wilberding was ecstatic. He remembered me from Pathfinder school and said the detachment could really use both of us, since it was short of qualified personnel.

The very next day, Wilberding, Reynolds, and two other members of the Pathfinder detachment came to greet us. Wilberding said Pathfinder-qualified personnel had priority in the division and he was personally going to division headquarters to ensure that our requests for transfer received approval.

In the few days that followed, our platoon finally acquired some leadership, so things became less hectic. As far as our transfers were concerned, Brad and I had not heard anything and began to lose hope. Perhaps the first sergeant was right, our transfers wouldn't be approved. But one day, just as Brad and I returned from a detail loading equipment at the railway yard, we received word to report to the orderly room. We both felt apprehensive. Anytime a private is told to report to the orderly room, it's usually something bad. Needless to say, we were pleasantly surprised to see Lieutenant Wilberding and another Pathfinder waiting with First Sergeant Saul. Wilberding displayed a wide grin as he held up some papers. "These are your orders; pack your gear. You two are being reassigned."

He handed us the papers and then held out his hand. "Welcome to the 101st Pathfinders."

The mission to transport the 101st Airborne Division to Vietnam was named Operation Eagle Thrust and was the longest and largest aerial troop deployment in the history of modern warfare. In one month, 10,356 paratroopers would be flown more than ten thousand miles, ready to fight in a combat zone. The division's advance party had deployed a few weeks earlier, and a steady flow of C-141 Starlifters continued to fly in and out of Fort Campbell every two hours, transporting troops and equipment.

The 101st Airborne Division comprised three brigades, each with three infantry battalions. The rest of the division was composed of various supporting units organic to the division. The 1st Brigade had been in Vietnam since 1965 and won an excellent combat reputation. Helicopter support for the division came from its only aviation battalion, the 101st Aviation Battalion. Although Pathfinders are considered elite infantry and assist ground commanders, they are responsible for the control of aircraft and therefore assigned to aviation. Accordingly, we Pathfinders were part of the 101st Aviation Battalion.

The 101st Aviation Battalion's distinctive insignia was an eagle diving for its prey. Above the eagle, a scroll carried the battalion's motto: "Wings of the Eagle." As Pathfinders, we guided the eagle.

We had approximately six weeks to improve our Pathfinder skills before deploying to Vietnam. Vietnam was steadily becoming a helicopter war, and therefore the infantry battalions trained for airmobile operations by practicing combat assaults (CAs).

Generally, a combat assault consisted of a company- or battalion-size infantry unit assaulting an objective with the use of helicopters. The location where the infantry would land by helicopter was called a landing zone (LZ). Usually, standard operating procedure was for a two-man Pathfinder team to be on the LZ beforehand or be on board the first helicopter landing into the LZ. The team would then guide the rest of the aircraft into the area.

We worked our butts off, since there were only fourteen of us in the whole division. It was a remarkably hectic period. We also attended classes, filled out forms, packed equipment, and received our combat issue of clothing and equipment. We were struck by the light weight and numerous pockets of the jungle fatigues. We were also issued brand-new M-16 rifles.

None of us had ever been in combat, except for our detachment sergeant, Staff Sergeant Guerra, who pulled his first tour in Vietnam with the 1st Air Cav. He wasn't too thrilled about going back for another tour; he had a family and was close to retirement. Still, he was a soldier, and if his country ordered him back for a second tour, he would comply. The rest of us, however, were especially eager and excited about deploying.

Some of us were lucky enough to participate in a farewell jump out of the C-141 Starlifter, the air force's new, large jet transport. It turned out to be a great jump, right at dusk. It was the last time many of us would conduct a parachute jump for a year or more. (Actually, it was the last parachute jump the 101st would perform as an Airborne division.)

A few detachment members also received promotions. Ron Reynolds, another member, Joe Bolick, and I were promoted to the rank of corporal (E-4). (Primarily, Pathfinders were always promoted to corporal rather than specialist when attaining the grade of E-4. A corporal is a noncommissioned officer, a leadership rank, and thereby more appropriate to the position because of the immense responsibility, leadership, and decisiveness required of Pathfinders.)

As the date for deployment drew near, everyone in the battalion was given leave to go home if they desired. Single soldiers received ten days and married soldiers twelve.

I wasn't going to miss out on the opportunity to say farewell to my family, so I went home for ten days.

During my entire stay at home, no one in my family discussed my going to Vietnam. They attempted to behave the way they always did when I was home, but the atmosphere was different. My stepfather, Bob, was a career navy man of nineteen years and close to retirement. Although I had elected to serve in the army, he was very proud of me. On past visits home, we discussed politics, the Vietnam War, and cracked jokes about each other's branch of service. This time proved different as we both fumbled through our talks together, keeping the subject of the war far out on the fringes of any discussion.

My mother stayed exceptionally busy around the house. The few times she found herself alone with me, she centered the conversations on frivolous topics like the weather or the price of groceries. My little brother Bobbie was too caught up in the world of a nine-year-old to take such matters seriously.

I was certain my presence at home was the most difficult for my sister, Debbie. Although she was five years younger than I, we were extremely close, especially after the death of my father. I could tell by her eyes that she wanted to express her feelings, but either didn't know how or didn't think that she should. The thought that she might never again see her brother, her most trusted family ally, must have been frightening.

The most uncomfortable time for everybody was during the evenings after supper. While I remained glued to the war coverage on the six o'clock news, everybody else remembered something they just had to do, eventually leaving me all alone in the room. Didn't anybody care about what was going on over there?

My time on leave was ultimately boring. Most of my friends worked during the day or were away in the military. Unfortunately, I didn't have much in common with those who stayed around. They seemed immature, and their priorities were very different. Somehow, my experiences in the military had caused many of my perceptions to change.

Perhaps it was just as well that the subject of Vietnam wasn't discussed during my stay. Quite a few young men from Brockton had enlisted in the various services, and the majority of my friends and many high school acquaintances joined the army or Marines. Although America's regular forces had been fighting in Vietnam for just two years, many young men in and around my town had already been wounded, maimed, or killed. Sadly, while on that leave, I learned that two more of my hometown friends, Danny Goodwin and Ronnie Berrisford, had been killed in action.

My last day home, while saying good-bye, my stepfather finally said something that alluded to Vietnam. He shook my hand and said, "Make sure you keep your head down over there." I nodded.

The night before our unit left for Vietnam, our entire area was sealed off. No automobiles or civilian personnel were allowed into our sector of the division. All streets were roadblocked and guarded by military police. Married soldiers whose families lived nearby met them at the barriers to say their last farewells. Practically everyone else assembled at the enlisted or officer clubs and partied late into the night.

Roll call was conducted at 0430 hours. All detachment members were present, at least physically. Then, our equipment and rucksacks already packed, we loaded onto trucks and headed for Campbell Army Airfield. Clad only in jungle fatigues, we stood in the morning cold, snow visible in the surroundings, waiting to board the C-141 transports that would take us to Vietnam. The Screaming Eagles were once again forging a place in history, and we felt fortunate to be a part of it.

The detachment was divided among three different aircraft. Ron Reynolds, Joe Bolick, Larry Foracker, and I were manifested on the same plane. After waiting in the cold for some time, we hurriedly grabbed our rucks and weapons when the loadmaster motioned us aboard. As we proceeded onto the ramp of the aircraft, I turned around and took one last look at Fort Campbell, just in case it was the last time I would ever see the United States.

Our aircraft was loaded down with three-quarter-ton trucks. Larry remarked, "Man, where are we going to sit? This plane is packed!"

We spread out and found a few seats grouped together. It was really tight and difficult to move around. Actually, I had it a little easier than the others. Ron, Joe, and Larry were all well over six feet tall, so their knees touched the vehicle in front of us. Since I was shorter, I had a bit more legroom. Of course, I caught a lot of harassment from them.

Larry Foracker was well built and always joked about being half wetback because his mother was Mexican. It was all in fun; he was quite proud of his heritage, continuously bragging about his mother and how well she could cook. I got along well with Larry. He was a warm, caring person who maintained a sense of humor under even the worst of circumstances.

Joe Bolick had a more slender build and was kind of wiry. Joe didn't like me. I never could figure out why. I got the impression that, to him, I just wasn't worth much. He always wanted to spar with me mentally, but I tried not to engage. Still, no matter what situation we found ourselves in, regardless of our personal feelings, we'd cover each other's ass. That's what I thought. In any case, I'd find out soon enough.

Ron Reynolds and I were steadily becoming close friends. We both liked being soldiers and wanted the most from the army. If a challenge was involved, we'd volunteer for it. Ron, however, was a much better soldier than I. Soldiering for Ron seemed to come naturally, and he exhibited all the traits of a fine leader. He was intelligent, tough, fair, and compassionate. He seemed to possess more confidence than I did. We constantly assisted and motivated each other. He was a true friend.

In the C-141, after remaining crammed in one position for a very long time, my knees began to stiffen. With Vietnam over ten thousand miles away, I could see it was going to be a long flight. Sitting bedside me, Ron became frustrated as well. "Damn, there's just no way to get comfortable. I can't take much more of this."

Ron poked me in the side and chuckled, "Hey, lil' man!" (I was still being harassed!) "Why don't you climb up on top of that truck and see if it's comfortable?"

Larry leaned over. "Yeah, Rich! Go up there and see if it will hold you," he said, referring to the truck's canvas cover.

Joe nodded his approval.

I glared at all three of them. "Wait a minute! Why me? Even if it will hold me, it can still cave in if one of you goes up there after me. You guys are heavier!"

"If it does cave in, at least you won't do as much damage as one of us would. Don't be so selfish," Larry said.

Ron stood up. "C'mon, Richie, I'll give you a hand." Ron clasped his hands together as a step for me to climb.

If I didn't go, they would just get together and throw me up there anyway. I slung my weapon over my shoulder and stepped into his hands.

"Yeah! Sure! If it breaks, I'm the one who's going to get the Article 15, not you guys."

Larry guffawed, "What are they going to do? Send you to Vietnam?"

We laughed. That had become a very common response by division soldiers during the previous several weeks. It seemed to make sense, though. What the hell would happen to me if the canvas did cave in? Send me to Vietnam? I'm probably going to be killed anyway.

Grabbing onto the truck, I stepped into Ron's hands. He gave a shove, and I was flung easily atop the canvas. I lay down and stretched out. No problem. Man, that was heaven.

I heard Larry's voice. "Well, Rich, how is it? Will it hold us?"

The canvas was strong enough to hold everyone, but they'd been harassing me all day. "Nah! I don't think any of you should come up here. It'll probably break."

Ron grabbed his weapon. "Hell, let it break. I'm coming up." He reached out his hand for assistance, and I yanked him up.

Joe looked at Larry. "What are they going to do, send us to Vietnam?" Larry and Joe climbed on top of the next truck.

I was awakened by the plane's touching down on the runway in Anchorage, Alaska. It was nighttime and snowing lightly. The cold ripped through my jungle fatigues as we stepped into the brisk air and walked about a hundred meters to a small cafeteria. Nothing was open, so we just hung around for an hour while the plane refueled. The few locals present were unimpressed by our appearance. It was obvious they had viewed the same scene many times before.

It was damn near as cold inside as it was out. I guess the heat wasn't on. The locals were bundled in thick, warm jackets.

I think Ron started a conversation to get the cold off our minds. "Hey, do you guys know what day it is?"

Joe replied, "Yeah, that's a tough one to answer. It's the day we're going to Vietnam!"

Ron scoffed, "No, I mean the date."

Immediately it dawned on me. The date was 7 December 1967. My answer was energetic, as if I were participating in a game show. "I know! It's the day the Japanese bombed Pearl Harbor!"

Ron's voice became excited. "That's right! December seventh! Isn't it ironic? We're going to Vietnam on the anniversary of the bombing of Pearl Harbor."

Larry injected his humor as always. "Yeah! That's really great, Ron! I don't know about the rest of you, but that just makes me feel a whole lot better, man. If I remember my history, mostly Americans got killed at Pearl Harbor!"

Everyone chuckled.

Finally we got the signal to reboard. No one spoke as we trekked across the ramp back to the plane.

Crawling back on top of the truck, I lay down and wrapped the sling of my weapon around my arm, keeping it tucked close beside me. I bet that weapon and I were going to become real close friends. With the hope that it would take care of me, I made a solemn promise to take care of it.

It was dark inside the plane. The truck's canvas had that new-equipment smell to it. The only sound was the plane's droning. I could barely make out the silhouettes of the others. I laid my head back down and pondered the situation.

The time had finally come. I was going to experience combat. I tried hard to fall asleep, but my mind raced. Would I make it back home? Would I ever see my family again? What would happen if I became dismembered or was blinded, or captured?

My biggest fear was that I might not perform when the chips were down. That terrified me. Sure, I was a paratrooper and a Pathfinder, but no one really knows how he's going to function in combat until it happens. I pleaded with God, asking Him to honor just one request. "Please, God, whatever happens, don't let me be a coward."

Chapter Three

It was three in the morning when we landed at Bien Hoa Air Base, Vietnam. Over twenty hours had elapsed since our departure from Fort Campbell. The four of us conducted a quick inventory, then gathered our rucksacks and weapons while the plane taxied to a stop. Eagerly we assembled to the rear of the aircraft and waited to exit the plane.

The loadmaster let down the ramp and, accompanied by a foul, unfamiliar smell, a blast of heat engulfed us. Stepping down the ramp and advancing into the damp night air, I felt as if I were in a sauna. The heat and humidity were unbearable even though it was still dark.

A lone figure motioned for us to follow. In the distance I could make out the outline of a bus. It was difficult to breathe as we trekked across the asphalt, and my lungs were gasping for oxygen. Our rucksacks were weighted down with team equipment, making the jaunt all the more difficult. Already sweat was dripping off my forehead and down my back.

Larry let out a loud gasp. "Man, it is really hot, and it's still nighttime. Can you imagine what it must be like during the middle of the day?"

Ron answered in a drawl. "Shoot, this is just a little hotter than the summers back home."

I grabbed the top of Ron's rucksack strap, then let my body go limp. "Good. You can drag me along, since you're used to this kind of weather."

Ron stopped short, forcing us both to collide. "Get off

me, you damned Yankee! You mean yawl don't have hot weather like this in Bawston?"

"No! We're too smart to live in weather like this."

Everyone laughed, then Joe hit us all with a dose of reality. "Well, we better get used to it. We're going to be in it for a long time."

Nearing the bus, I gave serious thought as to how in the hell I was going to hump a rucksack in that kind of heat for a whole year. I immediately put that kind of thinking out of my head; it caused too much anxiety.

There were just enough seats on the bus when we boarded. I don't know how long the others on the bus had been waiting, but they looked uncomfortable sitting there in the heat.

Some leg (non-Airborne) REMF with an olive drab floppy hat introduced himself as our "tour guide." Mindful of our discomfort, he assured us that it was a short ride to the 101st Airborne Division compound, since it bordered the Bien Hoa Air Base. Gesturing for the driver to proceed, he launched into a well-rehearsed speech.

"Well, gentlemen, welcome to Vietnam. I guess by now you have all noticed the chain-link fencing covering all the windows? This, gentlemen, is to protect you from hand grenades or other explosives that may be thrown at the bus."

I gazed at the metal mesh, the first sign that I was actually in a hostile environment.

The guide continued his lecture while the bus journeyed along. Dawn was breaking as we neared our destination, causing most of us to focus our attention on the unusual countryside and people.

Suddenly the guide beamed with excitement. Interrupting his presentation, he pointed to two Vietnamese males who were walking down the street together, holding hands. "That, gentlemen, is a prime example of some of the cultural differences you will encounter during your 'all expenses paid' tour of duty in Vietnam. It is common in this culture for close male friends to hold hands in public as a sign of friendship. It does not mean they are homosexual, as some of you might assume."

Someone in the back yelled, "They look queer to me!" Others followed suit, shouting various comments; the conversation went downhill from then on. The tour guide attempted to regain control, but he eventually sat down in disgust.

Ron and I were surprised by the clusters of wooden buildings scattered throughout the division area. We had expected to be housed in tents; this was luxury. Later, all of us learned that the 101st Airborne Division had taken over the rear area of the 173d Airborne Brigade, which had moved to another region. (Although the 173d insignia was present everywhere, it was quickly painted over and replaced by our division's Screaming Eagle in a few days' time.)

Our unit was located in the Bien Hoa army compound, a relatively built-up area adjacent to the Bien Hoa Air Base. This was referred to as the "rear area" or the "rear." Rear areas were safe locations most of the time. Nonetheless, both the Bien Hoa army compound and the Bien Hoa Air Base had been hit by enemy rockets on occasion.

A person's living quarters in Vietnam was referred to as a hootch, whether it consisted of a building, a tent, or just a plain poncho hung overhead out in the field. Ours, like most of those at Bien Hoa, consisted of an open bay with cement floors and metal roofing. Each of the buildings was surrounded by fifty-five-gallon fuel drums filled with sand, topped with four layers of sandbags. Moreover, sandbag walls had been erected in front of the doorways. All the barrels of sand and layers of sandbags were placed around the buildings to protect the occupants from the shrapnel of enemy rockets and mortars.

We each slept on a cot covered with a mosquito net. With the exception of Lieutenant Wilberding and Staff Sergeant Guerra, the whole detachment resided in the same hootch. (Wilberding lived in the officer hootch and Guerra in the senior NCO hootch.)

Unit morale steadily declined during the weeks following our arrival in Vietnam, especially for the lower enlisted. Since our unit was located in the rear and none of us was getting shot at, we remained isolated from combat. Consequently, our leaders still treated us like we were back in the States. Given the unpredictable nature of guerrilla warfare and the hostile surroundings, we should at least have had easy access to our individual weapons. However, they remained locked in a conex (see Glossary), where we had to sign for them and await the armorer to show up and issue them to us.

A typical day began with roll call at 0630 hours, during which the first sergeant would funnel out various details. As lower enlisted, the majority of us were tasked with filling sandbags to replace the old, tattered ones that surrounded the buildings. It was an all-day affair, laboring in the hot sun with the temperature well over one hundred degrees. Everyone present chipped in, however, regardless of rank. Except for the presence of barbed wire, sandbags, and outhouses, we wouldn't have known we were serving in a combat zone.

As Pathfinders, we became increasingly frustrated. We had expected to be thrown into the midst of the fighting, performing dangerous missions; not remain in the rear, pull details, and put up with Stateside bullshit. Although assigned to aviation, Pathfinders were infantrymen, and all of us were hungry for action.

Given the environment, attending three formations a day and parading around in shined jungle boots and unsoiled fatigues seemed totally asinine to most of us. Failure to comply with the slightest regulation, however, resulted in threats of disciplinary action. Moreover, many soldiers were sunburned but dared not say anything or seek medical assistance; any soldier who acquired a sunburn received automatic Article 15 punishment and the possible loss of a stripe.

Staff Sergeant Guerra was a nice guy, but he was an old-timer who followed orders without question. Furthermore, he was nearing retirement and didn't want to rock the boat or let anything threaten his career. Lieutenant Wilberding attempted to go to bat for us every now and then, attempting to exempt us from details and involve us in missions, but he was just a lieutenant and usually overridden.

On one of those noneventful days, Ron and I were walking back to our hootch. We rounded the corner and saw a little puppy clumsily trying to push his body between some sandbags in an attempt to hide from three Vietnamese kids who were chasing him. It was a rarity to see a puppy in Vietnam, so we immediately became interested. The children must have been allowed on base to help fill sandbags. The puppy was genuinely frightened of them, so I picked him up while Ron talked with the kids.

A girl spoke a little English and, at first, tried to claim that the dog belonged to them. We knew that wasn't true because they never would have gotten through the gate with him. Eventually they told the truth: they were foraging for food around a nearby garbage dump when they spotted the puppy doing the same. They figured he was a stray and would be good *chop-chop*, which meant they would take him back home, fatten him up, and eat him (one reason dogs were so rare in Vietnam).

Ron and I had the same idea: there was no way we were going to give this puppy up for *chop-chop*. Even though I knew they didn't have a claim, I asked the kids what they wanted for the dog. I ended up giving them the equivalent of five dollars in Vietnamese piasters and threw in some C rations.

The puppy took to me right away. I guess he felt protected. He looked up at me with his bright eyes. He was one of the cutest puppies I had ever seen. Except for his floppy little brown ears, his body was white. He had a unique tail that curled on his back to form a circle, and a large black nose.

Ron came over to pat him. "Well, now that we've got him, what are we going to do with him?"

I had already wrestled with that question. "Keep him!"

Ron loved dogs. He talked fondly of the times he and his dogs went squirrel hunting back in Arkansas. It didn't take him long to agree. "Yeah! Okay! We'll make him the Pathfinder mascot."

We brought him back to the hootch. We didn't know how the others would react to a dog being part of the team. A few griped a little bit, mostly about who was going to clean up after the dog. All the team members knew how badly we wanted to keep him, however, so the decision was unanimous that he stay.

Later that day we had to decide on a name. Traditional names like Spike and King were considered. I was adamant that the dog's name be Pathfinder related. Other names like Chopper, Pathfinder, and Call Sign were contemplated. While all of this discussion was going on, Ron was sitting on a footlocker, heavily lost in thought. He kept staring at my Pathfinder badge. After a while I confronted him. "What?"

"The Pathfinder badge!"

Bewildered, I asked, "What about it?"

"The dog's name should have something to do with the Pathfinder badge."

I glanced over at Ron's badge. "Well, it has a flame streaking across it."

"Naw! I already thought of that."

He had his head resting on his chin, mumbling out loud, "What is the symbol of a Pathfinder?"

Suddenly I felt like I was in a game show again and had to come up with the right answer. "The torch is the symbol! The flame comes from the torch. The torch lights the way and guides the aircraft."

Ron's face sparkled. "That's it!" He sounded like someone getting ready to yell "Bingo!" "We'll call him Torch. It's the symbol of the Pathfinder." The rest of the team thought the name appropriate. From that moment on, the mascot of the 101st Pathfinder Detachment was duly named Torch.

Lieutenant Wilberding agreed with the idea of keeping Torch. Staff Sergeant Guerra, being a member of the Old

Army, thought it highly irregular. I reminded him that the
mess sergeant had a German shepherd, which he'd brought
over with him from the States. Also, the army was using
scout dogs in the field. Sure, both were American dogs, but
we didn't know where Torch came from; he might be an
American. Even if he wasn't, the army had Kit Carson
Scouts (enemy soldiers who'd defected to our side). Torch
was too young to be involved in any enemy activities anyway. Besides, he was an orphan. And he voluntarily joined
our outfit after trying to escape from the Vietnamese. Why,
those kids could have been VC!

Sergeant Guerra still wasn't convinced, that is, until
Torch looked up at him with those big, dark eyes. Sergeant
Guerra was one of those NCOs who looked hard as nails
on the outside but was easygoing inside. "Well, maybe we
can keep him as long as there's no trouble."

As if he understood, Torch loped over to him wagging his curly tail. Guerra reached down and picked him
up. "He sure is a cute little fella, isn't he?" That was the
end of the confirmation hearing. Torch was officially
enlisted in the United States Army, 101st Pathfinder
Detachment, with the rank of private first class.

It took only a couple of days to train Torch to go outside and perform some tricks. He was an intelligent creature. We figured his age to be about eight to ten weeks old.

Eventually Torch won the heart of every team member.
Even the most skeptical enjoyed having him nearby. There
was something therapeutic about having Torch around. I
don't know if it was because of his innocence or the way he
always greeted us as if we were special. Maybe he reminded
everyone of their own dogs back home. Whatever the reason, Torch was a full-fledged member of the detachment,
and every one of us cared for him. He accompanied us on
every activity. Torch's past remained a mystery. We never
did find out where he came from or how he got on base.

The majority of the detachment had just returned
from detail when Lieutenant Wilberding sent word that

all detachment members were to gather at the team
room. The team room served as the place we all con-
gregated for detachment meetings or recreation. It
possessed a makeshift bar, a few stools, plus a large
cooler stocked with cold drinks.

Ron stepped behind the bar, handing out beer and sodas.
Joe "Mitch" Mitchell just finished guzzling his soda.
Although Mitch was short, he was athletic and sinewy,
with dark hair and features. Normally a guy who would
give you the shirt off his back, he had a quick temper. It
didn't take much to piss Mitch off. He'd met a girl,
Martha, while at Fort Campbell, and they married right
before we left. He really loved her, and she was all he
talked about. "I'll bet the LT [pronounced "ell-tee"] is
going to tell us we're all handpicked for some exotic detail, like removing water buffalo shit from a rice paddy."

Larry's expression became serious as he said, "Sounds
to me like that could be a real shitty detail."

Everyone was groaning at his near pun when Lieutenant Wilberding entered the room.

Wilberding was tall with a slim build. At times he looked
physically awkward. He was intellectual in demeanor and
wore thick, black, army-issue, horn-rim glasses. By appear-
ances, the bookworm type. He did not fit the image of a soldier chosen as honor graduate of the grueling six-month
infantry officer candidate school who went on to become
Airborne, Ranger, and Pathfinder qualified.

His major deficit seemed to be that he lacked interpersonal skills. He was uncomfortable communicating on a
personal level. Moreover, he was a perplexing person to
figure out; oftentimes his actions were totally unpredictable. For instance, we figured he would be the stumbling block to our keeping Torch, since he was usually
"by the book." Instead, he readily agreed with the idea. I
respected his accomplishments, however, and felt a certain sense of loyalty. If it hadn't been for Lieutenant
Wilberding, I wouldn't have been in the 101 Pathfinders.

Wilberding was grinning. "What's going on? Did I

miss something?" Something wasn't right. Wilberding was actually beaming.

Bolick was quick to reply. "No sir! We were just wondering what kind of detail was in store for us for you to call a meeting."

Wilberding's grin broadened. "Well, I have some good news for a change. We've just been tasked with our first combat mission."

Man! It was like watching a bunch of little kids excitedly opening presents at Christmas. Everybody started speaking at once: "What kind of mission?" "Who's going?" "How many guys are going along?" "When is it taking place?" "What unit are we supporting?"

Wilberding held up his hands as he raised his voice. "Okay! Hold it! Just calm down!"

The room fell silent. Lieutenant Wilberding was still smiling. I had never seen him so happy. It was then that I realized he was just as excited as the rest of us.

"An element of the 2d Brigade is conducting a combat assault and has requested Pathfinder support. The Pathfinder team will consist of two men. Whoever is selected will stay with the unit from insertion to extraction. The mission will probably last around seven days."

Bolick was the first to address the question we'd all been thinking. "Who's going to go on the mission, sir?"

"Well, since it is the detachment's first mission, I was going to ask for volunteers. But I can see by everyone's reaction that isn't going to work." Wilberding kept his smile, but we could tell he felt uneasy. I couldn't blame him. Ten of his men were going to be real disappointed no matter what method of selection he used.

Immediately a debate ensued among us as to who should go. Just as Wilberding started to become annoyed, Ron yelled, "Everyone be quiet for a minute." He turned to Wilberding. "Sir, a fair way would be for all of us to draw straws. That way, each of us would have an even chance."

"Well, that seems like a fair system," Wilberding said. "Does anyone disagree?" We all agreed.

Ron grabbed some thin red-and-white cocktail straws from a container on the bar. He took his knife and cut two of the straws, making them shorter than the others. He then balled all of them in his hand. From the way he held them, no one could tell which were the shorter, since they were all even at the top. He then said, "To make it fair, I'll get the last one."

I thought Ron's idea was clever. It was the detachment's first mission, and each member should have an equal opportunity at going. Besides, no one could complain later. I knew I didn't have a prayer, however. The only time I ever won anything in my life was at a bingo game in the second grade.

Ron extended his hand, holding the straws out over the bar. Every selection seemed to take an eternity as each member pondered which straw to select. So far, four members had labored over their selection, only to follow it with a cussword.

Finally, Bolick cried out, "I don't believe it. I've got a short one!" You would have thought he'd won a new car at a TV game show. Hell, I didn't blame him. What a lucky guy!

The tension grew. Finally, it was my turn. Three straws remained. Miraculously, no one had yet chosen the second short straw. As I viewed the straws to my front, I attempted to figure out some sort of strategy. The room fell silent. I reached out my hand, my finger almost touching one of the straws, but I immediately drew my hand back. Please, God, let me pick the right one. Damn, which one is it? Eventually someone yelled, "C'mon, Richie, pick the damned thing!"

The hell with it, I'm not going to win anyway. I quickly grabbed a straw. Reluctantly my eyes drifted down to my hand. It took a moment for my choice to register before I heard my voice howling out, "Holy shit! I picked the right one."

Ultimately the grumbling ceased from the group, and

some of them left the team room to eat. Ron approached me, grinning from ear to ear. He slapped me on the shoulder. "You sure are lucky for a Yankee!"

I shook my head. "I know, man. I can't believe I picked the right one. I never win anything."

Even though Ron was disappointed because he didn't win, he was genuinely happy for me. "Well, you won this time, Richie! Makes all the times you didn't win worth it, doesn't it?"

I thought about that for a minute. "Yeah, I guess you're right!"

"Man! You and Bolick are going on the detachment's first combat mission. I'd give anything to trade places with one of y'all."

I glanced around to see if anyone was in earshot. "I sure wish you were going along instead of Bolick."

Ron appeared a little surprised by my remark. "I wish I was, too, but Joe's okay. You two will do fine together."

Ron and Joe Bolick had been together for some time, and Bolick didn't act toward Ron the way he did toward me, even though we were all corporals. "If I know Bolick, he's going to be real bossy, and anything I say isn't going to be right, no matter what."

"Well, I have a solution!"

My face lit up. "You do? What is it?"

"I'll take your place, and Joe and I will go on the mission instead."

I started laughing. "Yeah, right! No way, buddy! Forget it!"

I had to give it to Ron. He knew just what to say for me to put things in proper perspective. I'd have teamed up with the devil himself to go on that mission. Besides, Joe was a good soldier and a competent Pathfinder. That's what really counted.

Just then Joe walked over to us. He had been chatting with Wilberding. "Richie, the LT is going to meet with us at the hootch in an hour to brief us on the mission."

Ron reached out to shake Joe's hand. "Congratulations, Joe! You two sure are lucky; I wish I was going."

Joe smiled warmly at Ron. "Thanks! I can't believe it myself. I wish you were going along, too." Joe glanced at me, and for a moment his face changed.

Ron looked down at his watch. "We still got time for chow. Let's all go get something to eat."

Joe turned toward the door. "No, thanks. I'll open up a can of Cs. I'm going to start a list of some of the equipment we're going to need for tomorrow."

Joe stepped out of the team room, then quickly stuck his head back in the doorway. In a serious tone, he blurted, "Remember, Richie, one hour. Be there."

I stared down at the corporal stripes on my sleeve and then at Ron. I raised my eyebrows, and we both broke out laughing.

Ron and some of the other detachment members joined us for Lieutenant Wilberding's informal briefing of the mission. Joe and I would be supporting an infantry company from the 501st. The unit would conduct a heliborne combat assault, followed by a weeklong search-and-destroy mission. It was also this unit's first combat mission since its arrival in Vietnam. Joe and I would accompany the first bird going into the LZ, remain with the unit to assist in its airmobile operations, and then depart on the last bird on extraction.

After the briefing, some of the guys hung around to help Joe and me get ready. It was great; they were as excited as we. Since we'd be in the jungle for seven days, in a combat environment, we had to bring enough equipment to be prepared for any situation. The group helped us brainstorm and offered suggestions regarding equipment. Joe and I both felt it was better to bring something and not need it than to need something and not have it.

We talked and packed late into the night. By the time we finished, it seemed like we'd stuffed our rucksacks with enough Pathfinder equipment to control the invasion of

Normandy. Besides the usual tools of the trade like two PRC-25 radios with extra batteries, VS-17 panels, strobe lights, ammo, and smoke and fragmentation grenades, we carried such exotic items as an SE-11 light gun that a pilot could see five miles away and two of the beanbag landing lights usually used for fixed-wing landing strips.

I racked out on my cot with the hopes of getting at least two hours' sleep. Well, I was as ready as I was ever going to be. Man! It was really happening. I was going on a real combat mission. I would find out what I was made of. Damn, I might even get shot at . . . Shit, I might even get wounded . . . God, I could even be killed.

I reflected on the day's events. My mind replayed drawing the straws. Ordinarily, I never won at anything. Boy, I couldn't believe my luck. I sure was a lucky guy this time . . . wasn't I?

Chapter Four

A furious wind blew through the chopper's cabin, offering a welcome reprieve from the heat. Unbuttoning the top buttons of my jungle-fatigue jacket, I let the gale blow through my shirt, causing it to flap frantically.

I felt secure sitting on the floor beside the door gunner on the right side of the helicopter. Joe was seated on the other side, across from me. Turning my head, I yelled over to ask how he was doing, but he couldn't hear me. The only sound was the *whopping* of the chopper's blades.

The doors of the helicopter remained open to allow a quick exit when we hit the ground. Although I was close to the edge of the opening, I didn't have to worry about falling out; my rucksack was so heavy, I felt anchored to the floor. My M-16 rifle rested on my lap. It was locked and loaded with a twenty-round magazine. (Though our magazines were equipped to hold twenty rounds of ammunition, we packed them with only eighteen to lessen the tension on the magazine spring and help prevent the bullets' double feeding.)

The Vietnamese countryside was beautiful from a thousand feet up. Miles of lush vegetation ranging from open meadows to thick jungle spread across the whole region. The landscape was decorated with every shade of green imaginable. Small ponds and soggy rice paddies speckled the area. The sun's brightness temporarily blinded me every time I caught its rays as they reflected off the water. Although the view was breathtaking, I had to remind myself that a menacing, deadly enemy lay concealed beneath all that lavish undergrowth.

I heard the blades of the helicopter changing pitch just as the door gunner tapped me on the shoulder, signaling our descent. Joe and I were on the lead bird, accompanying a flight of five helicopters onto the LZ. We were only a few minutes out. I had controlled numerous combat assaults in training, but this was completely different; this was for real. In my mind, I rehearsed the plan Joe and I had devised for when we landed.

Once we were on the ground, two other flights consisting of five helicopters each would follow at approximately two-minute intervals. It was imperative that we keep them abreast of the enemy situation, wind velocity, terrain, and any obstacles on the LZ. Based on those factors, we would also recommend the best landing formation (staggered left, staggered right, wedge, etc.) to utilize. (If possible, it is always desirable to land aircraft in the same formation in which they are already flying.)

We each carried a PRC-25 radio and had performed commo checks before our departure to ensure that both radios were operational. Joe's radio would serve as the ground-to-air radio. He would control the aircraft and issue instructions to the lead pilot of each flight. I would check the winds, throw smoke, and provide security. My radio was also set on ground-to-air so I could listen in and take over if Joe was hit or if his radio went dead. Furthermore, I could switch frequencies to the command-and-control net to request or control artillery or gunship support without interrupting control of the flights.

Approximately thirty seconds out, I could see the LZ off to our front, a huge, open, grassy field surrounded by thick jungle and trees. My heart started thumping violently, my hands began perspiring. I searched the faces of the three grunts sitting to my right. They were lost in their own thoughts. One guy, who appeared to be of Hispanic descent, was making the sign of the cross. He then held a religious medal to his lips. Somehow it was comforting to know that I wasn't the only one who was scared.

Suddenly the fear seemed to swell in my gut. I felt

extremely vulnerable sitting there with the wide-open space to my front, like one of those moving metal targets at an amusement park booth. I thought about all the kids my age back home. Their biggest problem was trying to figure out what party to attend or what movie to see. I started to question myself. What the hell was I doing here? I could be sitting at home, safe, in a comfortable chair, watching TV or going to a movie. Maybe I really wasn't tough enough for the job after all.

The fear intensified. My mouth and lips dried. I wanted to reach for my canteen to get a drink of water, but it was too late. We'd be landing any moment. I could feel my heart beating in my throat.

Deliberately, my eyes glanced down to my left shoulder at the white screaming eagle with the yellow-and-black Airborne tab arced above it. Damn it! I'm a paratrooper. A proud member of the 101st Airborne Division. The finest Airborne unit in the United States Army. I thought about all those who had served before me, and who had fought in places like Normandy and Bastogne. I thought about my family being safe back home and my friends having the freedom to choose what movie they wanted to see.

Besides, I was a Pathfinder. The first man on the ground during the parachute drop in Normandy was Capt. Frank Lillyman, a 101st Pathfinder. Like him, my job was to go in first and safely guide my fellow paratroopers into the battle. I was trained to do that. I chose to do that. No one forced me. My country had always relied on its Airborne soldiers to get the job done, and they had never failed her. I'd be damned if I would.

Abruptly, my thoughts were interrupted as our helicopter skimmed just above some tall trees and went sailing toward the middle of the LZ. The door gunner beside me opened up, his M-60 rapidly spitting bullets. I watched the red streaks of tracers stream into the trees. He screamed over at us, "Shoot! Shoot!"

I flicked my weapon from "safe" to "automatic." I didn't observe any enemy, so I aimed at the door gunner's tracers and squeezed the trigger in short bursts. The grunts immediately followed suit. Suddenly my chest was on fire. It continued to burn all over. Glancing down, I watched in amazement as the door gunner's spent hot brass from his M-60 whipped down the front of my fluttering shirt, scorching my chest.

"Oh shit!" I jolted back and watched the brass zoom by me just as the chopper flared into a quick hover.

I was fumbling to change magazines when the door gunner screamed, "Go! Jump out!"

I stared up at him. My mind was swirling. Everything was happening too quick.

Thrusting my torso toward the edge, my eyes gawked at the ground below. The long blades of elephant grass were pressed down from the chopper's blades, disclosing a drop of about ten feet.

I shouted back, "We're too high up!"

The door gunner stopped shooting and grabbed the frame of my rucksack in an attempt to shove me forward. "Get the fuck out of here!"

All eight of us seemed to leap at once. It felt like I was in the air for a long time. There was a mixture of moans, thumps, and equipment clanking as we slammed into the earth. I was stunned. I hit hard on my tailbone, and it took a moment for my legs to work. Glancing up, I witnessed the last of the helicopters abandon the area. A lonely feeling spread over me, like when your mother waves goodbye to you on your first day of school.

There was shooting everywhere. The sound resembled thousands of firecrackers going off all over the place at once. Leaders were shouting commands, and everybody took off running toward the tree line, which was at least fifty meters away. Joe and I moved with them for about ten meters, then sat down. Bullets were zinging by us as we took off our rucks and turned on the radios. We were sitting ducks out there in the middle of the LZ, but we had to stay and control the choppers.

God, those were real bullets zipping overhead.

Someone was actually trying to kill us. A soldier about twenty meters to our left toppled over; I didn't see him get back up. I heard the familiar sound of M-79 grenade launchers, followed by explosions. Maybe being a coward and sitting at home wasn't such a bad idea after all. I must have been insane to volunteer as a Pathfinder.

Part of me felt like there was a little boy inside just wanting to cry. I was hoping that I was living a bad dream, and if I was, I wanted to wake up right now. I'd heard somewhere that a person used only a small portion of their brain; I thought that maybe, if I concentrated real hard, I could use my whole brain and will myself out of here.

A voice barked over the handset. "Pathfinder Control! This is Black Widow Lead with a flight of five, approximately one minute out. Request landing instructions. Over?"

I looked over at Joe to see if he had heard the transmission as well. He was about five feet away and, like me, was hunkered down low behind his equipment, his handset to his ear. Bullets continued piercing the air around us. A few made a loud *crack* as they whipped by.

He seemed to be in his own little world, so I tried to shout above all the noise. "Joe, the choppers are inbound!"

He looked angry and snapped back, "I know, damn it! Cover me!"

For an instant I got pissed. This was the first time Joe and I had spoken since departing on this mission, and he was already barking orders at me. Right! Cover him? Who the hell was going to cover me?

I noticed something very unusual about Joe's face, however. Staring into his eyes, I recognized that Joe Bolick was as terrified as I was. At that moment I felt a peculiar alliance with him that I could not explain. He was also right. It was my job to provide security and cover him while he brought in the birds.

I brought my weapon up to my shoulder. "No sweat, Joe. I got you covered. Bring them in."

The elephant grass was so high I had to stand up to see

above it. Searching the tree line, I spotted a few gray puffs of smoke from enemy weapons. Making sure I had a clear field of fire, I let go some short bursts at them. I was amazed at how fast the weapon emptied. As I changed magazines, I could hear Joe giving instructions to the pilot.

"Black Widow Lead, this is Pathfinder Control. Land one five zero. Staggered left formation. Winds calm at this time. Receiving enemy small-arms fire from the south and southwest. Continue approach. Over!"

"Pathfinder Control. This is Black Widow Lead. Roger! Continuing approach!"

Joe and I took a moment to remove our helmets and don our black hats so the pilots could distinguish us from the grunts. We hated wearing steel pots anyway. They limited our vision and were hot and uncomfortable to wear. (We hadn't wanted to bring them, but we were ordered to because of some division policy when in the field.)

Anticipating Joe's next request, I grabbed a yellow smoke grenade from my LBE (load-bearing equipment) and ripped off the tape that secured its lever. (Each smoke grenade had its color painted on the top for easy identification. The colors were yellow, green, violet, and red. Red was used only to identify enemy or danger and to abort missions and aircraft landings.)

We could see and hear the aircraft in the distance. Joe called out, "Richie, pop smoke."

Selecting a spot far enough away from us and downwind, I pulled the pin and threw the smoke grenade. There was a metallic *ping* as the lever flew off, followed by a loud popping sound, an eruption of sparks, and a resounding *whoosh* as the smoke roared out of its container. (Deployed improperly, a smoke grenade could cause a fire that would be spread by the rotor wash of helicopters, thus endangering future landings and soldiers on the ground. If thrown too close and upwind, the smoke would encompass us, hindering our vision. Luckily, our position was surrounded by wet, damp elephant grass. The likelihood of it creating a fire was low.)

Joe waited until the smoke had time to billow up from the grass. "Black Widow Lead, this is Pathfinder Control. Smoke out! Identify!"

(It was extremely important never to inform the pilot ahead of time what color smoke you were using. At times, the enemy monitored American radio transmissions. Early in the war, incidents occurred in which pilots were instructed to land on a certain color smoke, for instance green. From monitoring the transmission, the enemy would understand ahead of time what color was being used and would release green smoke at a different or multiple locations. This either confused the pilots or caused them to land in the middle of an enemy ambush. Therefore, the practice was to pop smoke and then have the pilot identify the color.)

"Roger, Pathfinder Control. I spot yellow smoke!"

"That's affirmative, Black Widow. Yellow smoke. You are clear to land!"

The flight of helicopters darted onto the LZ laden with troops. Door gunners carefully scanned the area for enemy; however, none could fire their machine guns because they might accidentally hit Americans already on the ground. By that time most of the fighting was occurring closer to the tree line. More paratroopers bounded from the choppers, tumbling into the elephant grass. Their leaders quickly began to bark orders. So much had happened since we landed on the LZ with the first lift, it was hard to believe that only a few minutes had passed.

Joe had just completed relaying landing instructions to the third and final flight of helicopters when a different voice crackled over the radio.

"Pathfinder Control! Pathfinder Control! This is Medevac One-three, approximately five miles to the northeast. Request landing instructions. Over."

Joe called out, "Richie, there's a dustoff inbound!"

"Yeah, I heard! I was monitoring! The unit commander must have called it! I'll find out where he wants it to land."

Turning the knob on my radio to the command-and-control frequency, I contacted the unit commander. I learned he was assembling casualties who needed evacuation on the southwest portion of the LZ near the tree line. There were six in all, one critical, another KIA.

Since one man was critically wounded, it was essential that we land the dustoff as close as possible to the injured. Joe would continue to control the flight of five that was on its way in while I trekked over to the approximate spot where the commander wanted the dustoff to land, roughly seventy meters away.

"Hey, Joe! When the medevac comes on station, tell him that I'll be there to guide him in visually. I'll link back up with you once he leaves."

"Okay! I'll instruct him to guide in on you when he gets about one mile final. You better get going."

I needed to get there quickly. The dustoff would be inbound in minutes. Searching for a prominent tree in the distance, I located one that I could easily recognize above the others in order to keep my bearings. I had plenty of smoke and ammo attached to my LBE, so leaving my rucksack and radio behind with Joe, I grabbed my weapon and plunged through the thick elephant grass.

Pushing through the dense grass required a great deal of exertion. Movement was rough. It was extremely hot, and my jungle fatigues were drenched from moisture and sweat. Besides my being eaten by insects, blades of grass sliced at the exposed portions of my skin. I couldn't see three feet in front of me, so I kept moving toward the tree I had selected. Hearing the last flight of helicopters approach, I turned and watched them land on the LZ next to a stream of green smoke. Damn, the medevac would be next on station any minute.

About ten meters from the tree line, the elephant grass ended, and it was as if the whole world came into view; I could see again. Noticing a small group of soldiers off in the tree line to my right, I called out, "Hey, where's the wounded?"

Someone from the group replied, "Over here! Are you the Pathfinder?"

I heard another mutter, "Of course he's a Pathfinder, man. Can't you see the black hat?"

As I ventured toward them, one of the group walked hastily in my direction. He seemed especially concerned.

"I'm a medic! Listen! We got to get these guys out of here ASAP [pronounced "ay-sap"]."

I touched him on the shoulder. "I know! No sweat! There's a chopper inbound, and it should be here any moment."

I proceeded with him over to the group. Gazing at the injured, my eyes fell upon a still, lifeless body covered with a poncho. Mud-soaked jungle boots protruded from beneath it. The scene was like something out of a movie, but it wasn't a movie; it was reality. A fellow paratrooper was dead. Forever. I wondered if he was one of the guys that had been on my helicopter coming in. I remembered the Hispanic kid praying and kissing the medal. I was grateful the soldier's face was covered, because I didn't want to know who he was.

A deep feeling of sadness encompassed me. I thought about how terrible it would be for his family when they received the news. I also wondered if the people back home could even slightly fathom the immense sacrifice the soldier and his family endured for the preservation of a people's freedom.

I pushed those thoughts out of my head and redirected my attention to the mission. Stepping out from under the trees, I searched the skies. Sure enough, off in the distance a lone chopper was heading our way.

I was certain Joe had already informed the dustoff pilot to proceed to the southwest portion of the LZ and guide on me, so I had to move fast.

I shouted to the group, "Okay, guys! We got a dustoff inbound. Let's get the wounded out into the field." I instructed the medic to load the litter on first, then the ambulatory, once the bird landed.

Running about twenty meters out into the LZ, I snatched a violet smoke from my web gear and tossed it off to the side. (Joe was in contact with the pilot and, once he saw the smoke, would ask the pilot to identify.)

Raising my arms straight above my head, palms inward, I faced in the direction of the aircraft. That was the signal for him to guide on me.

The dustoff was coming in fast. When it was approximately twenty-five meters to my front, I extended both arms out to my side, horizontally, palms downward. That signaled the pilot to hover. Once I had the helicopter at the desired spot, I moved my arms in a downward motion. Then, crossing my arms to the front of my body, I signaled him to land.

Racing around to the side of the medevac, I assisted in loading the wounded, then ran over and tapped the right-side window of the helicopter, catching the pilot's attention. I knew that the best departure route for him would be to his ten o'clock, thereby avoiding some tall trees as well as possible enemy fire. Making a circular motion with my right hand above my head, I then pointed in the direction I wanted him to depart. This also signaled him to take off. He acknowledged with a thumbs-up. Immediately the aircraft bolted skyward.

The medic and the others expressed their thanks. I didn't have time to converse; I was worried about Joe, who was all alone in the middle of the LZ. Besides, we still had to gather up our equipment and be ready to travel with the unit. With my weapon at the ready, I thrust back into the thick vegetation.

After trudging about fifteen meters, I discovered a path leading in the general direction I was moving. It had been created by our guys treading off the LZ during the assault. The trampled grass sure made the going a lot easier.

Eventually reaching the section I thought to be Joe's approximate location, I called out softly, "Joe! Hey, Joe!"

"Over here!" To my surprise, his voice sounded fairly close.

Proceeding about twenty feet, I stumbled upon a
small opening. Joe had his equipment packed and was attaching his helmet to the back of his rucksack. I felt a
profound sense of relief.

"How's it going, Joe?"

"Good! The pilots reported that the whole operation
went real smooth."

Joe placed his arms through the shoulder straps of his
ruck and struggled to his feet. "Did all the wounded get
out okay?"

"Yeah!" I headed toward my equipment. "Everything
went like clockwork."

"Airborne!" He seemed genuinely pleased.

While I secured my gear, we discussed the success of
the operation. Joe and I certainly worked well together as
a team. Something had changed in the way we interacted, something I'm sure neither of us could explain.
Somehow a strong feeling of trust and camaraderie had
developed between us in that short period of time.

We decided to keep Joe's radio operational while we
moved off the LZ to link up with the unit. Staying in
communication with them was vital to our survival. The
last thing we needed was to get wasted by our own troops
while entering their perimeter. Moreover, if we ran into
any enemy along the way, we could summon help.

It was remarkably quiet on the LZ. I couldn't hear the
faint voices off in the distance anymore. An eerie feeling
came over me, that kind of feeling I used to experience
when I was a young boy all alone in the house while
watching a horror show on TV. I could tell Joe felt it, too.

Joe's voice interrupted my thoughts. "We better get
going! They're probably waiting on us."

"I'm with you. Let's get the hell out of here."

Examining the area to make sure nothing was left behind, we set out for the tree line.

Since I had already crossed the LZ once, I took point.
As we moved through the elephant grass, my mind began
to race. What if the unit had already left the area and for-

gotten about us? What if the gooks saw me returning to the LZ and were waiting to ambush us? Damn, what if we ended up getting captured?

Finally, it occurred to me that it was only the first morning of day one of the mission. It was amazing how much had already taken place; it seemed like an eternity had passed. I felt more secure knowing Joe was with me.

No troops were visible when we arrived inside the tree line, so Joe got on the horn and relayed our location to the unit company commander. The commander instructed us to proceed on about forty meters south for linkup. He had informed his troops of our approach so they wouldn't fire on us. I hoped no one was trigger-happy or just plain spooked.

As we neared their perimeter, we saw some soldiers eating chow while others provided security. It was hard to believe they were the same guys we had flown into the LZ with earlier. They all appeared older and looked like they had been in combat for weeks instead of just a few hours. Even their eyes looked different. I wondered if Joe and I looked like that.

While going by, I addressed a small group: "Which way's the CP?"

Giving us a puzzled stare, one of them pointed to his rear. "Just keep straight ahead, Sergeant."

I thanked him but didn't bother to correct him on my rank. Corporals were an oddity, and the darkened stripes on my sleeve were continuously being confused with those of a sergeant. After a few more inquiries we found the company commander, a captain. Following introductions, he briefed us on his overall mission.

His company was assigned to patrol a specific area for six days, then be extracted by helicopter on day seven. There were not any villages or inhabitants in our AO (area of operations) and no other friendly troops, so the entire area was a "free-fire zone," which meant anyone we came upon was considered the enemy.

While on the move, Joe and I would remain with the

CP. Anything involving aviation was our show. The captain instructed us to wear our steel pots, but we would don our black hats when performing Pathfinder duties. He looked like an amiable person, and it seemed like his soldiers thought highly of him.

Within moments of the end of the briefing, we moved out.

Humping through the jungle was hotter and more laborious than I ever could have imagined. When we were moving, there was never any relief from the heat. I thought walking under the jungle canopy would provide shade, but the humidity was so stifling, it sapped the body's strength. When we marched out from under the trees, in the open, the sun's hot rays sweltered down relentlessly. There was no escape, and sweat streamed from every pore. The salt from my sweat stung my eyes and painted white blotches all over my fatigues.

A wide range of insects ceaselessly attacked us throughout the move. The strangest was a colossal flying bug with a snout and big horn. It looked like a rhinoceros. We called it a B-52, as it buzzed around out of control. It was so big it actually hurt when it slammed into someone's face.

The straps from my rucksack bit into my shoulders, and the steel pot felt like a hundred pounds resting on top of my head. We stopped for a ten-minute break every hour, and within minutes of recommencing I found myself silently begging for the next halt.

I remembered instructors during infantry training, relaying stories of how American soldiers actually cast equipment aside, only to have it recovered by the enemy and used against them. At that time, I'd wondered how in the hell anyone could be so negligent or foolish. But I soon found myself debating whether to dump a smoke grenade or a radio battery just to relieve myself of some of the weight and pain. I don't know if it was faithfulness to my duty as a soldier or the possibility of being caught that stopped me from doing it. But I questioned my ability to be a paratrooper.

My thoughts continually drifted back to home: I could be swimming in a lake right now or taking a cold shower. Tonight I'd be hanging with my buddies or going out with a girl. I could have taken the easy way out. Why did I volunteer for this?

I viewed the soldiers around me. Surely they must be hurting, too. Maybe some of them questioned themselves. The buck sergeant in front of me was short but stocky. In addition to his regular equipment, he carried a complete 292 antenna strapped to the top of his rucksack. I couldn't even conceive of lugging a 292 antenna around. The weight had to be unbearable, but he was making it. If everyone with me could do it, so could I.

Nearing the end of the first day, we sat down for a well-needed break. My shoulders ached, even though the weight of the rucksack was off them. Man, was I tired. I didn't even bother to swat at the mosquitoes anymore. I unsnapped my canteen from its cover. Careful not to spill a drop, I ravenously took a few swallows. It required all of my willpower not to just guzzle it down; the water in my canteen had to last.

I wondered how Joe was faring. I couldn't see him. We'd been moving in a single file, and he was a few soldiers behind me. (To decrease the chance of both of us being wounded or killed at the same time, we did not stick together.)

Checking my watch, I knew we had about two minutes before the break was over. The guy behind me tapped me with a piece of straw he had been chewing. He mumbled something, but I couldn't make it out. I thought he was asking for water and figured he better have one helluva good excuse to get any water from me. Bending forward, I asked, "What'd you say?"

Nonchalantly, he pointed the piece of straw in my direction. "I said there's a scorpion on your right arm!"

I glanced down. I had never seen a scorpion before, and there one was, crawling up my arm. Swiftly I swiped it with my left hand and stood up, chills running down my back. Stunned, I stared at it while it made its way toward a thicket. Hell! They were poisonous. All I needed was to die in Vietnam by a scorpion sting.

Within moments everyone arose. It was time to move out. The guy took the butt of his rifle and crushed the creature. Shrugging my shoulders in an attempt to adjust my ruck, I glanced over at him.

Still chewing on the piece of straw, he shook his head in disgust. "Must be a city boy."

The second day of humping wasn't any easier than the first, particularly since we didn't get much sleep. As darkness crept around us, Joe and I shared some of our thoughts on the day's events and talked a little bit about home. Afterward, we listened to the radio transmissions of another 101st unit, at a different location, heavily involved in a nighttime firefight. Unfortunately, during their battle an artillery round fell short, causing American casualties.

Around midday Joe and I were traveling behind the lead platoon. I was so tired that it took all my effort just to keep placing one foot in front of the other. Suddenly there was loud yelling, followed by small-arms fire. I hit the ground. Immediately my stomach started churning, that intense fear swelling deep in my gut again. Those around me jumped up and started moving forward. I found myself going with them. Although my mind kept telling me to stop, my body wasn't listening. At least I didn't feel tired anymore. Eventually we slowed to a halt at hearing the words, "Cease fire!"

A few moments passed, then Joe and I accompanied the captain to the front of the column in case a medevac was needed. When we arrived, all the platoon members were alert on one knee or in the prone. They seemed fairly relaxed for just having been in a firefight. Two men were attempting to calm down a black soldier. He was approximately six feet tall, thick-bodied, and muscular. He was pacing back and forth, flapping his arms, and speaking hysterically. Before the captain could ask what was going on, the platoon sergeant came forward. His weapon slung, he had his hands extended to his front, like he was motioning someone to stop.

His voice was very apologetic. "It's okay, sir, just a little misunderstanding. That's all!"

The captain seemed puzzled. "A misunderstanding? What the hell happened?"

"Well, sir—" Before the platoon sergeant could finish, the black guy skittered forward, gasping as he spoke. "It was Jake, sir. A no-shoulders, sir. A big goddamn no-shoulders."

The captain put his arm around him, taking him to the side. "It's okay. Take it easy now. Take it easy."

I could hear the soldier continue to ramble. "You know me, sir. I don't run. I'm telling you, sir. The biggest Jake in the world. I'd face a hundred dinks before I'd mess with something like that. That's how goddamn big it was."

I grabbed a blond-headed guy who had initially tried to calm the soldier down. "What's going on? What the hell is he talking about?"

The guy rendered me a confusing stare. "It was a no-shoulders, man. Jake."

Now I was really perplexed. "No-shoulders! Jake! I don't understand!"

My confusion irked him. "Man! Where you from? New Yawk?"

Oh great! Just what I needed! Another country boy from Arkansas. Damn, where was Reynolds when I needed him? I could have used an interpreter right about then.

The guy sounded like a teacher instructing a young student. "Son, the man was talking about Jake the snake. Snakes ain't got no shoulders. Get it? Jake the snake is a no-shoulders."

When it finally registered, I burst out laughing. Unfortunately, the guy didn't think it was so funny. He shook his head, mumbled something, and stomped away. He probably said, "Must be a city boy." I thought to myself, Thank God!

Soon after, the whole story unraveled. The black guy was a good soldier who even volunteered to walk point when he came upon "Jake, no-shoulders." Afraid of snakes and obviously surprised by one of Jake's magnitude, he yelled and ran back toward the others. The rest of the platoon, thinking he had run into the enemy, got spooked and opened fire. Since it was a free-fire zone, they didn't have to worry about injuring other friendlies or innocent civilians. Once the platoon sergeant realized that no one was shooting back, he shouted for everyone to cease firing.

One of the other platoon members killed the snake with a machete. As we continued on, each of us passed its body. It was the largest and most colorful snake I had ever seen. It had to be at least twelve feet long and was remarkably thick in diameter, with triangular patches of reds, greens, and yellows covering its body. It was sliced clear through near the head. It seemed a shame that it had to be killed; I figured a snake that size had been around a long time. Besides, we were trespassing on his property. If I had come across it first, I don't think I would have killed it. Chances are, I probably would have run like hell, too, though.

A day seemed like a week, humping through the jungle with a helmet on and all that equipment. It was difficult to maintain a high state of alertness. Occasionally my mind slipped into daydream mode, contemplating all kinds of thoughts, only to be startled back into reality by a whipping branch or some other interruption.

The nights were not any better. Besides the muggy weather and abundant attacks by mosquitoes, the hard, rugged ground combined with the threat of an enemy attack obstructed any semblance of quality sleep.

On the morning of the fourth day, we moved out at first light. We had been humping only about an hour when small-arms fire erupted to our front. It wasn't a snake that time; it was a firefight. Joe and I stayed with the captain as he maneuvered closer to the action. The lead platoon was in contact. The captain ordered the second platoon in line to move up and support the lead platoon. He then instructed the third platoon to perform a right flanking maneuver while keeping the last platoon for reserve, in case something went wrong.

I felt fortunate remaining with the CP. Although a few rounds sliced at the trees above us, most of the action was happening at the immediate front. Still, it took only one bullet to end a life, and that fear was swelling in my gut again.

Despite the circumstances, it was quite a learning experience for me to watch the company commander carry out his tactic against the enemy. Infantry tactics finally made more sense observing them in action than out of a textbook or on a blackboard. Within moments the shooting stopped, and Joe and I went forward with the captain.

Miraculously, no one on our side had been killed or wounded. It seemed amazing that so many rounds could zip through the air and not hit anybody. We remained with the point element and inched forward. Although we didn't find any enemy bodies, we did encounter some blood trails.

Cautiously advancing about a hundred meters, the point man held up his hand, signaling danger. Instantly we all crouched. Continuing forward, we discovered a recently abandoned enemy base camp. The captain surmised that enemy trail watchers had spotted us approaching and opened fire, probably alerting others in the camp of our presence. We proceeded into the encampment in case any enemy were staying behind to ambush us.

There was no way anyone could have spotted that place unless they were right on top of it. It consisted of a series of foxholes and tunnels concealed by thick foliage. The dense jungle canopy overhead made it impossible to observe from the air. After an initial search, two platoons provided security while the rest of the company broke up into small patrols to conduct a more thorough investigation. Joe and I could have sat around and enjoyed a break, but we didn't want to miss out on anything, so we each latched on to a squad.

It didn't take long before the squad I accompanied came across a small tunnel. The squad leader told us to spread out and search for others in its proximity. I found something that at first looked like a foxhole. A closer examination revealed it to be another tunnel. On the ledge of the entrance, in soft dirt, was a grenade with a wooden handle. It looked very similar to the old German potato mashers of World War II. I thought I could keep it as a souvenir if I completely disarmed it. Bending to pick it up, I remembered the words of an instructor during infantry training who had served a tour in Vietnam. "Don't touch nothing! It doesn't make any difference what it is. Chances are it's booby-trapped. Forget souvenirs. No souvenir is worth losing your life or a limb over." Heeding those words, I backed away from it.

Then a more solemn thought hit me: What was it doing right there at the opening? What if somebody had been getting ready to throw it at me and changed his mind? Withdrawing farther, I kept my weapon aimed at the opening until another squad member neared.

"Whatcha got, man?"

"Another tunnel."

He stepped closer, attempting to peek into the entrance. I put my hand out to caution him. "Watch out! There's a grenade lying right there on the ledge."

Quickly retreating from the opening, he called out to the others.

A total of three tunnels were discovered close to each other. We assumed they were connected. A few of us were stationed at each entrance, then the squad leader shouted for any enemy who might be inside them to come out. There was no response. After waiting a few seconds, he had one man at each entrance pull the pin on a grenade. Yelling "Fire in the hole," he had them toss the grenades into the tunnels simultaneously.

The ground shook under my feet, but the noise wasn't as loud as I thought it would be; the earth muffled the sound. The way the dirt, gravel, and smoke shot from that hole, however, left no doubt in my mind that anybody remaining in there was not around anymore. The squad leader seemed satisfied, so we headed back to the CP.

On our way back, we heard some loud voices and

commotion off to our right. Curious, we ventured over. A bunch of guys were milling around, including Joe and the captain. They had located a tunnel with a larger entrance than the others.

One of the soldiers grabbed a smaller guy standing next to him. "You go down there, Pete. You're always saying what a badass you are."

The guy pushed the other's hand away. "Forget it, man! I'm bad, but I ain't stupid. You go in there, asshole."

Everyone laughed as others began challenging their buddies. The captain smiled, entertained by it all.

I wondered why they bothered sending a guy in at all. Not wanting to appear ignorant, I whispered to Joe so the others couldn't hear me, "Why don't they just frag it?"

Joe didn't seem surprised by my question, which led me to assume that he had probably asked the same thing to himself. "It might be a cache and have supplies or something, since it's a lot bigger than the others."

Finally, a small, pale, wiry individual came forward and volunteered to go in. A couple of his fellow squad members had urged him on. Patting him on the back, they bragged to the rest of the company while he took off his shirt. Someone handed him a .45-caliber pistol. With the weapon off safe and a round in the chamber, he crouched down in front of the entrance.

Man, talk about eerie. There was no way in hell anyone could ever get me to go down in there. (Well, maybe for an R & R week in Australia.) It was a dark, ominous, mysterious-looking hole, more like a cave. The outer sides of the walls were damp, and stringy, thick vines grew from it. It was like out of some horror movie. I imagined that soldier going down into Dracula's tomb without a cross. He was either real brave or just plain crazy. There was no telling if it was booby-trapped or if the gooks were just waiting down there to blow him away.

As he entered the opening, everyone became silent; not even a whisper could be heard. Each second that passed seemed like an hour. He was gone about fifteen seconds when, all of a sudden, we heard him yelling and cursing. The fun was over. While some of the men sprang toward the tunnel, others backed away. Every one of us, however, had his weapon aimed at the tunnel opening.

Unexpectedly, something huge came soaring out of the opening, actually clobbering some of us. People were ducking and swatting. Finally, it stopped, clinging to the bark of a nearby tree. The captain was the first to identify it. "It's a damn bat!" Someone else muttered, "Holy bat shit, Batman! Look at the size of that thing!"

An instant later, a human body propelled itself from the tunnel. It was the little guy. His arms and legs moved so fast it actually looked like he was swimming through the dirt. His elbows, face, and chest were all scraped and dirty. He was still shouting and cussing.

"Christ! Something attacked me down there. Some kind of animal. It was a huge son of a bitch. I was lucky to get out of there alive!"

With the tension lifted, everyone erupted in laughter.

The bat had latched itself to the tree at about eye level. We had some bats back home, but that thing was enormous. It had at least a two-foot wingspan. A few guys went over to examine it while others debated whether to kill it or not. The captain told them to leave it alone and ordered us to prepare to move out. Walking over to my equipment, I chuckled to myself. With the bat and all, I hadn't been far off in my comparison to Dracula's tomb.

Day five was one of pushing through dense jungle. Movement was extremely slow and difficult because of all the wait-a-minute vines. By afternoon the vegetation thinned out to intermittent patches of thick bamboo. Becoming frustrated by the lack of enemy contact, the captain decided to let the lead element conduct a recon by fire every once in a while at their discretion. (Recon by fire is a tactic used to trick the enemy into giving his position away. An area is selected and fired upon at random, say a clump of bushes to the front, with the hope that the enemy is there, either watching or waiting. If the enemy is indeed present, he will think he has been spotted because he is being fired upon, and he will return fire, giving his position away.) Although the lead element conducted a recon by fire on several occasions, that tactic proved uneventful.

Around noon of the sixth day the captain received word that we had to arrive at the PZ (pickup zone) that same day in order to be extracted by early morning. To reach the PZ before nightfall we would have to move rapidly with few breaks. Although we were all dog tired, our morale was high, and everyone hustled. Nobody wanted to miss the ride home. We arrived at the PZ right before dusk. It was too dark to recon the area, so Joe and I decided we would check the terrain at first light.

During the night, sporadic bursts of gunfire broke out on two or three occasions, accompanied by explosions from grenades. I didn't know if the enemy was probing the perimeter or if someone was just spooked.

Just before first light, Joe and I were awakened by whispering. It was the company RTO.

"Just wanted to let you guys know there's going be a mad minute in around zero five" (five minutes).

He caught us by surprise and scurried off before we could thank him. If he hadn't alerted us, we would have thought the enemy had attacked in full force.

A mad minute was similar to a recon by fire but with a twist. Legend had it that a few years back an infantry company from the 173d Airborne Brigade was waiting for an early morning extraction, the same as we were. Since the troops were weighed down with ordnance and leaving the field anyway, their commander decided to let everyone shoot their weapons simultaneously for one minute to expend some of their ammo. When he gave the signal, everyone started firing, not knowing that the enemy had surrounded them during the night and was going to attack them either directly or when the choppers landed to pick them up. When the firing stopped, not one American was injured, but a number of enemy lay dead. The number ranged from fifty to two hundred, depending on the storyteller. I didn't know if it was true or not, but it sure was a great tale. Besides, allowing soldiers to shoot the hell out of their weapons is a great way to relieve stress.

The mad minute began, and the perimeter erupted in a continuous crescendo of small-arms fire and explosions as a company of Airborne infantry blasted away with M-16 rifles, M-79 grenade launchers, and M-60 machine guns for a solid minute. The firepower was majestic. If any gooks had been out there, they weren't around anymore. As a matter of fact, if there had been insects out there, they were probably dead.

Since Joe and I would control the extraction, we radioed the rear and learned that there would again be three flights of five helicopters each. The flights would be landing in one-minute intervals. Once all the troops were extracted, Joe and I would depart on the last aircraft leaving the PZ. We secured our rucksacks and took off to recon the landing site.

The PZ was a relatively open area encircled by tall trees. Numerous obstacles such as stumps, bushes, and bamboo thickets were strewn about the location. Two tall trees stood almost in the center, blocking any approach. It didn't take us long to decide it was a Pathfinder's nightmare. Perhaps we could find another location. If not, the extraction would have to be delayed. A lot of work would have to be done for even one helicopter to land in that place, let alone five of them. We headed back to inform the company commander.

We surveyed the map with the captain, confirming that no other landing sites were available in the area. The extraction would have to be delayed until the PZ was clear of obstructions. The captain took the news gracefully. We radioed the rear and delayed the extraction for three hours. We explained what needed to be done, and the leaders relayed the bad news to their soldiers.

The captain decided most of the work could be accomplished by explosives, so his soldiers wouldn't labor in the hot sun. Thank God I had my steel pot on. You would have thought we were in the middle of a demolition range. All I heard was one "Fire in the hole!" after another, followed by chunks of wood, dirt, and stones slamming the top of my helmet. I watched the two tall trees blocking the approach crash to the ground.

About an hour passed when we received a request for landing instructions. The pilot informed us that he was a Charlie Charlie bird (command-and-control helicopter) carrying the unit's battalion commander on board and his estimated time of arrival (ETA) was zero five.

Since Joe had been the ground-to-air on the insertion, it was my turn to control the aircraft during extraction. There was no way the helicopter could land on the PZ at present, so I gave the pilot some basic instructions, advising him to continue his approach and call me on one-mile final. Meanwhile, Joe would call a halt to all demolition work and scout out a clearing somewhere for the bird to land.

I was starting to get a little nervous. Joe had not returned yet, and the pilot was going to request final instructions any minute. Finally I heard his voice behind me.

"Richie, I found a place over to the east behind that clump of trees. It's really tight, but I think he can fit in there." Joe grabbed a smoke grenade and took off running. "Tell him I'll have to guide him in visually."

The bird reported on one-mile final. I spotted the smoke Joe threw to mark the landing site. After the pilot identified the color, I instructed him to guide in on Joe.

A few moments later, a tall, very erect soldier came tramping through the clump of trees where the chopper had just landed. He had an officer's bearing. As he stomped by, all the leaders saluted him. He was wearing his steel pot, LBE, and a holster with a pistol. You didn't have to be a rocket scientist to figure out the guy was the battalion commander. My assumption was verified when I viewed the silver leaf of a lieutenant colonel on his helmet.

He halted about twenty feet from me. His face was stern as his eyes scanned the area. They stopped abruptly, locking themselves on the colorful Pathfinder badge sewn on my left breast pocket. A moment later he started hastily in my direction. He had more than a serious look on his face. As he got closer, I could tell the look was one of anger. I immediately thought to myself, Oh shit!

Keeping the radio handset in my left hand, I saluted him with my right. Before I could finish saying "Good morning, sir," he barked, "Who's in charge here?"

I knew he was impatiently waiting for a reply, so I swallowed the lump in my throat and answered, "Well, ah, sir! . . . I guess I am."

"Do you mean to tell me you are the soldier responsible for delaying the extraction of my troops?"

Before I responded, I again thought to myself, Oh shit!

"And just who in the hell do you think you are, Sergeant?"

"That's corporal, sir!"

"What?"

"I'm not a sergeant, sir. I'm a corporal! Corporal Burns!" Immediately after I said it, I realized I had just corrected a colonel. He had a strange look on his face. I didn't know if it was one of increased anger or confusion.

I continued, "That's okay, sir! Everyone makes the same mistake! Pathfinders are promoted to corporal instead of specialist because of the responsibility incurred with our jobs."

For some reason, my explanation didn't seem to help his composure. He became more agitated.

"All right! All right! Do you mean to tell me that a corporal delayed the extraction of one of my rifle companies?" He paused, staring me in the eyes, then continued. "Maybe you have overstepped your responsibility just a little, Corporal?"

Well, that was it. I'd be shipped to a line company if I were lucky enough to stay with the division or even keep my rank. My heart began pounding.

"No sir! The safety of those aircraft and their crew are

my responsibility. It's my job to see that they land safely. This PZ is far from safe."

He became even more upset. "Soldier! My troops have been out here for the last seven days. They're tired and hungry, and I want them out of here ASAP." He paused to make sure he had my attention. He did. He continued, "I picked this spot myself on an overflight, so why don't you explain to me just what is wrong with this landing zone?"

I was surprised that the colonel didn't interrupt while I explained the many obstacles that could puncture the fuselage, the debris that could get caught in the rotor wash, the formula for approach, the length in feet of the helicopter blades, and the minimum safe distance needed between each aircraft.

He was still steaming but remained quiet for a few more minutes. He appeared a bit more cordial.

"Okay, son! I'll tell you what. We've got a little over an hour. I'll get all the leaders together and see what we can do."

As he turned to walk away, he blared, "But understand this! At ten hundred hours, my troops are being lifted out of here and brought home no matter what. Is that clear, Corporal?"

I didn't respond as he paraded away.

It was getting near ten o'clock. Joe was busy supervising the clearing party and coordinating with the leaders to arrange sorties. Although the main obstacles like stumps and tall trees had been taken care of, there were still numerous small trees and bamboo sticks protruding from the ground. Many were cut and jagged at the top, standing two to four feet high, and dispersed all over the landing site. Joe informed the leaders that the protrusions would have to be leveled with machetes and entrenching tools, but they stated their battalion commander didn't want the troops laboring in the hot sun. There was no way five helicopters could land and load troops without the possibility of puncturing an aircraft's fuselage.

I saw the colonel glancing at his watch as he advanced toward me. He didn't look as mad as before. "It's getting around the time for those helicopters to contact you, don't you think, Pathfinder?"

"Yes, sir! They should be on station any minute."

Then I took a deep breath and tried to keep in mind that regardless of his rank I was the expert and what I was telling him was true.

"Sir, the PZ is not clear yet, and I've got to tell those birds they can't land here until it is."

Oh-oh! He was angry again. "Soldier, obviously you didn't hear my instructions. I told you earlier that at ten hundred hours my troops will be on board those helicopters and on their way home. Is that clear?"

I took another deep breath. This was definitely developing into one of the worst days of my life.

"No, sir . . . I mean, yes sir . . . it's clear. I mean, no, sir, I'm not going to clear those helicopters to land."

I couldn't believe it was me, standing there telling that to a lieutenant colonel; he was really pissed. "And just why the hell not?"

My heart was pounding again. "Sir, see all those small trees and bamboo that's been cut. They'll act just like big punji stakes; they can puncture the fuselage of the aircraft. I can't allow that to happen, sir."

"This is ridiculous! You will land those helicopters! I've been around a long time, and I know that a helicopter can land just about anywhere."

"Sir, the pilots are the ones that can land just about anywhere and usually they do, especially when troops are in trouble, but we're not in contact. Besides, there's no way five helicopters can land here. We were lucky to get your bird in that small clearing over where you landed. A group of your men are going to have to physically cut all that stuff down."

"Now you listen to me, soldier. Your job is to support me. I'm the ground commander."

God, I was getting into worse trouble than I thought. "Yes, sir. My job is to support you, but not at the risk of an aircraft or its crew. Even though I'm an infantryman, I'm assigned to aviation. That's why Pathfinders are assigned to aviation, so that pilots have their own people with expertise on the ground."

I was so involved in the conversation, I didn't recognize Joe until he was right up on me. Everyone looked alike with a steel pot on. He stood about three paces to the side. He could tell that the colonel and I were in a pissing contest and gave me that do-you-need-my-help look.

By this time, the colonel was furious. He was ready to say something, but a voice came over the radio.

"Pathfinder Control. Pathfinder Control. This is Black Widow Lead, with a flight of five, approximately five miles to the northwest. Request landing instructions, over."

I grabbed the handset. "Roger, Black Widow Lead. Wait one."

I then stared into the colonel's face. "Well, sir?"

He didn't hesitate for an instant. "You will land those aircraft! That's an order!"

That fear was swelling in my gut again, but it was a different kind of fear. I knew in my heart I couldn't compromise my position. I never dreamed I would disobey a direct order from a field grade officer. I pondered a few more seconds, then answered, "No, sir!"

The colonel was stunned by my reply, and I could see his mind racing. He looked at Joe, then back at me. "You are relieved. I'll deal with you later."

He turned to Joe. "Soldier, I want you to get on that radio and bring those helicopters in here right now."

Joe was quiet for a moment, pondering the situation. Finally he answered, "I can't do that, sir."

I had to give the colonel credit. I never saw anyone keep his composure while being that angry. He never raised his voice even once. He had remarkable self-discipline.

"Son, unless you want to end up with the same consequences as your friend here, you had better land those aircraft immediately."

I could see Joe's struggle with himself. I knew Joe

would stick to his guns once he was committed to something and believed in it; this was no exception.

"I'm sorry, sir. I can't do that. It's too dangerous."

I guess the pilot figured he had waited long enough and wanted instructions. "Pathfinder Control. This is Black Widow Lead."

The colonel spoke at both of us. "Well, gentlemen, this is your last chance." I placed the handset down in the radio's carrying handle and left it there.

"Damn it!" The colonel snatched the handset and brought it to his mouth. "Black Widow Lead. This is Shining Alpha Six. You are clear to land."

"This is Black Widow Lead. Request landing instructions from Pathfinder Control. Over."

"Black Widow Lead. This is Shining Alpha Six. The Pathfinders are relieved of their duties. You will take instructions from me. Over."

There was a hesitation on the pilot's end. I bet he was confirming with the copilot what he thought he heard. "Shining Alpha Six, this is Black Widow Lead. Say again. Over."

"This is the ground commander, Oscar Five [lieutenant colonel pay grade]. I say again, I have relieved the Pathfinders. You will take instructions from me. Over."

The pilot hesitated again before replying. "Negative. Request landing instructions from the Pathfinder. Over."

The battalion commander was furious. I noted a slight elevation in his voice. "Now, you listen to me. Your sole purpose for flying out here is to support me. My troops are tired and need to go home. You will land and pick them up. Is that clear? Over."

This time the pilot was quick to respond. "Let me talk to one of the Pathfinders. Over."

God, the colonel was angry. The flight was in view about two miles away, and the colonel was staring at the helicopters as if the pilot could see him while he conversed. "Negative! I told you they are relieved. You will take orders from me. Over."

This time the pilot's voice was stern. "Shining Alpha

Six. This is Black Widow Lead. I will not land unless I can talk with one of the Pathfinders. Over!"

Now the colonel was the one pondering the situation. He rendered me a this-is-all-your-fault look and passed me the handset.

"Black Widow Lead. This is Pathfinder Control. Over."

"This is Black Widow Lead. What's going on down there? Over."

"This is Pathfinder Control. We did not clear the Papa Zulu (PZ) so the ground commander relieved us. Over."

"Roger, Pathfinder Control. How long before the Papa Zulu can be cleared? Over."

"If everyone cooperates, approximately one hour. Over."

"Roger! Pathfinder Control, wait one."

The colonel stared impatiently. Quite a bit of time elapsed before the pilot came back on the radio. "Pathfinder Control. We're going to return to base. Inform us when the PZ is ready. Please give me back to the commander. Over."

"Roger! Wilco!"

I handed the handset back to the colonel. "He wants to talk to you again, sir."

"It's about time." The colonel spoke with his best command voice. "This is Shining Alpha Six. Over."

"Roger! Shining Alpha Six, this is Black Widow Lead. We will return to base and come back once the PZ is cleared by the Pathfinder. He will also control the airlift. Over."

I think the colonel was in shock. I don't believe he had ever been in a situation like that and just didn't think the pilots would refuse to land. He was losing face and grasping for some kind of control.

"Listen here! I'm giving you a direct order to land. Is that clear?"

"This is Black Widow Lead. Negative! We are returning to base at this time. Over."

Man, the colonel was beyond furious, but he still

didn't yell. "You can't do this. I will report you to your commander for disciplinary action."

"Roger, Shining Alpha Six. Be advised I am in contact with my commander, who supports this decision. You will be contacted by your higher headquarters. Out!"

The flight was turning course as the colonel spoke. The soldiers watched the flight turn away instead of picking them up. They were unaware of what was happening and started to voice their frustration. I couldn't blame them. The colonel stomped off.

About ten minutes later the colonel called a quick meeting with his officers and senior NCOs and instructed them to cut down and level everything to a foot or lower. The leaders handled it well, but when they relayed the news to the men, there was a great deal of complaining. The colonel made himself visible among the troops, stating that once the work was accomplished they would get out of there. He even chipped in with some of the labor. His presence calmed the men. A senior NCO came to us when the work was finished. Joe and I checked the PZ and it looked great. I notified the birds to proceed for the pickup.

Joe went off to place the troops into sorties to make the airlift run smoother. I was checking the winds when the colonel approached. "How's everything going, Pathfinder?"

I stopped what I was doing and stood at semiattention. "Fine, sir. The helicopters should be arriving in about twenty minutes, and we'll all be on our way."

He acted completely different from before. "Do you know this incident went all the way to division?"

Joe and I were happy we had been supported, but we didn't know it went that far up the chain. "No, sir. I didn't!"

"Well, it did. And everyone in command seemed to agree with you, so I guess I was the one at fault." He waited a moment to see if I would comment, but I was speechless.

"Listen, I want to apologize to you. We are all a bit new

in country, and I shouldn't have interfered with your work. My job is running an infantry battalion, and your job is controlling aircraft. I sure as hell don't like it when someone tries to tell me how to do my job. You two are very competent, and I can tell you are both good soldiers."

I felt a bit uneasy and didn't know what to do. "There's no apology necessary, sir. You were just looking out for your men."

"Well, that's kind of you, but an apology is necessary. You stood by your guns when you were right, and I know that was extremely difficult for you. A leader needs soldiers who will tell him what he needs to hear, not what he wants to hear. That's true loyalty. Don't ever stop standing up when you are right. Just make sure you are, like you did today."

"Thank you, sir. I appreciate it."

The colonel shook my hand. "If you want to trade those corporal stripes for those of a sergeant, you just let me know. I need men like you. If you come to my unit, I'll promise you a leadership position."

"Well, I appreciate it, sir, but I like being a Pathfinder."

"I know you do . . . and obviously you're good at it. Give it some thought when you get some time, and if you change your mind, let me know. That goes for your partner as well."

"Yes, sir. I'll let him know."

"Well, I'll get out of your way so you can do your job. I'm flying back to my headquarters so I can do mine." I saluted him, and he walked off.

A few minutes later I cleared his helicopter for departure. That was the last time I ever laid eyes on that colonel. I didn't even get his name; his name tag was covered by his LBE suspenders. I'm sure he never realized the impact his words had on me. I never forgot what he said about loyalty and standing firm when you knew you were right. I promised myself I would try to carry that principle with me throughout life. I also gained a great deal of respect for him. In the future, I would come in contact with many senior leaders, and few would have the humility of that man.

The extraction went off without a hitch. Joe and I didn't have to fly back with the infantry battalion; once the extraction was completed, a separate helicopter was sent to pick us up and flew us directly to our own unit.

When we arrived at the helipad, Ron, Larry, and some of the other guys were waiting to greet us and, of course, Torch. It felt great to be back with the detachment; it was like coming home to family. They asked a thousand questions as they helped carry our gear.

There was definitely a difference in the way Joe and I interacted with each other. I was sure Ron and the others noticed but didn't say anything. Sharing the experience together on the LZ brought Joe and me closer, maybe because we had to rely on each other so much. In any event, we would remain friends forever.

At the debriefing, Joe and I reported that, in our opinion, it wasn't necessary for Pathfinders to remain with the infantry for an extended period of time. The infiltration and extraction were a necessity, but we were not really utilized throughout the rest of the mission. Lieutenant Wilberding stated that he had formulated that assumption earlier, but thought it best to have a Pathfinder team confirm his supposition with facts. He was certain that as Pathfinder missions increased, the division's units would not be afforded that luxury anyway.

That night, Torch lay on the ground beside my cot. I think he was glad to have me home. I finally had a chance to play back the whole operation in my mind. I thought about the door gunner's hot brass burning my chest and the leap into the elephant grass. The enemy bullets whizzing by and my shooting back at gray puffs of smoke. The dead American soldier with his jungle boots protruding from under the poncho. The insects, the snake, the bat, and the scorpion. Finding the grenade and blowing the tunnel. The intense heat, the jungle, and the wait-a-minute vines. Last, but certainly not least, the altercation with the battalion commander. God, all of that happened in just seven days! What adventures would an entire year bring?

I had finally experienced combat and performed okay. I felt pretty good about myself. I made it through the fear. Perhaps I was cut out to be a Pathfinder after all. If I could just hang tough for the rest of my tour . . . Surely, nothing could be worse than what I had just experienced.

Soon it would be a new year, 1968. In a little over a month the Vietnamese would celebrate a holiday called Tet. I was lost among my young thoughts and naïveté as I lay there. How could I possibly know that the Communists would then launch the largest single attack of the war, and the 101st Airborne Division would be right in the thick of it?

Chapter Five

The Christmas holidays were over and so was the Christmas cease-fire. Many politicians had lobbied for it, and maybe the American people thought it was a great idea, but quite frankly, most of the experienced soldiers I talked with thought a cease-fire, for any reason, was foolish. All it did was allow Charlie a chance to move and regroup, thus improving his ability to attack or ambush us at a later date. The Communists had utilized the same tactics during the Korean War.

Also, the Bob Hope show came to the area, but very few infantry soldiers attended. They were busy patrolling the surrounding countryside, attempting to prohibit the enemy from launching rocket attacks on the rear while the show was in progress. It seemed a shame, since the infantrymen bore the brunt of the war. Most of our detachment was out in the field as well.

In the beginning of January 1968, our detachment had been in country approximately one month, and we still sought to define our role as Pathfinders within the division. To give us an idea of the range of activities supported by a mature Pathfinder unit, Lieutenant Wilberding coordinated with the 1st Infantry Division Pathfinders out of Phu Loi so that Joe Bolick, John Johnson, Joe Mitchell, and I could work with their detachment for ten days. Pathfinder detachments are particularly small units, and a close brotherhood exists beyond just being Airborne. The 1st Infantry Division Pathfinders went all-out to welcome and include us on their operations.

Luckily, their division had a few significant operations going on during our stay. We paired off with their Pathfinders and conducted a variety of missions, including: sling loading, coordinating sorties, air traffic control, and combat assaults. Their Pathfinder detachment also had parachutes and a qualified parachute rigger. We planned to get a jump in while we were there but were unable to obtain the proper air clearance during our short visit.

Thanking the 1st Infantry Division Pathfinders for their hospitality, we brought back some valuable tips to our own detachment. For instance, it was decided not to get involved in the sling-loading business unless unavoidable, since those functions took time away from actual combat operations. Besides, a rigger unit organic to the 101st Airborne Division was better able to support those types of tasks already. Working closely with a seasoned Pathfinder detachment helped confirm most of our assumptions regarding the type of missions we would ultimately support within our own division.

As the end of January neared, the Tet holidays approached. Tet is the Vietnamese lunar New Year, a sacred holiday during which for several days the Vietnamese people participate in traditional celebrations, hold street festivals, and worship revered ancestors at family altars. This time the Communists decreed a truce, claiming it would last from 27 January to 3 February 1968.

A few days before the Tet cease-fire, rumors started circulating that the enemy was going to launch a major attack on a number of rear-area installations, including Bien Hoa. Intelligence reports had supported the assumption all along. But the South Vietnamese leaders thought it inconceivable. Surely the Communists would not attack on such a hallowed occasion, especially since it was the North Vietnamese themselves who called for the cease-fire agreement.

The American military knew that the Communists had a long record of breaking agreements. As far as the

North Vietnamese were concerned, a war was in progress. Their only goal was to win, and by any means. Therefore, the U.S. military wasn't taking any chances, including the 101st Airborne Division. Every Screaming Eagle was put on alert, and infantrymen from the 502d Infantry relocated to our compound at Bien Hoa to help strengthen the perimeter.

Flak jackets and steel pots became everyday wear. We kept extra batteries and ammunition on hand and drilled rushing to our assigned bunkers. Chopper crews practiced getting gunships armed and into the air quickly. More fighting positions were created and older ones fortified.

Most of the guys I talked with hoped the Communists would attack in large numbers so we could fight them outright for a change, without having to search the jungle and engage them on their terms.

At three in the morning on 31 January 1968, three days after the beginning of the Tet holidays, mortar and rocket fire began pouring into our compound. It sounded like the Fourth of July, except louder. The Communist 122mm rocket was particularly menacing. It weighed 112 pounds and had a range of ten miles. Carrying an immense warhead of forty-two pounds, each one sounded like a low jet fighter ripping through the sky overhead. It made a thunderous explosion, which shook the ground. Although extremely inaccurate, it scattered huge chunks of jagged metal, which tore through anyone and anything in its kill radius.

Rushing into the bunkers, we stumbled and fell on top of one another like the Keystone Kops. Explosions continued, jolting the ground around us. The bunker was a four-foot-deep, four-foot-wide trench, protected by a steel culvert and a few layers of sandbags. It probably would not have withstood a direct hit, especially from one of the rockets.

Within a short while, Lieutenant Wilberding came by and informed us that a ground attack was highly probable. He told us to proceed to the helicopter revetments and protect the aircraft until the flight crews got the choppers into the air. He, Sergeant Guerra, and a few others remained behind to coordinate additional support. (Revetments were parking sites for helicopters. Each such site was surrounded by barrels filled with sand to protect the aircraft from shrapnel and other projectiles.)

In addition to our M-16 rifles, we grabbed two radios and plenty of ammo, then rushed to the revetments. Although it was still dark, the incoming explosions illuminated the night sky, allowing us to find our way easily. Once at the revetments, our group spread out in two-man teams and took up positions behind the sand-filled barrels.

We could hear sporadic gunfire in the distance, and every once in a while a bullet zipped overhead or slapped into one of the barrels protecting us. It was a frustrating situation, because we didn't know the enemy's exact location and friendly units were scattered around us. Consequently, we couldn't return fire for fear of hitting fellow Americans. Anyway, our primary concern was a possible assault by enemy sappers.

Sappers were elite enemy soldiers highly skilled in the art of infiltration. They could penetrate just about any perimeter given the right circumstances and a little luck. Generally they were fully clothed and armed like other NVA soldiers. Sometimes, however, they simply wore a scanty loincloth with a type of grease covering their bodies. That made it easier for them to slither through barbed wire, trip wires, and other obstacles.

Normally, sappers toted explosives attached to their bodies, usually a satchel charge that they could easily throw into a bunker or building, or beneath an aircraft. Since they were not expected to survive or to return from an attack, it was not uncommon for them to blow themselves up along with the intended target, if necessary, to ensure its destruction. The probability of their successful penetration increased when they were assaulting under the protection of a mortar or rocket attack.

In short time, helicopter crews showed up and manned their assigned choppers. Fortunately, none of the choppers appeared to have been seriously damaged by any of the incoming rockets or small-arms fire. While the gunships relocated to load their armament, some of the utility helicopters received orders to immediately transport an infantry platoon of Screaming Eagles to the U.S. embassy in Saigon, which was under attack. Lieutenant Wilberding radioed us that he and another Pathfinder already at his location would coordinate the pickup zone of the platoon.

Suddenly, intense small-arms fire broke out all along the installation's perimeter. By the sound of it, one hell of an attack was under way. Wilberding's voice blared over the radio. He informed us that the enemy was assaulting the perimeter in large numbers. Our group was directed to leave the revetments and immediately proceed to the perimeter to find any position that needed additional reinforcement. By the sound of the gunfire, we had to get there fast.

Hurrying to a nearby road, we hitched a ride on a truck delivering supplies and ammunition along the perimeter. When we arrived at the perimeter, we discovered a place with a forty-meter gap between fighting positions. As the truck screeched to a stop, a few rounds zinged by. The driver yelled for us to get off. Quickly jumping from the bed of the truck, we all crouched low off the side of the road. Hastily, the vehicle sped off, the driver obviously happy to be away from the scene.

The site we picked contained two deteriorating sandbag walls about ten feet long and four feet high for use as cover. Larry Foracker, Ron Reynolds, Joe Bolick, and I bolted behind one stack of sandbags while the rest of the detachment members dashed behind the other. The position had a clear view to our left front, which encompassed a large open area with shrubbery, rolling hills, and ditches. The right front overlooked the Bien Hoa Air Base and its runway in the distance.

Instantly, bullets cracked all around us, some slamming into the sandbags shielding us.

Larry was on my left, Ron and Joe to my right.

Breathing heavily, Larry gasped, "Damn man, that was close!"

Ron slowly raised his head to peek above the sandbags. "Maybe I can see where it's coming from."

Sand splattered in his eyes and on his face as bullets impacted into the sandbags. He quickly dropped to the ground. "Goddamn! Someone has us zeroed in."

Watching Ron wipe the sand from his eyes with his sleeve was so humorous we all started laughing.

I turned to Larry. "Hey, Larry! Poke your head up there and tell us if you can see anything, will you?"

"You're crazy, man. This shit's for real. My mother will be real upset if I get killed." I would have given anything to have a photo of his face; his expression prompted us to laugh all the harder.

It was Joe's turn. "Richie, weren't you the one bitching about having to wear a steel pot and flak jacket?"

I shook my head. "Yeah! But not now, brother. You won't hear me complain about wearing this stuff again."

Bullets continued zinging overhead and slapping into the sandbags. Afraid to aim our weapons for fear of exposing our heads and getting them blown off, we sat huddled together, paralyzed. Glancing over at the other position, I saw our fellow Pathfinders trapped in the same predicament.

Finally, out of frustration, Ron cried, "We've got to do something! We just can't sit here like this."

Larry agreed. "He's right! For all we know an entire company could be charging across that field at us right now and we can't even look up to see them."

That scary thought was emphasized further when someone on the perimeter cried out, "Fix bayonets!"

That did it! As if Ron and I read each other's mind, we switched our weapons to automatic and lifted them above the top of the wall, exposing just our hands. We sprayed the area to our front once, then repeated the procedure. Within seconds the rest of the detachment followed suit, saturating the area with bullets.

We stopped shooting just as a jeep squealed to a halt on the road directly behind us. Two more members from our detachment jumped out of the vehicle and ran toward our position. One lugged an M-60 machine gun while the other hauled ammo. The one with the machine gun was Corporal Elliot. Elliot was the only black soldier in the detachment. They took cover behind our barrier. Elliot smiled and pointed to the M-60. "Thought you guys might need a little help."

Since Elliot had just arrived, we updated him on the little that had been happening so far. While listening, he straightened up for a moment to stretch his back. Bullets ripped through the air around him. Terrified, he fell to the ground and scampered behind the nearest sandbagged protection he could find. We tried hard not to laugh but couldn't help it.

"Yeah! Go ahead! Go ahead and laugh! You all might think it's funny, but that little bastard just tried to kill my black ass."

As the laughter grew louder, tears streamed down my face. Even though Elliot was upset, he eventually shook his head and grinned.

Suddenly our attention was diverted by explosions occurring inside the air force compound. Portions of a building blew apart, hurling shattered wood and debris into the air. At first we thought the explosions were the result of enemy mortars. To our surprise, however, fifteen to twenty armed figures clad in brown uniforms rushed past the buildings and onto the runway. One of them tossed something at a parked jet on the strip; the plane exploded in a ball of fire. Sappers had penetrated the air base.

Later it was reported that a sapper unit along with approximately two hundred enemy soldiers had broken through the ARVN compound, whose weakened perimeter bordered the air base. Half of the South Vietnamese soldiers were away on leave visiting with family for the holidays.

The sappers were approximately three hundred meters from our position and caught in the open. We couldn't believe our luck. Someone shouted, "Let's get them!" We opened fire.

Instantly, many of the figures fell. Some lay completely still while others squirmed and writhed on the ground. Moments later we stopped shooting to assess the situation. Only a few continued running; others struggled to their feet, some hobbling for cover.

Elliot got excited; he shouted, "Let me have that damn machine gun!" Since the machine gun was too heavy and awkward to lie on top of the wall, it had not yet been put to use. Elliot motioned for Larry and Mitch to carry the gun around to the side of the sandbags.

Once the machine gun was in place, Elliot quickly positioned himself behind it, crossing his legs. With the gun's barrel pointing in the general direction of the runway, Elliot snarled, "I'll get the rest of those bastards!"

Instead of firing short bursts as every infantryman is taught, he just held the trigger back and let it rip. The machine gun began spitting out a continuous stream of bullets. It sounded like a runaway jackhammer. The rest of us opened fire again.

Joe Bolick had been monitoring the radio. Suddenly he frantically waved his arms and shouted for us to cease firing. Sensing his concern, we all stopped. Elliot, however, continued blasting away with the M-60, oblivious to anyone around him.

Joe shouted at those of us standing near. "I was just told that some of our rounds might be hitting air force personnel who have left the security of their bunkers."

Joe screamed for Elliot to stop. "Elliot! Corporal Elliot! Cease fire! Cease fire, damn it!" We all attempted to capture Elliot's attention but he just continued, his face expressionless, the machine gun steadily spitting bullets. The gun's barrel grew hot and began to glow.

Continuing to scream in Elliot's ear, Joe slapped him on the top of his helmet. Someone else tugged at the back of his shirt. Finally Ron cried, "Twist the belt! Twist the belt! That'll stop the gun." Snatching the ammunition belt close to the feed tray, I gave it a hard twist, immediately silencing the weapon.

Elliot remained motionless, his finger still bent on the trigger. It was as if he were locked in some kind of deep trance. His face looked weird, almost euphoric. He never uttered a word. Pulling him to his feet, we grabbed the machine gun and retreated back to the safety of the sandbags.

Although most of the sappers had been killed, enemy soldiers continued to fire at us from both inside and outside the perimeter. Of course, those inside the perimeter were trapped, and they knew it. Daylight only promised their demise. Nonetheless, some remained cleverly concealed, taking occasional well-aimed shots at us from hidden or fortified positions. And every once in a while, a Communist bullet found its mark.

The sun rose steadily, along with the heat. Without the benefit of shade, my flak jacket and helmet grew even more uncomfortable, and I began to gripe again about having to wear them. I stopped complaining when I watched a soldier get hit right in his steel pot. The enemy bullet pierced his helmet, spun around the inside, and then exited from the same hole it had entered. Other than a crease around his head, the man was fine.

At one point I thought I detected an object in a drainage ditch about two hundred meters away. Inadvertently glancing to my left, I witnessed a soldier fall from a guard tower. His limp body struck the ground like a sack of potatoes. I gazed back at the location where I'd first spotted the object; it had disappeared. Surely the appearance of the object and the soldier's being shot at the same time were not a coincidence.

My eyes remained fixed on that spot for a long span. After a good while I concluded that it was just my imagination and was about to give up when the object reappeared. This time I clearly recognized it as the torso of a man. A moment later it vanished once again. I peered over at Foracker; it looked as if he was staring at the same location. Damn, I was hoping he had not seen the enemy soldier.

Perhaps I should have revealed the soldier's whereabouts, but I wanted him all to myself. I don't think I was being selfish really. I saw it more as my reward for having been the one who discovered him. Well, maybe I was being selfish, but that son of a bitch had just killed a fellow Screaming Eagle, and I wanted to be the one to take him out.

Resting my weapon on the sandbag, I aligned the top of the front sight post with the contour of the ditch and waited for what seemed an eternity. At last the object rose again. My body trembled. Taking a deep breath, then slowly letting it out, I forced my body to relax. Making certain the rear sight and front sight were aligned, and with the enemy's torso resting on top of the front sight post, I slowly squeezed the trigger. *Bang!* Without hesitating I fired a second shot. The figure disappeared from my sight picture. I stared for quite some time and never saw him rise again.

I couldn't believe it. That was the first enemy soldier I was certain I had killed. An immense feeling of elation rushed through me. Not because I had taken another person's life but because I pulled the trigger when it was time. It was different from the chaotic shooting I had done in the jungle. Most soldiers wonder if they could actually pull the trigger when the time comes that another human being is actually in their sights. I'd performed when it was time, and I did the right thing. That enemy soldier would not be killing any more Americans. I made a mental note of the exact spot in case the opportunity arose for me to check him out later.

It was about eight in the morning when shouting began all along the perimeter. Looking in the direction where everyone was pointing, I was awestruck. It appeared that, some ten miles away, an atomic bomb had detonated. I watched the massive, dark cloud mushroom high up into the atmosphere.

Wide-eyed, Larry blurted out, "What the hell is that?"

Just as perplexed, Ron remarked, "God, I don't know. I've never seen anything like that in my whole life. It looks like an atom bomb!"

I was thankful that Ron voiced what I had been thinking, so I added my two cents. "It sure looks like the atomic bombs they show on TV."

Joe Bolick was skeptical. "It can't be an atom bomb! It has to be something else."

Mitch piped in. "Okay! If it's not an atom bomb, then what the hell is it?"

Bolick shook his head in confusion. "I don't know. I've never seen anything like it before either. It sure looks like an atom bomb, but I just know it isn't."

The enemy must have noticed it, too, because most of the firing stopped. All of our eyes remained fixed on the mammoth cloud of smoke as it continued to ascend skyward, growing bigger and greater. Finally, upon reaching its peak, it sprouted a colossal ring that began to ripple across the sky.

Buz Harding, another detachment member, switched one of the radios to the command frequency, hoping to find some answer. Kneeling on one knee and holding the radio handset close to his ear, he waved his free hand to get our attention. "Hey! Listen up, guys! Listen up! I found out what's going on."

You would have thought a general had just showed up, the way everyone immediately became silent. Buz continued, "Sappers blew up the ammo dump at Long Binh." Long Binh was an enormous American installation, which housed one of the largest ammunition dumps in all of Vietnam.

Bolick was the first to respond. "Wow! No wonder it looks like an atom bomb."

Mitch let out a sigh of relief. "Well, I guess you were right, Joe; it wasn't an atom bomb after all." Pausing for a moment, something still on his mind, he continued, "But what the hell is that weird-looking circle in the sky that's coming right for us?"

Ron answered before Bolick could reply. "I think that's the shock wave from the explosion."

Larry echoed my thoughts precisely. "Oh great! Look at the size of that thing. That's one hell of a shock wave. I wonder what happens when that thing passes over us?"

With a tinge of anxiety lingering in his voice, Mitch muttered, "I guess we'll find out real soon, won't we?"

Ron snickered. "I can't believe y'all. This is a piece of cake, especially after going through the last few hours with bullets whizzing by and all."

He had a point!

Watching the shock wave move toward us was one of the most fascinating occurrences I have ever witnessed. A huge spherical ring was actually distorting the sky as it rippled toward us. Ironically, none of us sought cover; we just remained stationary, in awe. I was wondering how many people get to see something like this in their lifetime. What a sight! It passed over with a thunderous *boom*, and for a moment it felt as if the earth had quivered on its axis. After the shock wave traveled by, we returned once more to the fighting.

By late morning we were informed that the enemy's main attack on the installation had failed. Standing toe-to-toe, slugging it out with American forces, the Communists proved no match. However, the fighting carried on for days. Other than those trapped inside the compound, the enemy forces retreated to the town of Bien Hoa and the surrounding villages.

Early in the battle, General Barsanti, the division commander, had ordered elements of the 2d Battalion, 506th Infantry, to relocate from their base camp to our location at Bien Hoa as a reaction force. Lieutenant Wilberding and Staff Sergeant Guerra had set up an LZ near division headquarters to land those infantry companies. The 2d Battalion, 506th Infantry, under the command of Lieutenant Colonel Grange, would have the job of chasing down and destroying the remaining enemy forces.

As the day wore on, our section of the perimeter quieted down so dramatically that it was basically secure. It surely didn't require our detachment's augmentation anymore, so we decided to go back to the hootch and get some chow. We caught a ride on one of the trucks heading in that direction.

Torch wagged his curly tail at the sight of us. The little guy sure was happy to see someone, especially after being closed up in the hootch all morning. We broke out some C rations and sat around eating and telling war stories.

About an hour later an intense firefight broke out about a kilometer away. Some of us stepped outside the hootch to watch the helicopter gunships go to work, followed by air strikes from air force jets. We learned that the majority of enemy soldiers, still trapped inside the compound, were locked in battle. It gave me a strange, guilty sort of feeling to be back at the barracks, fairly safe, when only a kilometer away a major firefight was going on and men were dying.

While observing the action I noticed a plane pull up from an air strike. At around five hundred feet its engine sputtered and it starting losing altitude. The aircraft banked a hard right, turning in our direction. As it neared, I recognized it as an A-1 Skyraider, a large fixed-wing aircraft with a propeller and a piston engine. Used for escort missions and close air support, it was slower than the newly designed jet fighters, therefore more susceptible to ground fire.

The plane was trailing smoke, the pilot obviously in trouble. It continued losing altitude, and as I watched, began descending right toward us. I decided to warn the others.

"Hey, guys! There's a plane in trouble, and it looks like it's heading right for us."

Locked in some debate about who did what, none of them really bothered to take me seriously. Larry was his old humorous self. "Oh, sure! Where's it going to land, on top of the hootch?"

My voice grew louder and I pointed at the aircraft. "No! I don't think it's going to land on the hootch. I think it's going to crash right into us."

Finally they decided to look; I heard mutters of "Oh shit!," "Damn!," "I don't believe it!"

Bolick responded with, "Goddamn! It's coming right at us!"

By now the plane was a hundred meters away and closing fast. I felt like I was part of a World War II movie, watching a plane plunging head-on at me, trailing smoke. I picked up Torch and began to run for it.

Luckily, at only thirty meters away, the plane overshot us, but not by much. It flew right above our heads about the height of a telephone pole, still sputtering and smoking. I could actually see the pilot, a Vietnamese. The expression on his face was one of terror mixed with determination.

Instead of crashing behind us, the plane snatched a bit of altitude at the last second and banked right again, this time in the direction of the runway. The hootches obstructed our view, so we never knew what happened to the aircraft. But, since we didn't hear a crash, we assumed the pilot had landed it safely.

Later in the day, most of us were ordered back to the perimeter for the night. Along with one of the door gunners from our battalion, Ron Reynolds and I occupied a well-fortified, three-man bunker. Ron and I had our individual M-16s; the door gunner brought along an M-60 machine gun. My weapon was also equipped with a starlight scope, a telescope that could be easily mounted to the M-16 rifle and other weapons. The starlight scope was an image intensifier that used ambient light to enable one to see at night. It was truly remarkable.

We three decided that two of us would remain awake while one person slept, rotating shifts every two hours. That seemed fair enough.

While Ron and I set up the position, the door gunner kept complaining about how unfair it was that the unit had put him on bunker guard, since he would have to fly the next day. He was a decent guy, so we agreed to let him sleep first and nap past the two-hour shift until one of us became too tired to stay awake.

Throughout the night, sporadic gunfire continued as units remained locked in firefights. In the distance a stream of bright red showered from the sky as gunships sprayed the surrounding areas with their miniguns. The minigun was an awesome weapon that shot six thousand rounds a minute and generated a thunderous sound that was truly all its own.

The night air was extremely humid, causing my fatigue shirt to stick to my back. Even through the noise of gunfire, the insects and reptiles persisted with their unmelodious sounds. Around midnight I was scanning the area with the starlight when I saw five silhouettes patrolling slowly across our front about a hundred meters away. At the guard briefing we were instructed to notify the OIC (officer-in-charge) if we saw anything suspicious. I radioed the OIC, asking if any friendly patrols were in the area. After checking with higher headquarters, he radioed back that no friendlies, American or allied, were patrolling the vicinity. Still, he instructed me to open fire only on his approval. Given the circumstances, I thought that was pretty stupid.

Well, maybe I was just tired and my eyes were playing tricks on me. I stared back into the starlight. There they were again, five figures strolling horizontally across my front. The door gunner was sound asleep, so I asked Ron to look through the scope.

"What do you think?"

Ron exhaled. "Hell! I don't see anything!"

I guess I had a sorrowful expression on my face, because he continued, "But just because I don't see anything, doesn't mean nothing's there!"

"Yeah! But I don't want to look stupid or get in trouble if I open fire."

Ron paused for a moment, then continued. "If you fire,

how the hell is anybody going to know that it came from this bunker?" He paused, then chuckled. "Besides, the whole damn berm is going open up once they hear a gunshot."

I stared back into the starlight scope at the location where I had last seen the figures. Nothing! I continued scanning the area and was about to give up when there they were, just like before. It couldn't be just my imagination!

Excitedly, I turned to Ron. "Shit! I still see them!"

Ron put his face close to mine. "Let me have another look."

I steadied the weapon while he placed his eye on the scope. "They should be right where you're looking!"

I could see the weapon move slightly as Ron scanned the area. "Sorry, Richie! I still don't see any movement."

I was getting frustrated. "Can you see the bush that's about five feet high and shaped like a fan?"

He moved the weapon slightly, then responded. "Yeah! I got it in sight!"

"Well, scan to the right of that and you'll see them."

Ron continued searching for a few moments, then gave up. "Sorry, man! I just can't find them."

"Damn! I know they're out there!"

Ron was a good friend and knew that I was debating whether or not to open fire. He grabbed the M-60 machine gun, placing its bipod on top of the sandbags. "Tell you what! You got any magazines with tracers?"

I nodded. I always carried some magazines, with the last three rounds being tracers. On missions where it didn't matter whether you gave away your location, the last rounds of a magazine containing tracers proved useful, especially when firing on automatic. The tracers alerted you that it was time to change magazines. It might sound ridiculous, but a lot of precious moments can be wasted when changing magazines in the heat of a firefight.

Ron slammed the M-60's feed tray and pulled back the bolt. "Okay, Richie! Go ahead and find them again; when you do, open up. I'll follow your tracers with the sixty."

Quickly I located the bush and scanned to its right

with the starlight. It took a while, but there they were, five figures moving ever so cautiously across the field.

"I see them! You ready?"

Ron took aim behind the machine gun. "Roger that! Let it rip!"

I flicked the selector switch of my weapon to automatic and pulled the trigger. In seconds my magazine emptied, and Ron was blasting away with the 60, showering the area with bullets.

I slammed another magazine into my weapon. This time I had to bead in on Ron's tracers. Every fifth round of M-60 ammo was a tracer. Since each tracer scorched an erratic, bright green streak across the lens, my starlight scope became useless once he began to fire the area up.

Behind us, we heard the door gunner bellow, "Christ! What the hell's going on? Are we under attack? We got gooks in the wire?"

Once we stopped firing, Ron and I turned to inform the door gunner of what was going on; both of us burst out laughing. There the guy was, on the floor, with a flak jacket draped over his head, his fatigues covered in dirt.

Ron continued to laugh as he spoke. "Richie thought he saw some gooks out there, so we opened up on them."

The poor door gunner was not amused. "Damn! You guys should have woke me! You scared the shit out of me!"

I shrugged my shoulders and tried to act serious. "You're right, man. Sorry!"

Ron was right about everyone else firing once we opened up. The whole berm had erupted in a volley of small-arms fire. I guess all the guys on bunker guard were just waiting for an excuse to fire their weapons. They weren't taking any chances after the day's battle.

Ron cleared the 60 and shook his head. "Damn! I bet that poor lieutenant who's the OIC is going crazy right about now."

Morning came and the three of us immediately traveled to the area by the bush where I'd seen the five figures. I was hoping to find either bodies or blood trails. To my disappointment, we didn't find any indication that anyone had ever been there. Had I hallucinated? Ron tried to raise my morale by telling me how clever the gooks were at not leaving any traces when they policed their dead. I appreciated the gesture. We made it back to the hootch just in time to grab some C rations before being placed back on the perimeter. It was going to be another long day.

This time we were positioned on a different part of the perimeter, but still close to the Bien Hoa Air Base. Enemy stragglers were still fighting inside the compound. Since we had two radios, we kept one in contact with Wilberding and the other on the aviation frequency. We agreed to take turns monitoring each radio. During my shift on the aviation frequency, I sat behind the safety of the sandbags and listened intently to elements of the 506th heavily engaged with a large enemy force. They were only about a kilometer away from us.

Some Cobra gunships in support of the battalion's reconnaissance platoon dived on the enemy. The Cobra was the army's new helicopter gunship and a flying weapons arsenal. Equipped with 2.75-inch rockets, 40mm grenade launchers, and miniguns capable of firing six thousand rounds a minute, the helicopter wreaked havoc on the enemy. During its attack, one of the Cobra's rockets either malfunctioned or fell short, blowing up in the midst of the platoon. The rocket killed two soldiers and seriously wounded some others.

The platoon leader immediately started screaming over the horn. The Cobra pilot was devastated. His voice was cracking with emotion. "Oh my God! Oh God, is there anything I can do?"

Angrily the platoon leader ceased the gunship support and requested a dustoff to evacuate his injured.

When the dustoff pilot arrived on station, he announced that he dare not land because of the intense enemy fire. I listened while the Cobra pilot, understandably still shaken up by the mishap, pleaded with the dustoff pilot to set down. At one point the Cobra pilot threatened to blow the medevac out of the sky if it did not go in and pick up the wounded.

Ultimately the dispute ended with the Cobra pilot declaring that he would land his gunship and tie the wounded onto its skids. Shamed into acting, the medevac retrieved the wounded soldiers successfully. Since monitoring the radio was like having a front-row seat to the many happenings of the battle, everyone wanted a turn. When my time was up, I passed the radio on to Ron.

Of all the assorted firefights and engagements taking place, the one that received the most attention involved two enemy soldiers who had barricaded themselves in an old French colonial bunker inside the Bien Hoa compound. Constructed of enormously thick concrete on its top and sides, the bunker offered stout protection. Throughout the day, the two had fought off everything thrown at them; it was nearing dusk.

The battle gained such notoriety that everyone not on the perimeter was watching the show. For an hour, Cobra gunships took turns diving on the bunker, saturating it with rockets and minigun fire. But after every pass the enemy soldiers returned with a burst of machine-gun fire.

Each attack by a Cobra ended with the same result. The Cobra would dive on the target, firing its rockets, many hitting the bunker. The gunship would then complete its run by blasting away with its miniguns before ascending back into the sky. The red tracers from the Cobra's miniguns resembled a bright red stream of water showering down on the structure. As soon as the Cobra's miniguns ceased firing, however, green tracers from the enemy's machine gun would reach up for the aircraft once again.

In some of the units inside the compound, groups of watching soldiers actually gathered around with beer and soda. Congregating on tops of bunkers and sitting in chairs, they could be heard cheering after every pass. Although nobody wanted anything to happen to the Cobra pilots, a certain admiration had developed for the two daring defenders.

As soldiers, you had to give them credit. They could have surrendered, but they chose to fight to the end. Secretly, I hoped that if I was ever caught in the same situation, I would fight with the same tenacity. The commitment displayed by those two soldiers, and that of the sappers who blew themselves up to ensure success, left no doubt in my mind that we faced a formidable enemy. The two soldiers actually fought through the night and into the next day before being killed.

For the following few days, the battle continued with house-to-house fighting in the town of Bien Hoa. Some enemy soldiers, donning civilian clothes, dispersed into the holiday crowds. Others, including entire units, shielded themselves behind women and children, confident that American soldiers wouldn't fire on them. Some of those soldiers escaped and others surrendered, but many were killed after a lengthy standoff.

While the infantry companies battled in the city and villages, most everyone else participated in some form of cleanup of the compound. Members of our detachment were distributed out to various details. Ron and I ended up overseeing the gathering of debris at the perimeter. Ironically, the place was close to the site of our first-day firefight.

Dead enemy bodies were scattered all over the place. And they were already decaying. A stench hung over the area. I remembered some of the old-timers saying that a dead body had its own distinctive smell; it was definitely true. Details wearing work gloves and gas masks policed up the enemy bodies and placed them on two-and-a-half-ton trucks. They were then transported to giant holes and covered with dirt by bulldozers. I was glad we didn't get stuck with that chore.

During a break, Ron agreed to go along with me to the spot in the drainage ditch where I was certain the enemy soldier I had killed might be lying. I told Ron about my feeling selfish about the way I hadn't told anybody, wanting the guy all to myself. He assured me that he probably would have done the same thing.

As we stepped across the field, it looked completely different from the other day. Then, amidst all the excitement and confusion, everything was so frenzied, it was downright exhilarating. Now the place seemed drab and desolate, almost colorless.

To our immediate front was the drainage ditch. We walked farther, and there lay the enemy soldier. He didn't look real. His clothes were all crumpled and his body twisted, resembling a large rag doll. His skin looked like wax. I'd thought I would feel some kind of power surge, my first kill and all, but I didn't. Even though he had killed Americans, I didn't feel angry toward him either. I guess what I really felt was a certain respect for him. He was a fellow soldier who'd put his life on the line like the rest of us.

He had sustained two wounds, which meant I'd hit him with both shots. He had a bullet hole in his side and another higher up in his chest. The latter must have ricocheted off a rib, because the exit hole was a lot higher up his back. Ron searched the immediate vicinity for his weapon, but the cleanup detail had already been through the area and probably scavenged any souvenirs.

When Ron was searching for the weapon, I stared into the dead soldier's face. For a brief moment, I wondered if he and I had met under different circumstances, could we have become friends. I dismissed that notion immediately. That was fantasy. He and I were both soldiers. He was sent to represent his country, and I was sent to represent mine. It could just as easily be me lying there instead. Moreover, he wasn't going to kill any more Americans, and that's what really counted. Perhaps before the year was out, I wouldn't make it either.

The overall battle in and around Bien Hoa lasted about five days. Our division was credited with having killed well over six hundred enemy soldiers. Unfortunately, we lost around forty-five Screaming Eagles.

A few sections in the city of Bien Hoa were utterly destroyed, and numerous reports confirmed that many South Vietnamese civilians were murdered—selectively and at random—by the North Vietnamese during their withdrawal. Observing all the devastation, many of us wondered why we just couldn't fight the enemy in his own country, North Vietnam. It didn't seem to make sense to limit the ground fighting to the country of South Vietnam, because that made the South Vietnamese populace the overall losers. Oh well, I was only eighteen years old and fresh out of high school. Most, if not all, of our political leaders were of the World War II generation, many of them veterans of that war. I had confidence that they had some plan for us to win.

Within a few days after Tet, the news media and military intelligence sources related the full account of the battle. The North Vietnamese Army along with the Viet Cong had attacked a number of military installations and urban centers throughout the country. With a force of over eighty thousand soldiers, their objective was to destroy South Vietnam's military and rally the civilian population to their Communist cause. Labeled the Tet Offensive, their assault failed miserably, with over forty-five thousand of their soldiers being killed, many captured, and the entire Viet Cong infrastructure in South Vietnam destroyed.

Conversely, among all the free-world forces we lost about four thousand soldiers. Unfortunately, 1,001 Americans were included in that number. The Tet Offensive proved to be a tremendous victory for the U.S., South Vietnam, and all our allies.

Our euphoria and pride turned to shock and hurt when we discovered that the news media had negated our victory to the people back home. Instead, they reported it as a "psychological" victory for the Communists since they had attacked so many installations by "surprise." What crap! We knew they were coming all along and had prepared for it. We would not have been so victorious if we hadn't. Moreover, the South Vietnamese population never rallied to the Communists' side. As a matter of fact, after the Tet Offensive, most of the populace stood firmly behind the South Vietnamese government.

Initially, the news reports were a blow to our morale, but that didn't last long. Those of us who fought at Tet knew we had performed well. In my opinion the Tet Offensive was a good thing for the 101st Airborne Division. As a newly arrived division to Vietnam, we fought a major battle with the same spirit and determination as those Airborne soldiers before us. After experiencing a significant battle like Tet, the 101st Airborne Division proved it was ready for anything the enemy could throw at it.

In the months that followed, the enemy would attempt to do just that.

Chapter Six

Not long after Tet, Lieutenant Wilberding received a request for a Pathfinder team to deploy to a place called Song Be, where units from the 101st Airborne Division had been sent to protect that city and its locale, thus increasing the flow of air traffic in that area. Wilberding decided to assign a three-man Pathfinder team consisting of Joe Mitchell, Brad Bradford, and myself. I would be the senior Pathfinder, since I outranked Mitch and Brad. Our mission would be to control a much-needed refueling point for helicopters and to assist any units or aircraft in that vicinity requiring Pathfinder skills.

Historically, Song Be had been the site of numerous battles. Its close proximity to the Cambodian border made it vulnerable to the North Vietnamese. In previous engagements the enemy had launched attacks, then withdrawn back across the border into Cambodia, knowing that American troops were prohibited from pursuing them.

Intelligence reports predicted that in the near future the Communists would attempt to capture a major city in the south because they desperately needed a military victory after their devastating defeat at Tet to boost Communist troop morale and bolster the American antiwar movement back home. Enemy activity around Song Be had increased so significantly during the previous week that intelligence sources determined the city of Song Be might well be the Communists' intended target.

We had heard that the air force operated a runway at Song Be. Everyone knew that air force personnel usually lived pretty well. Hell, they probably had ice for their drinks and hot chow every day. While gathering equipment and packing our rucks, we boasted to the other detachment members about what a "get-over" assignment we had been given. Imagine, a few weeks of sitting around, getting tanned, and sipping cold drinks while controlling aircraft, and receiving sixty-five dollars a month combat pay to boot!

Although the mission wouldn't be as exciting as a combat assault or an aircraft recovery, running a major fuel point would allow us to utilize our air traffic control skills, so they wouldn't become rusty. Besides, someone had to perform the get-over jobs.

Flying into Song Be was like slipping back into the past in a time machine. Situated close to the Cambodian border, the terrain around Song Be had a primitive look about it. An enormous river, seemingly untouched by civilization, wound its way through the region. Small villages of thatched huts were scattered among its dense forests. Pigs and oxen could be seen moving within the hamlets, while dark-skinned men and women, naked from the waist up, labored in the hot sun. I later learned those villages were the homes of the Montagnard tribes, staunch allies of U.S. Special Forces. Were it not for the signs of modern warfare technology, one might well have stepped backward in history a thousand years or more.

Gazing out from the floor of the chopper, my eyes beheld a huge mountain jutting straight into the sky. It certainly stood out in relation to the surrounding terrain, which lay generally flat. Although thick jungle blanketed the mountain's slopes, its face was pockmarked by an endless number of artillery and bomb craters. With all those battle scars, I imagined that that old mountain had lots of war stories to tell.

Not far from the bottom of the mountain sat a large airstrip with a small control tower. An air force C-123 cargo plane was barreling down the runway for takeoff as we approached. The small airport seemed rather forlorn. Instead of buildings, sandbagged bunkers lined its sides. Bundles of supplies sat in disorderly heaps at the end of the runway. The surroundings were not as luxurious as I'd hoped they might be, but what the hell, maybe the three of us would share a section of the tower with the air force. Perhaps they even had a fan!

Our chopper continued its approach toward the control tower, but instead of landing on the airstrip, the helicopter banked right and continued flying until it hovered across a road and descended toward an old helipad.

As we lowered onto the pad, the wash of the blades generated a tremendous whirlpool of dust that rose high into the air, then swirled violently across the ground. After waiting for the dust to halfway settle, I checked our immediate surroundings. On one side of the helipad was jungle and trees; the other bordered a dirt road. The helipad was about the size of a small parking lot back home. A tiny, dilapidated, sandbagged bunker sat on the edge of the pad near the road.

It was evident that the pad had not been used for quite some time, perhaps when the French had fought the Viet Minh a number of years earlier. Surely this was not the refueling point, and that decrepit structure was not going to serve as our Pathfinder hootch and control center.

The crew chief pointed to the ground, then shouted, "This is where you get off!"

Perplexed, the three of us stared at one another.

I yelled back at him, "Are you sure?"

His face was expressionless but his voice confident. "This is it!"

I hoped for some sign that would prove him wrong as my eyes continued to scan the pad. They fell on some fuel bladders sitting in the corner on the opposite edge of the pad, confirming the location. The fuel bladders contained hundreds of gallons of helicopter fuel, most commonly referred to as JP-4.

Brad and Mitch had also noticed the fuel bladders. I

tried to cheer them up. "Well, at least we're not humping through the jungle and getting shot at."

The three of us off-loaded the chopper and gave the crew a thumbs-up. As the bird lurched forward, the crew chief cried out, "Have fun! See you back at the ranch."

Brad, Mitch, and I just stood in the middle of the helipad for a few moments, dumbfounded. The helipad's surface was saturated with pentaprime, a thick petroleum-base product poured onto dusty surfaces to harden the ground and keep the dust to a minimum. I didn't know if the pentaprime would make much difference there, however, because everything in sight was covered by a reddish-brown dust.

The dust was about four inches thick on the ground surrounding the pad. Off the helipad, footsteps produced small clouds. After walking just a few paces, my fatigues and boots were stained red from the knees down. Each time a military vehicle traveled by on the road, an enormous cloud of the reddish powder blanketed us.

I hailed a passing jeep carrying three MPs (military police). The jeep came to an abrupt halt, completely covering me in dust. An MP sergeant addressed me from the passenger seat.

"Whatcha need?"

Waving away the dust with my hand, I choked while responding. "Hi, Sergeant! We just arrived in the area, and I was wondering if you could orient me as to what's around us."

The MP sergeant's response was cordial. "Sure! Down the road, the way we just came, is Song Be City. I don't know why it's called a city though, it would just be a small town back home. If you take the road in the other direction, you'll end up in the middle of nowhere."

I was curious about the wooded area bordering the helipad. "What's past this vegetation behind me?"

"Well, beyond those woods, about fifty meters, is the perimeter." The sergeant glanced at my 101st patch, then continued, "A unit from your division protects that sector."

My curiosity heightened. "Really! Would you happen to know what unit?"

He glanced at his driver, who shrugged his shoulders. "Nah! But I think it's a Cav unit because of the armored vehicles and the red-and-white flags."

There was only one Cav unit in the 101st and that was 2/17th Cav, the same unit Brad and I were initially assigned to at Fort Campbell. If it was B Troop, that meant Stump and Ed Brown (from the 187th Pathfinders) were just fifty meters away. I couldn't believe it. The four of us were together at Benning, then Campbell. Now, halfway around the world, we stood a stone's throw away from one another.

The MP sergeant had eyed my black hat throughout our exchange. He obviously needed to satisfy his interest. "What is it you do?"

"I'm a Pathfinder. We're going to run a refueling point here for helicopters."

My answer sparked a look of surprise in him. "You mean you're going to land helicopters in all this dust?"

I nodded in affirmation.

Shaking his head, he continued, "Good luck, buddy. You're gonna need it." Motioning to his driver, he muttered, "Let's go."

I thanked the MP for his time. The jeep jolted forward, leaving a trail of dust behind it and all over me.

We were operational the next day at first light. Brad held the beginning shift on the radio. Mitch remained with Brad while I went on a scrounging mission. I decided to visit the unit guarding the nearby perimeter, hoping it was the 2/17th Cav. I followed a well-used path through the woods until it widened into a field containing shrubbery and bushes. Scattered about the thickets were foxholes and small bunkers. Behind the bunkers sat armored personnel carriers and gun jeeps; their red-and-white markings were those of B Troop. I greeted a few old friends, then came upon Stump and Ed. Ed was playing cards with a few other fellows, and Stump was off to the side cleaning an M-60 machine gun. They were surprised as hell to see me. After exchanging pats on the back and swapping stories, they updated me on the enemy situation.

Their patrols were running into the enemy more and more frequently, and their perimeter was being probed almost nightly. Stump and the others believed it was only a matter of time before the gooks launched a serious attack. I stayed for a couple of hours, scrounging some C rations and Kool-Aid. Before I departed, Stump gave me his platoon's radio frequency out of concern. Since we three Pathfinders were alone at night and fairly isolated from any close friendly force, the Cav's frequency would enable us to monitor the enemy situation as it unfolded. Moreover, we could radio them for help if we got into trouble.

When I returned to the pad, Brad insisted that a bullet had whizzed by him while he was controlling aircraft. Mitch was in the bunker at the time and hadn't heard it. Just for the hell of it, Mitch and I harassed Brad about the claim and his imagination. That is, until the next day, when we found a single bullet embedded in the sandbags near where I sat monitoring the radio. Every day afterward, around midmorning, a single bullet would strike a sandbag close to whomever was visible. We figured it was only a matter of time before one of us would be hit.

Our job required the man controlling traffic to be exposed most of the time, and as each midmorning approached, an intense feeling of vulnerability swept over that person. It was strange knowing that there was a gook out there whose sole purpose each morning was to end your life. Thank God the sniper was either a bad shot or using iron sights from a good distance away. Incredibly, after six days the sniping simply ceased.

The bunker proved to be a tight squeeze for three people, so one of us usually slept outside on top. We put a poncho by the bunker's blast wall to stop dust from the road and built shelves along the inside ledge with wood from artillery shell crates. The biggest problem turned out to be the centipedes and the rats. The centipedes seemed to reside under every third sandbag. Colored with bright orange-and-black horizontal stripes, their bodies ranged from six to ten inches in length. A large number of rats ran across our bodies at night searching for food. They were huge, causing me to rethink why the cat population was so scarce. It seemed like everything in Vietnam was gigantic in size: the rats, the insects, the plants, the trees, everything but the people.

Within a week of its first operation, our helipad became a beehive of activity. In addition to refueling, pilots began using our pad to shut down their helicopters for breaks or mechanical repairs. Units placed supplies and equipment at our location to be sling-loaded out, and wounded were brought to the pad for medevac.

Actually, we found ourselves controlling far more aircraft than the air force runway nearby. We had to remain particularly alert at all times in order to avoid a midair or ground collision since the dust blinded both us and the pilots. At one time or another, every type of helicopter landed on our pad, including a CH-54 Sky Crane, which brought in a downed aircraft.

Every day it seemed as if something interesting or unusual occurred that challenged us either personally or professionally. One afternoon a jeep screeched to a halt at the end of the pad. Two soldiers jumped out and lifted a third soldier on a litter from the back of the jeep. Carrying him onto the pad, they set him down gently. Mitch was on the horn, so I ran over to find out what was going on. The two said they had to report back to their unit right away, but that a dustoff had already been requested to medevac their buddy. They said farewell to the injured soldier and departed, leaving him lying all alone in the hot sun.

He was naked on the litter, and I had never seen wounds like his before. From the neck down, his body was coated with some kind of salve or ointment and wrapped in yards of gauze bandages. Portions of his skin had been stripped away, revealing bright red and pink blotches. He looked really bad off.

I knelt beside him. "What the hell happened to you?"

He appeared to welcome the company. "I got burned!"

I paused, not knowing what to say.

His face saddened. "Looks bad, doesn't it?"

With his eyes looking straight into mine, I knew better than to lie. "Well! Let's put it this way: I'm glad I'm not you right now."

He chuckled. "Yeah. I don't blame you."

Just then a chopper approached the pad, and the wind from its blades blew at his bandages. I hunched my body across his until it landed. I needed to tell Mitch to keep the choppers as far away as possible from this guy and to let me know when the dustoff was inbound. I touched the litter case on his shoulder. "Hold on! Don't move! I'll be right back. I just have to tell my partner something."

The guy smiled. "I'm not going anywhere."

As I ran to Mitch, I thought about how stupid I must have sounded.

A few moments passed before I returned. When I arrived back at the litter, the guy looked real uncomfortable, more so than before. "Are you in a lot of pain?"

He seemed uneasy. "Yeah! But they shot me with some stuff that makes you not give a shit."

Even with the hot sun beating down on the pad, I noticed him shiver. "Are you sure you're okay?"

He was becoming lethargic, too, his words slurring. "I'm getting kinda cold!"

I wondered if he was going into shock. During infantry training, the instructors taught us that a soldier could die quickly if the symptoms for shock were not treated at once. Their instructions were to cover the person with a blanket or something, but I couldn't do that in this case because of his burns. It was also important to keep the person talking by asking personal questions. I decided to give that a try.

"Hey, I forgot to ask you, where are you from?"

It was as if he had to search his mind for a few moments before answering. "California. I'm from California!"

"How old are you?"

Sluggishly, he responded. "Twenty-one!"

"You got a girl back home?"

Suddenly his expression appeared a bit more lucid. "Yeah, yeah! I got a girl."

Well, I finally struck a chord! Maybe thinking about his girl would keep him attentive. Perhaps everything would be okay after all; I relaxed a little.

Instead, he became agitated, his head moving slowly from side to side. He started mumbling. "No! What's going to happen when she sees me like this? I can't let her see me like this!"

Damn! Where was that medevac? It should have been there already. Suddenly his eyes rolled back. I was really scared that the poor guy was going to die right there on the pad.

I placed my face directly in front of his and stared into his eyes. I hoped like hell I had his attention. "Listen, buddy! You got to get your shit together. You're on your way home. Your family and that girl you got waiting for you back there wouldn't appreciate you dying on them over here."

After a second or two, his eyes widened a bit. He muttered feebly, "Damn, man, you don't give up!"

Finally, Mitch yelled and gave me a thumbs-up. "Richie, dustoff's inbound!"

I grinned at him. "Your bird's here, man. You're going home."

Mitch must have advised the pilot to be careful, because the dustoff stopped at the other end of the pad, then slowly hovered toward us. Still, the wind from its blades blew all over the bandages, and as the medevac crept closer, some of the dressings flew off. Dust and grit swept into his wounds, sticking to the ointment. Lying on the ground beside him, I fumbled with the bandages as best I could, grabbing at each one as it started to blow away. Unfortunately, many of them disappeared in the dust storm.

With the dustoff at a complete halt, two crew members rushed toward us and grabbed each end of the litter.

Tears welled in his eyes as the medics carried him toward the bird. I heard him say, "Thanks, man! God bless you!"

The medevac lifted up, propelling forward. I turned around and covered my eyes from the dust. After the bird departed and the dust settled, I stood there and watched the aircraft shrink into the sky. I wondered how many years it would take for that guy to recover. How much suffering and pain would he have to endure? I thought to myself, No, buddy, you got it all wrong. God bless you!

A couple of days later, Mitch and I went to a nearby infantry unit in need of a class and demonstration on hooking various types of sling load to helicopters. When we arrived back at the helipad, Brad informed us that a crew chief had accidentally walked into a helicopter's rotor blade. He was hit in the head and killed instantly.

Brad appeared very detached and nonchalant as he related the incident. I was startled by his manner. Brad was an extremely compassionate person, to the point where I sometimes worried about him. I thought about it later and realized that we were all getting kind of callous about death.

The site of the accident was about thirty meters from our bunker. There wasn't much blood, but the guy's brains were lying on the pad. I guess in their haste to medevac him, nobody noticed his brains lying off to the side. It was the first time I had actually seen a human brain. Staring at it, smeared on the ground like that, I wondered how people could experience thoughts and emotions because of that small heap of gray substance. It was really gross, with flies buzzing around it, so none of us ventured over there or volunteered to clean it up. Besides, with the aid of the hot sun and insects, it didn't take long to decompose. Whenever possible, we landed helicopters a safe distance from it so the flight crews wouldn't be bothered by the sight.

During the second week, some Cobra pilots asked if they could park their birds on our pad overnight. In no time, two to four Cobras were there every evening. Soon afterward, an ammo dump housing armament for the Cobras was placed on the other end of the pad, allowing them quick access to rockets and ammunition. Unfortunately, the fuel bladders, the ammo dump, and the Cobras all presented inviting targets. Since the pad was not far from the perimeter, we knew it was only a matter of time before Charlie mortared us. Sure enough, within a few days enemy mortar rounds dropped into the trees in front of the pad.

After the first night of being mortared, none of us slept on top of the bunker anymore. The enemy continued mortaring us about every third night. Luckily, the rounds usually hit in the woods immediately to our front, close to the pad. Once in a while, one or two rounds hit the outer edge of the pad. Fortunately, the choppers were not hit.

By the end of the second week we had everything down pat. One morning, Mitch was controlling aircraft, Brad was down in the bunker, and I was sitting on top, cleaning my weapon. Glancing to my side, I noticed an old papa-san strolling near the helipad. Something seemed strange about the way he was walking, however. Normally, the Vietnamese took short, quick-paced steps, but the papa-san's steps seemed exaggerated and systematic. My mind flashed back to a class we had attended at Fort Campbell. The instructor explained that, at times, "civilians," who were really Viet Cong, would pace off an area and memorize or copy down the distance and other dimensions. Later, the information was relayed to enemy mortar crews or sappers.

I yelled for Brad to come up from inside the bunker. A moment later he was beside me.

"Brad! Take a look at that papa-san over there. Do you notice anything funny?"

Now, Brad was a very smart and inquisitive person. He studied the old man for a few moments before answering. "No! Not really. Why?"

"Doesn't it look like he's pacing off the area by the way he's walking?"

Brad watched the old man again. "No, Richie! He's

just an old man. Maybe you're letting your imagination get the best of you."

I glanced back at the papa-san. He looked harmless enough. Hell, next thing you know, I'd be seeing gooks behind every tree. I slid the carrying handle and bolt back into my weapon, unaware that Brad was continuing to observe the old man's movements. A few moments later he nudged me.

"Hey, you might have something. Do you see the way he just stopped?"

I had just finished performing a function check on my M-16. "No! I wasn't paying any attention!"

The papa-san glanced in our direction. We both tried to look nonchalant, proceeding about our business. The old man then turned right, staying on the outer edge of the pad. Again, his walk was deliberate.

Brad continued, "Did you see that? I think he *is* pacing the area."

Since Mitch was busy controlling aircraft, Brad suggested we contact the MPs with the other radio. I was hesitant, however. What if the MPs came all the way out there and it was just our imagination? Man, would I be embarrassed.

As fate would have it, an MP jeep happened to be traveling down the road toward us. It had a machine gun mounted on it. Two MPs sat in the front while a third stood behind the M-60 machine gun. We waved them down. I briefed them on our suspicions about the old papa-san.

The two MPs got up out of their seats and advanced toward the papa-san. The third MP continued to man the machine gun. As the papa-san watched them approach, he appeared terrified. I started to feel bad for the old man; the poor guy was probably innocent, and it was all my fault. Neither MP spoke Vietnamese, so they questioned him in English. Frightened, the papa-san kept shaking his head that he didn't understand. Frustrated, the MPs began searching his person. Now I was feeling really bad for the old man and strolled over to possibly lighten the situation.

To my surprise, they pulled out a few sheets of paper from under his shirt. A closer look revealed a map of some type, an outline of our helipad and some scribbling. Son of a gun! The old man was a VC after all.

The MPs were ecstatic. It made their day. The MP in charge approached Brad and me while his partner placed the papa-san in the jeep.

"Good job! Most of the time these things don't pan out, but we got this guy dead to rights. By the looks of it, he was surveying your area here for an attack of some kind."

Brad and I just stood there, flabbergasted. The MP said the papa-san would be interrogated by military intelligence and that we might be contacted as well. Brad and I went back to our work. No one ever contacted us, and we were too busy to ever follow up on it, so we never knew the outcome.

The next day I decided to visit Stump and Ed and spend the night at their location. I also wanted to tell them about catching the old VC. Brad and Mitch didn't mind my being away, because the Pathfinder bunker would be more bearable with one less person sleeping in it. While at the Cav, I ended up drinking beer and playing cards. Someone passed around a bottle of booze he'd purchased locally. It was a lot stronger than any of us anticipated. Around midnight, in my drunken wisdom, I decided to make my way back to the Pathfinder bunker instead of staying put. Stumbling through the dark, I had just about reached the pad when I came across some wooden crates. Pausing to take a break, I sat on the wooden objects and passed out.

During the night, my sleep was interrupted by tremendous claps of thunder and bright flashes of lightning. Fortunately, it never did rain. In the morning I awoke to the sound of helicopters hovering by. Checking my immediate surroundings, I discovered that I had fallen asleep on top of the ammo dump.

When I arrived back at the bunker, Brad and Mitch were not only surprised to see me, they were pissed. They had radioed Stump earlier that morning to find out when I was due to return, only to learn I had left the Cav area during the night. The noise and flashes of light, which I believed to be thunder and lightning, were actually mortar rounds impacting all over the pad. One of the helicopters had been destroyed. Brad and Mitch thought I'd been blown away. And of course, I had been, but not by the mortars.

Lieutenant Wilberding radioed that he was sending Larry out to replace me. He wanted to rotate detachment members through Song Be every two or three weeks to keep us proficient in air traffic control skills. He planned for me to return on the same bird that would drop Larry off. Instead, I convinced him that I should stay the night to acquaint Larry with the situation, since I was the senior Pathfinder and the operation was rather complex. I would catch another bird back to Bien Hoa in the morning. Wilberding agreed. In reality I just wanted to spend some time with Larry because I hadn't seen him in a while.

That night we all had a pretty good time, sitting around the bunker, shooting the breeze. Unfortunately, when it came time to go to sleep, the bunker was really crammed with the four of us in it. Around three in the morning, a shot rang out. The noise was deafening. The bullet hit close to Larry's foot, spraying dirt on him. Since we all slept with our weapons, everyone popped up instantly with their fingers on the trigger.

Larry was the first to yell. "Goddamn! Anybody see anything?"

Mitch answered, his voice overly calm considering what had just transpired. "Take it easy, everyone. Just take it easy."

Larry was furious. "Take it easy? What the hell are you talking about? Someone just shot at us, dammit!"

Brad and I stayed quiet but at the ready. My feelings told me something strange was going on.

Mitch continued, "Nobody shot at us. I just shot at a rat, that's all."

By now I had acquired my night vision, and I could see the disbelief on Larry's face, coupled with anger.

Larry was pissed. "A rat! You shot at a rat with all of us in here. Goddamn it, Mitch! You almost blew my foot off."

Mitch was aggravated but apologetic. "Sorry, man, but I had the flashlight on him. I knew where I was shooting. That's the same son of a bitch that got into my crackers the other night. I'm sick of his shit."

This time Larry remained speechless.

Mitch continued. "Damn! I had that thing right in my sights, too. I can't believe I missed him at this close range."

Brad and I started to chuckle. Mitch was more concerned about missing the rat than he was over scaring the shit out of Larry.

Larry mumbled something in Spanish, but I couldn't understand it. After a few moments the excitement died down and everybody attempted to get back to sleep.

Lying there with everyone so quiet, I couldn't help myself. I whispered, "Hey, Larry!"

His voice still possessed a tinge of anger. "What, dammit?"

"Welcome to Song Be."

Chapter Seven

It was around noon when I landed back in Bien Hoa. Lieutenant Wilberding greeted me at the pad. As we walked to the hootch, I updated him on the situation at Song Be. Torch greeted me in his usual fashion as I entered the Pathfinder quarters. He was dancing around, his curly little tail wagging, acting as if I was the most important person in the world. I dropped my rucksack beside my cot and patted him for a few minutes. Ron, Joe, and Buz gathered around, welcoming me back. They all remarked about the great tan I had acquired while at Song Be.

Although I was hungry, my first order of business was to turn in my weapon, then take a shower. The guys headed off to chow and promised to bring me something to eat. Back at Song Be, there weren't any shower facilities; we simply washed out of a five-gallon water can. I couldn't wait to bathe my whole body.

The shower stall at Bien Hoa consisted of a fifty-five-gallon drum filled with water, resting on a wooden frame. I eagerly pulled the cord to release some water and was startled to see red dye streaking down my arms and legs. At first I thought someone had played a joke and colored the water in the drum, but the water was clear coming out of the nozzle overhead. A pool of red, murky liquid collected at my feet. Finally, I realized that all the red substance was Song Be dirt rinsing from my body. As I continued to scrub, my skin turned white, eventually washing away the great tan that everyone, including myself, thought I had.

It felt great to be back with all the guys. That night we

120

sat around the team room drinking beer and soda. I related my experiences at Song Be, then asked how everyone else was doing.

Ron patted Torch as he spoke. "Well, Brad is presently on a mission with one of the battalion recon platoons from the 1st Brigade. Some of us have been on a few one-day operations, but that's about it."

Buz chimed in. The tone of his voice was upbeat. "At least things have gotten a little more lax around here since you left, Richie."

"What do you mean?"

"The lifers have cut back on a lot of the bullshit. There's still the ongoing details like bunker guard duty, but having to wear pressed uniforms, spit-shined boots, and all that shit has gone by the wayside."

Joe elaborated. "Yeah! The first sergeant only holds one to two formations a day now, and it's no big deal to miss one once in a while."

I was getting ready to ask why they thought the rules had become more relaxed when Ron cut in. "I think the attack on the rear during Tet, along with pilots and crew members being killed on missions, has finally convinced the lifers that there's a war going on around here."

In the two days that followed, I cleaned my equipment, played with Torch, and enjoyed the nightly gatherings at the team room. Around day three the routine became boring. I was finding out something very peculiar about myself. When I was in the field, I couldn't wait to get back to the rear; but when I was in the rear, I couldn't wait to get back to the field. I asked Lieutenant Wilberding if there were any upcoming missions I could go on. Unfortunately, he said that other detachment members were scheduled in front of me, since I had just returned from an operation.

The next morning, a few of us arose early to eat breakfast at the mess hall, a wood-frame structure topped with a tin roof. Inside was a cluster of benches and tables. As we searched for a place to sit, someone at one of the far tables called out, "Hey, Richie, over here!" It was Charlie

Bartlett, a buddy who lived about three miles from me back home. We decided to join him and the other enlisted flight crew members of the unit at their table.

After a few introductions, everyone settled down to eat. I liked Charlie. He was probably viewed by some as hyper, but he was just a friendly, gregarious person who always went out of his way to say hello or lend a hand. Charlie flew as a crew member on one of our battalion's gunships. We had UH-1 Bravo and Charlie model helicopters, configured with an aerial weapons platform that, unlike Cobras, required enlisted crew members to fly along.

"Still flying guns, Charlie?"

Charlie seemed surprised. "C'mon! Is there anything else?"

Some of the guys around him groaned. A fellow sitting across from Charlie threw a piece of bread at him. "Yeah! Did you ever hear of slicks, asshole?" Slicks were the most commonly used UH-1 Delta model helicopters for the tactical transport of troops, supplies, and other support missions.

Charlie didn't look up from his plate as he answered, "No, thanks! Slicks are too much work and not enough glory. Besides, you can kill more dinks flying guns!"

Another person chimed in, "He's right about the work. I've been flying my ass off with no relief."

Someone else muttered, "Hell, we all have."

We listened while the group complained about the endless flying they had done since being in country. It was then mid-February 1968, and none of them had had any time off since their arrival in December. They claimed that the increasing number of missions combined with a shortage of door gunners and other flight personnel was taking its toll on them physically and emotionally. It didn't make any difference if they were sick or just plain burned out, they still had to go up every day.

Any infantryman, with all the hardship of that profession, might have seen those guys as simply whining, but their complaints had merit. The 101st's being the only aviation battalion in the whole division put an enormous demand on the unit's crews and aircraft, both of which had to remain in peak condition because of the lives at stake, including those of the infantrymen they transported and protected.

As the crew members debated who had it rougher, those flying guns or slicks, Ron leaned toward Joe and me. "This is incredible. These guys are complaining about going on too many missions, and we can't get enough."

Charlie grabbed my shirtsleeve. He had a surprised expression on his face. "Did I just hear him right? You guys got some downtime?"

I felt kind of embarrassed answering that question after just hearing about all their problems. "Yeah! Right now we do. Division still doesn't quite know how to use us, and Wilberding is just a lieutenant, so it's not like he has a lot of clout."

Charlie slapped his hand on the table, his voice booming. "Well, shit! Why don't you guys help us out?"

Everyone stopped talking. I felt like all eyes were on me. "What do you mean?"

Charlie appeared excited. "Why don't some of you Pathfinders volunteer to fly door gunner during the times you're back in the rear? You can't fly on gunships, but you can help out on the slicks. It would give the rest of the guys some slack time."

A couple of other crew members chimed in, "That's a good idea!" "We could sure use the help!"

Ron seemed interested. "Don't you have to be school trained to fly door gunner or be assigned to a permanent slot or something?"

The crew member sitting across from Ron answered. "Hell no! We already got a few guys who permanently fly that are not school trained. They get their MOS after they completed their OJT. You guys would just be flying temporarily anyway, filling in every once in a while."

Another chimed in. "Shit! When operations gets really strapped for door gunners, they even let some of the clerks-and-jerks tag along. Christ! Most of them don't even know how to fire the damn machine gun!"

We discussed it among ourselves. As Pathfinders, we were already assigned to the unit and personally knew many of the enlisted crew members and pilots. Moreover, we understood aviation jargon, the helicopter's capability, radio procedures, and each crew member's responsibility. Our primary task as door gunners would be the operation and handling of the M-60 machine gun. There were only minor differences between an infantry M-60 and the helicopter M-60, the biggest being the difference in triggers. The helicopter's machine gun had a butterfly trigger that you pushed down with your thumbs.

It was agreed that the crew members would run the idea by flight operations while we cleared it with Lieutenant Wilberding.

Those of us who wanted to fly door gunner presented the idea to Wilberding that same morning. We did not have high hopes that he would approve our request; most commanders do not like to lend their people out to other units. But to our surprise, he was all for the idea. From his perspective as the detachment commander, he thought it served as an excellent way to maintain rapport with the flight crews. Furthermore, the detachment would be helping its parent unit.

Of course, our reasons were not as lofty. We just wanted to fly door gunner for the experience, and also viewed it as a good way to get out of pulling details. Wilberding made it very clear, however, that Pathfinder duties came first, and flight operations had no authority to schedule any Pathfinders who might volunteer to fly door gunner without his permission. That seemed fair enough to those of us who wanted to participate. Remarkably, the very next afternoon I received word to report to a Sergeant First Class Hunt in flight operations to receive a briefing.

The flight operations hootch was covered with maps, personnel rosters, and flight schedules. Scanning the area, I noticed a field table in the corner. Behind it sat a sergeant; his name tag read "Hunt."

Approaching the table, I introduced myself. Sergeant Hunt didn't bother to look up at me. Instead, his eyes stayed fixed on the paperwork in front of him. "Yeah! I already got the word. Wait one!"

While he continued whatever he was involved in, I walked over to a board that had aircraft numbers with names written beside it. I studied it to see if my name was anywhere on it. A grease pencil hung alongside the board on a string.

Sergeant Hunt must have observed me staring at the pencil, because his voice bellowed, "While you're waiting, don't touch anything!"

I turned around to respond, but he was in the same position as before, looking down at the papers on his desk.

Maybe the guy didn't like the idea of Pathfinders flying door gunner. Maybe it created more work for him or something. While I waited, others, including officers, queried Hunt about different issues, and they were treated in the same abrupt manner. That made me feel more at ease. At least it wasn't anything personal. Hunt seemed to be curt with everyone. Perhaps he was just having a bad day.

A moment later he motioned me over to his desk. "Burns—Okay! Listen up! You're scheduled to fly tomorrow."

He handed me a small slip of paper. "This is the aircraft number. Be at the revetment, ready to go, at 0545 hours. We don't have any Nomex for you, so make sure your shirtsleeves are rolled down." (Nomex was a flame-retardant material used in flight suits to protect crew members in the event of a fire. Therefore, the entire flight suit was simply referred to as a Nomex.)

"You'll be flying a log bird . . . basically ash and trash." A "log" bird was a utility helicopter used for logistics and resupply. "Ash and trash" meant we'd be hauling anything from C rations to ammunition. Most flight crews disliked ash-and-trash missions, finding them mundane in comparison to flying troops into hot LZs, etc.

I nodded.

"Any questions?"

"I do have one question, Sergeant Hunt. What about drawing the 60s?" Usually the door gunner was responsible for maintaining the machine guns and assisting the crew chief when directed. So I needed to know if obtaining the machine guns would be my responsibility.

"Don't worry about the guns. Since you're just temporary, the crew chief will take care of them. Anything else?"

I thought for a moment. "No, I guess not."

"Well, that's it for now. We'll see how you make out." He stared back down at the table.

As I turned to leave, Hunt grumbled, "By the way, the crew chief said to make sure you bring your flak jacket along with you tomorrow."

"Roger that!" Strolling back to the Pathfinder hootch, I wondered why the crew chief wanted me to bring along my flak jacket. The only thing I could figure was that he wanted me to wear it because I didn't have a chicken plate, the bulletproof ceramic plate that the crew chief and door gunner usually wore to protect both the front and back of their torso.

Oh well! Wearing the flak jacket wouldn't be that bad while flying; it was pretty cool upstairs. It would be hot as hell when the helicopter was on the ground, however, when loading supplies or personnel.

It was still dark when I arrived at the revetment at 0540 hours the next morning. To my surprise, someone was already at the aircraft. I assumed it was the crew chief, since he was attaching the M-60 machine gun to the mount on the door-gunner side of the helicopter. The two enlisted soldiers on a helicopter were the crew chief and door gunner. The crew chief was the senior of the two and ultimately responsible for maintaining the aircraft. The door gunner sat on the right side of the chopper and the crew chief on the left.

I approached apprehensively. Chopper crews were a

tight lot, and I didn't know what the crew chief's feelings were regarding my flying in place of his own gunner. For all I knew, he may have resented the idea. I also felt a twinge of guilt at watching him mount the guns, a chore that should have been mine as door gunner.

He was the first to speak. "Good morning!"

"Morning!"

"You all set to fly with us today?" The guy seemed exceptionally cheerful for any human being who was up and working so early in the morning. His good-hearted attitude appeared genuine, and I didn't sense any animosity in his voice.

"Yeah! I'm really looking forward to it." I held out my hand. "My name is Burns."

After brushing his hand on the side of his pants, he reached out and shook mine. "You probably already guessed that I'm the crew chief." He then turned and jumped up inside the helicopter. "The pilots will be along shortly."

With my anxiety diminishing, I decided to feel him out. If there was any ill will, I'd rather have it out in the open. "I hope you guys don't mind me flying door gunner today."

He was busy fooling with something overhead. "Hell! Not at all! We're glad to have you."

Pausing for a moment, he continued, "Joey's been complaining about that toothache for the past week. Now he can have the damn thing pulled or filled."

The crew chief finished whatever he was doing and moved up front between the pilot seats. It looked like he was adjusting a strap or something. "We're just flying ash and trash anyway. No big deal."

I felt awkward just standing around. "Can I help you with anything?"

"Nah! Just making some last-minute checks."

Jumping back out of the helicopter, he pointed to the flak jacket slung on my left shoulder. "I see you got the word on bringing your flak jacket."

I slipped the flak jacket off my shoulder and held it in my right hand. Since he was the boss and seemed to be a nice enough guy, I thought I would try to get out of wearing it before the pilots showed up.

Putting on my most pitiful look, I mumbled, "Yeah! I got the word." I lifted the flak jacket in an up-and-down motion. "Sure is heavy, though!"

The crew chief smiled. "Yeah! Good thing, too!"

Talk about no sympathy. I wasn't going to get anywhere with this guy.

He pointed to the place behind the gun where I would be sitting. "Best thing to do is fold it once so that it's doubled, and then just lay it down right here."

I was confused. Maybe I'd missed something. "Fold it and lay it on the seat?"

This time he looked perplexed. "Yeah! If you fold it in half, it's thicker . . . and more comfortable to sit on."

I was definitely missing something here. "To sit on?"

The crew chief's expression was either one of bewilderment or annoyance; I couldn't tell which. The tone in his voice changed to that of an older brother offering advice. "Well, the way I look at it, you got two choices: You can either wear the damned thing and sweat your ass off, or you can sit on it and protect your baby maker. It's up to you."

My baby maker? What the hell was this guy talking about? All of a sudden I understood quite clearly. Quickly folding my flak jacket in half, I placed it on the seat. We heard some voices and saw two silhouettes strolling toward us. The crew chief hopped back inside the cabin. "Here come the pilots. We'll be taking off in a few minutes!"

Standing all alone, I eyed the flak jacket, wishing I'd brought two instead of just one. Later, I discovered that the crew chief kept an extra chicken plate that he sat on.

The pilots introduced themselves. One was a captain and the other a warrant officer. Both appeared friendly and stated they were glad to have me along. The crew chief untied the helicopter's blade, then came around to my side. While the pilots conducted a preflight inspection, he provided me a quick refresher on the M-60, basic do's and don'ts, and the use of the monkey straps, a harness designed to strap the crew chief and door gunner to their seats. He stated he didn't use the straps sometimes because the harness was too restrictive.

When finished with orientation, he handed me a flight helmet. Since many Pathfinder duties required the use of a flight helmet, I was more than accustomed to it. Each flight helmet had a cord dangling from it that plugged into the aircraft's main internal communication wire.

My seat vibrated uncontrollably as the chopper's blades spun faster with each revolution. We were ready for takeoff. There was a short pause over the intercom, followed by the crew chief's voice. "You all set, gunner? Any last-minute questions?"

I grabbed the tiny mouthpiece that extended out to the front of the helmet on a small boom, rotated it to my lips, then pushed the button located on the wire. "That's a negative!"

Since the crew chief and door gunner each had a full view of his side of the aircraft, it was their responsibility to warn the pilots about obstructions or hazards. As the chopper lifted itself from the confines of the revetment, I examined my side to make sure the aircraft was not in danger of striking the sandbags. The crew chief's voice came over the intercom, "Clear left!" I followed with, "Clear right!" The helicopter lurched into the morning sky.

With the morning air sweeping through the aircraft, it was actually quite chilly. I was glad my sleeves were rolled down. A few moments later the chopper touched down on a unit log pad. We were still on the Bien Hoa compound. Three "pax" (passengers) loaded some radio equipment, cases of C rations, and mailbags, then hopped on board. Within minutes we were airborne again. I had no idea where the bird was headed and didn't feel it was my place to ask. We flew for about twenty minutes, then landed at a small firebase, where the troops and equipment off-loaded. Two soldiers from the firebase got on board for the return trip to Bien Hoa.

During the flight back to Bien Hoa we maintained an altitude of approximately one thousand feet. As I sat behind the gun, with the whole sky to my front, I realized how much I missed jumping. The cool wind whisked across my face while I listened to music over the intercom. The armed forces radio station was playing the latest hits from back home. I wondered about my family and what I would do when I returned home.

Not all of my daydreams were pleasant, however. I also envisioned Charlie hiding under the jungle, preparing to take a shot at us or, even worse, the possibility of our chopper crashing in the middle of nowhere. All in all, however, flying door gunner seemed to be a really neat job. I was thoroughly enjoying myself. In no time we landed back in Bien Hoa. After dropping off the two pax, we flew to another log pad to shuttle more troops and supplies.

Our next stop was a small LZ in the jungle. Yellow smoke billowed to our front as our helicopter hovered toward the tiny clearing, and soldiers scrambled to grab clothing they had hanging out to dry, while others scurried to secure their ponchos. As the chopper's skids touched the ground, troops, heads bent, ran toward us to off-load the ammunition, C rations, and other supplies.

While the supplies were being unloaded, I jumped out to stretch. Gazing at all the grunts, with their mud-caked uniforms and droopy eyes, I realized how fortunate I was to have a reprieve from that hardship. On the other hand, however, I longed to be with them. As the helicopter lifted skyward, I wondered how my feelings could be so much in conflict simultaneously.

We had been flying for about five minutes on the return to Bien Hoa, and I was caught up in the song "When a Man Loves a Woman" by Percy Sledge. Suddenly my tranquillity was interrupted by a voice blaring over the intercom. "Hey, door gunner!" It was the AC (aircraft commander).

Although it seemed awkward to be addressed by that title, I responded immediately, "Yes, sir!"

"Think you're about ready to shoot that thing?" He was referring to the M-60 machine gun.

"Yes, sir! More than ready!" Was I ready? Damn right! I had shot expert with every weapon I ever fired. This would be a good opportunity to show these guys how good I was with a machine gun.

Our altitude was approximately one thousand feet, well inside the range of the M-60.

"Do you see that old structure?"

"Yes, sir!" The structure was easy to spot, since little vegetation surrounded it. By its outline and large colored stones, I guessed it to be an old pagoda that had been destroyed long ago.

"I'll make a go-around. Let's see if you can hit it."

He had to be kidding. The old pagoda was about the size of a house, maybe bigger. A few large stones lay in front of it. I could easily hit those instead.

"I'll go for the stones off to the front of it, sir."

"Okay! If you say so." I detected a bit of laughter in the pilot's voice.

Something was up. I wondered if the crew was playing some kind of joke on me. Maybe the crew chief had messed with the gun, and it was going to misfire.

The helicopter completed the circle, and the structure reappeared. I slammed a round in the chamber and clicked off the safety. As I put my thumbs on the butterfly trigger, I imagined what it must have been like to be a gunner on a bomber during World War II.

I heard the pilot's voice. "Clear to fire!"

Taking careful aim, I pressed the trigger, reminding myself to fire in short bursts. Every fifth round was a tracer, so it was easy to see where the bullets traveled. To my astonishment, instead of the rounds going straight, they swerved sharply, like a sliced golf ball. I missed not only the stones but the whole damn structure.

The crew chief snickered, "How'd you do, gunner?" I was sure the pilots were chuckling as well.

Embarrassed, I responded, "Not worth a shit!"

He had that big brother tone to his voice again. "It's a lot harder than it looks. You're gonna have to learn to lead the target. It takes practice."

The crew chief beckoned the pilots to make another run on the pagoda. I improved my shooting some, but not much.

Later, flying over a murky, brown river, I had a chance to practice again. The target was an abandoned sampan beached on the shore. It was rotting away, its bottom gutted. The chopper dropped to five hundred feet. I deliberately aimed way in front of the sampan before firing. Even though I still did not hit the target, the rounds came much closer. In addition to following the path of the tracers, I could also see the rounds impacting along the water, which helped me to adjust better.

Quickly firing again, I hit the target.

The pilots turned the chopper around, situating the sampan on the left side of the aircraft so the crew chief could have a run on it. I heard his machine gun popping on the other side of the aircraft. After firing only a few short bursts, his gun ceased. He claimed to have destroyed the sampan on the first try. Although I couldn't see for myself, I didn't have any doubt he was telling the truth. Once our helicopter turned around to head home, I viewed the remains of the sampan; it had been chopped to pieces.

It was around 1800 hours when we touched down at the revetment, ending the day. The sun was lowering in the distance, shadowing the area. It had been a busy day, and I lost count of the number of sorties. We probably logged nine or ten hours of flying time. Although that might not sound like much, all the loading, shuttling back and forth, and refueling consumed the time—and our energy—rather quickly.

I couldn't have flown with a better crew. They were great guys and treated me as one of their own. I especially thanked them for allowing me to shoot the M-60. It was not only an added thrill, but a humbling experience.

The crew chief finished tying down the blades and came around to my side. I grabbed my flak jacket from the seat.

"Leave it!"

I didn't know if I'd heard him right. "What?"

"Leave the flak jacket in the aircraft. It will be secure until tomorrow."

I must have had that puzzled look on my face again, because he added, "You're flying door gunner with us again tomorrow."

I was stunned, but happily surprised. "I am?"

"Yeah! The AC radioed back a few hours ago about Joey's status. I guess he had his tooth pulled and is on some kind of medication containing a narcotic or something. We figured we'd use you for one more day to give him a break."

It was great news, but I had some concerns. "I can't fly until I clear it with Lieutenant Wilberding."

He had that older brother tone in his voice again. "That's already been taken care of. It's been cleared with operations and your lieutenant. No sweat, GI!"

"What about the other guys from my detachment? I feel kinda bad flying two days in a row."

"I don't know about that. You can check with operations, though." He grinned. "We decided to stick with you so we don't have to break in a new guy."

The crew chief jumped inside the chopper, performing whatever last-minute things he usually did before securing the bird.

It was late, and I felt compelled to help him out. "Do you want me to take care of the guns?"

"Nah! Leave 'em. I'll take care of everything. You just be here tomorrow at 0600."

Oh well, I wasn't going to argue. "Take care. See you then." I decided to go straight to the team room. That's where most of the guys would be gathered.

I was pleased and relieved to discover that Joe had flown that very same day, and a few of the other guys were scheduled for subsequent days. While we all drank and had a good time, I told the guys how difficult it had been to hit anything with an M-60 from a chopper. Of course, I got thoroughly harassed once I opened my mouth about it. With their exceptional skills, none of them, it was said, would have had the slightest problem hitting the target.

I had only two beers before calling it a day. It was amazing how much one day of flying had taken its toll on me. Besides, I wanted to get to the bird a little before six the next morning just in case the crew chief needed help.

Arriving at the revetment around 0550 hours, I was not surprised to see the crew chief already on station and the guns mounted. The guy was amazing. The day before, he told me that he really loved his job, and I believed him. If the other crew chiefs in the battalion were half as competent, the pilots had nothing to worry about.

Our pilots showed up at 0600 sharp. While they and the crew chief discussed the day's missions, I checked to make sure my flak jacket was thoroughly secured in its proper place, then loaded a waterproof bag containing sodas; I had drunk a few of their sodas the day before and thought it only fair to bring some in return.

The day's mission was another ash and trash. It began as the day before: we flew to a unit log pad where supplies and pax loaded onto the chopper, and we then proceeded to a drop-off destination. Once more, I did not know where we were headed. I was content just to have the opportunity to fly door gunner again. Usually I felt a sense of vulnerability when flying in a helicopter over Vietnam. But it felt different sitting behind the gun in the door gunner's seat. I felt more powerful than vulnerable. I hoped the opportunity would arise to allow me to practice with the M-60 again.

It was around midmorning as we proceeded on our third mission. So far we had completed the first two assignments, refueled, and were transporting another load. That time our cargo consisted of C rations, cots, radios, mailbags, and two pax. Between daydreams, I noticed that the terrain looked very familiar. A while later a huge mountain appeared off in the distance; I realized we were heading toward Song Be.

As we flew closer, the scene below startled me. A tremendous battle was raging beneath us. Pressing the talk button, I asked if anybody knew what was happening down there. The AC said he learned that, after we left that morning, gunships from our battalion were dispatched to Song Be because the city was under attack. He, too, was stunned at the intensity of the action and would have said something sooner had he known the fighting was so extensive. I inquired as to our destination and was told that we would be dropping off the supplies and pax on the top of the mountain.

The situation below was incredible. Explosions and smoke from artillery and other ordnance covered the countryside. The land area comprising the battlefield was enormous. I had no doubt that the major battle would go down in history. I thought about my fellow Pathfinders down there and my friends in the Cav. I prayed they would all be okay.

It was weird flying high above the battle, watching the whole show from a safe distance. Then I remembered my camera. Normally I didn't take photos, but I thought the countryside was so beautiful while flying door gunner the previous day that I'd brought along my camera. It even had color film in it. Hastily yanking it out of my pocket, I snapped a few pictures.

Our chopper approached Song Be airstrip, then veered left toward the mountain. Sitting on the strip below, an air force C-130 transport was engulfed in flames. Instead of flying directly to the top of the mountain, the pilots climbed the last three hundred meters flying low-level. Man, what an eerie place. The mountain looked even more menacing up close.

A small cleared area surrounded by barbed wire was situated on the very top. The number of antennas protruding from a large bunker led me to assume it was a radio-relay site. A few other bunkers were scattered about, probably sleeping quarters. The bunkers were linked by pathways of wood from ammo cases. Sandbagged fighting positions surrounded the perimeter. Being stationed at the bottom of the mountain was a luxury compared to that hellhole. Not only was it small, but I imagined it could become extremely boring.

A couple of soldiers ran down some makeshift stairs carved out of the dirt and helped the two pax unload the supplies. Once finished, we departed empty and headed back to Bien Hoa. The AC switched to our unit's gunship frequency so we could monitor the battle. Their call sign was Black Angel. I knew my buddy, Charlie Bartlett, was flying guns.

Just a few minutes into the flight, the AC received a distress call. An aircraft was desperately needed to evacuate wounded. Since we were a 101st aircraft and in the vicinity, it didn't take two seconds for the AC to respond. "Roger. This is Eagle one-one-five. We're on our way. Over!"

Holy shit! Although I wholeheartedly agreed with him, I still found it hard to believe that we were dropping down into that mess. It was like flying into the gates of hell. My heart and mind began racing as the helicopter descended rapidly. The closer we got to the fighting, the less powerful and the more vulnerable I started to feel.

The AC's voice rang over the intercom. "You two keep those guns ready and hang on. It looks pretty nasty down there."

The crew chief barked, "Burns! Stay alert! Looks like we're going into the shit."

I slammed a round into the chamber and switched the weapon off safe. I wished I could have replied with some cavalier response, but my fear allowed me to mutter only, "Roger that!"

I wondered where we were going to land. From my seat, every piece of earth seemed consumed by the battle. Artillery rounds slammed into one section, gunships worked another, armored vehicles blasted an area, and small-arms fire loomed everywhere. Damn! Maybe being a door gunner wasn't such a neat job after all.

As our aircraft flew closer, some clear spots appeared.

Still, clouds of smoke shadowed most of the terrain below, obscuring our vision.

At about two hundred feet, the AC announced, "Okay! We're going in!"

As we soared across the landscape, I leaned out over the gun to see if I could observe anything, my shirt flapping frenziedly from the wind. I heard popping sounds and a metallic *whack!* The chopper banked a hard left, throwing me back into the seat.

After gaining altitude, the AC's voice came back on the intercom. "It's damn hot down there. A lot of small-arms fire. We're going to try a different approach." I thought to myself, Where's a Pathfinder when you need one?

The crew chief blurted to the pilot, "Gee, sir, Joey's going to be pissed when he finds out he missed out on this one."

The bird descended rapidly, the blades *whopping.* In no time we were soaring across a narrow clearing. All I could see were trees to my front. My eyes furiously searched for movement.

All at once the tree line came alive with an array of little bright flashes. I heard a voice bark, "Gunner, clear to fire."

Instinctively my thumbs pressed down on the trigger. I tried to fire short bursts, but something inside me said to hell with it. I let the gun rip, tracers streaming into the trees. My mind was stuck on slow motion, photographing every detail from a distance. What seemed like an eternity was in reality only a few moments. Then I felt the chopper flare into a hover, and I immediately ceased firing for fear of hitting Americans on the small LZ.

The wounded were loaded on the crew chief's side. Some of the guys were really torn up. In seconds the pilot swung the chopper's tail boom around, positioning us to fly out in the same direction we'd entered from. As much as I wanted to shoot gooks again, part of me was glad the enemy would be on the crew chief's side. This time he would be the main target instead of me.

The pilot pulled pitch, springing the chopper forward. Immediately upon clearing the friendly area, I heard the crew chief's gun open up. The guy wasn't waiting for an invitation. I heard popping sounds again, some *whooshing* sounds, and a couple more metallic *whacks*. Whooping and hollering noises came from up front along with more popping sounds, like loud caps going off. Later the crew chief told me the noise was from the AC shooting his .38 revolver out his side window.

In no time we were out of danger. The AC's voice came back calmly over the intercom. "Everyone okay?"

The crew chief responded first. "I'm okay, sir! Sounded like the aircraft took a few hits, though. Gunner, you all right?"

Personally, I couldn't believe none of us was injured. "Roger! I'm fine!"

The crew chief and I took turns caring for the wounded while transporting them to a surgical hospital at Long Binh. Afterward we returned to Bien Hoa to shut the aircraft down. I guess the bird had sustained at least three hits that needed patching. The crew chief said those were the metallic *whacks* I'd heard. He explained that the *whoosh* sounds were actually bullets going through the open cabin and out the other side. My hands started trembling.

It was still early afternoon and the floor of the bird was caked with blood and dirt from the wounded. I asked the crew chief if he needed any help cleaning the aircraft or the guns. Again, he said he would take care of everything. The two pilots shut down the aircraft and joined us.

The captain reached out his hand to say good-bye. "Well, how did you like the flight today?"

I hesitated for a moment. "Ah, pretty exciting, sir!" The three of them laughed.

The warrant officer reached out his hand. "Yeah! This was just an average day for us!"

Chuckling along with them, I responded, "Shit! If this is an average day for you guys, you can have it."

The captain slapped me on the shoulder as he and the warrant officer turned to leave. "You're all right! It was a pleasure having you with us."

The warrant officer chimed, "Same goes for me. Hope to see you again sometime."

I nodded my head. "Thanks, sir! But the next time you guys see me again, it will be from outside the aircraft, while I'm guiding you in somewhere." Actually, a few of us from the Pathfinder detachment flew door gunner many more times during our year in country. I personally flew approximately twenty more missions as a door gunner. For me, however, none would prove as eventful as the Song Be trip.

I said my farewell to the crew chief and thanked him for everything. As I started to leave, he grabbed my sleeve and grinned. "Don't forget your flak jacket!"

"Oh yeah . . . thanks!" We both laughed.

While walking back to the hootch I reflected on the events of the past two days. I had always held a deep appreciation for helicopter pilots and crews. As a Pathfinder, I considered myself just as much aviation as infantry anyway, with a strong sense of loyalty to both. Flying door gunner elevated my admiration and appreciation for helicopters and their crews.

A few days later the photos I had taken while flying over the battlefield came back. Viewing the color prints of the actual battle, with the smoke rising from explosions everywhere, it was hard to believe we had flown into that inferno.

The battle we'd participated in was recorded in the 101st Airborne Division's history as the Battle for Song Be City, and it lasted approximately three days. As with any battle, all sorts of bizarre events and individual acts of heroism occurred. At one point the enemy even took over an American quad fifty (a vehicle mounted with four .50-caliber machine guns that could all be fired simultaneously) for a time.

The 17th Cav along with our 101st Black Angel gunships fought exceedingly well. As usual the Communists paid a high price, leaving behind 243 dead. Charlie Bartlett flew away unscathed and was credited with quite a few kills. He had a smile plastered across his face for a week.

Unfortunately, I was saddened to learn that Staff Sergeant Fedoroff, one of my NCOs while I was in the

Cav at Fort Campbell, had been killed along with approximately thirty other Screaming Eagles. Sergeant Fedoroff was assigned to B Troop, 17th Cav, from drill sergeant duty and frequently remarked about how excited he was to be back in the "real" army, especially with a unit like the 101st Airborne Division.

Stump received a Purple Heart for wounds; it was the first of several he acquired. As for my fellow Pathfinders on the ground, I was elated to discover that they had weathered the battle unscathed.

Through the end of February, I went on a few combat assaults and controlled a couple of extractions, mostly routine stuff. My birthday was steadily approaching, and I eagerly awaited its arrival. In March 1968, I would be nineteen years old and only two years from being able to vote or walk into any establishment back home and legally purchase a drink.

Lieutenant Wilberding informed us that most of the division was moving to I Corps, way up north by the DMZ near a place called Hue. Our Pathfinder detachment would be included in an advance party, so we'd be leaving right away. Supposedly, I Corps was a really hot AO, and rumor kept on referring to one place, a large valley. Supposedly it was a vast Communist stronghold literally crawling with NVA. The valley had a peculiar name, one that sounded almost as if it could be American Indian. It was called the A Shau Valley.

Chapter Eight

It was close to midnight as the wheels of the air force C-130 transport touched down on the runway, ending our approximately one-hour flight from Bien Hoa to I Corps, the northernmost sector of South Vietnam. Brad and I took turns holding Torch throughout the trip. Luckily, the young pup slept most of the way. The night air seemed cooler in I Corps than down south, at least it felt that way after stepping out of the cramped cargo bay of the aircraft. As we trekked across the tarmac, I noticed a large sign on the building to our front. It read WELCOME TO HUE PHU BAI.

We proceeded to the building, which turned out to be the air terminal. Before long an NCO from the division staff led us from the airport's main terminal up on to a dirt hill. An old master sergeant greeted us as we crested the top of the knoll.

A wide grin stretched across his face. "Welcome, men, welcome!"

He pointed to his right and continued. "C'mon! Keep moving! Right over there. We'll have some transportation for you shortly. Keep moving now, men."

Directly beside him was a newly painted sign, WELCOME, YOU BATTLING BASTARDS OF BASTOGNE.

Airborne units are steeped in tradition, and paratroopers are extensively taught, and reminded of, their division's past accomplishments and victories. The sign referred to the 101st Airborne Division's valiant stand while holding the besieged town of Bastogne, Belgium, during World War II. Although surrounded by German armored divisions, desperately low on ammunition and supplies, with over four hundred wounded, the 101st fought off the Germans for approximately ten days in the dead of winter. On 22 December 1944 the German commander requested the paratroopers' honorable surrender or every American soldier would be annihilated. The 101st commander's reply was "Nuts!"

A twinge of pride swelled through me. What most people didn't know regarding that historic event was that at 0935 hours the following morning, on the twenty-third, two Pathfinder teams parachuted into Bastogne and set up drop zones for resupply planes. Ninety minutes later the planes came. As a direct result of Pathfinder expertise, 241 planes dropped 144 tons of supplies in a mile-square drop zone by 1600 hours that afternoon. The recovery of bundles was 95 percent. If not for the courageous actions of that small team of Pathfinders, Bastogne might have fallen. I hoped that our detachment could continue to live up to that legacy.

We rested on our rucksacks until morning, when a truck finally arrived to transport us to the division's new base camp. The drive through the countryside lasted only about thirty minutes, and we were dropped off on a large, desolate, open plateau surrounded by small hills. The immediate ground was barren and rocky. To the west lay vast rolling hills, which slowly rose in elevation. To the east, the landscape appeared to slope gently downward, lush with vegetation and tropical trees.

We broke out some C rations and ate. An hour or so later a major from division headquarters came by and talked with Lieutenant Wilberding. The two went on a walk, the major periodically pointing in different directions as he spoke. Afterward, Wilberding informed us that the place where we were presently positioned, and the surrounding plateau, was indeed the division's new base camp. Our job for the next few days was to provide security for a portion of the perimeter about a hundred meters to our immediate south. Although there were no other soldiers within view, the major had assured Wilberding that the rest of the perimeter was secured by paratroopers.

We set up two-man poncho hootches, then went on a recon. Ron and I were particularly interested in some small stone structures scattered about the plateau approximately fifty meters from our makeshift tents.

A closer look revealed them to be grave sites or shrines. Several of them were very elaborate, with beautiful etchings of birds and other animals. Some of the tombs were more ornate than others and painted in various colors. The most elegant was a twelve-by-twelve-foot tomb surrounded by etched white carvings on blue walls averaging about four feet high. Ron went to gather the rest of the guys for a look while I took some photos. We all joked about how ironic it was that our division's new base camp was going to be built around a graveyard.

There wasn't time to dig foxholes as night rolled in. Besides, the ground was so rocky and hard, it would have taken us days with just an entrenching tool. There was no way our small detachment could cover the length of perimeter that was our responsibility either, so Lieutenant Wilberding decided that the best way to provide security and still maintain control was to have a three-man LP (listening post) to our front. The LP could radio warning of any danger or enemy activity to the rest of the detachment, which could then respond in force. Those not on LP could try to get some rest, but had to remain fully clothed and ready to react at a moment's notice.

Thank God I wasn't detailed the first night. Man, was I beat! I shared a poncho with John Johnson, and the two of us attempted to get comfortable among all the protruding stones. Torch was so small he just rolled into a ball between us and went right to sleep.

I considered John to be the other intellectual in the detachment besides Brad. He carefully thought about a subject and chose his words before he spoke. Whenever the opportunity arose, he had a cigar in his mouth.

John groaned for the umpteenth time as another stone stabbed into his back. "Damn! This ground is rugged. I swear, we'd probably be more comfortable if we slept on a bed of nails."

I decided to lie on my back instead of my side; the rock poking my back was smaller than the one jabbing my hip. "Yeah! There seems to be a fine art to maneuvering your body around this stuff and still sleep."

"Well, if there is, Richie, it's obvious that I haven't even come close to mastering it."

Since John read quite a bit, I decided to run something by him that had been weighing on my mind. "Let me ask you something, John. Do you know anything about Vietnamese history or folklore?"

John pondered for some time before answering. "That depends. Before we left the States, I did brush up on some of the military and political past of this country."

It would probably sound stupid, but I had already ventured this far. "No, John. I mean, you know, Vietnamese folklore. Tales handed down through generations."

I must have sparked his curiosity or intellectually challenged him somehow, because John's voice was a bit irritable. "You'll have to be more specific!"

"Well, I heard they had a lot of superstitions. I just wondered if sleeping or fighting over their graves was a bad omen or, you know, some kind of curse is put on the guys that do—like you die of a bad case of jungle rot, where your skin decays slowly away while you're alive. Or—"

"Christ!" John interrupted. "Here we are, Richie. Just a small detachment, about the size of a squad, on some hill in the middle of nowhere in I Corps. There might be a hundred gooks out there, sneaking up on us right now. And you're thinking about curses and omens. I don't believe it!"

He had a point. "Yeah! I guess you're right. I was just wondering about it."

John shook his head, adjusted his poncho up over his shoulders, and turned away from me. "Shit! You got some imagination."

I adjusted my poncho liner so that most of my body was covered. Right before I dozed off, however, I heard John mumble, "I wonder where I can get some information on that subject."

The next day a few trucks arrived from Phu Bai with supplies, and finally some of our fellow paratroopers could be seen milling around. That night it was my turn on LP. The three of us decided to set up the LP in one of the graves, which made sense, since the stone walls offered excellent cover and concealment. It sure felt eerie, though, sitting on top of a grave, wondering about ancient curses and such. I had to strain to keep my imagination in check. Even when using the starlight scope, I often saw a bush move or an imaginary figure appear, even if just for an instant. The practice of using the graves for LPs continued, although we used a different shrine each night to confuse the enemy.

As each day went by, more division soldiers and equipment poured into the base camp, which was eventually named Camp Eagle. Since the eagle was the division symbol, most of us considered the title appropriate.

Luckily, the presence of more troops offered us a reprieve from full-time perimeter security. Our detachment manned the LP in front of the perimeter for the time being, however. As far as base camps went, the Eagle was quickly building its nest. With the increase in American activity, we knew it was only a matter of time before the enemy would arrive to check out the area.

Hence, shortly after the troops arrived, the detachment members on LP reported enemy movement, prompting Wilberding to increase the LP to four members. That worked out better because two guys could stay awake while two guys slept. The enemy continued probing our area for the next four or five nights, so just about every detachment member got a chance to experience a harrowing night on LP.

My most interesting night occurred while on LP with Ron Reynolds, Buz Harding, and Mike Gibbons. Mike was the other member in the Pathfinders, besides myself, who was from Massachusetts. He was short and thin. Although he was small in stature, he was big in guts. Mike would do anything if you dared him.

Mike took a liking to me right away since I was a home boy. He was about three years older than I, and although I outranked him, he treated me like a younger brother. I never minded because, in reality, Mike should have been my senior in rank; he had more time in the army. But he had one problem that always got him in trouble, one that kept him from getting promoted. At times Mike got carried away when drinking, and when he did, look out. When Mike got drunk, anything could happen. Before we left Fort Campbell, some of us went to Nashville and had to flee the hotel because Mike was throwing smoke grenades off the room's balcony.

At Bien Hoa, Mike got into a fight at the enlisted club and then fell into barbed wire on the way back to the hootch. By the time we got him untangled, his body was a mass of cuts and scrapes. The good thing about Mike was that he was loyal; when the chips were down, he'd cover your ass. That's all that really mattered to me.

It was about one in the morning. Ron and Buz remained on watch while Mike and I slept. It was overcast, so the starlight scope wasn't much use. Ron thought he heard movement and alerted Buz. After a few moments Buz heard it, too. Ron told Buz to wake us.

Buz lightly nudged me. My fatigues were damp. Tired and chilled, I tried to convince myself that I was really home and Vietnam was just a dream. Buz nudged me again, this time more forcibly. The alarm on his face thrust my mind into reality. Quickly but quietly, I awoke Mike. The two of us slowly positioned ourselves behind the grave's wall.

At first I prayed that the noise was just some animal moving about, but the motion sounded too calculated and cautious. Ron got on the horn and called in a sitrep (situation report), alerting the perimeter. Whispering into the handset, he kept the volume low on the radio. Since most of the soldiers guarding the perimeter came from other units, those of us out on LP insisted that only a fellow Pathfinder monitor the radio on the other end. If the situation became such that we had to vacate the LP and run back toward the perimeter, we wanted someone we could depend upon to ensure that our own troops would not fire on us.

After we listened for a while, the noise faded away. I hoped the enemy was leaving for good. About ten minutes later, however, some bushes rustled and twigs snapped. The noise continued to grow louder. Earlier the movement seemed to push across our front; now it sounded like it was heading right toward our position. They probably didn't even know we were out there.

Ron sent another sitrep. Since Ron and I were both corporals and had been promoted on the same day, neither one of us outranked the other. However, that was never an issue between us. I considered Ron a better soldier and a more mature leader than myself. For him, soldiering came naturally; I had to work hard at it. Moving alongside him to confer, I whispered, "What do you think?"

Ron's eyes remained fixed to the front as he spoke. "Sounds like they're coming right at us."

Damn! I hated to hear him confirm my suspicions. I didn't want to hear the answer to my next question, either, but I had to ask it. "How many do you think there are?"

At first Ron shook his head, indicating he was unsure. Then he raised his hand in front of my face, displaying four fingers. Even though I knew there was absolutely no way that Ron could actually tell how many were out there, I felt a slight sense of relief. If his guess was right, at least the odds were even.

The four of us listened intently. It was too dark to observe anything, and the blackness just magnified the slightest sound. My heart began beating rapidly in my throat. The waiting was nerve-racking. Part of me just wanted to open fire and get it over with. I knew that would be a stupid thing to do, however, since the muzzle flash would give away our exact position.

Forcing myself to stay calm, I carefully moved the selector switch on my weapon from "safe" to "semi." My hand crept slowly across my LBE and worked free a grenade. I squeezed the open ends of the grenade pin together, making the pin easier to pull if needed. I cautiously placed the grenade on the wall to my front.

Even though the noise was clear, it was difficult to tell how close it was or how many enemy soldiers were actually out there. Ron was skillful at not showing his emotions during times like that, but I knew him well enough to know that he was scared, too.

Mike and Buz each placed a grenade on the wall to their front. They both expressed looks of impatience, anxiously waiting for Ron and me to initiate some kind of plan. Overall, Buz appeared calm, his grenade within reach and his rifle shouldered. Mike, on the other hand, was fidgeting and eager for us to act. Mike was a good soldier who didn't mind following orders, but he had little patience for a leader who hesitated when making a decision. I knew if Ron and I didn't act soon, Mike would.

Ron tugged at my sleeve. "What do you think?" he whispered.

Although that should have been an easy question for me to answer since I had been pondering that issue all along, it was not. "Hell, I don't know. But we got to do something!"

Ron paused for a moment. Finally he whispered, "Let's try a grenade and see what happens."

I gave the idea some thought. Tossing a grenade was probably the best strategy given the present circumstances. A grenade was an excellent weapon to use at night because it didn't give away your position the way the flashes of a rifle did. Moreover, with a grenade, it didn't have to hit the target to be effective.

It was still risky, however. What if the gooks out there

were the point element of a much larger force? Throwing the grenade would let them know we were close by, and we'd be in for one hell of a firefight. But, after swiftly weighing the alternatives, I nodded in agreement.

While Ron radioed the perimeter to explain our "plan," I waved my hand across my rifle, letting Buz and Mike know we would not use M-16s, at least initially. I then pointed to Mike's grenade and gestured for him to wait for the signal to toss it. Letting Mike throw the grenade would ease his tension.

Ron put the handset down and grabbed his weapon. We all crouched beneath the wall for cover, weapons ready. Anything could happen once that grenade exploded.

I gave the signal to Mike, and he threw the grenade. A bright flash and earsplitting explosion erupted. We waited for all hell to break loose, but nothing happened. Nothing! No screaming! No moaning! No gunfire!

We stared at one another in disbelief. Surely the grenade must have hit at least one of the bastards. Maybe it killed them all. The four of us remained completely still and just listened. The perimeter radioed for a sitrep, which Ron supplied. A long time passed, perhaps twenty minutes, without a sound or anyone's stirring. It seemed like hours. My left leg began to cramp from remaining in the same position for so long.

Finally I thought I heard movement again. The others heard it, too. The only thing I could figure was that Mike's grenade had totally missed the enemy, and they were smart enough not to fire their weapons and give away their position. Obviously they had just been lying low for a while.

I grabbed my grenade and gestured to Ron. He nodded in agreement and radioed the perimeter to let them know we heard movement again and would be throwing another grenade. This time the enemy's movement was periodic and much more controlled, so I listened very intently, hoping to hear some sound that might help me track their general location. Making sure everyone was ready, I pulled the pin on the grenade and threw it.

Another flash and loud explosion followed. Again nothing happened.

The perimeter requested another sitrep. The guys back there probably thought we were just hearing things on LP, and were enjoying a good laugh at our expense. Ron radioed the situation while the rest of us remained alert.

Suddenly an explosion occurred about twenty meters off to our right, scaring the hell out of us. Mike almost fired his weapon but thought better of it. Ron was pissed; he kept his voice low as he spoke on the horn. He assumed someone from the perimeter had fired an M-79 grenade launcher in our direction. The voice at the other end, however, assured him that was not the case.

The four of us were baffled. What the hell was going on? Within moments another explosion occurred, this time impacting closer to us, toward our front.

Immediately, Buz echoed my thoughts. "It's the gooks. They're throwing grenades back at us!"

Unfortunately, Buz was right. The enemy had decided to play the same cat-and-mouse game, probably hoping either to hit us or force us to give away our position by firing our weapons. The four of us had to act fast. We couldn't just lie low and wait. If they continued throwing grenades and one of them landed in our midst, we'd all be killed. Using gestures and light whispers, we quickly began racing through our options.

If the four of us opened fire, we might get lucky and hit the gooks, but our muzzle flashes would definitely give away our position. We could vacate the LP and head back to the perimeter, but if the gooks happened to be between us and the perimeter, they could ambush us. Besides, the possibility of our getting shot at by our own troops was very high if the shit hit the fan.

Each of us had carried two grenades to the LP. That meant we had six remaining. It was agreed that the best thing to do was stay put and throw grenades back at the gooks, in a different direction each time, starting from left to right across our front.

Ron relayed another sitrep, then Buz threw his grenade to our left side. Nothing happened. After a few minutes of waiting, Ron threw one in a different direction. Again nothing happened. Instead of throwing more grenades as initially planned, we decided to wait and see what transpired.

We listened intently for movement throughout the rest of the night. Any minute I imagined a gook grenade landing in the middle of us. I couldn't wait for morning to come. It was one of the longest nights in my life. Later in my tour, however, there would be other nights that seemed a lot longer.

At daybreak the four of us split up and checked the immediate surroundings for any signs of bodies or blood trails. To our surprise, we didn't find anything. On our walk back to the perimeter we concluded that the enemy had thrown their grenades to divert us while making their escape. Hell, I had to give them credit; it worked!

Ron and I figured we would be harassed a bit while passing the guys on the perimeter, but I guess the four of us looked so emotionally and physically burned out that everyone decided to leave us alone.

Camp Eagle built up rapidly during the weeks that followed. It wasn't long before the perimeter was surrounded by a berm and permanent bunkers, negating the need for an LP. Unfortunately, the many huge holes the engineers dug for bunkers and living quarters needed to be covered with tents and surrounded by sandbags. Each day consisted of laboring in the hot sun filling sandbags, setting up tents, or carrying equipment and supplies.

One evening, two armored vehicles moved in at the bottom of the slope about seventy meters from our new battalion area. Most likely they had escorted one of the many convoys arriving at Camp Eagle with supplies, and they probably needed a place to park overnight.

Around ten the next morning, most of us from the detachment were placing sandbags around what was to be our new Pathfinder hootch. Sergeant Guerra arrived with some water, so we gathered around him, taking a break. Suddenly Guerra's body became rigid. His eyes grew wide as he stared toward the armored vehicles. Puzzled, Ron, Joe, and I looked in that direction.

About seven men were lounging beside or on top of the vehicles. Some had their shirts off. Surely, Sergeant Guerra wasn't upset about that. Sometimes we took off our shirts and nothing was said. Just as Guerra started to shout something, I heard a loud *whoosh* and saw a rocket trailing smoke soar toward the vehicles. It exploded about five feet in front of them.

As the men by the armored vehicles yelled and scrambled for cover, we glanced to the left, across the open clearing from where the rocket came. To our surprise there stood two gooks, right out in the open. We all watched in astonishment as the one closer to us fired a second rocket, which impacted directly on a vehicle. As the gooks turned and ran, the other armored vehicle opened up with its machine gun, saturating the area.

Medics arrived to care for some of the men wounded by shrapnel. Luckily, none of them was severely injured. At that point, Sergeant Guerra told us to get back to work. We never did find out if they killed the two gooks or not.

A few days later, some South Vietnamese children were helping us fill sandbags, two girls and a boy. Vietnamese civilians assembled at the front gate of Camp Eagle every morning in the hope of obtaining some kind of employment from any of the units. I don't think any of the kids working with us were over twelve years old. Without warning, something with the sound of a freight train screeched overhead. The projectile smashed about a hundred meters from our hootch, making a colossal explosion that sent dirt and gravel high into the air.

It took us completely by surprise. Fear surged through my body as I dropped to the ground. Sergeant Guerra yelled out, "Try to find cover! Everyone run for cover!"

Frantically I searched for a place to hide until I heard screaming and saw the children. They just stood there horrified, frozen with terror. Just as a second freight train came overhead, I lunged for them. I wasn't alone. At least four other Pathfinders had the same idea. The three children were completely covered by us.

All around me I heard voices. "What the hell is it?" "What's going on?" "It's some heavy artillery!" "Is it ours?" Whatever it was, it made a 122 rocket sound like a hand grenade.

Under the pile of bodies, a little girl's face was next to mine, tears streaming down her cheeks. I tried to calm her as the third round came screaming in. God, it sounded like it was on top of us. Larry must have been somewhere in the pile, because I heard his voice. "Hold on! Here comes another one."

The third explosion hit fifty meters away. The noise was deafening. Pieces of shrapnel whizzed by. Dirt, gravel, and rock poured down on us. Everyone was quiet as we all lay there for a few moments. Eventually each person got to his feet. It was over.

Afterward, the explanation was that a U.S. Marine 155mm artillery battery from another military compound had erred in calculating a fire mission.

Sergeant Guerra wasn't himself the rest of the day. Finally he admitted that he felt bad for the children, since they reminded him of his own back home. He was thankful his kids lived in America and admitted that was one of the reasons he remained a career soldier. For a brief moment I got to observe a different side of Sergeant Guerra than just an old hard-faced NCO. I thought about how sad war was for the children. I also felt very privileged to be serving with a group of guys who, without hesitation, spontaneously put the lives of those kids ahead of their own.

After two weeks, working around Camp Eagle and filling sandbags was getting old. I knew work had to be done, but I was getting itchy. I hadn't joined the

Pathfinders and come to Vietnam to fill sandbags and pull guard duty. Finally a few missions came down to support the division's 1st Brigade. I readily jumped at the chance to go on one of them. The next day Lieutenant Wilberding selected me for a mission and I departed the following morning.

One of the brigade's infantry battalions was getting ready to push toward the A Shau Valley and would need close artillery support. My mission was to link up with an infantry company on a hilltop and establish a landing zone for an artillery battery of 105mm howitzers.

I was a little surprised when Lieutenant Wilberding told me I would be operating alone. Usually that type of mission called for a two-man Pathfinder team. I wasn't overly concerned; I knew he must have had a good reason to make such a decision. Perhaps other missions were anticipated, and he didn't want to be left short-handed. In any event, I didn't question his judgment. I knew I was going to be working my ass off, though.

Since I would be alone, I tried to pack light. Even so, my rucksack felt like it weighed a ton. I carried the minimum Pathfinder items, which included a PRC-25 radio, extra batteries, ammunition, M-16 rifle, fragmentation grenades, rations, VS-17 panel, strobe light, flashlight, poncho and liner, and beaucoup smoke grenades. Luckily, Pathfinders didn't have to carry or wear helmets anymore.

My departure time was 0800 hours at our unit helipad. I arrived about thirty minutes early, which gave me time to conduct a last-minute commo check to ensure the radio still functioned properly. I then test-fired my weapon by shooting a round into the sand-filled fifty-five-gallon drum that had been placed beside the pad for that purpose. After making sure my radio was turned off and my weapon was placed back on safe, I rested on my rucksack and waited for the chopper that would transport me to my destination. Since I was heading toward the A Shau, I assumed one of our battalion slicks would pick me up, along with gunships to provide cover.

Even though it was early morning, the sun had already made the tarmac hot. While waiting, I pulled the small notebook from my left breast pocket and began memorizing the important radio frequencies I would be utilizing.

An unusual buzzing sound caught my attention. Off to my right I noticed a small observation helicopter, an OH-13 flying in my direction. The tiny chopper was just a round plastic bubble with a tail. It looked like a big insect, a type of helicopter that was scarce and long since outdated. I remembered seeing similar ones in old army training films. The aircraft could seat only two people, the pilot and a passenger, and it lacked any protection or weaponry. With all the new helicopters and latest technology, I wondered what the hell that little thing was even doing in Vietnam. I chuckled to myself as it flew near, then returned to my notes.

The buzzing sound got louder. To my surprise the tiny chopper landed right in front of me. I continued to stare at it after it touched down. The pilot waved me over. Damn! The guy was probably lost and looking for division headquarters to fly some high-ranking officer around Camp Eagle. Loosening the straps on my ruck, I slipped my arms out, stood up, and walked over to the bird. There were no doors or enclosures on the aircraft. Both sides of the bubble were completely cut out and exposed, making it easy to talk to the pilot. He was an older-looking guy. Most of the pilots I knew were a lot younger.

I shouted, "Whatcha need, sir?"

"Grab your equipment and let's go!"

His words took me completely by surprise. "Go, sir?"

He appeared flustered. "You're the Pathfinder, right?"

I paused for a moment, making sure I understood his words correctly over the sound of the blades. "Yes, sir! I'm a Pathfinder!"

He spoke firmly. "Well, jump in! Let's go!"

I got it! I thought he had to be taking me to another helipad at Camp Eagle to board a different chopper. "Okay, sir! Let me grab my ruck!"

After squeezing my rucksack, weapon, and body into

the tiny bubble, I asked the pilot, "What pad are you taking me to, sir?"

The pilot had a bewildered look on his face. "Pad? What pad? What are you talking about?"

Now I was really confused. I tried not to appear irritated, but I had to find out just what the hell was going on and end all this nonsense. "Just where are you taking me, sir?"

His mouth widened into a big shit-eating grin as his hand pulled back on the throttle. "Hell, son, we're headed for Indian country!"

Holy shit! You got to be kidding me! There's no way this little piece of plastic is taking me out on a mission near the A Shau!

Like a big insect, the tiny bubble buzzed up into the sky.

Chapter Nine

The A Shau Valley lay in the northernmost region of South Vietnam, encompassing a network of rivers surrounded by mountainous, heavily vegetated terrain. For years the A Shau remained an impregnable Communist stronghold. Thousands of NVA soldiers moved about freely and manned heavily fortified bunker complexes protected by antiaircraft guns and artillery. Trucks, weapons, ammunition, and other material lay hidden in huge underground caches. Even hospitals thrived in caverns connected by intricate tunnel systems. Situated close to the Loatian border, the A Shau was continuously used by the North Vietnamese as a major route for infiltrating personnel and supplies into South Vietnam.

I couldn't believe I was flying on a mission toward the A Shau in a little OH-13 observation helicopter. It was really cramped inside the plastic bubble with the heavy rucksack resting on my lap. The only armament on the entire aircraft was my M-16. Flying at a thousand feet with a sheet of plastic to my front and nothingness on my whole right side gave me a strange feeling. With everything above, around, and under me in full view, I felt like I was sitting in a flying seat.

As the mountains and jungle came closer, the pilot dropped to low-level flight; the enemy would have a more difficult time spotting the aircraft at treetop level than at a higher altitude. The OH-13's slow speed and lack of shielding made it a particularly vulnerable target, so the pilot wasn't taking any chances. He had the little bird buzzing at full throttle, literally skimming the tops of the trees. On more than one occasion, branches and treetops slapped the bubble right under my feet. I didn't know if the pilot was doing that to impress me or scare the shit out of me; he accomplished both. Every time I glanced over at him, though, he seemed to be enjoying the hell out of himself.

I could understand why the OH-13 helicopter was used for observation. Its slow speed and excellent view allowed me to see through the trees and vegetation significantly better than when flying in a slick. It was also less noisy. If we'd ever gone down in that thing, though, it would have been all over. I doubt very seriously that either of us could have survived a crash in such a light aircraft, especially at the speed we were traveling.

As I thought about the mission, I wondered why I would be operating alone. Setting up an LZ from scratch, controlling all the aircraft, and coordinating the placement of the artillery was a lot of work for just one Pathfinder. Perhaps all of our helicopters were committed elsewhere, and the tiny bubble, which could carry only one passenger, was the only transportation that could be allocated. In any event, I bet Lieutenant Wilberding was having a good laugh for himself back at Camp Eagle.

I held on tight as the light helicopter popped up the side of a mountain, grazed its peak, then sailed down the next valley, scraping the tops of bushes and trees. In some ways the trip resembled a roller-coaster ride. We had been flying about thirty minutes when the pilot tapped me on the shoulder, then pointed to a hilltop at our two o'clock.

The east side of the hill facing our approach had a steep drop. The terrain on top of the hill was long and narrow, containing obstacles like small trees and bushes. The pilot circled the hilltop in search of an adequate spot to land, which allowed me to get a complete view of the ground. The western side of the hill had a more gentle incline.

I observed about thirty soldiers scattered below, resting on their rucksacks. They appeared to have just arrived. The infantrymen had probably spent the night in the thick vegetation at the bottom of the slope, then humped up the hill at first light. By the looks of their clothes and equipment, they had been in the field for at least a few days.

The pilot returned to our original approach from the east and maneuvered the tiny helicopter into a small, tightly confined clearing. With the skids firmly on the ground, I shook the pilot's hand and struggled out of the tiny cockpit, tugging along my rucksack and weapon. It was only then that I noticed the tail of the aircraft extending over the sheer cliff. The pilot, still smiling, rendered me the traditional thumbs-up. The little bird popped to a hover about ten feet up, spun around, and buzzed away. I just shook my head in disbelief, then scanned the hilltop, hoping to find someone in charge.

Eventually the infantry company commander, along with another officer who was probably the artillery FO (forward observer), greeted me, and we began to lay out the LZ. It was agreed that the artillery should be positioned on the western slope, which was a more gradual incline. Since the guns would primarily be firing in support of troops to the west, wind permitting, I would direct all aircraft to approach from the east. That would keep the flights clear of outgoing artillery fire.

CH-47 Chinook helicopters would be arriving first thing in the morning. A Chinook could transport a 105mm howitzer artillery piece, one load of ammunition, and the gun crew on a single flight. The big cargo helicopter carried the gun and ammo slung beneath its belly while hauling the artillery gun crew inside. There was only one piece of ground flat and large enough to use as an LZ that could land a Chinook and unload the crew, so I immediately went to work on having it cleared.

It was late afternoon by the time the LZ was prepared and the proposed sites marked for the guns. I was beat and decided to take a break, perhaps even settle down for the night. I found a spot beside some bushes, spread out my poncho, and sat down. The poor grunts had been laboriously chipping away at the rock-hardened clay in an attempt to dig their foxholes, and the sounds of entrenching tools whacking away at the ground echoed through the hills. An old, hard-faced first sergeant trooped up and down the line, repeatedly telling the men to dig their foxholes deeper.

I had just finished taking a swallow of water from my canteen when the first sergeant approached me. "What do you think you're doing here, son?"

God! He looked even older up close. "I'm getting ready to shut down for the night, First Sergeant!"

His reply was cordial but serious. "You can't stay here!"

After busting my ass all day, the last thing I needed was to get involved in a pissing contest with a first sergeant. Obviously he wanted to assert some authority. The hell with it, I wasn't budging. "Why not, First Sergeant?"

Surprisingly, he didn't appear upset by my response. "Because you don't have any cover. You need to be in a foxhole." He glanced over to where the troops were digging, then at his watch. "We're going to get hit in a few hours, soon as it gets near dusk."

What the hell was he talking about? The commander didn't mention anything to me about reports that we were going to get hit. This guy just wanted to exhibit some supervisory authority over me. I decided to put him off, but tactfully. "I appreciate your concern, First Sergeant, but I've got to be up and functioning by first light tomorrow, controlling all the aircraft coming in here. I guess I'll just have to take my chances if we get hit."

I expected him to be at least slightly irritated by my response, but instead his composure was rather serene and matter-of-fact. "I'm afraid I can't let you do that, son. You stay here, and you might not live till tomorrow."

He searched the surrounding area for a moment, then glanced back at me. "Too late to dig a hole of your own. C'mon with me."

Damn! The old guy seemed so calm and so genuinely

concerned about me, I couldn't help but grab my equipment and follow him.

The infantry company was actually the size of about two platoons, approximately sixty men in all. The majority of the men were spread out in two-man foxholes across the crest of the hill, forming a perimeter. The rest remained nearby, entrenched right on the hilltop. The first sergeant stopped in front of one of these foxholes. A lone soldier stood inside a newly dug hole, frantically chipping away at the earth with an entrenching tool.

"You can share this hole with Davis here. He's all alone and can use the help."

He gave Davis a wry look. "Maybe the two of you can have it deep enough before the mortars come in."

The first sergeant stomped away, pausing in front of the next foxhole. I heard him bark, "Not deep enough, men, keep digging. You can bet your ass the dinks are out there watching us right now, setting up their mortars. It won't be long before they hit us. I can smell the little bastards."

Davis shook my hand, welcoming me. He looked worn out. His foxhole was only about two feet deep. I set down my equipment, grabbed his entrenching tool from him, and started hacking away at the ground. Damn! It was like trying to dig through rock. No wonder the poor guys were exhausted.

Maybe Davis could fill me in on what was going on. "What the hell is he talking about, getting hit?"

"The first sergeant's been around a long time and knows his shit. If he says we're going to get mortared, believe it!"

I was already tired of slamming the entrenching tool into the ground. "Man! I'll say he's been around a long time. That's the oldest NCO I've ever seen in the field. I can't believe he's out here doing this stuff."

The soldiers in the next foxhole had been listening in on our conversation. One of them chimed in, "Top's old, all right. They say the old fart pulled KP at the Last Supper. Don't let his age fool you, though, he's harder than woodpecker lips."

The soldier had my curiosity. "Do you believe him when he says he can smell the gooks?"

"You can bet your ass he can. He's been over here a long time. I think he even fought in Korea."

Davis and I spent the next few hours hacking away at the clay. Right before dusk, the first sergeant came around to inspect all the foxholes again. He loomed over us, hands on his hips. "That hole ain't nowhere deep enough, you two!"

Davis's look was pitiful. "Damn, Top! I've been digging at this hole all day. It can't get any deeper."

The first sergeant remained expressionless. "Well, it's too late now. When those mortars start coming in, you'll wish to God it was deeper."

As he strutted off to the next position, we heard him mumble, "I guess you boys are just gonna have to learn the hard way."

Just as dusk set in, I heard some sounds, like hollow, metallic thuds, off in the distance. *Thump . . . thump . . . thump . . . thump.*

Davis and I looked at each other. "Incoming!" We plunged down into the hole. The first round crashed about fifty meters to our front, then another, followed by others. As the explosions continued, Davis struggled to fit his entire body inside his steel pot. Since I hadn't brought a helmet along, I tried my best to become one with the earth. About twelve mortar rounds exploded in all.

After the barrage ended, the first sergeant sped past our position. He spoke softly. "Okay, stay down now! They got two tubes firing on us. If they have an FO out there, he'll adjust their fire, then they'll drop some more on us."

Sure enough, a few moments after he left we could hear mortars coming out of the tubes again. *Thump . . . thump . . . thump.*

This time the first few rounds hit about twenty-five meters away. The sound of the explosions grew increasingly louder with each detonation. Damn, the gooks were walking them right toward our position. Quickly I reached out of the hole and pulled my rucksack in on top of me, hoping to protect my radio from shrapnel and also to provide myself some possible cover. The last round hit about ten meters short of our foxhole.

Once the barrage ended, the first sergeant hurried by again. This time his voice expressed more concern. "Okay now, men, this is it. If they drop them again, it's gonna be right on us. Stay down now."

Stay down?! He didn't have to tell me twice!

Davis and I remained frozen, each of us lost in his own thoughts. For some reason my mind reflected back to when I was a kid and used to toss pebbles onto a group of ants. It was only a matter of luck as to which ant would be hit by one of the small stones. In my situation, I felt just like one of those ants. I vowed never to do that again.

A few moments had elapsed. Both enemy tubes had fired six or seven rounds in the previous volley. Perhaps they were out of ammunition. Suddenly the metallic thuds broke the silence once more. *Thump . . . thump . . . thump . . .* The first rounds exploded, immediately producing cries for help. The explosions crept toward our foxhole from two directions. Each explosion was louder than the last. Finally one detonated about five meters away. Instinctively I placed my hands over my ears waiting for the next one to hit, praying it would not land right on top of us.

Another enemy mortar round exploded about a meter past our foxhole. A deafening, high-pitched blast showered us with dirt and gravel, causing our ears to ring and engulfing us in a cloud of dark gray smoke. I guess the shrapnel flew over the foxhole, because neither Davis nor I was hit. Stunned, I listened as the mortar rounds continued thundering by, the sound of their explosions fading. Abruptly the bombardment ceased. Several cries for help pierced the night air.

Davis was the first to speak. "Shit! That was close. Think they'll hit us again?"

"Hell! I hope not!" I pushed the rucksack off me and placed it back outside the foxhole.

Davis remained hunched down in the hole, listening intently for the sounds of mortar rounds leaving their tubes. Finally he took off his helmet and wiped the sweat from his forehead with his sleeve. "Man, I'll never complain about digging another hole again. If we stay here, I'm going to work on this hole all day tomorrow."

American artillery rounds screamed overhead, slamming into the surrounding hillside in an effort to counter the enemy mortars.

I pulled the radio out of my rucksack and jumped out of the foxhole. "Hey, Davis! Do me a favor and watch my stuff."

Davis looked bewildered. "Where the hell you going? They might lob some more in on us any minute!"

"Some of the guys are wounded. They're probably going to need a dustoff."

Just then someone called out, "Pathfinder! Where's the Pathfinder?"

"Over here!" I quickly checked my LBE to make sure everything was still in place, grabbed my radio and weapon, and took off in the direction of the voice.

A sergeant led me to the company commander. The commander was standing near the center of the hilltop talking with two soldiers. It was dark as we approached. "Did you find the Pathfinder?"

I moved to the front of the sergeant. "I'm right here, sir!"

The commander appeared calm but weary. "Good! I radioed for a dustoff. I'm going to need you to bring him in!"

"Roger that, sir! How many WIAs need to be lifted out?"

"At present, the count is four, but that may change." He turned to one of the soldiers beside him and told him to check and make sure the count was still accurate.

"Will we have any problems getting the dustoff in here?"

"No, sir! I'm going to bring him in on the LZ we cleared earlier. It would help if the wounded were ready to load as quick as possible, though, so the chopper's not on the ground long. Charlie would like nothing more than to take out a helicopter."

"No problem! Do you need anything else from me?"

"No, sir!" I pointed to my LBE. "I'll bring the dustoff in with my strobe light."

I immediately went to the LZ to help prepare the wounded for transport. The number of WIAs being lifted out increased to five, which still posed no problem as far as transporting all of them out on one lift. Once the wounded were situated at the LZ, I ran back over to the eastern side of the hill and waited for the aircraft. Minutes later I noticed the green and red lights of a helicopter several miles off in the distance. I waited for the pilot to contact me.

"Pathfinder Control! This is medevac one-two, approximately five miles to the east. Request landing instructions. Over!"

"Medevac one-two! This is Pathfinder Control! Enemy situation negative at this time. Continue approach to the west. Over!"

A few moments passed, then the pilot's voice came back over the horn. "Pathfinder Control! This is one-two! Can you give me a short count? Over."

"Roger! Short count now! One, two, three, four, five, four, three, two, one. Short count. Out!"

To the pilot, the ground was a sheet of utter blackness with nothing to show exactly where we were located. In darkness or extremely poor weather it was possible for the pilot to become lost or disoriented. Helicopters were outfitted with FM, UHF, and VHF radio and navigational frequencies. FM was the main frequency most commonly used for ground to air. Each helicopter was equipped with an FM directional homing needle to guide in on. A short count was nothing more than a procedure used to keep the radio handset keyed for approximately ten seconds by counting to five and back. That allowed the pilot time to home in on the FM radio's location. A long count consisted of counting to ten and back. Although a fairly simple procedure, it was very accurate.

The aircraft continued its approach until it was about two miles out. "Pathfinder Control! Medevac one-two. Over!"

"This is Pathfinder Control!"

"This is one-two! Can you give me one more short count? Over!"

"Roger, one-two! Short count now! One, two, three, four, five, four, three, two, one. Short count, out!"

"Roger! Thanks!"

When the helicopter was a half mile out from the hilltop, I contacted the pilot.

"One-two! Lima Zulu is located on the western side of the hilltop. Winds calm! Enemy situation negative at this time. Be advised that you could receive mortar fire while on the ground. Land and depart to the east. Guide in on strobe light. Over."

"Roger! This is one-two! Will land to the east and guide in on strobe."

I quickly removed the strobe light from its case and pressed the black rubber button to turn it on. The distinct whining noise of the battery was followed by a brilliant, flashing blue light. *Blip . . . blip . . . blip!* I extended the light above my head. Unfortunately, it lit me up like a neon sign; the whole world could see me.

"Pathfinder Control! One-two! I've got the strobe in sight!"

The dustoff passed over the hilltop, banked right, then slowly approached the strobe light, lining up on my signal. It was so dark the pilot had to be cautious. As the dirt and sand slammed into my face from the chopper's wash, I couldn't help but visualize a sniper's bullet smacking me in the chest or mortar rounds hitting the helicopter and blowing us all to hell.

About fifteen feet above the ground, the pilot turned on his searchlight. The beam lit up the entire LZ. If the gooks were ever going to drop mortars, that would have been the perfect time.

My strobe light was tied by a cord to my LBE, so I shut it off and let it drop to my side, then guided in the dustoff with hand-and-arm signals. As soon as the bird's skids touched the ground, the pilot turned off his light. Thank God!

About a minute later the pilot's voice came over the horn. "Pathfinder Control! This is medevac one-two. Over!"

I blocked my other ear so I could hear through the handset above the *whopping* of the blades and yelled, "This is Pathfinder Control. Over!"

"This is one-two! Departing Lima Zulu to the east. Have five pax on board. Over!"

"Roger! One-two! This is Pathfinder Control! Affirmative, five pax! You are clear for departure to the east. Over!"

The dustoff hovered up about ten feet, then quickly pulled pitch. I covered my eyes as a cloud of dirt and fine gravel blew over me. Thank God no sniper or mortar rounds came into the LZ. The only thing I could figure was that the gooks were either out of ammo or the previous friendly artillery fire had scared them off. I tucked my strobe light back into its case and waited until the aircraft was well off in the distance before shutting down the radio. As I stumbled around trying to find my foxhole, a voice whispered, "Over here!" It was Davis. He must have recognized my silhouette carrying the radio.

I placed the radio beside my ruck and jumped into the hole. Davis appeared relieved to see me back. "How did everything go?"

"Great! I got all of the wounded out okay!"

"I thought for sure the gooks were going to drop mortars on us while that chopper was landing."

"Yeah! Me too! Maybe we were lucky and the artillery nailed them earlier."

Davis opened up a pack of Chiclets from a C-ration packet and handed me one. "Man, I couldn't believe you were standing out there, lit up like a damn Christmas tree. You guys do that often?"

I popped the gum in my mouth. "Sometimes!"

Davis shook his head. "You can have that shit!"

I smiled and winked. "Yeah! I love performing for an audience."

We both tried to get some sleep, but it was just too cramped in the tiny foxhole. I volunteered to sleep on the ground behind it. I seriously doubted that Charlie would hit us with mortars again. Hell! He would have used them on the chopper when it landed. I grabbed my poncho and liner out of my ruck and spread them out in back of the foxhole. Using my rucksack as a pillow, I strapped my M-16 through my arm by my side.

I awoke to the sound of voices. It was just getting light. My fatigues were damp from the morning dew. My mouth tasted like the 82d Airborne had jumped in it wearing muddy boots. The first thing I always did in the field, situation permitting, was brush my teeth. Somehow that made me feel clean.

I crawled out of the foxhole, brushed my teeth, then filled my canteen cup with water. I carried a small block of C-4 plastic explosive, which I used just for cooking. Although a powerful explosive, C-4 resembled soft, white modeling clay and could easily be shaped. It burned with intense heat when lit. A piece about the size of a quarter would heat a can of C rations or boil water in seconds.

I tore off a little piece and heated the water in my canteen cup. Davis and I combined our packets of coffee and cocoa and mixed them together. Once finished, I strolled over to the eastern edge of the hilltop, turned on my radio, and waited for the first aircraft to report when it was inbound.

At about 0800 hours the first Chinook came on the horn. "Pathfinder Control! This is Big Windy Six. Over."

"Big Windy Six! This is Pathfinder Control!"

"This is Big Windy Six, inbound from the east. Over."

Searching to the east, I attempted to spot the aircraft but couldn't see anything. "Roger! Continue approach."

I then yelled for everyone to get ready, that an aircraft was inbound.

After a while I observed the Chinook in the distance. As it moved closer toward us, I spotted the artillery gun hanging beneath the Chinook's belly. Dangling below the gun was a cargo net carrying the weapon's ammo.

"Pathfinder Control! This is Big Windy Six. Approximately five miles out. Request landing instructions. Over."

While relaying instructions to the pilot, I kept a sharp eye on the sling load. It was oscillating a little. I was sure the Chinook's crew chief had an eye on it as well, but if the swinging got any worse, I would let the pilot know. On more than one occasion a pilot had to "punch" a load, dropping it from the sky to save the aircraft. Back at Song Be, I'd watched a Chinook release a Caterpillar from around five hundred feet. Luckily the heavy equipment crashed into a side of the mountain that was uninhabited.

When the helicopter was one mile out, I ran over to the western slope and popped smoke. The large bird whipped dust and dirt across the slope as it hovered toward me. Like a miniature tornado, it snatched up everything in its path. A poncho darted by me and was flung up into the rotary blades. I hoped it wouldn't cause any damage. Before the aircraft arrived, I'd instructed everyone to gather up ponchos or any other debris that could get sucked up into the big aircraft's rotor wash. But there's always someone who never gets the word!

I clipped the radio handset to the left strap of my LBE so I could talk and still have both hands free. The pilot awaited my guidance. He had no problem identifying me as the Pathfinder; I was the only one standing erect. Everyone else had sought cover. Dirt, gravel, and other debris continued to sting the exposed areas of my skin.

Extending my right arm out to my side at a ninety-degree angle, I waved my left arm across my chest in the direction of my right. This signaled the pilot to move the Chinook to his left. I continued this gesture until I had the load of ammunition where the artillery unit desired. I then signaled the pilot to hover in place and gave him the sign to set free the load. The ammunition dropped to the ground.

With the ammo in place, I extended both of my arms to

the front and brought my hands toward my chest, waving the pilot forward. With a few instructions on the radio, the gun was eased gently to the ground. The Chinook released its grip on the gun, and the straps toppled around it.

Once the artillery piece was properly positioned, I waved the bird over to the cleared portion of the LZ to unload the gun's crew. As the Chinook lowered its tailgate, passengers hastened from the ramp. In no time the Chinook launched itself skyward. A second Chinook called for instructions and repeated the same drill without mishap.

The third Chinook arrived on the scene, releasing the artillery piece and ammo it was carrying. Then, like its predecessors, it hovered over to the LZ to unload passengers. Just as its wheels touched the ground, however, mortar rounds began crashing around us. Immediately everyone hit the dirt or scattered for cover.

The Chinook continued to lower its tailgate. It was evident that the flight crew was unaware of the exploding enemy rounds. One impacted about thirty meters from the aircraft.

In desperation I shouted into the handset, "Big Windy Two-seven! Pathfinder Control! Be advised we are presently under mortar attack. Clear for immediate departure to the east. Over."

The pilot's voice boomed over the radio. "Christ! Roger! Big Windy Two-seven. Departing to the east at this time."

Mortar rounds continued exploding around the hilltop. In the movies, mortars and grenades discharge big flashes of fire when they detonate. In reality, the explosions are not as fiery. They are more like puffs of gray smoke sometimes mixed with brown clouds of dirt. The mortar attack ceased momentarily, only to be followed by a second volley. This time they impacted all around me. I had nowhere to go, so I crouched down, placed my head behind my rucksack, covered my ears with my hands, and just prayed I wouldn't get hit. One mortar round exploded so close that I felt the windlike heat from the blast. Later I discovered that pieces of shrapnel had actually torn through my rucksack, cutting the metal frame almost in half.

The mortar attack stopped, and unbelievably, nobody was wounded. It never ceased to amaze me how, on some occasions, bullets or shrapnel could be whizzing all over the place and not one person would get hit. I also wondered why the gooks hadn't lobbed mortars on us when the dustoff landed the night before, with the whole LZ lit up like a damn shopping area. It was difficult to figure out war sometimes!

By early afternoon all the artillery guns were in place. I felt pretty satisfied with myself. I had set up the LZ from scratch, brought in a dustoff at night, got all the wounded out safely, controlled all the Chinook and helicopter sorties, and directed the placement of artillery. All within a twenty-four-hour period.

After making sure my services were no longer needed, I gathered my gear and called for a chopper to take me back to Camp Eagle. I had about an hour wait, so I decided to search out Davis and bid him farewell before leaving. Eventually I found him nestled beside some shrubbery, monitoring a radio.

"Hey, Davis! What's happening?"

He placed his hand up to his eyes to block out the sun. "Richie! What's going on?"

His eyes were squinting, so I walked around to his side. "Well, it's time for me to go. My mission's completed. I just wanted to say good-bye."

Davis placed the handset into the carrying handle of the radio he was monitoring and stood up. "Gee! I hate to see you go so soon. You guys sure don't stay in the field very long, do you?"

I chuckled. "Well, actually it depends on the mission, but, hey, you know, somebody's got to get over."

I held out my hand. "Listen! I wanted to thank you for sharing your foxhole with me. The old first sergeant was right! It sure came in handy!"

Davis shook my hand. "You don't have to thank me. I

was glad for the company, especially while all that shit was going on."

There was a short pause as we both struggled for some kind of quick-witted farewell, but it just wasn't there. "Well! I got to go, Davis. My bird will be in any minute. You take care of yourself!"

As I turned to leave, Davis uttered, "Hey, Richie! I hope you make it."

I turned back and for a brief moment glanced into his eyes, my voice solemn. "Yeah! I hope you make it, too!"

I often wonder if he ever did.

Chapter Ten

The slick dropped me off right at the unit pad, so I proceeded directly to the Pathfinder hootch. At around 1400 hours, I was cleaning my equipment when Lieutenant Wilberding stopped by. I debriefed him on the results of the mission. He and some of the other detachment members enjoyed a good laugh when I recounted my momentous flight toward the A Shau in the tiny flying bubble.

The next day a few members from the division's Long Range Patrol (LRP) Company dropped by with their mascot, a young female pup that resembled a miniature German shepherd. She actually looked like a stuffed animal with huge, towering ears. Her name was Dixie. The LRPs (pronounced lurps) heard that we also had a dog for a mascot, so we brought out Torch and the puppies began playing together. The division LRPs lived right across the road from us. Since the LRPs were a newly activated unit within the division, they had adopted the lineage of the 58th Infantry and were designated F Company, 58th Infantry (LRP).

Members of our detachment got along well with the LRPs, since we had a lot in common. For one, they were the only other unit in the division besides Pathfinders that wore black baseball hats. They wore their jump wings in front of a 101st Recondo patch on their hats, while we displayed our wings on a blue, oval background. The LRPs were also elite infantrymen who worked in small teams and whose duties required proficiency on the radio, map reading, call for fire, and other specialized training. Like us, most LRPs were basically young and enthusiastic. Their job also demanded a great deal of skill, control, and responsibility. While gulping down beer and sodas, we updated each other on the happenings of our units. I was surprised to discover that our detachment was faring better than the LRPs as far as missions went.

Since the LRP company had a lot more members than our small detachment and for that reason was commanded by a captain, I just assumed their commander would have more clout with division headquarters than our lieutenant as far as securing missions for his LRP teams. Instead, the LRPs told us they also felt they were being misused and complained about having to pull details and provide perimeter security. Moreover, their company was plagued by internal problems. As a unit new to Vietnam, it had to endure the process of defining its new role within the division.

During their visit, one of the LRPs drank a few too many beers and became a bit rambunctious. He tried to get the puppies to fight each other, boasting that a LRP dog could easily kick the shit out of a mere Pathfinder mongrel. Although he truly didn't mean any harm, his fellow LRPs protested. Still, he tried every means to provoke the two pups. At one point he even opened a C-ration can and tossed some beef on the ground, hoping the animals would fight over the meat; nothing worked. As the two young dogs politely shared the food, the disgruntled LRP left in total disgust while the rest of us laughed.

While swapping gripes, a short, well-spoken, animated LRP named Kenn Miller told us about his unit's arrival at Camp Eagle.

"Hell! Our unit was the advance party here! The day we got here, there wasn't anything but a few graves in this whole goddamn area. Nothing! Our small group provided security for most of the perimeter until the rest of division showed up."

The young LRP's story quickly got our attention. Ron turned and pointed his finger at the perimeter. "Only about ten of us from our detachment were the advance party that guarded that whole portion of the perimeter over there. During our first night at Eagle, we were told by some major not to worry if we got attacked because 'other units' were guarding the opposite side of the perimeter. Now we find out that it was just your small group."

Miller pondered momentarily, then grinned, trusting that Ron was only joking. "You're shitting me, right?"

Ron answered with that honest Andy Taylor look that left no doubt he was telling the truth. "Nope! I'm not shitting you at all!"

Miller glanced at his fellow LRPs. "You got to be kidding me! Those bastards! You mean to tell me that just a handful of LRPs and Pathfinders pulled security for this whole goddamn place before the rest of the division arrived? I can't believe this shit!"

One of the other LRPs chimed in, "What the hell would have happened if we'd been attacked by an NVA battalion or some other large force?"

Kenn offered a quick but probable comeback. "We probably wouldn't be having this conversation right now!"

A few of us laughed while Miller continued, shaking his head. "Damn! You would think that a famous, historic Airborne division like the 101st would know how to properly utilize its Pathfinders and LRPs."

Miller was right. His remark echoed what every one of us had thought at one time or another.

As their visit came to an end, the LRPs thanked us for our hospitality and told us not to be strangers.

They called to their mascot, "C'mon, Dixie Dog. Say good-bye! We got to get going."

Dixie started to leave, then thought better of it and continued playing with Torch. A tall, lanky fellow with blond hair shrugged his shoulders, then reached down and grabbed Dixie. "Typical LRP, always ignores commands!"

After a few steps he set Dixie back on the ground, pointing her in the right direction. "C'mon, Private. It's time to go."

Ron seemed lost in thought as we watched the LRPs

stroll away. Before they got too far, he hollered, "Hey! Your dog Dixie's a private?"

The tall blond LRP answered, "Yeah! The mutt's a typical private, all right! Can't you tell?"

Another member spouted, "Dixie's actually a PFC, a proud fucking canine!"

The three LRPs made their way across the road with Dixie shuffling in and out among their feet.

I could tell something was on Ron's mind after the LRPs departed. Later that evening he shared his thoughts over a few beers.

"We got to do something about Torch! We need to make him an official member of our unit and the army."

Ron paused for a moment, then continued. "The LRPs said their dog was a PFC [private first class]. Torch deserves to have his own rank in the army, too!"

Joe Bolick stood up. "That's a good idea! Let's get him over here. Hey, Torch!"

Buz chuckled. "Hell! He crawled under one of the cots when he heard his name mentioned. Must have thought he was getting a bath!"

Joe frowned. "Well, somebody get him over here, and we'll make him a PFC!"

Ron motioned for Joe to sit down, his expression serious. "No! That's not what I'm talking about! We need to give Torch his own rank, but it has to be official!"

Larry's face beamed. "Yeah! Hey, that's a great idea! We can make Torch a PFC in front of a detachment formation."

Mitch jumped on the bandwagon. "We can get one of the tailor shops to sew a Pathfinder badge and some PFC stripes on a piece of cloth that we can tie around Torch whenever we have formal ceremonies and stuff."

Although Ron was pleased that everyone was backing his idea, we could tell he still wasn't satisfied. "Those are all good ideas, but they still don't make it official. We need to have orders made up giving Torch his rank; that would make it official."

Buz scooted his chair closer to Ron. "Don't get me wrong, Ron. I think it's a good idea. I just don't think the army cuts orders on dogs to give them rank."

It was obvious Ron had already thought that one through. "What about scout dogs? They're actual soldiers in the army, ain't they?"

Buz nodded. "Yeah, but Torch isn't a scout dog."

Mitch chimed in. "That's right! Torch isn't a scout dog; he's a Pathfinder, dammit."

Afraid he was treading on sacred ground, Buz shrugged his shoulders. "You guys know what I mean. Torch's situation's a lot different."

Ron slapped his hands on his knees. "Well! There's a REMF in the orderly room who's a pretty good guy. I bet he'll type us up something if we make it worth his while."

He took the group's silence as an agreement. "We'll write down what we want and let him put it into an official format. Somebody grab some paper."

While Mitch went for the paper, a thought came to my mind. "Before we begin, I have a suggestion!"

Ron grabbed the pen from his fatigues' pocket and glanced up at me. "What's that, Richie?"

"Well, since the LRPs' dog is a PFC, we ought to make Torch a corporal!"

Joe agreed. "Richie's right! We can't let the LRP's mascot outrank Torch. Besides, most Pathfinders eventually get promoted to corporal, anyway."

Ron glanced around to see if anyone was in disagreement. "Okay! Corporal it is!"

A few days later Buz and I were cleaning some of the radios when Staff Sergeant Guerra suddenly stormed into our hootch. He seemed flustered.

"Burns, Harding! Where's the rest of the men?"

I stood up quickly and answered, "The guys are at chow, Sergeant Guerra!"

Guerra peered down at his watch. "I want everyone to be here in thirty minutes. Is that clear?"

I peered over at Buz and then back at Guerra. "Airborne!"

Sergeant Guerra hit his head on the tent flap on the way out, almost knocking off his black hat.

Buz snickered. "What the hell was that all about?"

I sat back down on the cot. "I don't know. Maybe we're going on an aircraft recovery operation."

Buz immediately destroyed my hopes. "Looked more to me like he was pissed off or something. We're probably going to go on some kind of shit detail."

There were only a total of six of us in the rear. Luckily, Buz and I didn't have to go out and hunt anyone down. We anxiously waited for Sergeant Guerra. He entered the tent right on time. And he still seemed upset. His right hand tightly clutched a piece of rolled white paper. "Do we have everybody, Burns?"

Even though I had already taken a head count, I glanced around the room one more time to make sure before answering. "Roger that!"

He waved the piece of paper around like a wand as he talked. "Does anyone know anything about a new member being assigned to this detachment?"

We all looked at each other with blank faces. A few members shrugged their shoulders.

Sergeant Guerra appeared distraught. "Damn it! The first sergeant had a piece of my ass this morning. He said I didn't let him know that a new man had been assigned to the Pathfinders and that he also hadn't approved any promotions. He was pissed because we're not authorized any more people under our TO&E. I had to stand there with my head up my ass and tell him that I didn't even know who or what the hell he was talking about."

Sergeant Guerra paused for a moment to see if any of us would respond. His face became flushed and he was breathing heavily. "A little while ago I found out that *division* doesn't even know anything about this guy!"

He paused again, a pitiful expression on his face. "Has

anyone seen a new guy walking around the area or someone you don't know?"

Looking at one another, we all shook our heads. It was immediately evident that all of us were just as bewildered as he was.

Bolick was the first to say something. "Sergeant Guerra! You got a name on this guy?"

Guerra began unrolling the paper in his hand. "He's got a real funny name. I don't know what nationality it is!"

We waited curiously while his eyes scanned the paper. "His last name is Torch, Corporal Trooper T. Torch!"

Holy shit! I couldn't believe it! Sergeant Guerra was talking about our dog! He never made the connection. Everyone's eyes widened. I was sure they were experiencing the same thoughts as I.

Finally, Ron broke the silence in that Andy Taylor manner. "That's Torch, Sergeant Guerra!"

Guerra's expression was one of utter confusion. We all tried hard to hold it in, but just couldn't. There was an explosion of laughter.

Guerra became furious. "Goddammit! Somebody tell me what's going on right now or I'll have you all doing push-ups until you reach China."

We wanted to stop laughing, but whenever Sergeant Guerra got mad, his accent became more pronounced. It made the situation only more hilarious.

Unfortunately, Buz was the first one to open his mouth. "Sergeant Guerra, we're already there!"

Guerra was more confused than ever. "What? I don't understand!"

Buz gave him a sly look. It was a particular expression Buz used regularly, but it usually tended to piss Sergeant Guerra off. "We're already in Southeast Asia, right next door to China."

Sergeant Guerra went ballistic. "Well, goddammit! You drop down and do push-ups until you reach home."

Buz quickly assumed the front-leaning-rest position

and started counting. "One, two . . ." The rest of us had tears rolling down our faces.

Sergeant Guerra stared at Ron. "Reynolds, do you want to tell me what the hell is going on here?"

We tried to settle down while Ron explained. "A group of us made up a full name and service number for Torch, then gave a clerk in the orderly room a case of beer so he could type up official orders making Torch a corporal."

Staff Sergeant Guerra listened in horror. He was a soldier with over eighteen years in the army. That was definitely not the way things were done.

Guerra glanced back down at the paper, then slowly shook his head. "I don't believe this shit!"

His expression had eased a bit, and he directed his attention back toward Ron. "How the hell did the first sergeant find out about it?"

Anyone could tell Ron's sincerity was genuine. "I don't know. Honest! The clerk promised me that the orders wouldn't go anywhere."

Guerra let out a sigh. "Damn! How am I going to explain this shit to the first sergeant?"

He glanced over at Buz, who was still doing push-ups. "Harding, recover!"

I felt sorry for Sergeant Guerra. Ron must have read my thoughts. "Sergeant Guerra! I'll go explain everything to the first sergeant!"

Joe stepped forward. "Hell! We'll all go! We all did it."

Sergeant Guerra's body straightened a bit. "No, dammit! I'm in charge of this detachment. I'll go! If the first sergeant wants to see any of you, I'll let you know."

As Sergeant Guerra walked out of the tent, we heard him mumble something in Spanish, followed by "promoting the dog!"

Later in the day the first sergeant stopped by our tent and wanted to know the name of the clerk we'd bribed. We wouldn't tell him. He said he'd figured as much, but had a pretty good idea who it was. Eventually we got ahold of the clerk and found out that he'd left an onionskin copy of the orders on his desk and that an overzealous REMF had placed a copy on the first sergeant's desk. The clerk was pissed. He said, "It was the first damn time the son of a bitch did anything right!"

Surprisingly, at dusk Sergeant Guerra came by our tent with a case of beer and a bottle of booze. He said that even though we were all a bunch of shitheads, we were right about Torch's needing to be promoted officially. We had a formal ceremony for Torch followed by a promotion party, and even Torch drank a little too much.

A couple of days after Torch's promotion party, I was resting on my cot when Lieutenant Wilberding entered the hootch.

"Richie, you ready to go out on a mission?"

I sprung to my feet. "Yes, sir! What's up?"

"Tomorrow morning you'll be going out with the 1st of the 327's recon platoon."

I didn't even attempt to hide my enthusiasm. "You mean the Tiger Force, sir!"

Wilberding gave me a slight grin. He knew I would like that one. "Roger that!"

"Damn, sir! That's great! What's going on?"

"You'll be inserting into an LZ at first light and remain with them while they conduct a recon of an area."

Tiger Force was the reconnaissance element for the 1st Battalion, 327th Infantry, part of the 1st Brigade. Its size usually varied from twenty to forty soldiers. In addition to reconnaissance, the Tiger Force conducted ambushes, raids, and intelligence gathering. The unit had been in country for quite some time and had a notable reputation. Rumor had it that the Tiger Force had one of the highest body counts in Vietnam for a unit its size.

I considered myself lucky to be going on an operation with the team. I was puzzled, however, as to what my role would be.

"Why do they need a Pathfinder, sir?"

Lieutenant Wilberding pulled a map out of his right

cargo pocket, spread it across a field table, and flattened it with his hand.

"Intel reports conclude that there's a large NVA unit somewhere in this area, possibly battalion strength or larger."

His finger circled a four-klick square, then stopped at a small clearing on the map. "This is the LZ where you'll be inserting."

Wilberding glanced up for a moment to see if I had any questions, then continued. "The Tiger Force will conduct a reconnaissance of this section in hopes of locating the NVA unit."

His finger moved about two klicks and stopped at a much larger clearing. "If the Tigers locate the enemy and time permits, you will bring in a company-size or larger reaction force at this location here."

It all sounded good to me. I just didn't understand why a Pathfinder had to tag along during the reconnaissance phase of the operation. Why not go in on the first bird with the reaction force?

Lieutenant Wilberding must have guessed my thoughts. "It would be an asset for a Pathfinder to already be on the ground, especially if the Tiger Force makes contact with a superior element and the shit hits the fan."

He paused for a few seconds, then proceeded. "Besides, I've been working hard to convince Division of the need for Pathfinders on all combat operations. There's even a proposal that, as part of our overall mission, we might permanently attach a Pathfinder to each battalion recon element. I'll want your input regarding that subject when you return."

"Airborne, sir!" I wasn't going to question anything that might permit me to go out on a hunting expedition with the Tiger Force.

I examined the LZs and their surroundings on the map for a few moments. The LZ selected for the Tigers and me to land in looked a little small. "Are you sure the one I'll be inserting in tomorrow with the Tigers is big enough, sir?"

Lieutenant Wilberding nodded. "I personally conducted an aerial recon of both LZs yesterday."

We discussed a few more details, then he left. I began making a list of everything I would need for the operation. My thoughts drifted to the mission. Even though the Tiger Force was a small reconnaissance unit, it could surely hold its own in a fight regardless of the enemy's size. After I finished my list, I studied it once more to make sure I hadn't omitted anything. There were two items on the list that I had packed considerably more of than usual: fragmentation grenades and ammunition. If the Tigers lived up to their reputation, it would not surprise me if we stepped into a world of shit.

Chapter Eleven

I knew that in a few moments I'd be running from the cool air blowing through the helicopter into the stifling heat of the jungle. I took a swallow from my canteen along with two salt tablets. The Tigers and I were about three minutes from our insertion LZ with a flight of three helicopters. As always, I was on the first bird and had a front-row seat.

I expected the Tiger Force to be a platoon-size element (thirty men), but there were only about seventeen members on this mission. Hence, only three helicopters were needed to carry all of us to the LZ. I was surprised to discover that there wasn't an officer leading the group. I assumed that the NCO in command was either a sergeant first class (E-7) or a staff sergeant (E-6).

Before we left, the NCO made himself very clear to me. "Listen, while you're with us, you'll stay close to me! You don't even fart without asking me! Any problem with that?"

"No! No problem at all!" Actually, I expected as much. I wouldn't be all that excited about having an outsider patrolling with my unit either.

I didn't want to start off on the wrong foot and alienate him, but I had a job to do as well. "When it comes to helicopters, though, I have to be able to do my thing! Okay?"

He stared straight into my eyes, paused momentarily, then said gruffly, "Fair enough!"

My thoughts returned to the mission. I glanced at the men surrounding me in the cabin of the chopper. I was struck by how each soldier, including me, camouflaged his face with his own unique pattern. I checked out their uniforms. Each wore tiger-stripe fatigues along with a short-brimmed, tiger-striped bush hat. My uniform was different. I wore the leaf-pattern camouflage fatigues that were issued to our detachment. Some of the Tiger Force members' tiger-stripe uniforms were sterile, absent any patches, while others wore various insignia along with their infamous Tiger Force scroll.

Many infantry battalions in Vietnam possessed a small reconnaissance element that the commander could use to seek out and find the enemy without committing a whole company or his entire battalion. The theory was much the same as the small groups that scouted ahead of the cavalry in the old west.

Since this type of work could be considerably more dangerous than patrolling with a larger force, the recon elements were usually made up of volunteers. Considered the elite of the unit, those men customarily enjoyed relaxed standards, sported different uniforms and weapons, and wore an insignia that set them apart from the rest of the unit.

Most recon units in Vietnam wore a shoulder scroll made by local tailors. The scroll was usually worn above the unit patch or alone; the Tiger Force was no exception. Their scroll was approximately four inches long and over an inch wide with gold letters on black twill. It read: 1ST TIGER FORCE 327. Their sister battalion, the 2d/327 Infantry's recon platoon, had the same-size scroll and the same color scheme, but it read: 2 HAWK RECON 327.

The crew chief signaled that we were about one minute out. As we flew into the LZ, the three helicopters kept a tight formation. Everyone leaped from the choppers, then immediately crouched, motionless and silent. It was a much smoother operation than the commotion and confusion of a company unloading during a combat assault.

In seconds, the choppers ascended skyward. A moment later two trailing gunships streaked across the tree line and vanished. In no time, all the aircraft had left. It became quiet. The Tigers lay low, listening for distinct noises, especially the metallic sounds that are almost always the sounds of men. I tried to remain completely still while my eyes scanned the trees for the slightest movement. Already beads of sweat had built up around the rim of my hat and dribbled down the sides of my face. Finally the sergeant signaled us to move toward the trees.

Just as we arose from the grass, the enemy opened up. Instinctively the Tigers responded, pouring bullets into the jungle. Their aggressiveness was contagious. With my weapon on automatic, I pulled the trigger. *Zip!* In two or three seconds, my magazine was empty. Eighteen rounds gone!

I flicked the selector switch to semiautomatic and grabbed another magazine. Earlier I had contemplated taping two magazines together, opposite one another. That way I could have just flipped the empty one around and slammed the other into the weapon. I wished I had.

I fumbled getting the next magazine into my rifle just as two figures in black pajamas popped up from inside the trees and took off running. I aimed and pulled the trigger; others beaded down on the two as well. They fell dead in their tracks. My body felt like it was speeding on amphetamines. The adrenaline rush was unreal. The sergeant motioned everyone to assault the tree line. Hurrying behind him, I reached for my radio handset.

My lungs strained for air. "Do you want me . . . to get the gunships . . . back here?"

The sergeant turned his head slightly but kept running at a mad dash. "Let's wait . . . until we get to the tree line . . . see what we got!"

Once inside the trees, the sergeant ordered the Tigers to cease all firing. The leaders took a quick head count. Everyone was accounted for. Two teams branched out, to our left and right, to conduct a hasty recon. The rest of us stayed put and provided security. I could tell the Tigers had been through this drill a number of times. I was going to bring up the matter of getting the gunships back for support, but thought better of it. Hell! The sergeant knew what he was doing. Besides, it was his show.

After a while, the team from the left returned. One of them whispered, "We got two dead gooks!"

The sergeant didn't seem overly concerned. "Anything else?"

"Negative!"

The team from the right arrived moments later. "Found two spider holes and a small trail . . . no signs of any more gooks, though."

The sergeant pondered the information for a moment, then glanced around at us. "Anybody see any other dinks besides the two we wasted?"

Every man shook his head.

"Seems to me they were trail watchers, keeping an eye on the LZ. There's probably more of them keeping an eye on other clearings in the area."

He paused to see if anyone wanted to add anything, then continued. "Okay! Let's go ahead and take a look at the dead dinks."

The sergeant sent four two-man teams to fan out into the jungle to provide security; the rest of us patrolled over to the two dead enemy.

As we approached the bodies the point man uttered, "The sons a bitches are dead all right!"

Once I got close enough to see them, I understood what he meant. Both bodies were riddled with bullets. One corpse was lying facedown. The point man used his foot to turn it over. The man's arm flung around like a rag doll. His eyes were wide open and had an empty, dull look. Alongside the bodies lay two SKS rifles, which a few of the guys argued over taking, since, as semiautomatic weapons, they could be legally brought back to the States.

The sergeant ordered two men to search the bodies. He then grabbed the handset from his RTO and called in a sitrep. Once finished, he motioned for the security teams to return.

"Okay! Let's saddle up! We're gonna move in the same

direction as the trail. It might be a long shot, but I got a gut feeling we might run into something."

As we departed, I fell in behind the sergeant's RTO. In back of me was a Tiger named Albee. I liked Albee; he was helpful and didn't mind me tagging along. Besides, Albee had to be the only other paratrooper in the whole 101st Airborne Division who looked as young as I. I was told that he was on his second tour with the Tigers; I was thankful he was covering my back. The jungle paralleling the trail was thick, so we slowly moved out single file. As we passed by the dead gooks, I noticed Tiger Force scrolls had been placed on their foreheads. It was the Tigers' "calling card." It let the enemy know who their comrades had messed with.

We had patrolled for hours. It was early afternoon, and the rucksack muscles in my shoulders were screaming. The humidity combined with the heat and the weight of my ruck seemed unbearable. I had a small green towel tucked under the rucksack frame, resting across my shoulders to cushion some of the pressure, and I used the corners of the towel to wipe the sweat from my forehead before the drops of salt stung my eyes. We were traveling slowly, and despite the danger, I caught myself daydreaming from time to time. I had to force myself to stay alert.

Signaling a danger area, the point man halted the patrol. Shit! Not again! I bent forward at the waist and heaved the rucksack up off my shoulders for some relief. A danger area was usually a place where the enemy could lie in ambush, such as a stream crossing, an open field bordered by a tree line, a trail, etc. The word was passed back that there was a creek ahead.

The sergeant went forward, then ordered the rest of us up to the creek's bank. The creek was about twenty feet wide with a slight current. It seemed to be shallow, about knee-deep. We stayed hidden inside the foliage and spread out in a line on each side of the point man so that all of our firepower was up alongside the creek in case the enemy hit us while crossing.

The point man lay low for a few minutes before stepping into the water. His eyes searched the bank on the other side for the slightest sign of movement while his ears listened intently for any noise out of the ordinary. Finally satisfied, he proceeded across. When he reached the halfway point, the sergeant motioned the next man to follow.

The rest of us remained concealed and alert until it was our turn. It seemed like an hour had passed before the sergeant finally ventured across, followed by his RTO. I was next in sequence, and slipped in the mud as I entered the water. After a few paces I understood why it was taking so long for the men to cross. With each step my foot became embedded in the muddy bottom; it felt like it was stuck in peanut butter. The weight I was carrying sure didn't help matters, either. Even though the crossing was slow, I wasn't overly concerned. The enemy would have hit us long before letting half our force occupy the other side.

I was just a few feet from the edge of the creek when small-arms fire erupted. Suddenly bullets whizzed by me. One round came so close to my ear that it made a loud *crack* as it zoomed by my head. My heart pounded while my brain raced. Somehow my body reacted entirely on its own. My feet stomped and splashed as they tried to break through the resistance of the water on my shins.

The yard or so remaining to the edge of the creek now seemed a mile away. My foot slipped on the creek bank, and I tumbled facedown in the mud. I started to get up, then realized that the ground wasn't such a bad place to be just then. I crawled the remaining few feet into the bushes.

Someone behind me yelled, "Get to the other side!"

I glanced back to see Albee and another Tiger still in the water. Albee got about three feet from me and was also having difficulty running through the mud. Bullets ripped through the air. I stood up and grabbed his right arm just as he began falling backward. I yanked him toward me, and we both fell into a thicket.

The other Tiger still thrashing through the water was a hefty guy called Ski. Ski made a big target. On his back, a rucksack looked like a butt pack. Bullets continued whizzing about as he splashed his way toward us.

"Son of a bitch! I'm going to kill every one of those bastards by myself! I'll slit their goddamn throats!" His huge body crashed right beside me.

Albee and I couldn't return fire because of the Tigers to our front. Frustrated, we just stayed down and waited. All firefights were chaotic; it was worse when you didn't know what was going on.

Ski patted his upper leg, then held his hand up to his face. He looked puzzled. "Son of a bitch! I thought it was blood! It's goddamn peach juice!"

He looked at Albee and me, then back down at his leg. Sure enough! A bullet had gone right through the cargo pocket of Ski's left pant leg, piercing a can of peaches he was carrying. I would have thought that a sticky liquid like peach juice was blood, too. Albee nudged me, and we both started snickering.

Ski's expression changed from one of disbelief to rage. "Those bastards shot my fucking peaches!"

He reached up to the suspenders on his LBE and withdrew a large knife from its sheath. "I'm going to kill the son of a bitch that did this!"

Springing straight to his feet, he charged off through the jungle like a linebacker. I watched in amazement. "Holy shit! That guy's crazy!"

Albee raised his eyebrows. "Nobody messes with Ski's peaches! He trades some good shit for them, too. Loves 'em!"

I nodded. "Oh!"

A second later I mumbled, "Damn! I'd hate to see what would happen if someone destroyed a whole meal of his."

A minute or so later the firing subsided, and Albee and I began creeping forward until we linked up with the others.

The sergeant tapped Albee on the shoulder. "Go back and tell the rest of the guys to come across to our side."

As Albee turned to go, the sergeant stopped him. He grabbed Albee's left sleeve. "What the hell happened?"

Tiger fatigues had a small pocket sewn high in the upper left sleeve of the shirt. It came in handy for small items that required easy access. Albee's shirt pocket was shredded.

The sergeant started laughing. "A round tore a hole through your pocket."

Albee put his finger through the material and wiggled it. "Damn! It must have happened when I was crossing the creek!"

Unbelievable! Albee and Ski both had their pockets shot off while crossing the creek. Talk about close calls. I then thought about the bullet that had cracked right by my head and shuddered.

While the sergeant waited for everyone to regroup, I asked him what happened. He said that when the first few Tigers crossed the creek, they fanned out and formed a perimeter. As more Tigers joined the group, two went forward to set up a hasty OP and act as an early warning system for the others. Just as the two crouched into place, four enemy soldiers stumbled right onto them. Surprised, the Tigers and the enemy soldiers simultaneously opened up on each other. After the exchange of gunfire, two of the enemy soldiers lay dead, and the other two had taken off into the jungle.

Once again the Tigers had not sustained any casualties. Except for his peaches, even Ski returned unscathed. Ski's knife was covered with blood. He said he'd stabbed one of the gooks for shooting his peaches. I wondered whether he had actually killed a gook or was just pulling my leg and had stabbed one of the dead bodies. As I watched Ski wipe the blood from the blade, I thought, Who am I to question his story?

Everyone remained on alert while a few of the Tigers searched the dead enemy soldiers for documents and placed Tiger scrolls on the foreheads. The two corpses were carrying a number of canteens.

The sergeant knelt beside the bodies. "These and

the two that got away must have been part of a water-gathering party."

He glanced up at me. "Hey, Pathfinder! You notice anything different about these dinks and the ones we wasted this morning?"

I didn't know if he was testing me or trying to put me on the spot. In any event, I hoped I gave the right answer. "The uniforms!"

He nodded in agreement. "That's right! These sons a bitches are NVA regulars."

The sergeant's expression turned serious as he stood up. I knew why. The dead NVA soldiers left no doubt that we were close to a large, well-trained, well-equipped enemy force.

The sergeant grabbed his RTO's handset and called in a sitrep. While he gave his report, part of me thought that an extraction would be nice. The enemy knew we were in the area. Moreover, a reaction force could be here in no time, and personally, I'd had enough action to last me for the rest of the day.

The sergeant finished his transmission. "Roger. Out!"

He handed the handset back to the RTO. "Okay! Listen up! We're gonna lay dog while they decide whether we continue with the mission or have a reaction force sent in to assist us."

A few of the Tigers let their thoughts be known with one-word comments.

The sergeant let out a grunt. "I know! I know! The headquarters pukes probably have a powwow every time someone has to take a shit."

While he waited for orders, the sergeant gestured for his leaders to assemble around him. The rest of us took a few moments to remove leeches and reposition equipment.

As Albee and I split a John Wayne bar (a chocolate bar from our Cs), we overheard the sergeant's instructions. "Make sure everyone keeps their shit together. I don't want any dicking around. That NVA unit can't be far away, and those two that got away are going to tell them where we're at."

The RTO signaled the sergeant that he was wanted on the radio. The sergeant grabbed the handset, listened for a few seconds, then responded. "Roger that!"

He gave the handset back to the RTO, then cinched down the shoulder straps of his ruck. "Okay! Saddle up!"

As the Tigers formed up into patrol order, they all had more serious expressions on their faces. Just as the point man stepped into the bushes, a low, gruff voice murmured, "Remember, stay alert!"

We moved even slower and more cautiously than before, and with good reason. The two NVA who got away had had ample time to warn their unit that we were close by. There was a lump in my throat that got larger with each step. If the handful of us stumbled onto the large enemy force, we'd be in big trouble.

We patrolled until dusk. Eventually the sergeant picked a place to RON (remain overnight), a clump of thickets that provided excellent concealment but little cover (physical protection). We proceeded past the location, then circled around and entered it from behind. If anyone was following us, we'd ambush them.

After setting up 360-degree security, we placed claymores around our perimeter. The claymore was an antipersonnel mine that, when detonated, propelled seven hundred small steel balls in a sixty-degree fan-shaped pattern. Although it could be detonated in a variety of ways, the most common way was command-detonation by means of a handheld device most everyone referred to as a clacker.

The night fell upon us like a dark blanket. Although there was a reprieve from the sun, the jungle moisture soaked our clothing and a musty smell filled the air. While some wildlife settled down for the night, other creatures began stirring, especially insects and reptiles.

The mosquitoes pestered the hell out of us. In no time they were buzzing and crawling everywhere. Earlier I had mixed insect repellent with my camo stick, making it easier to apply the camouflage paint to my skin. It had long since worn off. I debated on whether to use any more repellent, since the enemy might smell it. Eventually I couldn't stand the torture anymore and rubbed a small amount of repellent on my hands, face, and the back of my neck.

Albee watched in amusement, then whispered, "That bug juice isn't going to do any good! Mosquitoes love that shit! It works like alcohol on them; they get high off it!"

Sure enough! In no time it seemed the number of mosquitoes buzzing around me had doubled. Even the noise of them was driving me crazy.

I waved my hand across my head for the umpteenth time as another pest bit into my skin. "Damn! These son of a bitches are big!"

It was dark but I could make out a slight smirk on Albee's face. "You don't see any elephants around here, do you?"

I wondered how the conversation had changed from mosquitoes to elephants. "No! I haven't seen any elephants lately!"

"That's because the mosquitoes in Vietnam are so big, they trip and rape elephants."

I just shook my head. Even in the most miserable circumstances, American soldiers never lose their sense of humor.

The night went without incident. On a few occasions we heard some movement, which could have been animals. The Tigers stayed cool, however, and maintained fire discipline. About an hour after first light we pulled in our claymores and continued patrolling. Around midmorning we discovered an abandoned enemy base camp. The sergeant put out security, then inspected the camp.

I followed the sergeant and his RTO as he examined a fighting position. "Whoever was here left recently, and in a hurry! My guess is that this place probably housed a battalion-size unit. They must have hatted up when they found out we were in the area."

He motioned to the RTO. "Give me the radio."

The sergeant took the handset and called in the information to headquarters. While he waited for a response, he had a few of us scatter and look for equipment or documents that might have been left behind. He cautioned us to stay alert for booby traps and trail watchers.

During my search, I was struck by the large size of the base camp clumped under the jungle foliage and how cleverly the whole compound was concealed. Even though the area must have been half the size of a football field, it was undetectable by air. When I arrived back at the sergeant's location, he informed me that a decision had been made to insert both a reaction force and a blocking force into our vicinity. The commander hoped to use both forces on the ground as pincers to prevent the NVA unit's fleeing the area.

I would land the reaction force into an LZ approximately two klicks away. The blocking force would insert into an LZ farther to our northwest. The sergeant took out his map and, together with his point man, selected a route to the reaction force LZ.

The Tigers didn't waste any time falling into patrolling order. Although it was only midmorning, it would take us some time to make it to the LZ. Two kilometers on a map or by air doesn't seem like a long way, but pushing through wait-a-minute vines, danger areas, and thick jungle is a whole different ball game. Not to mention that at any moment we could stumble into an enemy unit containing hundreds of NVA regulars.

Moving cautiously but steadily, we reached the edge of the LZ by early afternoon. The tension of patrolling combined with the heat and very few stops along the way had taken its toll; all of us were beat. The sergeant sent out three-man teams to recon the LZ; he was especially concerned about the possible presence of trail watchers. Once the teams returned and gave the all clear, the sergeant radioed the rear that the LZ was secure. I set out to survey the clearing along with Albee, who also volunteered to assist me in landing the choppers once they were inbound.

The LZ had a few obstacles and some tall trees at one end, but basically it could land five helicopters in a staggered-right formation without any problem. Albee and I remained in the center of the LZ and awaited the arrival of the reaction force.

After a while we heard choppers off in the distance and then gunfire; the blocking force was inserting into its LZ to the northwest. Joe Bolick must have been on the first bird going in, because I recognized his voice controlling the CA.

Even though Albee and I stayed hidden in some underbrush, it was scorching just being out in the middle of the clearing. Albee took a swallow of water from his canteen and swished the liquid around in his mouth before swallowing.

He pretended he was gagging. "Damn! This water is as warm as piss!"

I was just getting ready to ask him how he became such a connoisseur of urine when an aircraft came up on the radio, requesting guidance. Along with the landing instructions, I reminded the pilots that friendlies were already on the ground. Throughout the operation, Albee popped smoke and relayed messages to the commander for me. With the LZ secure, and Albee's assistance, the operation went without a hitch.

I was thanking Albee for his help when a call came over the radio. "Pathfinder Control! This is Eagle one-one-five, over!"

"Eagle one-one-five! Pathfinder Control!"

"Roger! This is one-one-five! Be advised to remain at your location. We will transport you back to Eagle in two zero mikes. Do you roger? Over."

"This is Pathfinder Control! Roger! Wilco!"

"One-one-five, out!"

I placed the handset into the radio carrying handle and turned to Albee. "Well, looks like I'm going back to Camp Eagle. A chopper's gonna pick me up in about twenty minutes."

Albee cinched down the straps on his ruck. "Yeah, I heard! You know, I could get into pathfindering."

I slapped him on the back. "Well, you really helped me out, and I appreciate it. If we ever have any slots open, I'll let you know."

Since I had a twenty-minute wait, I kept my radio on and accompanied Albee to the tree line to thank the Tigers for their hospitality. We had gone about twenty feet when a voice blared over my handset.

"Pathfinder Control! This is Bold Eagle. Over!"

Damn! Bold Eagle was the call sign of Major General Barsanti, the division commander. Immediately I set down my ruck and grabbed the radio's handset.

"Bold Eagle! This is Pathfinder Control. Over!"

"This is Bold Eagle! Put out some smoke. Over."

I snatched a violet smoke grenade from my rucksack, pulled the pin, and threw it into the middle of the LZ. A thick plume of purple smoke surged from the container and billowed up into the air. I had the pilot identify the color, then cleared him to land. As the skids of the helicopter touched the ground, the door gunner hopped out from behind his gun to assist the general. Barsanti, however, was already strutting toward us.

General Barsanti was a short man with thick, black-rim glasses. He did not look the part of a general at all. It was hard to believe that he was a highly decorated officer who had fought in both World War II and Korea. I had to chuckle to myself as I watched him hunched over while passing under the chopper's rotary blades. Hell! He could stand up straight as an arrow and still have plenty of clearance above his head. When the general was approximately six paces from me, I rendered a salute.

Barsanti returned the salute. "Where's the commander?"

I assumed the CO had assembled in the tree line with the troops. "He's probably in the clump of trees behind me, sir!"

Although the general didn't say it, I had the distinct impression he wanted me to lead him there. I turned and headed for the woods with Barsanti and another officer in trail.

I quickly questioned the first NCO I encountered. "Where's the CO?"

He looked somewhat annoyed until he noticed the officer beside me had two stars on his collar. "I'll go get him!"

While Barsanti waited, I discreetly took side steps, hoping I would eventually be far enough away to make a break from the general and say good-bye to the Tigers. General Barsanti didn't seem a patient man. I had personally landed his aircraft a few times back at Bien Hoa and noticed that he wasn't well liked by a lot of the troops, especially soldiers of the 1st Brigade. Rumor had it that 1st Brigade members didn't appreciate Barsanti telling them how to fight a war when they had performed so well prior to his and the rest of the division's arrival.

I scanned the bushes until I located the Tiger Force. Now that the reaction force had arrived, the small band of Tigers was bunched together inside the tree line, taking a well-deserved break before proceeding on a new mission. The Tigers were fifty feet away from me, and I had just stepped off in their direction when I heard Barsanti bellow, "Who the hell are those vagabonds?"

He was referring to the Tigers. "Goddammit! Tell me they're not any of my troops!"

Someone mumbled, "That's the Tiger Force, sir! The recon unit for the battalion!"

General Barsanti stomped over to the small group of Tigers. "Who the hell's in charge here?"

Most of the Tigers were eating chow; a few clumsily rose to their feet while others simply gaped at one another. I noticed that, unfortunately, the Tiger Force sergeant was not present among them. He must have been off coordinating the next phase of the mission. One didn't have to be a rocket scientist to figure that the Tigers were not overly impressed by the general, either.

Barsanti became furious. "Well, goddammit! Someone speak up!"

One of the NCOs finally stood up and spoke. He either realized he had the most time and grade, had one hell of a pair of balls, was the most stupid son of a bitch in the world, or plainly didn't give a shit. "I guess I'm in charge, sir!"

I watched the veins pop out in the general's neck as he went into a tirade. "Dammit, look at you! You men are a disgrace to my division!"

Barsanti paused for a moment. If he was waiting for some kind of reaction, he didn't get it. The Tigers just looked at him like he was out of his mind. They honestly didn't know what the hell Barsanti was talking about. Yesterday they had a body count of four enemy soldiers and, moreover, they were the ones responsible for finding the enemy base camp.

Now Barsanti was fit to be tied. Even the officer who accompanied him began to distance himself from the general's line of fire.

"You men look like the sons of Genghis Khan! Pack up and get off this LZ immediately!"

Damn! It was true! Besides their crude appearance, a number of the Tigers brandished Fu Manchu mustaches and gold earrings. They did look like the sons of Genghis Khan!

Bewildered, the Tigers began gathering their gear to move farther into the jungle. Barsanti didn't know it, but he was doing the Tigers a favor. First of all, most recon units didn't like to be too close to conventional troops, anyway. Second, I was sure the majority of Tigers took Barsanti's comments as a compliment.

As the Tigers gathered their equipment, Barsanti swiftly changed gears and strutted off to meet with the CO of the unit. Damn, he sure was pissy.

I went over to bid the Tigers farewell before my bird arrived. One of the NCOs handed me a Tiger Force scroll. "We don't just give these out to anyone!"

I was sure they didn't. I felt extremely honored, especially since I was receiving it in my hand and not on my forehead. "Thanks! I really appreciate it."

Albee shook my hand and promised to keep in touch (which he did for the rest of my tour). I didn't have to wait long for the chopper to pick me up. Bolick and Mitch were already on board after landing the blocking force. As the helicopter lifted skyward, I watched the group of paratroopers grow smaller until they all faded into the jungle. Secretly, I wished them luck.

I was lost in thought until Mitch tapped me on the knee. "You look like shit!"

I grinned. "War is hell!"

The three of us harassed each other all the way back to Camp Eagle. It was great! I felt like I was back with my own family.

Ron really liked the Tiger Force scroll and felt our detachment should have a scroll as well. We designed it in the same fashion as that of the division's other elite infantry. The finished product, with gold letters on black twill, read 101 PATHFINDER 101.

The wearing of our scroll didn't last long, however. Staff Sergeant Guerra gave us a lecture on how the patch was not authorized. We pointed out that not only did all the other elite units in the division wear scrolls that were not authorized, but just about every Pathfinder unit in Vietnam wore them as well. In addition, our own helicopter pilots wore unauthorized pocket patches and nobody gave a damn. In the end, Sergeant Guerra remained inflexible. We took the scrolls off our uniforms and hid them away for another day.

The practice of attaching a Pathfinder to each of the battalion recon elements was short-lived. The 101st Airborne Division's objective was to eventually conduct an actual assault into the A Shau Valley. The division would have to set up a chain of fire support bases in order to support combat units with artillery as they fought their way closer to the valley. Since Pathfinder teams would be needed to control aircraft at the firebases, missions increased significantly for our detachment. One such firebase, Birmingham, had already been established and was in use.

The division's plan to assault the A Shau gained momentum when word came down that Special Forces reconnaissance teams had discovered a primary NVA staging area deep in the jungle about twenty-five miles southwest of Hue, toward the A Shau. The NVA staging area was located at the junction of a river called the Song Bo and a road built by the NVA, Route 547A.

The NVA staging area was referred to as Delta Junction. Delta Junction was an extremely crucial target, since the North Vietnamese used it to organize major attacks throughout the northern region. The mission of annihilating the target was given to the 1st Brigade.

The first phase of the operation would be to establish a "heavy" fire support base on a hilltop wide enough to contain 175mm, 155mm, and 105mm guns, and eight-inch howitzers, guns capable of reaching Delta Junction. In keeping with the historic tradition of the 101st Airborne Division, the fire support base was named Bastogne. In order for the huge, self-propelled 175mm and eight-inch guns to make their way to FSB Bastogne, infantry units would have to clear and secure Route 547, the road that ran all the way from Hue to the A Shau. The 2nd Battalion, 327th Infantry, under the command of Chargin' Charlie Beckwith, was selected to spearhead the attack.

Beckwith's battalion fought its way to Bastogne against a highly trained, well-equipped NVA regiment. His infantry companies continually engaged one bunker complex after the next, assaulting entrenched enemy in heavily fortified positions. On the night of March 26, Lieutenant Wilberding burst into our hootch.

"The second, three two seven just took Bastogne!"

Wilberding quickly scanned the hootch until his eyes fell on me, then Ron. "Burns! Reynolds! Pack your rucks. You two will be flying out to Bastogne in the morning."

I couldn't believe my luck. First of all, Ron and I would be working together. Second, we would be serving with Lt. Col. Chargin' Charlie Beckwith. Beckwith was a legend among Airborne soldiers. During his previous tour in Vietnam with Special Forces, he caught an enemy .51-caliber bullet through his right side. The wound would certainly have killed a lesser man. When Beckwith was triaged to the hospital's death row, he reached out and grabbed the nearest person discussing his imminent demise, a nurse major, and in his gruff voice bellowed, "Now let's got one thing straight here. I ain't the bear, and I didn't come here to pack it in." After some argument and a number of operations, Beckwith was back for another tour.

Ron and I didn't know exactly what to expect, so we packed everything but the water buffalo.

I even held up an SE-11 light gun and showed it to Ron. "What do you think?"

Ron stopped packing his rucksack, paused for a moment, then shrugged his shoulders. "Hell! Bring it along!"

Chapter Twelve

The following morning a lone helicopter landed at the pad, and Ron and I hopped aboard. The chopper followed Route 547 toward the A Shau. After about five or ten minutes of flying time, we passed a large firebase stretched out along a plateau, FSB Birmingham. On one side of Birmingham was the road, on the other was a river.

As we headed toward the A Shau, the jungle became denser, changing from double to triple canopy. The rolling hills turned into huge, steep mountains, vertically slanting from 10 to 70 percent.

The crew chief pointed out Bastogne off to our northwest. The hilltop sat nestled among other mountains, covered in thick green vegetation. It was hard to imagine it as a future firebase containing artillery batteries, troops, and bunkers. Our chopper banked right and landed on the very top of the mountain in a tiny, one-bird LZ. Ron and I jumped off the bird and gave a thumbs-up to the crew.

The paratroopers around us had their shirts off and were busily filling sandbags or unloading pallets. Ron and I sat down on our rucks and turned on the radios. While I transmitted to all the aircraft in the area that we were operational, Ron scanned the hilltop to locate Colonel Beckwith.

Eventually an NCO passed by and Ron stopped him. "Hey! Do you know where we can find the CO?"

The sergeant answered abruptly. "Yeah, man! He's right over there!"

Ron glanced over at some soldiers filling sandbags who were sweating terribly in the hot sun.

He shrugged his shoulders. "Where?"

The NCO looked at Ron like he needed glasses or something. "Right there!"

He pointed to a tall, large, older guy who Ron and I had both assumed was a senior NCO. "Where?"

The NCO became curt. "Hell! The one with the scar."

We both gawked at the horrendous, thick scar covering the older man's side and branching out around his torso.

It was then that we realized he was Chargin' Charlie Beckwith. He was a big, rough-looking man. I could immediately tell by his physique that he was a former football player. (In his younger days, Colonel Beckwith had been drafted by the Green Bay Packers but chose a career in the army instead.)

Needless to say, I was deeply impressed. "Holy shit! That's where he took the fifty-one cal."

"It looks like a damn road map!" Ron said.

My respect for Charlie Beckwith rose several notches as I watched him working alongside his soldiers; he was even the one wielding the shovel while a young soldier held the sandbag open.

Ron remained with the radio while I proceeded to report to the colonel.

"Sir! I'm Corporal Burns and over there is Corporal Reynolds. We're the Pathfinders sent here to support you."

Beckwith continued shoveling dirt into a sandbag, his voice coarse. "Fine! Fine! I'm busy now. Get with my sergeant major! He'll take care of anything you need!"

I thanked the colonel and headed back over to Ron.

"How'd it go, Richie?"

The conversation with Beckwith had gone by so fast, I had to think before answering. "Great! I didn't get my ass chewed or nothing!"

I paused momentarily, then continued. "I'll tell you one thing. He's definitely not the kind of officer you'd say to, 'Take off that rank, sir, and I'll kick your ass.'"

Ron chuckled. "He is a mean-looking son of a bitch, isn't he?"

Instead of looking around for the sergeant major, Ron and I decided to find a good site before all of the prime ground was taken by someone else. We needed a location high enough to control aircraft and, luckily, found a spot right at the uppermost point on the hill. For the next two hours, one of us remained there at all times so nobody would claim it from us.

Eventually we got in a pissing contest with a group of battalion headquarters staff who wanted the site. As we argued over land rights, a stocky, well-built, older soldier in an OD T-shirt approached us. His dog tags dangled outside his shirt. The headquarters people fell silent as he stepped up to us.

His voice was gruff. "What's the problem here?"

A senior NCO just about snapped to attention. "Hello, Sergeant Major! We were just trying to tell these guys that we need this location to set up a two-niner-two and some other equipment."

The sergeant major eyed us for a moment. I felt like I was being inspected. "You the Pathfinders?"

Ron cleared his throat. "Roger that, Sergeant Major!"

The sergeant major had a thick neck and a barrel chest. Although shorter than Beckwith, he looked just as tough. "Well, let me hear your side."

Both Ron and I explained that it was essential that we be able to maintain eye contact with all the aircraft in and around Bastogne. As the firebase grew in size, it would be crucial. Besides, we had laid claim to the site first.

As the sergeant major appeared to be rigid and uncompromising, we assumed he would side with his own people. Instead he said rather cordially, "The Pathfinders will go ahead and set up here. We're going to have a lot of aircraft coming in and out of this firebase. You men can set up your antenna and the rest of your equipment over by the TOC [tactical operations center]."

The group grumbled but immediately unassed the area. The sergeant major introduced himself. "I'm the battalion sergeant major, Command Sergeant Major Gergen. You men need anything?"

Ron and I replied simultaneously, "Negative, Sergeant Major!"

"Well, if you two need anything, let me know!" Sergeant Major Gergen politely turned and walked away.

Ron knelt beside his ruck and looked up at me. "You've heard of him, haven't you, Richie? That's 'Bull' Gergen."

Son of a gun. I didn't put the name together. Bull Gergen was somewhat of a legend himself. "Damn! I can see how he got his name. He looks just like a bull! He and Beckwith must make one hell of a pair!"

Ron snickered. "I'll tell you one thing! He's definitely not the kind of NCO you'd say to, 'Take off that rank, Sergeant Major, and I'll kick your ass.' "

We laughed.

Within thirty minutes of our arrival at Bastogne, scores of helicopters and Chinooks flew in with backhoes, sandbags, steel culverts, mechanical mules, and other materials to build bunkers, LZs, and fighting positions. Besides controlling all the aircraft, Ron and I had to set up a POL (petrol, oil, and lubricants) refueling point, establish two supply LZs, and oversee the VIP LZ. One of us controlled aircraft while the other supervised all the LZ preparations.

Most of the air traffic ceased as nightfall came. Just about everyone had some kind of cover to protect them except Ron and me. We'd been too busy to fill sandbags or dig a hole, so we laid our ponchos out on the ground and fell asleep. Around midnight we awoke to gunfire as enemy soldiers probed the perimeter. Around an hour after first light, enemy mortars exploded on the far side of the hill, overshooting the hilltop. Just as the mortar fire ceased, aircraft began calling for instructions.

Around midmorning, Ron was on the radio while I was popping smoke. I heard a loud whiz zoom right by me. A few minutes later, bark exploded off a tree to my left.

"Ron! Take cover!" He couldn't hear me.

I ran over and yelled in his ear. "Get down! There's a sniper shooting at us!"

Ron and I crouched behind our rucksacks, and he reported the danger to all the aircraft. I yelled to other soldiers standing around. A few men looked at me kind of bewildered until a round kicked up dirt in front of them. They immediately scrambled for cover.

Throughout the day and into the next, the sniper fired a round every five to fifteen minutes. One soldier was grazed in the head. It was soon discovered that the weapon sniping at us was an enemy .51-caliber machine gun. It made a distinct sound. Like our .50 caliber, this gun could fire an aimed round from over two kilometers away. The bullet was huge. Even though it wasn't super-accurate at that great a distance, it scared the hell out of anyone on the receiving end. Again, I thought about Charlie Beckwith's taking one of those monsters in his side. Damn!

By midmorning, air traffic was really hectic. Ron and I had to make sure all the aircraft remained at a safe distance from one another and also stayed clear of whatever direction the mortars were firing. And we had to ensure that the LZs were continually kept free of debris such as empty sandbags, ponchos, and plastic coverings. In addition to doing all that, while monitoring the radio I received a call from General Barsanti's pilot requesting landing instructions.

After relaying the information, I cleared the pilot to land on the VIP pad. Ron and I were flipping a coin to see who would have to physically guide in the general's bird. Unfortunately, I lost.

I was getting ready to turn the handset over to Ron when a voice boomed over the radio. "Bastogne Control! This is Bold Eagle!"

It was General Barsanti himself. "Bold Eagle! This is Bastogne. Over!"

"What the hell are all those soldiers doing down there with their shirts off? Over." I glanced around. Most everyone without a shirt had been laboring in the hot sun for hours. Surely the general knew how hot it was.

Maybe I'd misunderstood his transmission. "Bold Eagle! Say again. Over!"

"You heard me! I want the battalion commander to meet me when we land. Is that clear?"

"This is Bastogne. Roger!" I gave the handset to Ron. "Barsanti doesn't like the troops having their shirts off. He wants Colonel Beckwith to meet him when he lands."

Ron frowned. "You've got to be kidding! It must be over a hundred degrees out here."

I wondered if Barsanti knew we were fighting a war. I ran over and relayed the message to Colonel Beckwith, who didn't seem overly concerned. I then stood in front of the VIP pad and raised my hands above my head, giving the pilot the signal to guide on me. The general's helicopter slowed to a hover. The chopper's blades made their loud *whopping* sound over my head while gravel and dirt blasted my face and chest. Even the wind created by the helicopter was warm instead of cool. I crossed my hands, giving the signal to land. With the skids firmly on the ground, Barsanti hopped out of the cabin, followed by the tall and lanky General Clay, the assistant division commander.

Suddenly Barsanti stopped in his tracks like someone had kicked him in the chest. He had a perplexed look on his face. I was so busy landing the helicopter, I hadn't noticed anything behind me. I turned around, and there was Colonel Beckwith waiting to greet the general, shirtless.

As Barsanti stormed over to where Beckwith was standing, General Clay put his arm around Sergeant Major Gergen and steered Gergen from the scene. General Clay was much more even tempered and seemed to be an old hat at this sort of thing. I didn't stay around to hear what transpired. Barsanti's visit lasted about fifteen minutes, then he jumped back into his chopper.

Ron cleared the pilot for takeoff. "Roger! You are clear for departure. Stay south of the road. Over."

"Roger, Bastogne! Understand southern departure. Over!"

Ron and I kept an eye on the general's helicopter until

it was well on its way. Just as we both breathed a sigh of relief, a voice barked over the radio.

"Bastogne Control! This is Bold Eagle!"

Shit! It was the general. "Bold Eagle! This is Bastogne. Over!"

"This is Bold Eagle! I noticed artillery canisters and some other debris on that pad we just departed from. Make sure you get that cleaned up. Over."

Ron chuckled as he spoke. "Watch this. Roger! Wilco! Bald Eagle!"

The general's voice blasted over the handset. "Dammit! That's *Bold* Eagle. Over."

Ron tried to keep his voice from cracking. "Roger! Understand, Bold Eagle. Over."

From then on, whenever Barsanti came on over the radio, we would reply to "Bald Eagle." It usually resulted in an ass-chewing. I never knew the outcome of Barsanti's conversation with Colonel Beckwith, but Chargin' Charlie never told us to put on our shirts.

The next morning a two-and-a-half-ton truck loaded with various munitions parked about fifty meters down the slope from us.

Ron tapped me on the shoulder. "Is that truck in your field of vision? If it is, I'll go have it moved."

Since the truck was located on the downward side of the slope, it didn't obstruct my view. "Nah! It's okay!"

Jokingly I uttered, "It would be hell if the son of a bitch blew up, though!"

About an hour later the truck did explode. We had no idea what caused the explosion, but bullets and other munitions zipped past us for over a day.

To make matters worse, the battalion mortar crews worked feverishly to silence the sniper as well as support the companies in combat. Unfortunately, every once in a while one of their rounds fell inside the compound, sending shrapnel everywhere. It was not uncommon to hear someone yell "Short round!" and watch everyone scramble for cover. Ron and I quickly took turns filling sandbags to hide behind.

Around the third day I was clearing a helicopter for departure and happened to glance down into the jungle at the bottom of the hill. Although most of the thick vegetation within the firebase had been cleared, the jungle was still very dense from the perimeter on out. Three figures dressed in olive-drab uniforms sauntered out of the vegetation and into the open, halting right in front of one of the artillery batteries. The three appeared dazed and confused. There was something peculiar about their appearance as well. Shit! They were carrying AKs!

I pointed at the enemy soldiers and yelled, "Gooks! Gooks!"

A few of the artillery men looked up at me, then in the direction I was pointing. They, too, began shouting. Pretty soon everyone was hightailing it for cover. The NVA soldiers were obviously just as surprised as the rest of us. Momentarily in shock, they just stood there. Finally they spun around and scurried back into the jungle.

Ron heard the shouting and saw me jump behind the sandbags. "Richie! What the hell is going on?"

My eyes were still wide with excitement. "An NVA patrol just walked right into the firebase."

"You got to be shitting me!"

I snickered. "No! I'll bet their point man is going to get one hell of an ass-chewing when they get back to Hanoi."

Ron pointed at the artillery guns. "I don't think those boys are going to make it anywhere!"

We watched in awe as the artillery battery lowered all three gun barrels until they were horizontal with the ground. Called "direct fire," the crews were using the three cannons like rifles, aiming the huge barrels right in the direction the gooks ran.

Boom! Boom! Boom! The three guns fired in succession. Crashing, fiery explosions lit up the side of the hill. Chunks of trees, branches, and dirt flew violently into the air. The artillery fired again . . . and again. What a show!

Once the dirt and smoke settled, huge gaping spaces with jagged stumps were all that remained of that part of the jungle. The three NVA didn't have a snowball's chance in hell of escaping; the artillery rounds used were beehive rounds. Beehive rounds were loaded with eight thousand lethal steel flechette darts that slashed through anything in their path. The name beehive came from the deadly sound made by the hail of darts as they spun through the air.

At dusk the air traffic slowed to a halt. I broke off a small piece of C-4 and heated up a can of beefsteak and potatoes. As I stirred the succulent cuisine, a thought came to mind, and I laughed.

My actions sparked Ron's curiosity. "What's so funny?"

I shook my head. "There I was today, three NVA in the open, and instead of shooting them, I just yelled. Can you believe it? My big day and I blew it!"

Ron laughed, too, but then put his hand on my shoulder. "It is funny, but I wouldn't let it bother me. Those gooks didn't fire a shot either, and they had all kinds of Americans in the open. Besides, you're around to talk about it."

Even though I laughed, it did bother me a little. Ron always had a way of making a guy feel okay, even when he screwed up.

The beefsteak juice was boiling, so I held the can up to Ron. "You want some?"

"Hell, yeah!" Ron grabbed a white, plastic C-ration spoon from his top left pocket. It was covered with the dust and dirt stirred up by the chopper traffic.

I put out my hand. "Wait a minute! You're not sticking that nasty spoon in my Cs."

Ron held the spoon up as if to inspect it. "Sorry!"

He put the spoon in his mouth and pulled it back out. "How's that?"

I handed him back the can. "That's better!"

Within a week, with four LZs and all kinds of artillery batteries in place, Bastogne became one busy firebase. Air traffic remained continuous. The enemy pounded us with mortars during the day and beefed up probes of the perimeter at night. The casualties mounted. The engineers finally dug us a bunker for cover, and luckily, Larry Foracker's smiling face showed up to help us; his presence was more than appreciated.

The fighting around the mountains of Bastogne increased significantly. Every day at least one of the companies made contact or came up against another bunker complex. The complexes found in the A Shau were large, heavily fortified fighting positions made with logs, large stones, and earth and connected by trenches. Only five hundred meters to the north of us, a patrol stumbled into one such network containing a large enemy force. Beckwith's men repeatedly assaulted the bunkers, only to be driven off again and again by enemy rockets, machine guns, and grenades.

Their failure to take the bunkers wasn't due to a lack of guts. One NCO was wounded on three different occasions leading his men in the attack. The enemy was just so well entrenched and heavily armed that even the LAWs (light antitank weapons—a kind of throwaway bazooka) had little effect against the fortifications.

Colonel Beckwith was flying above the battle at treetop level, directing the troops and assessing the situation. When his bird returned to the firebase, he stormed straight to the TOC. A few moments later an NCO approached Ron and me.

"The old man wants to see one of you guys."

Since it was Ron's turn to control traffic, I followed the NCO to the TOC.

Stepping into the bunker, I paused for a moment to let my eyes adjust to the dark. Colonel Beckwith was shouting at someone on the other end of the telephone landline. Frustrated, he slammed the phone down, breaking it in half.

"Dammit! I got brave men being wounded and killed! Don't those sons a bitches know we're fighting a war?"

Surprised, I mumbled to a lieutenant sitting behind a field table. "Damn! I didn't think those phones were breakable!"

The lieutenant never spoke. He just eyed me momentarily, then went back to his work.

Hesitatingly, I walked over to the colonel. "You wanted to see me, sir?"

Colonel Beckwith towered over me, his eyes glaring. His mind must have still been shifting gears. Whoever was on the other end of the landline had really pissed him off.

"I'm one of the Pathfinders, sir!"

His expression began to change. "Good! Listen! I'm going to pull the men back and bring in an air strike before dark. We need some way of marking their position besides smoke."

The solution entered my mind immediately. "We've got some VS-17 panels, sir. They'd be perfect for the job!"

The colonel seemed genuinely pleased. "Good! Go get the panels and report back here ASAP. I'll have somebody take you up there."

I hustled back to let Ron and Larry know what was going on. Larry and I grabbed the panels and headed back to the TOC.

Two battered soldiers waited to escort us up to their unit. They looked exhausted and were covered in dirt. At the southwest portion of the perimeter there was a space in the concertina wire that could be opened for passage. The four of us slipped through and trudged our way up the side of the hill. Luckily, some paths had been beaten down by men hauling the wounded and ammunition. The two soldiers led us to their unit.

Most of the men were scattered in the vegetation. All of them looked haggard, staring nowhere. Larry and I moved forward a few meters and tied down a panel marking the center of the unit. Even though the men would be moving farther back, we still wanted to make sure there was a buffer zone. Once the panel was secure, we split up. I would mark the far left of the unit with a panel, and he would mark the far right. From the air the pilot would see the three panels in a line, identifying the front of the unit, and know to keep his bombs in front of the panels.

After slipping and stumbling through mud and wait-a-minute vines, I eventually linked up with the platoon on the far left.

An NCO I assumed to be the platoon sergeant spoke out. "You the Pathfinder?"

I crouched down beside him. "Roger that!"

He rubbed his eyes. "We got word you were coming. What's up?"

I explained that Colonel Beckwith wanted me to mark the friendly position for an air strike and that I needed to place the panel as far forward of the troops as I could.

The platoon sergeant glanced around at his men. "Hell! I'll go with you. My boys are beat!"

The sergeant and I stayed low, using the vegetation as concealment. He said that the enemy bunker complex was approximately a hundred meters away. I had to find a location that could be seen from above. We moved forward about twenty meters until I found a small clearing in which to lay the panel. I unfolded it and spread it out on the ground. As I was tying down one of the corners, an enemy machine gun opened up.

The bullets kicked up the dirt in front of me. The firing stopped, so I lifted my head to see if I could locate the gun. The enemy fired another burst. This time the bullets tore up the ground right by my head. I hugged the earth, my cheek pressed to the dirt. I dared not move for fear of having my head blown off. Again, bullets ripped up the ground around me.

I forgot all about the platoon sergeant until I heard him speak. "You see him?"

There was no way I could see anything, because I didn't dare look. I tried to talk but could only mumble, "No!"

"It's probably an RPD!"

I didn't care if it was called a Singer sewing machine; I wasn't budging.

I couldn't tell where the next burst of bullets went, but I knew it was only a matter of time until I was dead. I wondered if Larry was faring better than I.

Silently I started praying, Oh God! Please get me

through this. I know I'm not supposed to bargain, but I'll go to church every Sunday when I get back home—

My prayers were interrupted by the sergeant. "I'm going to throw a grenade, so get ready. When it goes off, stay low but move back to some cover."

He threw the grenade from the prone. I swear it went only about ten feet in front of us. There was a loud *Boom!* It took everything I could muster to move. When the enemy machine gun opened up, I was behind a tree.

I heard men shouting, and then the platoon sergeant yelled, "Get some suppressive fire on the son of a bitch."

Off to my right, an M-60 started spitting bullets. I took the opportunity to crawl farther back and immediately stumbled into some members of the platoon. After a while the M-60 stopped, and so did the NVA machine gun.

We made our way back to the rest of the unit, and I had them radio that my panel was in position. I found out that Larry was okay and had his panel in place as well. I decided to remain with the unit and watch the action. We moved down the hill another thirty to fifty meters.

Right before dusk a roaring, high-pitched noise filled the sky. The platoon sergeant shouted, "Coming in hot!"

A jet streaked overhead dropping three round balls. The three spheres tumbled as they soared above us, toppling into the area of the bunkers.

The explosion of napalm created a huge fiery blast. It felt like the heat from a furnace had spread over us. I thought the hair on my eyebrows was singed. I heard one soldier remark, "Christ! No one can live through that shit!"

Once the air strike was over, the jet flew by one last time. The pilot waved good-bye by waggling his wings. I could actually see the white helmet and face of the pilot.

The platoon sergeant looked at me. "Hey, Pathfinder! What the hell kind of jet was that, a Phantom?"

I was looking down at the hair on my arms to see if it was burnt. "No! It was a TFFTR!"

The platoon sergeant looked puzzled. "What the hell is a TFFTR?"

"Too fucking fast to recognize!"

The soldiers standing around burst out laughing. The platoon sergeant had a serious expression on his face. "All right! All right! That's enough! You bubblegum fuckers think that's funny, huh!"

I collected my panel while the platoon sergeant took a head count of his men. He then turned to one of the soldiers. "All accounted for, LT."

I was surprised that there was a lieutenant in the platoon. I hadn't noticed him earlier.

The platoon sergeant spoke to the men again. "You all chow down and get some rest. First light, we're gonna go see if we can find us some crispy critters."

I thanked the platoon sergeant for everything, then headed back down the hill to the firebase before darkness set in. I had gone about ten feet when I heard the lieutenant ask the platoon sergeant, "What kind of aircraft was that anyway?"

The sergeant replied, "Hell, LT. That was a TFFTR!"

What do you know? He did think it was funny after all. I shook my head and smiled.

A few weeks later, in mid-April, I was called back to Camp Eagle. Torch greeted me as usual. I'd missed the little guy, and it felt good to take a shower and eat hot chow. The next day I received word that Lieutenant Wilberding wanted to see me at operations. As I entered the operations hootch, Wilberding was seated behind a field table.

"What's up, sir?"

There was a folding chair next to the table, and Wilberding motioned me to take a seat. "There's a big operation taking place tomorrow. The 1st Brigade and the South Vietnamese Airborne are inserting close to the A Shau. Since it's our birds, we need to attach a Pathfinder team to the South Vietnamese."

Damn! I had to be the luckiest guy in the world. What a mission!

Wilberding's face took on a solemn look. "I want you

to take Gibbons along. If he stays around here any
longer, he'll end up receiving a court-martial."

"That will be fine, sir." Lieutenant Wilberding was
right. Mike had to get out of the rear and fast. A couple
of days earlier he had been drinking and drove a two-
and-a-half-ton truck right through the mess hall tent. It
probably wouldn't have been so bad if the pilots and
crews hadn't been sitting in there eating.

Wilberding briefed me on the mission. The operation
was named Delaware/Lam Son 216. The 1st Brigade and
the South Vietnamese Airborne would operate in the
Rao Nho and Rao Nai valleys to cut off enemy supply
routes leading out of the A Shau. Mike and I would link
up with the South Vietnamese and help establish a firebase, which would be called Vehgel.

After the briefing I went to let Mike know what was
going on. We would insert at first light. I couldn't believe
my luck. Although rumors had it that the average South
Vietnamese soldier was not all that good, the South
Vietnamese Airborne and Ranger units had fine reputa-
tions. They were always in the thick of a fight and had
been cited for bravery on numerous occasions.

The next morning Mike and I arrived early at the helipad.
We test-fired our weapons and conducted one last commo
check before boarding the chopper. We would insert on a
one-bird LZ and link up with the South Vietnamese Airborne on the ground. At least we didn't have to rappel in; an
aircraft hovering for any length of time over a place like the
A Shau was sure to get the shit shot out of it. Sometimes, if
there was not adequate space on the ground for an LZ, the
only way for us to get on the ground was by rappelling in.

Although it was early morning, it was already hot and
muggy. I gave Mike a thumbs-up as, flanked by two gunships, our chopper lurched forward. In no time we were
flying at a thousand feet and heading toward the A Shau.

Chapter Thirteen

As usual, the cool breeze blowing through the chopper's cabin was a welcome reprieve from the unbearable heat outside. I took out my notebook and began memorizing the primary frequencies and call signs that would be used during the operation. Once on the ground, I would attempt to radio the American adviser we would be working with. My thoughts were interrupted when Mike tapped me on the shoulder and pointed to the mountainous, triple-canopy jungle about a thousand feet below. We were well on our way to the A Shau.

Studying the frequencies kept my mind occupied and helped the twenty minutes or so pass quickly. Eventually the chopper's blades made a loud *whopping* sound and I knew we were beginning our descent. Just moments later we were skimming along a river at low-level flight. Our bird was hauling ass, with two gunships trailing. Suddenly our pilot banked hard right, and we began climbing the side of a mountain.

The crew chief signaled us to get ready for insertion. The familiar smell of jungle dampness filled my nostrils once again, and my heart began pounding. My fingers tightened around my rifle.

All of a sudden small-arms fire erupted from below, followed by a loud *whack*. Our chopper was moving so fast there was no time to return fire. Mike and I immediately scanned the cabin for damage.

The crew chief noticed our concern and swung his

mouthpiece to the side. "No sweat, GI. Probably just took a hit or two in the tail boom!"

I nodded and gave him my best hard-core look. What, me worry? As I tried to make myself smaller, I watched both gunships peel off to circle for their prey. A moment later our chopper flared into a quick hover over a tiny clearing.

Mike and I examined the ground below as we positioned ourselves to jump from the chopper floor. We would be damn lucky if the bird fit into the miniature LZ. I couldn't believe they'd selected this place as our insertion spot. Both the door gunner and the crew chief stood out on the skids to guide the chopper as it slowly inched its way down into the jungle canopy. It was going to be a tight squeeze. At any second I expected a rotor blade to whack a tree. I just hoped that the pilot holding the controls didn't flinch or sneeze.

The helicopter was still at least thirty feet off the ground as it continued to sink into the tall trees. The seconds ticked away, and I realized that rappelling would not have been such a bad idea after all. At least we would have been on the ground already.

When the aircraft was about fifteen feet off the ground I shouted in Mike's ear, "I've had enough of this shit. We've had too much hang time. Let's unass the bird!"

Mike didn't waste any time thinking things over. "Where you go, I go! I still remember how to do a PLF [parachute landing fall]."

We waited a little longer. When the bird was about ten feet off the ground, Mike and I leaped from the cabin. I landed hard on my rucksack and prayed the fall hadn't damaged the radio. Mike signaled that he was all right, so I flashed a thumbs-up to the crew. The helicopter ascended slowly back through the canopy opening. The instant it cleared the treetops, it was gone. I was certain the enemy knew we were in the area, so we crawled into the bushes and lay low.

Mike pulled security while I made a commo check with the choppers. I wanted to ensure that the radio was working properly so I could also bring the gunships back if the shit

hit the fan. I then tried to get hold of the South Vietnamese adviser on their frequency, but couldn't for some reason.

I studied the map and estimated the South Vietnamese Airborne to be fifty meters uphill from us. I wasn't briefed on any kind of linkup procedure, so I had two choices. Mike and I could stay put and wait for the friendlies to link up with us, or we could leave to go find them. I decided we would stay put for fifteen minutes, then reconsider moving out if nobody came.

Mike and I stayed close together, listening for any sounds out of the ordinary. The insects didn't waste any time feeding on us as the sweat dripped off our foreheads and down our necks. Already I longed to be submerged in cool water somewhere.

Mike moved his head closer to mine and whispered, "You're not too smart, Corporal!"

Shit! Did I forget to bring something along? "What do you mean?"

His voice had a sarcastic ring to it. "What are we doing here?"

Now I knew Mike was up to something. "We're waiting for the Vietnamese to link up with us!"

"That's right, Corporal Burns! Do you speak Vietnamese?"

"No!"

Mike snickered. "Neither do I!"

I had no idea what the hell he was talking about. "So what!"

Mike moved in a little closer. "Because, smart-ass, if we hear anyone or link up with anybody, how do we know if they're friendlies or if they're gooks?"

Damn! One more thing to worry about.

About fifteen minutes had passed. I was sick of waiting. "Mike, we move out in zero one. You walk point!"

Cautiously we arose. I waited for Mike to scan the jungle and select a route. A twig cracked. Mike and I stayed completely still with our weapons at the ready. My mouth was so dry, my lips felt like they were glued together. They couldn't have been pried open with a crowbar. If those were enemy soldiers, Mike and I were in a world of shit.

Slowly we crouched down. Within moments I spotted a figure about twenty feet away. Asian! I couldn't tell how many other soldiers were with him, but I suspected he wasn't alone. I aimed my weapon and sighted in on the center of his torso. I signaled Mike to get a grenade ready. If I had to take the guy out, Mike would throw the grenade, perhaps giving us a chance to escape.

Mike and I stared at each other. It's that look friends give each other in combat, right before some kind of action is going to happen. As if knowing they will never see each other again.

The soldier whispered something in Vietnamese. Surely an NVA soldier wouldn't give his position away like that. He stepped closer. I could barely make out his uniform. It was an odd camouflage pattern. I kept my finger on the trigger but remained patient. I didn't want to kill an ally who was risking his own neck looking for me. As I peered through the different openings in the thickets, I finally noticed the white South Vietnamese jump wings over his shirt pocket. I felt a tremendous sense of relief and quickly removed my finger from the trigger.

I spoke softly. "Over here! Over here!"

I waited until I was absolutely sure he'd heard me before slowly standing up. Mike stayed out of sight, covering me.

The South Vietnamese soldier had a big smile on his face. I couldn't understand what he was saying but, by his gestures, it was What the hell took you so long?

There were four other soldiers with him, and none of them appeared startled when Mike finally stood up.

The first South Vietnamese pointed up the hill, then stuck his hand straight out and began flapping it from the wrist. *"Lai dai! Lai dai!"* "Come here." As Mike and I stepped forward, the five soldiers turned and started up the mountain.

The South Vietnamese Airborne unit was located on a steep slope on the side of the mountain. The troops were digging foxholes along the perimeter as we passed. The soldiers led us to an American who wasn't wearing any headgear but did have on the same camouflage uniform as their own. I assumed from the mission briefing that he was our contact, Sergeant First Class Girard, the South Vietnamese Airborne adviser from MACV Team 162.

In my best military bearing, I reported to him. "Sergeant Girard! My name is Corporal Burns, and this is Private Gibbons."

Sergeant Girard cracked a welcome smile and reached out to shake my hand. "You guys must be the Pathfinders."

"Yes, Sergeant!"

As Sergeant Girard reached out to shake Mike's hand, he said, "Listen! Forget calling me sergeant. Everybody just calls me Frenchy."

I smiled. "Okay, Frenchy!" It seemed strange calling a senior NCO by anything other than sergeant, especially when coming from a unit like the 101st Airborne Division.

The first thing Mike and I did was get help from the South Vietnamese soldiers to clear an LZ for a helicopter to land. Around midmorning the slicks and Chinooks started arriving. The LZ was large enough for only one slick to set down at a time. South Vietnamese paratroops arriving on the Chinooks had to climb down through the cargo hold. The aircraft continually brought in supplies, equipment, three 105mm artillery guns, and plenty of ammunition. Frenchy was great; he never interfered with our work. He would just say where he wanted something placed, and Mike and I would do our best to put it there. By the end of the first day the three artillery guns were in place and firing.

As dusk set in, Mike and I had just cleared a spot to sleep when enemy mortar rounds came in. Luckily, they all exploded outside the perimeter.

Frenchy stood over us and laughed. "Give them a day or two, they'll get it right!"

As Frenchy strolled away, Mike pulled his poncho liner over him. "He's got some sense of humor."

I wrapped my arm through the sling of my weapon

and cradled it to me. "Yeah! The funny part is, he's probably right!"

The next few days went by pretty much like the first. Besides the language, Mike and I learned a great deal about the way the South Vietnamese paratroops did things compared to Americans. For one, the Vietnamese didn't bother to clear the vegetation in and around their firebase like Americans did. Moreover, the size of the firebase was a lot smaller than the ones we were accustomed to.

Leaving all the vegetation in place made the base more obscure, therefore harder for the enemy to detect. Of course, it made it easier for the enemy to probe and infiltrate once he'd found it.

Since the size of the base was smaller, the enemy had a tougher time landing mortars and rockets in a tinier area. The downside was that if the enemy was successful, more matériel and personnel could be destroyed.

Instead of foxholes or sandbagged parapets, the South Vietnamese artillerymen dug deep circular holes beside their guns. The hole was just large enough in diameter to accommodate a man's body if he jumped into it in the standing position. However, the hole was deep enough to cover the entire body of the man when he stood straight up. That technique worked well because an enemy mortar round or rocket had to hit directly within the small, circular opening of the hole to be effective, or the shrapnel just blew over it.

It rained every afternoon, but it was a lot different from the way it rained back home. About thirty minutes beforehand, we could predict the rain's arrival. First, our noses detected a fine vapor as moisture permeated the air. Next, the sky turned gloomy and black. In the distance, a thick, gray tower of water could be seen, slowly advancing toward us. When the rainfall finally did arrive, it came in a downpour.

The first time the rains came, Mike and I watched the South Vietnamese quickly strip off their clothing, then place their uniforms somewhere safe from getting wet.

Although some of the soldiers were naked, most wore colored bikini-type underwear. As soon as the rain hit, they all soaped down and quickly rinsed off the lather before the showers ceased. Mike and I had a good laugh.

Later, Frenchy explained that the enemy soldiers used the rain for washing and drinking, and how the Vietnamese people applied nature to their advantage. He said that his soldiers weren't plagued with jungle rot and immersion foot the way many Americans were. It made sense. Once we saw how clean and refreshed the Vietnamese soldiers were, Mike and I decided to give it a try.

Like most American soldiers, I didn't wear underwear. Mike, however, had on baggy, army-issue, olive-drab boxer shorts. I wished I'd had a camera to capture the scene of Mike standing in the open jungle sporting his baggy boxers, his skin lily-white except for his arms and neck, soap in hand, waiting for the rain. All the South Vietnamese paratroopers stopped what they were doing and roared with laughter. Typical Mike Gibbons: instead of being self-conscious, Mike performed a little dance, then shouted that boxer shorts were "number one."

The show was far from over. The finale came when the rain stopped. I was fortunate enough to rinse off all the lather while it was still raining; Mike wasn't so lucky. He was left with big clumps of suds and foam dripping from his body. The Vietnamese roared. Of course, Mike tried to tell them that he let the suds remain on purpose, claiming that once the soap dried, it warded off insects.

A few days after our arrival, Frenchy shouted for everyone to be quiet. We could hear enemy mortar rounds coming out of their tubes. It sounded like three tubes firing. The artillerymen leaped into their holes. Mike and I crawled into a narrow trench we had dug for just such an occasion. As mortar rounds exploded all around us, I watched in awe as Frenchy just stood erect with his hands on his hips. One round exploded so close to him, it was a miracle he wasn't hit. Frenchy never even flinched. He just calmly told the South Vietnamese soldiers to get out of their holes and man their guns to return counterfire. The South Vietnamese soldiers sprang from their holes and in seconds were spraying the hill suspected of hiding the tubes.

We immediately called for a dustoff to get out the wounded. While Mike stayed with the radio, I helped sort out the most seriously injured for the first sortie. Eventually Mike shouted that the dustoff was inbound. I popped smoke and guided the bird in. As soon as its skids touched the ground, mortar rounds began exploding. We hadn't heard them come out of the tubes this time because of the aircraft.

Although most of the explosions occurred about fifty meters away, one of the NVA tubes began walking rounds right toward the helicopter. Each round exploded ten meters closer. The crew saw the explosions as well, but stayed on the ground for the wounded. Just as we heaved the last casualty on board, a mortar round exploded about thirty feet away.

I shouted to the crew chief, "That's the last of the seriously injured. Take off now!"

The chopper pulled pitch, its nose forward. I watched the skids brush the tops of the trees just as an explosion hurled me into the bushes.

My ears rang and I was disoriented. I turned over onto my knees, then felt someone help me to my feet. It was Mike. "You okay?"

My head felt fuzzy. "Yeah! I guess so!"

I checked myself out; not a scratch. Mike chuckled. "Shit! You had me worried there for a minute!"

As my head cleared, I remembered that two South Vietnamese soldiers had been standing near me when the round exploded. I turned to see if either of them was hit. One was unharmed like myself, but the other had sustained fragmentation wounds to the leg and arm. Two of his comrades had hold of him. Even though his leg wound was a deep, open gash that must have hurt like hell, he was smiling amidst the pain.

I got the attention of one of the soldiers who spoke a little English. "Is he okay?"

The Vietnamese soldier grinned, nodding his head repeatedly. "He okay! He happy!"

He happy? I was at a loss for words. Maybe I was missing something. I turned to Mike for help, but he just shrugged his shoulders. "Maybe it's a big family-honor thing to get wounded."

This just didn't make sense. This guy was almost ecstatic. Besides, Frenchy told me that most of these guys had been fighting the war so long that practically all of them had been wounded more than once. Hell, one of the older NCOs had been wounded something like eighteen times.

I threw my arms up at the soldier. "Why he happy?"

The Vietnamese pointed to the sky. "He go Saigon. See family!"

"Oh!" I understood. It was his ticket home for a while.

Later, Frenchy explained that the South Vietnamese Airborne stayed in combat, always being sent to every hot spot. His soldiers had been fighting the war for years. Getting wounded was one of the only ways to return to their home base in Saigon and thus see their loved ones.

Around ten days into the operation, another adviser came out to bring Frenchy some personal supplies and mail. Like Frenchy, the adviser was a sergeant first class and appeared to be genuinely friendly. He stood tall and upright and had black, wavy hair. The guy looked like he belonged on an army recruiting poster.

That night the new adviser filled Mike and me in on some of Frenchy's history. Mike and I knew that Frenchy spoke fluent French because we'd heard him converse with the Vietnamese. What we didn't know was that Frenchy's father was a French paratrooper who'd fought the Viet Minh at Dien Bien Phu.

The adviser went on to say that Frenchy had been in Vietnam for quite some time, hated the Communists, and loved the South Vietnamese. The way the South Vietnamese reacted to Frenchy, we knew the feeling was mutual. Although the adviser left the next day, we were grateful to learn a little about Frenchy's background.

It didn't take long for Mike and me to make a few friends among the South Vietnamese. One of them was a gregarious, chubby fellow whom we dubbed Tooth because every time the guy grinned, all you could see was a big, bright gold tooth. Tooth must have been the unit scrounger, because if there was anything we needed, Tooth would get it. He spoke a little English and was constantly trading or bartering for something.

Tooth was always accompanied by his smaller, fairly thin buddy who didn't speak a word of English but smiled all the time. Naturally, Mike and I called him Smiley. Wherever Tooth was, Smiley was trailing close behind. I often wondered what Vietnamese names Tooth and Smiley had bestowed on Mike and me.

Around every third day, one of the chopper crews would bring us out a case of beer or soda. Those were hot trading commodities, along with C rations, cigarettes, and soap. One day Mike was saying how he would give anything for some whiskey.

Since few aircraft flew around the A Shau at night, Mike and I shut down the radios after dark. Of course, we would resume operations immediately for an exception, like a medevac. One evening Mike and I were chowing down on some Cs when Tooth approached, flanked by his cohort, Smiley.

Tooth took a small cloth bag from Smiley and held it out. "Whiskey!"

Excitedly, Mike sprang up from the tree stump he was sitting on. "Whiskey?"

Tooth nodded and grinned, revealing his bright gold tooth.

Mike seemed pleasantly surprised and pointed to the bag. "Let me see!"

Tooth opened the bag and uncovered a colorful, picturesque bottle with Vietnamese writing on the label. He handed the bottle to Mike. "Whiskey!"

Mike twisted the cap open and put it to his nose. "It damn sure smells like whiskey, Richie!"

He shoved the bottle under my nose and I took a whiff. "Yep! It's whiskey all right."

He handed the bottle back to Tooth. "What do you want to trade for it?"

Tooth looked puzzled. "No trade! We drink!"

Smiley held up a ceramic cup and acted like he was drinking something.

Mike was as excited as a kid at Christmas. "Hell! Let's get our canteen cups!"

We swished a little water in our cups to get rid of the dirt, then held them out. Tooth filled each cup about a third of the way, but instead of drinking, Tooth and Smiley just stared as Mike and I brought the cups to our lips. The liquid was definitely some blend of whiskey. It tasted smooth and didn't burn going down. It had a sweet flavor to it as well. With widened eyes, Tooth and Smiley concentrated on our every movement.

I brought the cup down from my mouth. "Wow! This tastes pretty good!"

Mike made a loud smack with his lips. "Good! Are you kidding? This stuff is great! Airborne, goddammit!"

Tooth and Smiley appeared more than happy. I was taken aback by their willingness to please us. Smiley pointed to the parachute wings sewn above his shirt pocket, then pointed to Mike's. *"Nhay du! Nhay du!"* (pronounced "nay you").

Mike pointed to everyone's parachute wings, then clasped his hands together. "That's right! *Nhay du . . .* Airborne, same-same brothers! Understand?"

Everyone understood.

The four of us sat quietly sharing the whiskey and

teaching each other a few words of our respective languages. Soon a few of Tooth's comrades gathered around us. We offered them beer and soda, but they politely refused. They all seemed unusually shy, even afraid of us.

I was curious about their behavior and questioned Tooth. Tooth explained that his fellow soldiers figured Mike and I had to be real important. The Vietnamese knew that neither of us was an officer or senior NCO, yet we told all the aircraft what to do and the helicopter crews even brought us sodas, beer, and other items. We all had a good laugh over that one.

It was getting dark. Tooth stood up. "Night come! We go!"

He pointed out into the darkness. "Beaucoup VC come!" When talking to an American, the South Vietnamese referred to all enemy, NVA and the like, as VC.

Mike pointed to his Pathfinder badge. "Don't you worry. VC come, I kill VC!"

I burst out laughing. "What the hell are you talking about? These guys have been fighting for years, and now Gibbons the American Pathfinder is going to show them how it's done."

Tooth and Smiley were trying desperately to understand what I was saying. Mike pushed me away. "Don't listen to him! He's just a corporal. He doesn't even shave, for Christ's sake."

Tooth pointed to Mike. "You want kill VC?"

Mike puffed his chest out. "Damn right! We're Pathfinders! You come get us, and we'll kill all them sons a bitches for ya."

Tooth gave a little bow at the waist. Although he was grinning, he was serious. "Okay! VC come, we get you, you kill VC."

Mike winked. "Airborne, goddammit!"

It was around midnight. Someone was shaking me awake. I heard whispering but couldn't understand what was being said. Instinctively I grabbed my weapon. As

my vision came into focus, I saw Tooth crouched beside
me and Mike.

"VC! VC!"

Mike's voice was groggy. "What? What's going on?"

Tooth was wide-eyed and excited. "VC! VC! You say
come get you. You kill VC!"

Mike mumbled. "Come back in the morning. I'll kill
all the VC then."

Tooth seemed utterly confused. "VC here now! Morning no VC!"

Mike sat up momentarily and looked in my direction.
"Is he bullshitting?"

I reached down and tightened the laces on my boots. "I
don't think so, unless he's playing some kind of joke on us."

Tooth became downright demanding. "You come
now!"

Mike took a swallow of water from his canteen.
"Okay! Okay! We're coming!"

He grabbed a few magazines of ammo and stuffed
them in his pockets, then turned to me and whispered.
"You don't think Tooth is a VC, do you? Maybe he's going to lead us into a trap, and we'll be captured."

I secured my LBE. "No, Mike! That's crazy. These
guys are Airborne."

Staying low, we quietly followed Tooth through the
darkness. I hoped like hell I was right.

It was dark, real dark. I could barely make out Tooth's
silhouette even though I was right behind him. I even felt
Mike grab my LBE a couple of times in an attempt not to
become separated. I prayed that Tooth knew where the hell
he was going. We must have been close to the perimeter, because Tooth motioned us to crawl the last few meters. Moments later we met Smiley, who was inside a foxhole.

Tooth pointed his finger and whispered lightly. "VC!"

He then cupped his hand to his ear, signaling us to listen. It wasn't long at all until we heard bushes rustle on
the slope below us. NVA soldiers were probing the hillside, looking for our positions.

Tooth beamed with pride, while Mike just gaped in astonishment.

A minute or two passed as the four of us remained completely still. Thoughts raced through my mind. How many enemy were out there? How close were they to us? What if one of them bumped right into us? The whole situation was eerie.

When I was a kid, I watched a World War II movie where the Japanese were crawling at night among the Americans. I remember thinking how scary that must have been. Right now, I didn't feel as afraid as I did impatient. Let's just get the damn show on the road.

Obviously Tooth felt the same way. He got Mike's attention, then ran his finger across his neck like he was slitting a throat. Basically he was saying, "Okay, asshole! I brought you here to kill gooks. Here they are!"

Usually Mike was the one who was always impatient. I couldn't see the expression on his face, but I bet that he didn't believe something like this would have happened in a million years. Mike brought his weapon up slowly. Immediately Tooth placed his hand over it, pushing it back down. Tooth then held up a grenade and simulated pulling the pin and throwing it. He was reminding Mike that the muzzle flash of the rifle would give our position away.

Quietly, Smiley brought a canvas bag from out of the foxhole. It was full of grenades. He handed them out, then motioned Mike to join him in the hole. There was no way all four of us could fit, so Mike declined. I gathered that he didn't want to go into the safety of the foxhole if I couldn't. Tooth stayed out as well.

Slowly, Mike and I pulled the pins on our grenades. We held the levers tight and silently listened for any movement. There it was, a rustle of bushes. Simultaneously, we both threw the grenades in the direction of the sound, then fell flat on the ground. *Boom! Boom!*

We heard a loud scream, followed by moaning. Tooth and Smiley were overjoyed. They each handed Mike and me the grenades they were holding. Tooth motioned for us to throw again. Making sure to throw at the same instant, we lobbed the grenades down the hill. *Boom! Boom!*

This time the explosions were not followed by any screams but we could still hear some moaning. Tooth did a little clap with his hands. "Kill VC! Kill VC!"

Mike had this serious expression on his face. He then pounded his hand to his chest like some Roman warrior. "Airborne Pathfinder, kill all VC!" He looked so stupid, I had to laugh.

Tooth led us back to our equipment. Mike and I thanked him for a good time. Neither of us went back to sleep. Mike was just too excited and wanted to talk. The rest of the night he kept saying, "Can you believe this shit?"

Early the next morning Mike and I were sipping some coffee before the aircraft started arriving. Frenchy walked over. "You two responsible for all that racket last night?"

We were momentarily at a loss for words. I was the senior Pathfinder, but before I could respond, Frenchy continued, "I don't mind you guys having a little fun, but I hope you got that shit out of your system. Your job isn't to be fucking around on the perimeter at night. I can't afford to lose either one of you guys. *Bic?*" (*Bic?* is Vietnamese for "Understand?")

Mike and I nodded.

As Frenchy turned to walk away, I just had to ask. "Did we get a body count?"

"No bodies, but some blood trails."

That made my day. "Thanks, Frenchy!"

He just shook his head and smiled.

A few hours into the morning we heard a flight of helicopters in the distance. They sounded like they were landing a few kilometers away. Sure enough, sounds of gunfire followed; some unit was conducting a CA. I searched until I found the frequency and listened in. The Pathfinder controlling the operation was Joe Bolick. The unit was a company from the 1st of the 327th Infantry.

Late in the afternoon, to our surprise, the American

paratroopers arrived at our firebase. They had humped all the way up the mountain from the LZ they had landed at earlier. Needless to say, they looked worn out. Our firebase was too small to accommodate another entire company of infantry, so the American unit set up right below us, basically attaching their perimeter to ours. In no time they were digging foxholes.

From above, Mike and I watched our fellow paratroopers work feverishly to dig in. The sound of their entrenching tools echoed through the valley as they repeatedly struck away at the claylike soil.

I shook my head. "I wonder if that's such a good idea."

Mike was replacing the battery in one of the radios. "What's that?"

I pointed to the troops below. "Those guys sure are making a lot of noise with their entrenching tools!"

Mike snapped the clasps shut on the bottom of the radio. "They got to dig in, Richie!"

"I know that's the routine, but now Charlie knows that new troops have arrived and where they're at. I'd be surprised if they get those holes dug before dark anyway."

Mike handed the plastic bag that held the radio battery to a South Vietnamese soldier standing near him. Earlier the South Vietnamese had asked if they could have them when available. The small bags came in useful for keeping items dry. The soldiers were very appreciative.

I grabbed my M-16 and said, "Those guys need to know that Charlie's been mortaring the hell out of this place. You stay here and monitor the radio. I'm going to go have a talk with their CO!"

Mike shook his head. "Roger that! I just hope you're not wasting your time!"

I took off down the hill. "Yeah! Me, too!"

I wanted to let the unit commander know that Charlie had a forward observer who was probably watching their every move, and that the chances were real good that they would be hit by mortars before the day was over.

Furthermore, I knew they didn't have a Pathfinder along, and I wanted to assure him that he could call on Mike and me for any assistance.

A number of the American soldiers eyed me funny as I passed by them in search of their commander. One of them was taking a break while his buddy whacked at the dirt with an entrenching tool.

He noticed the 101st patch on my shoulder. "You part of the division?"

I stopped momentarily to chat. "Yeah! I'm a Pathfinder! How you guys doing?"

Although the soldier appeared cordial, his face held a look of disdain. "What are you doing with the slopes?"

I hadn't expected a question like that, so I was taken aback for a moment. "I'm attached to their unit for the operation!"

He sounded sympathetic. "You better watch yourself. I heard that Marvin the ARVN ain't worth a shit."

Although I wanted to hurry up and find the commander, I felt that I needed to set the record straight. "Well, I got to be honest with you. I don't know what the rest of the South Vietnamese Army is like, but I'll tell you the truth. Those guys are Airborne soldiers, and they're all right. I mean it."

The soldier paused for a moment. His friends had been listening. I thought he was going to start some kind of debate, which was the last thing I needed just then. Instead, his response was rather congenial. "They're Airborne, huh! Well, that says a lot for them. Everybody's been concerned because we're linking part of our perimeter with theirs."

He glanced around at his buddies and then back to me. "Thanks, man! I'll pass the word around."

I was glad for the opportunity to put his mind at ease. "Airborne!" I continued my search for the commander.

Not long afterward, a young specialist led me to an older-looking NCO. I introduced myself. "Airborne, Sergeant! I'm Corporal Burns! I'd like to see the commander for a few minutes. It won't take long!"

I knew the sergeant had a lot on his mind because he was real abrupt. "The old man's meeting with his platoon leaders right now. Whatcha need?"

I really didn't care who I relayed the information to as long as it was someone in authority. "I'm attached to the Vietnamese Airborne, and I just wanted to let you guys know that we've been mortared daily. We're pretty sure the NVA has an FO. Also, if you need any Pathfinder assistance, my partner and I would be more than happy to help."

The sergeant looked like he was interested, but I could tell he wasn't. "Well, we appreciate your input, but we've been doing this for a while now, and I think we got a pretty good handle on it."

I could tell by the expression on his face that the sergeant thought I was lower than whale shit. "Anything else?"

"No! That's it! I appreciate your time, Sergeant."

As the sergeant turned and walked away, I kicked myself in the ass for even thinking that they would heed anything I said. To them I was just some young peon running my mouth. I should have known better. I made my way back up the hill.

Tooth had prepared an appetizing concoction of rice, C rations, and whatever. As we munched away, Frenchy complimented Mike and me on how proficient we had become at using chopsticks.

Tooth had a special treat for me. On the side of my bowl sat a tiny, reddish-orange pepper. I carried a bottle of Tabasco sauce everywhere I went and used it on practically everything I ate. So Tooth and the others knew I liked a little spice with my food. Tooth raved about this tiny pepper, unique to his country. I had to promise to wait until the end of the meal to eat it.

I had just about finished my rice when Tooth reached across and touched the pepper with his chopsticks. "Now time! You eat!"

I glanced up to see all eyes upon me. One soldier said something in Vietnamese and motioned others to come over and watch. It was amazing what little it took to entertain soldiers in combat.

Clutching the tiny pepper between my chopsticks, I slowly brought it to my mouth. Suddenly one of the Vietnamese stuck his hand out. "Hot!"

He was immediately chastised by the others. Mike butted in. "Shit! It's not too hot for Richie. Right, Rich?"

Mike was right. There wasn't a hot pepper in the world that I couldn't handle. Hell! I ate jalapeños like they were nothing. Wanting the show to last, I just held the pepper in front of my face. Finally I bellowed, "No sweat, GI!" and dropped it into my mouth.

Tooth had played a trick on me. It wasn't peppery at all. Like most soldiers, I learned to inhale my food early on in the army. Consequently, I must not have chewed it enough to get the spicy flavor. I hated to disappoint everyone, but that pepper was kindergarten compared to the hot stuff I had eaten in the past.

Moments later, without warning, a raging fire erupted in my mouth, tongue, esophagus, everywhere. The sweat under my eyes ran into the tears streaming down my cheeks. Coughing and gagging, I fluttered my hand in front of my mouth like a fan. "Water! Water!"

I must have looked really stupid. Nobody could help me; they were too busy laughing. Ultimately someone handed me a canteen. Even though water was at a premium, I didn't care. I guzzled it down. That tiny pepper was a natural incendiary device, and it was burning through my stomach lining. I wasn't going to live that one down for a long time.

It had to be a good five minutes before the burning sensation became tolerable. Eventually Tooth and the others stopped laughing. Some of the South Vietnamese patted me on the back for being so entertaining.

Once the show was over, the group calmed down. Then one of the soldiers got a surprised look on his face. He ran his finger along my name tag. "Burns!"

He instantly doubled over in laughter. "Burns!"

His comrades appeared puzzled until he translated my name out loud. The roaring of laughter started all over again. Even Frenchy and Mike lost it. I couldn't help laughing as well. Inevitably the fun ended as everyone dispersed to attend to various duties.

After chow, Mike and I sat on a tree stump overlooking our fellow 101st paratroopers, who were about fifty meters downhill from us.

Frenchy came over and stooped down beside us. "Did you talk to their commander?"

I took a sip of hot cocoa from my canteen cup. "No, I never got that far."

I offered Frenchy a sip, then continued. "Besides, I've thought it over. They got here so late, I don't think there's much the commander could do to prepare for a mortar attack anyway."

"Well, maybe they'll be lucky and nothing will happen." Frenchy's voice had a sincere tone.

He must have caught me staring, because he went on. "You know, my first tour was with the 101st. After that, I lucked out and got assigned to the ARVN Airborne."

I was surprised. For some reason, I couldn't picture Frenchy in a unit like the 101st. "Really! What rank were you?"

"I left a sergeant E-5 and have been with the advisory team ever since."

I conducted a quick calculation and estimated Frenchy to be on his third tour. "I was told you've been over here a long time!"

He nodded. "I'm going to stay over here, too, until the war's over or they carry me out in a body bag."

Frenchy took a deep breath. "I hate the Communists; they're bastards!"

Frenchy stood up and put his hand on my shoulder. "I got to go check out the perimeter before dark."

My cocoa was getting cold, so I took a big swallow and said to Mike, "Frenchy's really something!"

Mike had his pocketknife out and was whittling a piece of wood. "He's squared away all right!"

It was getting near dusk. I glanced back down the hill to see how the Americans were doing. All was peaceful. Most of the guys had erected poncho hootches to keep out the rain. A few were milling around, either relieving themselves or finishing chow. I reached into my rucksack to get my poncho liner when I heard mortar rounds coming out of the tube.

It sounded like one tube firing. I shouted "Incoming!" Others yelled as well. Mike was nearby, and we both dove into our ditch. The rounds exploded farther down the hill; the target was the Americans. The NVA dropped five or six rounds in all, but luckily they fell short, impacting about twenty meters east of the unit.

Mike brushed some of the dirt and mud off the knees of his pants. "Man, those guys are lucky Chuck missed!"

"Yeah! They sure are!" Unfortunately there was little doubt that the NVA knew the Americans were there and, more important, had a pretty good idea where they were located.

Faintly I heard someone calling my name off in the distance. I was half asleep, dreaming I was in Vietnam. The person calling my name was Mike Gibbons. It couldn't be. Vietnam was only a dream. I tried to drift back to sleep.

"Richie! Get your ass up!"

Some dream! Mike's voice sounded so real. I actually smelled dirt and stench. My clothes really felt wet and damp, sticking to my body. Finally awake, I realized it *was* Mike. Damn! It wasn't a dream. A feeling of depression fell over me, but only momentarily. As soon as I was up and about, it vanished.

It was close to first light. Almost everyone else was still sleeping. Mike had heated up some C-ration coffee and poured half into my canteen cup.

"Thanks, Mike! Damn, I had a hell of a dream. I dreamed I was in Vietnam."

Mike smirked. "You're strange, Richie! Most guys dream of home, but you, you dream of Vietnam. That's really weird."

It was pretty strange. I thought about it for a few moments. "When someone dreams of home, they wake up in Vietnam. Maybe, unconsciously, I'm dreaming of Vietnam, hoping I'll wake up at home."

Mike was about to respond when we heard mortar rounds coming out of a tube. By the sound, more than one tube was firing. The first round exploded, followed by screams, then another and another. The enemy mortar rounds were impacting the American perimeter where most of the men were still sleeping. With no overhead cover, the paratroopers were totally defenseless.

To me, watching from above, the scene was horrific. Helpless, I watched the rounds walk across the landscape, all hitting inside the American perimeter. One round crashed by a tree. The next hit a poncho with two men under it. The poncho blew apart; one man was still alive, his partner lay motionless.

Those were my fellow Screaming Eagles. Anger welled up in me. I had been under many mortar attacks, but watching it that way was different. I hated the Communists and wanted to kill every one of them. A sick feeling came over me as I observed the agony of our men under fire. Some men screamed in pain, others just moaned, and there were those who would never speak again.

Finally the attack ceased. As I stared at the bodies, a terrible thought entered my mind: Thank God, I am uphill with the South Vietnamese and not down below with my countrymen. My anger had company—guilt!

Mike raced down the hill to let the commander know that I was calling for a dustoff. Frenchy sent his medics to see if they could help with the wounded. About ten minutes later Mike returned.

I placed the handset between the radio handle. "How'd it go?"

Mike inhaled deeply to catch his breath. "I let them know that a dustoff's on the way. Some of them are in bad shape. I hope it gets here quick."

I knew Mike well; he appeared to have something on his mind. "What's up?"

"They told the South Vietnamese medics they didn't need their help. I think they were hurt by it. Maybe they're pissed at the Vietnamese in general—you know, lumping the good and bad guys all together."

I nodded in agreement and was about to say something when the medevac pilot came over the horn, asking for landing instructions. I told Mike to grab some smoke and pop it when I waved. Once the bird was on final, Mike would guide him in. The dustoff took the most seriously wounded on the first flight and made two more trips afterward. Everything went smoothly, and luckily the NVA didn't drop any more mortars the rest of the day.

Buz Harding came out around the third week. It was great having him help us. The rains got a lot worse, the mortar attacks continued, and the casualties grew.

On Buz's first night there it was raining heavily. The three of us were sleeping in a hole Mike and I had dug when we were awakened by water rushing in on us. Half of the hole was filled with water before we crawled out. It was dark, our fatigues were soaked, and we were freezing. The only vacant hole that wasn't filled with water was the ammo dump, which was about ten feet long and five feet wide. In it were wooden crates filled with various munitions. Although it also had water in it, the crates sat above the waterline. So we stripped off our wet fatigues, lay on the tops of the crates, and covered ourselves in poncho liners. Even wet, a poncho liner would keep a person warm. The next day we dug a bypass trench around our hole.

During the fourth week I was called back to Camp Eagle. Although I really enjoyed working with the South

Vietnamese Airborne, I was ready to go back to the rear for a few days. When my chopper was inbound, I said my good-byes to Frenchy, Tooth, Smiley, and the others, then walked down to the pad. I had mixed feelings when the chopper landed. Part of me wanted to go, but part of me wanted to stay. Mike, Buz, and Frenchy gave me a thumbs-up as my bird took off.

On the way back to Eagle, I realized how fortunate I was to have worked with the South Vietnamese Airborne, and especially with an NCO like Frenchy Girard. The South Vietnamese paratroopers dispelled any misconceptions I might have had concerning their esprit de corps and bravery. Likewise, Frenchy proved to be the perfect role model for a young NCO like myself. His professionalism and courage were contagious. I hoped one day to have the privilege of serving with him again.

Sadly, Sergeant First Class Christian "Frenchy" Girard was killed a year later, April 1969, while on a mission with MACV-SOG. The United States Army lost one of its finest leaders.

Chapter Fourteen

It felt good to be back in the rear once again, with clean showers and hot meals. Basically, it was kick-back time. I flew door gunner once or twice and a few resupply missions, but that was about it.

I was back at Camp Eagle about a week when I was told that, after a review of records and scores, my name had come down on a list for Infantry Officer Candidate School (OCS) along with Brad Bradford and John Johnson. I declined the offer. I didn't want to leave Vietnam; there was just too much excitement. Also, I found out that I would not receive credit for a full combat tour, and after thinking it over, I really didn't want to be an officer.

Sure, officers received a lot more money and privileges, but as far as I was concerned, they just didn't have as much fun and excitement as NCOs did. Officers had to pull staff time behind a desk, attend formal functions and social events, and had numerous additional duties. As an NCO, I had a lot more flexibility when it came to jobs and leadership positions. More important, an NCO got away with more. I could make a mistake or get in trouble and just blame it on my being an NCO.

Sergeant Guerra and a few other senior NCOs also cautioned me that if I became an officer without already having a college degree, the army would revert me back to the enlisted ranks once the war was over. They called it an RIF (reduction in force) and said it happened after every war. It didn't make any difference how good an officer you were or how much combat time you had, either.

Time proved the older NCOs to be correct. A vast number of dedicated, decorated officers were forced to leave the army or revert back to the enlisted ranks after the Vietnam War, regardless of their performance as leaders.

Brad and John accepted the offer, however; a few weeks later they were gone. I wished them well and knew they would not have any trouble completing OCS. I was certain both would make excellent officers. A couple of days later Lieutenant Wilberding informed me that I was going back out to Bastogne.

I arrived at the firebase to find Ron feeling really low. He had become friends with a guy named Dale Lambert. Lambert, who had been in Vietnam for quite some time, received word he was scheduled to leave for home in a few days. Since Lambert had to get back to the rear in a hurry to process out, Ron got him a ride on the next available aircraft heading toward Camp Eagle. Waving good-bye, Lambert brandished a big smile as his chopper lifted from the pad. Unfortunately, it was the last memory Ron would have of Dale Lambert: the enemy hit his chopper with an RPG (rocket propelled grenade), knocking it right out of the sky. To make matters worse, the bird was hauling about seventy-five pounds of C-4 explosive. It plunged to the jungle floor in a huge ball of fire. Lambert and all four crew members were killed. Ron felt guilty about Lambert's death.

I wasn't surprised to discover that Bastogne was still a hotbed of enemy activity. The NVA had become so bold that they used flashlights to move about the hillsides at night. At times they even probed our defenses using flashlights. Every so often, lights could be seen bobbing about in the darkness right beyond the perimeter.

As usual, the air traffic remained constant throughout the daylight hours. One afternoon I had just cleared a chopper to land at the POL point when Larry barked in my ear, "Who the hell is that?"

A white helicopter soared across the trees toward the

POL point, headed on a collision course with the aircraft I had just cleared.

I shouted into the handset, "Eagle Two-two-seven! Break left! Break left!"

Luckily the pilot responded quickly, banking hard to the left and barely avoiding a midair collision. The white chopper zoomed across the firebase and circled around.

I let out a sigh of relief. "All aircraft inbound for Bastogne, do not continue approach. You are not clear to land. Enter and remain in left traffic. Over!"

I was pissed. "Unknown aircraft over Bastogne, identify. Over!"

The mystery pilot did not respond, so I tried again. After soaring over the firebase two more times, the white chopper finally sat down at the POL point. Although the side doors were closed, from a distance I could see soldiers with various camouflage uniforms as well as camouflaged faces. Larry ran down to tell the pilot not to take off without instructions.

A voice came over the radio. "Bastogne Control! This is Dragonfly One-one. Over!"

"This is Bastogne!"

"Roger! This is One-one! Sorry about the mishap. We were in desperate need of fuel and did not have your frequency! We were just given it by your partner. Request takeoff instructions, over!"

"Roger, One-one! You are cleared for takeoff to the west!"

"This is One-one! Understand to the west! Thanks again, partner!"

The white helicopter hovered, spun around quickly, and soared back across the trees. The pilot sure was in a hurry. I cleared the rest of the aircraft on hold for landings.

Larry was breathing heavily after running up the hill. "Did he . . . call you . . . for takeoff?"

"Squared away! Thanks!"

I was somewhat bewildered, though. "I never heard of

a Dragonfly call sign before, and what the hell is a white helicopter doing flying around the A Shau?"

Larry's voice hinted of secrecy. "That was an Air America bird! That's why they were low on fuel and didn't have our frequency. The pilot said if it weren't for Bastogne being here, they would have gone down."

Air America was the name that CIA aircraft flew under. I assumed that the soldiers on board were either Special Forces or mercenaries operating in Laos. The white helicopters refueled at Bastogne on two other occasions during my stay. On both episodes the pilots called in on our frequency.

The Pathfinder bunker was a tight squeeze for the three of us, but it had adequate overhead cover. The rains remained heavy, and one night while we were sleeping, the bunker filled with water. The three of us must have been exhausted, because we didn't even notice until morning. Fortunately our poncho liners kept us warm. Larry and I had just our faces protruding out of the water. Ron, however, had scrounged an air mattress from somewhere and was floating on top of it. We laughed until the bunker started caving in, then got out quickly.

A few days later, with the help of engineers, a new Pathfinder bunker was constructed. It was roomy enough to sleep four soldiers comfortably. Since the South Vietnamese Airborne operation was over, Buz came out to join us.

Life was a lot easier having four Pathfinders to share all the work. One would control aircraft, another could relay messages from the aircraft to the units with a second radio, a third could oversee the LZs, while the fourth took care of miscellaneous functions such as assisting with sling loads and manifesting rides for troops trying to get back to the rear.

One day three privates arrived at our bunker after unloading from a helicopter. With their pale skin and new fatigues, it was easy to tell they were new in country. Although they were my age or a bit older, they looked remarkably young. They didn't have that look in the eyes that all of the other guys had after being in country for a while.

One of them acted as spokesman. "Excuse me, Corporal! We were told to report here, and you would tell us where our unit was located."

Ron was the closest to them. "What unit you guys with?"

The private cleared his throat, then glanced down at a handwritten piece of paper. "We've been assigned to A Company!"

Ron pointed to the TOC. "A Company's out in the field. You'll have to go over to that big bunker right there, and they'll take care of you."

The private nodded. "Thank you, Corporal!"

As the soldier turned to pick up his gear, Larry leaped off the bunker roof. "Hey! Wait a minute!"

The three soldiers had scared looks on their faces. Larry grabbed the private's sleeve and chuckled. "What the hell is this?"

Completely perplexed, the pitiful-looking soldier glanced up at Larry. "What is what?"

Larry unrolled the soldier's sleeve to reveal a set of black stripes, a rocker sewn under a chevron. "Damn, son! Your unit sees this and you're in a world of shit."

Larry showed the stripes to the rest of us. "Look what he did! He cut the two top chevrons off of some staff sergeant stripes and left the rocker underneath."

We all started laughing. Ron walked over and placed his hand on the soldier's shoulder. "You better get that shit off right now. If the sergeant major sees you, he'll tear your head off and hand it to you!"

Larry grabbed the sleeve again. "What rank do you call this anyway, a staff private?"

Buz and I almost fell off the bunker as our laughter grew louder. The soldier just stared at us like we were lunatics. Finally he broke his silence. "I'm a private first class!"

The other two soldiers wore one stripe on their sleeves. Larry pointed to their rank. "Who the hell do you think you're trying to bullshit? *Those* are PFC stripes!"

One of the two spoke up. "No! It's all changed. This used to be a PFC rank, but now it's E-2!"

We could tell by the young soldier's sincerity that he was telling the truth. Larry shook his head. "Damn! It figures! When I was an E-2 we didn't have anything on our sleeve. Now they give them a stripe!"

The three soldiers became a little more at ease knowing we were just unaware of the new rank structure and not lunatics who had been in Vietnam too long. We talked with them for a few more minutes, and they went on their way. For the rest of our tour we referred to every PFC we saw as a staff private. Personally, I thought the army could have come up with something better.

Ironically, a few days later Lieutenant Wilberding brought out our mail and informed us that the army had changed the Pathfinder badge as well. No longer could the large, colorful cloth badge be worn on the sleeve of the dress uniform. The army had developed a colored metal pin to wear on the pocket flap instead.

As the war continued, only Pathfinders assigned to Pathfinder units were authorized to wear the large patch on the fatigue pocket. All other Pathfinder-qualified personnel wore a small cloth badge identical to the metal badge, except subdued, on the pocket flap.

Around mid-June 1968, Ron rotated back to Camp Eagle. Larry returned to the rear as well, but just to pick up some supplies. He was to return to Bastogne in a few days. Buz controlled aircraft while I was taking a break in the bunker. A pilot from the 2d/17th Cavalry requested landing instructions and asked Buz if a Pathfinder would meet his bird at the log pad. I headed off down the hill.

When I arrived at the pad, the pilot told me that one of his unit's Cobra gunships had gone down a few kilometers away. I was surprised, because we had not even heard about it. The two Cobra aviators involved in the crash were rescued successfully, but the sensitive items like the radio and weapons systems had to be recovered before the enemy got their hands on them. Time was critical.

Since the ideal situation would be to sling-load the entire aircraft up from the jungle floor, the aviation unit commander wanted a Pathfinder to assess the damage and surrounding area to see if lifting the gunship out was feasible. My problem would be physically getting on the ground at the crash site. The pilot said that there were no clearings near the wreckage where he could land. I thought about rappelling in, but decided against it. If the enemy was nearby, I would be stranded all alone on the ground with no way of getting pulled back out.

The best I could do would be to examine the wreckage from above. The pilot waited while I ran back to the bunker and grabbed my weapon and LBE along with a few smoke and fragmentation grenades. Buz didn't want to miss out on the adventure, but he had to stay and control air traffic.

I jumped on the bird, and in no time we were hovering over the crash site. The pilot took the helicopter down until it was literally touching the tops of the trees. I climbed out onto the skids to get a better look at the wreckage. The Cobra pilots were extremely lucky they had survived the crash, because the gunship was messed up. Its skids had shattered and broken off, and the aircraft appeared to have broken apart in three places.

An eerie feeling came over me as I stared down at the fractured helicopter. A Cobra was a sleek, flying war machine that spewed destruction on the enemy. There, however, lying crumpled in the jungle foliage, surrounded by towering trees, it looked like a broken toy.

I turned the flight helmet's mouthpiece to my lips to talk to the pilot. "It looks really damaged, sir. It doesn't look like it can be sling-loaded out in one piece, that's for sure."

The pilot's voice crackled over the intercom. "What about the guns? They still in place?"

I stood out on the skids and stretched away from the aircraft as far as I could to get a good view. "Roger that, sir! So far it looks like nothing's been touched."

The pilot's voice sounded insistent. "We've got to get that stuff out of there!"

I was contemplating a solution when my peripheral vision detected movement off to my right. Through a small opening in the trees I spotted at least three figures dressed in green and carrying AKs. They were looking right up at us.

As I scrambled to get back inside the aircraft, I heard the door gunner yell, "Gooks! Gooks! We got gooks at four o'clock."

Crawling across the cabin floor, I grabbed my M-16, flicked the selector switch to automatic, and spun around to a sitting position. The door gunner's M-60 began spitting bullets. The gooks returned fire almost simultaneously, but not before two of them were cut down. Muzzle flashes were coming from some thickets farther back. Just as I aimed at the flashes and opened fire, bullets ripped through the cabin. The chopper bolted straight up and to the left; I felt like I was shooting from a Ferris-wheel seat.

The AC's voice barked over the intercom. "Everyone all right?"

After we all said we were okay, he continued, "Shit! We're never going to recover anything from that wreckage now!"

I did have one idea and figured I might as well express it. "Well, sir. There is one way. I believe the LRPs have a rope ladder. I know some of them would volunteer to help me retrieve the equipment."

The AC didn't even take a moment to ponder the idea. "Negative! There's no time now. The site is compromised. Everything will have to be destroyed."

After another lapse of silence the AC's voice returned over the intercom. "We'll keep the bad guys away until the gunships arrive on station."

Our chopper remained at the site, circling the wreckage. Although there were no enemy soldiers in sight, the crew chief and door gunner continued firing short bursts into the surrounding jungle just in case. I had a few magazines left and thought I might as well join in the action. Hell! You never knew when you might get lucky. A short while later the gunships transmitted that they were only a few miles north of our location. Once the Cobras came into view, our chopper hightailed it back to Bastogne.

I reached the Pathfinder bunker in time to watch the two Cobras conduct gun runs on the crash site. With each pass they blasted the wreckage with rockets and miniguns. I wondered if the aviators felt any emotion at having to destroy one of their own Cobras. Although it seemed like a waste, it was the right thing to do. It was much better to demolish the aircraft and its accessories than chance having the gooks get hold of anything or, more important, risk American lives trying to retrieve it.

The twenty-fourth of June started out like any ordinary day at Bastogne. We had gone through another night of sporadic engagements as the NVA probed the perimeter. Air traffic was moderate, so I was alone on top of the bunker, controlling aircraft. It was hotter than hell as the sun beat down unrelentingly. I received a call from a division helicopter requesting takeoff.

"Bastogne Control! This is Eagle Four-seven-seven, ready for takeoff. Over!"

I scanned the firebase and sighted the chopper starting to lift up. "Roger, Eagle Four-seven-seven! I have you in sight. Winds are calm at this time. Enemy situation negative. You are clear for departure to the south of the road. Over."

Keeping the aircraft in traffic patterns on the southern side of Bastogne allowed us better visibility and control. The northern side of the firebase remained covered with tall trees and dense jungle extending right up to the perimeter.

"Bastogne Control! Eagle Four-seven-seven! Request takeoff to the north. Over."

Unless the pilot had a good reason, I did not want him departing to the north. First of all, the chopper would pass in front of the artillery guns. Second, he would have to gain altitude quickly to clear the trees.

"Eagle Four-seven-seven! That's a negative! You are clear for departure to the south. Over."

There was a slight pause, then the pilot answered. "Bastogne! This is Four-seven-seven! We have a zero six on board who needs to view the firebase and artillery emplacements from that direction. Over."

A 0-6 was a full-bird colonel. The artillery batteries were not firing just then and there was no inbound traffic. "Roger, Four-seven-seven! You are clear for takeoff to the north. Be advised of tall trees upon your departure."

"Four-seven-seven, roger."

The chopper lifted up, flying along the pathway of the big guns. It banked sharply to the north, then cleared the tops of the trees by about three feet. Everything was perfect. It had just leveled off when I heard a loud *whack*. A puff of gray smoke shot out of the helicopter's engine housing, then a second puff of gray smoke appeared, followed by a loud whine. The chopper dropped out of the sky, falling backward as if a giant weight had landed on its tail boom. As it crashed through the trees, it disappeared from sight.

I was stunned. I'd never had a bird crash while I was controlling traffic.

I yelled below to Larry, who was inside the bunker. "Larry! Get up here right away. I just had a bird go down. Hurry up and take over the radio."

Larry came rushing out. "Are you shitting me?"

"I wish I was! Notify the TOC for help." I passed him the handset and leaped from the bunker. I had to get to the crew.

The spot where the aircraft crashed appeared to be about forty meters north of the firebase, straight-line distance. Unfortunately, I had to sprint to the southwest corner at the break in the wire to get through the perimeter's defenses, then double back. My adrenaline was pumping as I raced to the concertina wire. Sharp barbs punctured my hands as I yanked the spiked wire off an engineer stake. Before I entered the jungle canopy, I took one last look at the vicinity where the chopper had gone down. I needed to find a prominent terrain feature that I could use to maintain my bearings. I sighted two tall trees protruding above the skyline close to where the crash occurred. With their image in mind, I plunged my way through the jungle foliage.

The vegetation was immensely thick, covered with a mesh of wait-a-minute vines. As I twisted and shoved my way through the tangled mess, the underbrush and briars ripped at my skin and wrapped around my legs and ankles. Finally after twenty meters or so the jungle thinned out. I had to halt momentarily to get my bearings. Frantically I searched the horizon to locate the two tall trees. Unfortunately, from where I was the tops of all the trees appeared even. I felt myself approaching a state of frenzy. I had to get to the helicopter crew.

I was distracted by movement off to my left. To my surprise, I discovered soldiers hiding in the nearby bushes. The one closest to me was crouched down in a squatting position, staring up at me. The others behind him had turned around and were sort of duckwalking away through the underbrush.

I assumed they were all members of the battalion's Hawk Recon platoon, since all wore floppy boonie hats. I expected the soldier closest to me to follow the others. Instead, he remained absolutely still. I sensed something odd about him, however. As I studied him closer, I noticed his uniform was solid green instead of tiger-striped. His weapon looked different as well. Instead of being black like an M-16, it had a wooden stock like an AK-47. What's more, the barrel was pointed at my midsection. My eyes immediately traveled to the soldier's face, confirming my worst fear. The guy wasn't American at all; he was an NVA soldier!

My heart skipped rapidly. My legs weakened. He just continued to stare at me. I studied his face, hoping to anticipate his next move, but his expression was stony, completely absent of emotion.

As I stood there, unarmed, I didn't feel terrified really, just numb. At that moment I somehow resigned myself to the knowledge that I was going to die. My life was going to end at that exact instant, on that little plot of jungle, ten thousand miles from home, with nobody ever really knowing what happened.

I looked down at the barrel of the AK. It would be the last thing I would see before the end of my existence. My body stiffened, awaiting the impact of the bullets. To my complete and utter astonishment, instead of pulling the trigger, the enemy soldier just backed away slowly until he faded into the jungle.

I don't know how long I stood there. Somehow, significant emotional events in combat seemed to drag out in one's mind. In actuality, the whole incident probably occurred in a matter of seconds.

My thoughts returned to the downed chopper and its crew. Luckily, I spotted wisps of gray smoke billowing up from some trees about forty meters at my eleven o'clock. I ran as fast as I could to the location. When I arrived at the crash site, I found a member of the crew standing a few feet outside the aircraft. He was dazed and in shock. I asked him if he was okay, but he just mumbled. The man was well over six feet tall and still had his flight helmet on. I reached up and lifted the helmet from his head, then grabbed him by the shoulders and escorted him out of danger to a nearby tree.

The helicopter had landed upright, but it was easy to tell by the damage that it had hit hard. The tail boom was completely severed. I was facing the right side of the aircraft, which was exposed. The left side and the rear were embedded in dense jungle. The chopper's left skid had snapped off, causing the right side to tilt way upward. Smoke was coming from someplace inside the chopper.

A soldier lay on the floor of the cabin with his upper torso slumped over to the outside. His helmet, which was secured to his head by his chin strap, was pressed into the ground. He was a big man, so instead of trying to push him up from the front, I jumped up inside the cabin and grabbed him from behind by his LBE. Glancing down at his rank, I saw the eagle of a full-bird colonel.

I failed in my attempt to pull him upward; the rim of his helmet was caught on the underside of the aircraft. Reaching down, I released the chin strap to free his head from the steel pot. As I pulled his head out of the helmet, I realized that spending any more time on him was useless; the colonel's skull was crushed. He had obviously died on impact.

The smoke inside the cabin thickened. The air smelled like burning wires and I could hear crackling sounds. I turned my attention to a second soldier. His body lay lifeless, sprawled halfway out the other side of the cabin. Hurriedly, I scrambled over some twisted seats and other debris to get to him. The aircraft tilted slightly. Cautiously, I moved to where the man lay. As the top portion of his body became visible, it was evident that he too had been killed on impact. From the way he was positioned, I couldn't get a look at his rank or name tag.

I scanned the front of the aircraft to check on the pilots. Both were alive and stirring. I heard voices outside and noticed that a few members of the battalion had just arrived to help them out. The crackling was growing louder, and the fumes were making it difficult to breathe. I took one last look around, then hopped outside the aircraft.

I headed to the injured crew member I had left by the tree. I asked him how he was doing, but he was still incoherent.

A young lieutenant approached with a couple of men. "We're here to help!"

I pointed to the crew member standing beside me. "He was in the crash and needs medical attention right way."

The lieutenant motioned to his soldiers. "Help get this guy to the firebase. Be careful with him."

The soldiers placed the crew member's arms over their shoulders and carted him off through the jungle. I looked to the front of the helicopter and saw that the pilots were being led away as well. I shouted to the group, "Are all of the crew members accounted for?"

One of them yelled back, "We got everybody!"

I turned to the lieutenant. He was staring at the colonel's body on the cabin floor. "What about him?"

I shook my head. "He's dead, sir! There's a guy on the other side. He's dead, too. They were both killed on impact."

Just then someone with a voice sounding of authority shouted, "Okay! Let's clear the area. We got everybody! This thing's going to blow."

The lieutenant touched me on the shoulder. "Time to go. There's nothing more we can do. We got to get out of here!"

As we turned to move away, I thought I heard someone moan. The lieutenant halted; he'd heard it, too.

Suddenly from inside the chopper someone yelled, "Help! Help!"

I ran back to the aircraft. On the far side of the cabin floor, lying in a mound of twisted seats, lay a soldier. His flight suit identified him as the crew chief. He must have been lodged behind the door gunner well and struggled forward when he awoke. Although he had brought his knees forward in an attempt to get up, his chest was pinned to the floor by the seat webbing. His face was turned in my direction and his left shoulder looked like it was dislocated.

"Please . . . help me . . . I can't . . . move."

I made sure my voice was calm. "No sweat! We'll get you out!"

I placed my hands on the cabin floor to hop inside. The metal felt like the top of a hot stove; I had to pull away quickly. A strong odor of burnt petroleum filled the air as the crackling grew louder.

The young crew chief was stricken with panic. "Hurry! Please, get me out. I don't want to die!"

I turned to the lieutenant. "We've got to do something quick!"

He placed his hand firmly on my shoulder. "You can't go in there! It's going to blow any second."

I started to panic. I'd honestly thought we could get him out, but reality was setting in. I stared into the young crew chief's face. His eyes were pleading for me to help him. He began yelling, "It's hot! I'm burning! Oh God, please don't let me die!"

I watched in horror as JP-4 fuel started dripping down

on him from the top of the chopper. Each trickle ignited as it landed on him. His hair caught on fire, and he started to scream. Next I watched the back of his neck go up and then his shoulders. I lunged forward and reached my hand into the aircraft in a halfhearted gesture, but the heat singed my face and arm.

The lieutenant shouted for help to a small group of soldiers standing about thirty feet away. They didn't respond. Frantically my eyes searched the cabin for a fire extinguisher. The young crew chief stared into my eyes, his contorted in agony. He screamed, "Oh God! I'm going to die. I'm on fire! I'm burning! Please don't let me die like this!"

I cursed myself for not having my rifle with me. Frenzied, I turned to the lieutenant. "Give me your weapon!"

His voice apologetic, he threw his arms up in disgust. "I didn't bring it with me! I left it in the foxhole!"

The young crew chief let out a continuous scream as the flames engulfed him. The lieutenant grabbed me forcefully. "C'mon! You got to get back, right now!"

I didn't resist as he pulled me away; I knew he was right. As we moved back, the young soldier's screams pierced the jungle. Suddenly the entire helicopter shot up in flames. Eventually the screaming ceased. I just stood there, in shock.

The lieutenant tried to reassure me, but I shook my head. "I didn't get him out!"

He placed his hand on my shoulder. "You did more than anyone else. You would have been killed, too, if you went in there."

I walked a little way with the lieutenant. I told him about running into the small group of NVA. As we parted, he promised he would relay the information of the enemy sighting to the TOC. I headed back the rest of the way to the firebase alone. It never dawned on me that I could run into the NVA again. The vivid, horrific scene of the young crew chief being burned alive ran over and over again in my mind, causing me to question my actions.

Why didn't I notice him in the first place? Why didn't I

jump in to save him no matter what? Am I a coward? Why didn't I bring my weapon along? I could have ended his pain.

As I broke out of the jungle and started to cross through the wire, I ran into Charlie Beckwith. I must have appeared very distraught, because he stopped and snapped, "What's wrong?"

My voice trembled as I replied. "I just saw a man get burned alive, sir. It was the most horrible thing I've ever seen."

His reply was compassionate but stern. "You get your head on straight right now or you're no damn good to me or anyone else, you got that?"

I straightened up a bit and barked, "Yes, sir! No slack!"

Inside, I was angry. Didn't Beckwith hear what I'd just told him? As I continued walking, I pondered what he'd said to me. Charlie Beckwith was one tough soldier, and I had a lot of respect for him. Therefore I had to conclude that he was right. I wouldn't be any good to anyone, including myself, if I didn't get my head on straight.

When I arrived at the Pathfinder bunker, I told the guys what happened, both at the crash site and about bumping into the NVA patrol. In the latter, we concluded that the NVA soldiers were a recon team and did not kill me because they would have given away their position. Ironically, I was not a threat because I wasn't armed. I wondered how many guys had escaped death in combat because they didn't have their weapon with them. Unbelievable! Still, I was angry at myself for not having my rifle with me at the crash site. It could have ended the young crew chief's agony.

That evening I attended the battalion briefing in case anyone on the staff had questions concerning the crash. The only time the incident was mentioned was right at the end of the briefing, by Colonel Beckwith. He was informed that a captain on his staff had rescued the pilots, and he was putting him in for a Soldiers Medal. I didn't see the officer at the site, but that doesn't mean he wasn't there. I knew he wasn't in the cabin with me, however.

The next day a detail was sent to police up the charred remains. I didn't envy that job. The men returned later carrying the corpses in ponchos. It was a sad sight. I learned that the two soldiers killed on impact were Col. Richard S. Pohl, the division artillery commander, and his sergeant major, Leroy J. Browning. The crew chief's name was Sp5. William E. Badger.

A few days later some aviators came out to Bastogne to interview me with a tape recorder. They were investigating the crash. I was the only eyewitness who actually saw the bird go down. They had been informed that everyone died instantly. I told them that in the crew chief's case, that wasn't so. They took down my deposition and left.

A short time after the investigation I was told by one of Beckwith's NCOs from the TOC that I was going to be put in for a Soldiers Medal as well. I thought, For what? For running through the jungle without my weapon? For bumping into an NVA patrol unarmed? Or for not having enough balls to save the crew chief when the chips were down? Because of my actions, or lack of, I honestly questioned whether I could accept such an award if it was approved. In the end I didn't have to worry. As with all Pathfinder award recommendations from attached units, the recommendation was lost somewhere in the process.

I was surprised when Mitch showed up to replace me. I was told that I was going back to Eagle for normal rotation. Although that may have been true, I suspected that Lieutenant Wilberding felt I needed a break after the chopper crash.

As my helicopter lifted out of Bastogne, I stared at the crash site below. The small plot of jungle had been transformed into a blackened piece of earth. In its center lay a clump of twisted, charred metal. Sadly, my thoughts returned to the young crew chief. His face and the torment he endured would haunt me the rest of my life. I made a solemn promise to myself that I would never be without a weapon again, ever.

Chapter Fifteen

I arrived back at Camp Eagle to discover that, in a few short days, on 1 July 1968, the historic and famous 101st Airborne Division would convert from its Airborne status and designation to that of airmobile. In other words, the division would trade its parachutes for helicopters. That drastic transformation to a "leg" (nonjump) unit caused concern for most paratroopers about the loss of their jump pay, $55 a month for enlisted and $110 for officers. Luckily, the army decided to continue paying jump pay to everyone then assigned to the division until they departed the unit.

All Pathfinder detachments were Airborne regardless of what units they were assigned, so we didn't have to worry. The Pathfinders, LRPs, and the Riggers would remain on jump status, and their units continued to select only Airborne-qualified personnel.

Since the division would begin receiving a vast number of helicopters, our small aviation battalion was the unit most impacted by the new change. It would expand to over three times its size, becoming an aviation group. Our Pathfinder detachment was also scheduled to increase in both personnel and rank. Our new detachment structure would call for a captain, four lieutenants, and various NCO/enlisted positions, eventually totaling about forty members.

In order to support the division's increase in airmobile operations, having more Pathfinders on board as soon as possible was imperative. Lieutenant Wilberding was informed that within the next week or so, ten enlisted Pathfinders would be permanently assigned to our detachment from the

Pathfinder detachment of the 1st Aviation Brigade. It made sense for the army to immediately transfer combat-seasoned Pathfinders to our newly formed unit rather than for us to await newly assigned personnel from the States.

Although our new aviation unit, the 160th Aviation Group, would be formally activated on 1 July 1968, it would be months before all personnel and equipment arrived. Our small Pathfinder detachment would transfer, on paper, from the Headquarters Company of the 101st Aviation Battalion to the Headquarters Company, 160th Aviation Group.

The title of the newly designated 160th Aviation Group was short-lived. The following year, on 25 June 1969, the group was redesignated the 101st Aviation Group. In fact, a distinctive unit insignia was never designed for the 160th, which is quite uncommon considering the long tradition of U.S. Army heraldry. As young enlisted men, we never found out why. Since we didn't have a unit insignia when we departed Vietnam, we wore our old Wings of the Eagle crest.

Since a captain would be coming on board as the new commander of our detachment, Lieutenant Wilberding wanted all of the equipment checked out for accountability and serviceability. It was the first week of July 1968, and I was examining some radios and other equipment with Frankie Farino. Frankie was quite a character, an Italian from New York and very proud of his nationality. Since I came from the Northeast and grew up in a mixed Irish-Italian neighborhood, we got along well.

Frankie was about my height, stocky, and well built. He sported a crop of dense black, wavy hair and, because of his thick facial growth, always appeared to need a shave.

Frankie's call sign was Dealer, and for good reason. He was a fast talker who could get anybody anything, for a price. He was very loyal, however, so detachment members always received a good deal and, on occasion, freebies.

Frankie and I were conducting a commo check on one of the radios when Lieutenant Wilberding entered the tent. I detected a sense of urgency in his voice. "There's a unit in trouble and they need immediate extraction. I need to know if you two will volunteer for the mission."

Frankie and I answered in unison. "Sure, sir!" "No problem, sir!"

Wilberding's expression turned serious. "Good! You two need to get moving ASAP! There's a helicopter arriving here shortly to take both of you out to the unit's location."

I was going to ask a question when Wilberding cut me off. "I don't have time to answer any questions right now. You will be briefed at the pad."

Wilberding turned, walked a few paces, then stopped. "Oh, by the way! Wear your cammies. And make sure they're sterile, no insignia sewn on them at all!"

Frankie and I stared at each other. Not only did Wilberding ask us if we would volunteer for the mission, he was now instructing us to wear a specific uniform, and sterile at that. Perhaps something big or secret was going on.

Wilberding's next remark sent my imagination soaring. "Leave your black hats behind as well!"

Holy shit! Never, ever, had we been told not to bring along our black hats. Frankie and I couldn't move fast enough. We quickly changed into our cammies, gathered up the equipment we would need, and headed for the helipad.

As we hurried to the pad, Frankie couldn't contain his excitement. "Shit! My fiancée would have a fit if she found out I volunteered for something like this."

His remark took me completely by surprise. "What the hell are you talking about, Frankie? Every day you're a volunteer; you're a Pathfinder!"

"I know, but I haven't told her much about what we do. She thinks I just sit around and play cards all the time. She doesn't mind me gambling when it comes to money and other stuff, but if she found out I was taking any chances with my life, she'd kill me. We're getting married as soon as I get home."

"Frankie! There is nothing she can do to you if you are dead."

Frankie's harsh New York City accent always caused me to laugh. Sometimes he sounded like a Mafia hit man. "Hell, you don't know my girl! She'll put some kind of curse on me or something."

Lieutenant Wilberding and some captain we didn't know were waiting for us at the helicopter. The captain pointed at us as we approached. "These your men?"

Lieutenant Wilberding stiffened up a bit as he answered. "Yes, sir!"

The captain moved close to Frankie and me so he could be heard above the chopper's whine. "I understand both of you volunteered for this mission. Is that correct?"

We both thought the question was stupid but nodded anyway. "Yes, sir!"

The captain smiled slightly. "Good!"

He turned to Wilberding. "That will be all, Lieutenant! Thanks again for all your help!"

Lieutenant Wilberding gave Frankie and me a thumbs-up as he walked by. "The captain here will fill you in on the details of the mission. Looks like it's going to be a good one, guys! I'm envious!"

As Wilberding walked away, the captain motioned for Frankie and me to follow him. "Let's move over here a few feet away from the noise so I can brief you two on the mission."

Frankie and I stared at each other as we followed the captain. I knew just what Frankie was thinking. "Who the hell is this guy?" The unit patch he was wearing was unfamiliar. One thing was for sure: he was not a member of the 101st.

Once we were a few paces away from the chopper, the captain's expression became serious. "We don't have a lot of time! What I'm about to tell you is considered classified information. That means you are not authorized to relay this information to anyone else. Now realistically, I know you could tell some of your buddies over a few beers and no one would probably ever know. I trust, however, that neither of you will do that. Your lieutenant speaks highly of you both."

The captain paused for a moment to let his words sink in, then continued. "Yesterday a Special Forces Mike Force operating out of Phu Bai was conducting an operation along a mountain range and ran head-on into a large NVA unit accompanied by tanks. During the encounter the Mike Force destroyed one of the tanks and killed a number of NVA soldiers before finally breaking contact. Unfortunately, hundreds of enemy troops immediately surrounded the base of the mountain, blocking all avenues of escape. Luckily the Mike Force made its way to the mountaintop and called for an extraction."

I had been exposed to a number of Special Forces officers while a Pathfinder at Fort Benning. I knew that a Mike Force generally consisted of a handful of Special Forces advisers leading a large number of indigenous troops in various missions, such as reconnaissance or rapid reaction into denied areas. This unit's home base was the Special Forces FOB (forward operational base) at Phu Bai.

The captain looked at us momentarily to make sure he had our attention, then went on with the briefing. "A rescue attempt was launched earlier this morning by the Kingbees. Just as their flight got close to the LZ, the NVA opened up with 37mm antiaircraft guns. One of the Kingbees' choppers was shot out of the sky and burst into flames. Everyone on board was killed. The rest of the flight had to abort the mission and return to the FOB."

The Kingbees, a CH-34 helicopter unit, regularly supported Special Forces. Unfortunately the CH-34 was a much older and slower-moving helicopter that resembled a grasshopper with wheels. The old, seasoned chopper was certainly no match for lethal enemy antiaircraft guns.

I heard our chopper's engine grow louder. The pilots were motioning for us to hurry on board. The captain gestured that he understood.

Until then the captain had appeared emotionally

detached. Suddenly a hint of despondency shadowed his face. "At present the Mike Force is severely outnumbered, low on ammunition, and has a number of wounded needing immediate medical attention. With the enemy steadily closing in, it is estimated that if they are not extracted from the mountaintop by dusk, all of its members will be annihilated."

His voice grew harsh. "Special Forces command is not going to let that happen!"

He looked as if he were waiting for me to agree with him. When it became evident that I was not going to respond, he continued. "The Kingbees have informed us that the extraction LZ is just a tiny clearing that at best can hold only one helicopter. To make matters worse, there is only one opening for the aircraft to both enter and exit, making it impossible for their type of helicopters to turn around. Every available Huey in your unit is being rounded up as we speak. Since the LZ is questionable, the pilots have insisted that you Pathfinders be on the ground."

I knew time was short, but I had to ask a few quick questions. "How many men are we talking about extracting, sir?"

The captain's expression remained grave as he glanced downward. "Ten Americans and 154 indigenous!"

Slowly his eyes rose until they were level with mine, his voice solemn. "A total of 164 men!"

Frankie and I stared at each other. God! That was a lot of men to pull off a mountain before sunset. Especially using a one-bird LZ and with the surrounding ridges covered by enemy antiaircraft guns.

The pilots were now gesturing feverishly for us to get on board. I motioned for Frankie to board the chopper. I had one more question I needed answered. "How many choppers have been rounded up for the extraction, sir?"

The captain's head dropped. "Last count was five or six . . . but we're hoping for more."

I didn't respond. I reached out and shook the captain's hand, then climbed on board the chopper. Frankie saw the concern on my face. I would fill him in on the way. Once the aircraft gained altitude, the crew chief handed me a headset and motioned that the aircraft commander wanted a word with me.

I plugged into the aircraft's intercom and introduced myself. "This is Corporal Burns, the senior Pathfinder, sir!"

As with most pilots, the AC was cordial and calm. "I take it you were thoroughly briefed on the mission. Just wanted to know if you had any questions or immediate concerns I can answer."

"As matter of fact, there is! You wouldn't happen to know the exact number of aircraft supporting the operation, would you, sir?"

The AC seemed genuinely pleased that he could answer my question. "Just minutes ago I received word that there will be a total of eight aircraft!"

Eight helicopters was better than five or six. However, given the time constraint, the large number of soldiers to be evacuated, the small number of aircraft involved, the turnaround time for each load, and the problem that only one helicopter could land at a time, this operation was going to be almost impossible to pull off.

I scooted across the floor to where Frankie sat and briefed him on the operation. Both of us were ecstatic at having been selected for such a mission. Our excitement was overshadowed, however, by the reality that if we did not succeed in getting everyone off the mountaintop before dusk, those left behind would be killed or captured. Included in that number would be Frankie and me, since, as Pathfinders, we would be the last two persons extracted from the LZ.

Time would be critical once we landed, so I took out my notebook and started planning the extraction. I was attempting to calculate the number of sorties when something crossed my mind. If the unit was in such deep shit, why weren't they receiving air support in the form of air strikes? Whenever the annihilation of a unit was imminent, every available jet aircraft was called upon to assist. To me, it was the perfect scenario for the jet jockies. Hell, here was a chance to wipe out a bunch of NVA, along with their tanks and antiaircraft guns.

I pressed the button on the intercom to talk to the AC. "Sir! Corporal Burns!"

"Whatcha got?"

"Well, sir! I was just wondering why someone hasn't called for air strikes or a reaction force to help out these guys. Since this unit's in deep shit, shouldn't they be considered top priority?"

The AC began to reply, but stopped. After a long pause, he came back on the intercom. "You were thoroughly briefed on the mission, right?"

I thought his response was odd, almost guarded. "Well, I guess so, sir!"

Again there was a pause before he spoke. "I'm sure there's some reasonable explanation why air strikes and other support were not feasible!"

I felt something strange was going on but decided not to question it. "Roger!"

I continued to plan for the mission. Every so often I peered at the ground below. I recognized the A Shau and assumed we would be landing any moment. Instead, it looked as if we were flying beyond the valley. Huge mountain ranges stretched across the landscape as far as I could see. The vegetation was remarkably lush and thick. Also absent was the familiar sight of bomb craters.

Frankie tapped me on the knee. He then pointed to his watch and shrugged his shoulders, indicating that the flight was taking much longer than usual. There was definitely something more than peculiar about the mission.

As I pondered the situation, things just didn't add up. We were specifically asked to volunteer for the mission. We were told to wear sterile cammies and leave our black hats behind. Although a unit was in a position of being wiped out, it was not receiving support in the form of air strikes or a reaction force. Furthermore, it was taking almost double the usual flight time for us to get to a destination.

Another thought occurred to me. I don't know why I hadn't thought about it earlier. I guess I was just caught up in all the excitement. There we were, en route to evacuate a besieged unit surrounded by enemy antiaircraft guns, yet our helicopter was not accompanied by gunships.

I couldn't erase the feeling rolling around in my gut. Something strange was going on, and Frankie and I both had the right to know. As the senior Pathfinder, it was my responsibility to find out.

I pushed the button on the intercom to talk to the AC, my voice somewhat sarcastic since I felt that I was getting the runaround. "This is Corporal Burns, sir! It sure is a long flight to the LZ!"

This time the AC's reply was curt. "We'll be at the location any minute!"

The hell with it. The worst thing that could happen to me was an ass-chewing. "What the hell is really going on, sir?"

This time the pause was so long, I was beginning to think the AC honestly hadn't heard me. I was just getting ready to ask him again when his voice broke the silence.

"We're crossing the fence!"

Crossing the fence? It took a moment or two for my mind to comprehend. I might have been a little slow at times, but I wasn't an idiot. Holy shit! We were crossing the border! We were going into Laos!

Now everything made sense. The Mike Force running into tanks and being surrounded. The absence of air strikes. Wearing sterile fatigues and no black hats. The long flight time. No gunship escort. Even though Laos was like New York City for the NVA, it was, unbelievably, off-limits to U.S. forces. If the helicopter we were flying on got shot down or captured, America could just claim that the pilots unwittingly strayed off course.

The AC's voice came back over the intercom. "I wasn't supposed to disclose that part of the mission, but screw it. As far as I'm concerned, since you two are putting your asses on the line, you have a need to know. Remember! Once this is over, it never happened!"

I had a much greater concern on my mind than going into Laos. "Where are the pax being transported to, sir?"

"Once they're on board we'll be taking them straight to the FOB at Phu Bai."

Damn! That's what I was afraid of. Not only was the turnaround time going to be long, the aircraft would also have to refuel more often between sorties.

Frankie slapped my boot to get my attention. He wanted to know what was going on. I placed my finger on the cabin floor, drew an imaginary line, then slid my finger across it. Frankie's eyes widened as his mouth formed the word "Laos!" I nodded my head in affirmation. As I pondered the situation, a funny thought occurred to me. If we ended up getting captured, Frankie would probably strike up some kind of deal with the enemy.

Towering mountains lay off to our front, covered by scattered layers of fog that lingered hauntingly. Our chopper was descending straight toward a particular mountain. As we got closer it looked as though the pilots were going to deliberately fly us right into the mountainside.

All of a sudden a cleared depression appeared on the edge of a sheer cliff about fifty meters below the mountaintop. It looked as if some fairy tale giant had just hollowed out that small piece of the jungle with his hand. I waited for enemy antiaircraft guns to open up and blow us out of the sky. Instead, our chopper flared into a hover and set down hastily into the tiny clearing without incident.

Frankie and I quickly unassed the bird and were greeted by a Special Forces adviser. While Frankie cautiously guided the chopper back around, I instructed the adviser to have a group ready to get on board as soon as the helicopter was facing back out of the depression.

The adviser pointed to a group of about thirty "little people" lying clumped together in a heap. Many had torn and bloody uniforms and were bandaged. "These are my wounded. I need to get them out first!"

Although a few were unconscious, most could walk with assistance. "Okay! Let's get them on the chopper ASAP!"

Hurriedly we carried and aided the wounded soldiers onto the aircraft. Usually a chopper can safely carry six to eight soldiers with equipment. Since we didn't have a whole lot of time and the little people were smaller in size, I didn't stop the loading until I counted ten placed on board.

Just as I grabbed the radio handset to clear the pilot for takeoff, the Special Forces adviser ran up to me. "I need one of the Americans to go with this load. That way we'll have an adviser already in place to help out at the other end."

I was afraid that I might have overloaded the aircraft. Under normal circumstances I probably would not have loaded any more personnel and equipment on the helicopter. But it was not a normal situation.

I tapped the adviser on the shoulder. "Tell him to hurry up and get on board!"

I had to clear the pilot for takeoff. There wasn't time for formality. "This is Pathfinder Control. You're ready to go! Be advised you are riding heavy with ten WIAs on board and one big guy. Over."

The pilot's response was more of a question than a reply. "I understand eleven pax in all? Over."

I glanced into the open cabin of the chopper. It was just a big heap of bodies with arms and legs protruding everywhere. "That's affirmative! You are clear for takeoff!"

As the helicopter lifted a few feet I could hear the strain on the engine. The pilot's voice blared over the radio. "Wish us luck!"

The chopper lurched forward out over the edge of the cliff and sailed across the mountains.

I felt good that the first chopper had gotten out okay. I hoped our luck would continue. I glanced around at my surroundings. Within my view were five or six American Special Forces advisers and about forty indigenous personnel. Most everyone was down on one knee, weapon at the ready, and staring up at the slope to our left. All of the little people were dark skinned with very bushy, jet-black hair. I guessed them to be either Montagnards or Cambodians; they were definitely not Vietnamese. Everyone was clad in tiger-stripe fatigues and bush hats.

The Special Forces adviser who was with me at the chopper approached. He appeared to be in his thirties, and I assumed by his manner that he was the senior person. I didn't know if he was an officer or enlisted, and I didn't ask.

His voice was friendly. "Glad you guys could make it. Appreciate your help."

I didn't know whether to refer to him as "Sergeant" or "sir." I'd heard that Special Forces soldiers, although highly professional, were real informal. "Thanks!"

I glanced over at the wounded. "Looks like you can definitely use some help, too!"

The adviser reached into a small plastic pouch and took out some of the contents. It looked like chewing tobacco. Although the situation was serious, he smiled. "Hell! We could have used some help for the past few days."

He placed the tobacco in his mouth and began chewing. "I guess you've been told that we've got to get everyone off this mountain ASAP."

I nodded. "Roger that!"

While we were talking, I looked over the unit. It was evident that the troops were well disciplined. Although it was searing hot in the sun, the troops stayed remarkably still and quiet.

The adviser noticed my interest. "The Yards are great soldiers. I wouldn't trade them for anything in the world." "Yards" was a term fondly used by Americans to describe Montagnard tribesmen. They were fierce, loyal fighters, equipped, trained, and led by American Special Forces.

The Special Forces adviser continued, "We got security spread all around the LZ, but my guess is that the NVA are going to come at us from up above there." He pointed to the top of the mountain on our left, where most everyone was focusing their attention.

My curiosity needed to be satisfied. "Why do you think they'll hit us from that direction?"

He pointed to the surrounding peaks, then back to the one overlooking us on the left. "The other sides are all too steep. The backside of that mountain has a ridgeline they can traverse without too much difficulty. I've placed a small security force on the top. They'll signal us if they suspect anything."

Frankie monitored the radio while the adviser and I set out to arrange the men into sorties. Each sortie was composed of eight to eleven men, depending on their size and the type of weapons or equipment that would accompany them onto the helicopter. It wasn't long before an aircraft called in for landing instructions.

The chopper was approximately one mile out on a straight-in approach when enemy antiaircraft guns opened up. The helicopter banked a hard right, then swiftly ascended. Instead of landing at our location, he dashed right over the top of the mountain.

We couldn't see the antiaircraft guns from the LZ, but we could hear them. They were positioned on the ridges beneath us.

The pilot barked over the radio. "Dammit! That was too close! Have a load ready for me. I'm going to make my approach from the backside."

That pilot had guts. No one would have said anything if he'd just turned around and left; a helicopter was no match for antiaircraft fire. I was concerned about his approach from behind us over the top of the mountain, however. If enemy soldiers were there, he would be a sitting duck, since he would be hovering at treetop level.

I gave him a chance to change his mind. "Roger! Understand you will be approaching from the southwest. Be advised I do not know the enemy situation. Over!"

We could hear the chopper but couldn't see it. It and the crew would never be recovered if it was shot down in that area. Suddenly the helicopter popped into sight right above me. Quickly I extended both arms in the air, signaling the pilot to guide in on me. Frankie assisted on the radio while I continued using hand-and-arm signals. Eventually we brought him down into the tiny clearing. The second group of wounded was quickly loaded on board. I asked the pilot if he wanted the load lightened to better his chances of a speedy exit, but he declined.

Frankie pressed the handset. "You are clear for take-off!"

The pilot acknowledged. "Roger! It's been fun. I'm going to request some suppressive fire on those guns."

The chopper lifted up a few feet, hovered momentarily, then bounded out of the tiny clearing. We held our breath waiting for the antiaircraft guns to fire on the helicopter, but for some reason they didn't. Although the operation was covert, I hoped that the pilot's request for suppressive fire would be approved. Otherwise, it was only a matter of time until the antiaircraft guns blew another chopper out of the sky the way they had the Kingbees' CH-34.

Quite a bit of time passed after the second sortie departed, or at least it seemed so. More aircraft would have to start arriving pretty damn quick if all of us were going to get off the mountain before dark.

Finally a voice blared over the radio. "Pathfinder Control! This is Kingsmen Two-five approximately five miles to your northeast. Request landing instructions. Over."

I gazed out into the horizon and spotted four aircraft. "Roger, Two-five! This is Pathfinder Control! Winds gusting six to ten knots from the south. Enemy antiaircraft guns positioned on the lower ridges on both sides of the Lima Zulu. Continue approach! Are you part of a flight of four? Over."

"This is Two-five! That's affirmative! Accompanying me is a Kingbee aircraft on a separate mission and a light fire team to take care of those enemy guns. Over." A "light" fire team consisted of two gunships; a "heavy" fire team had three.

We watched the four helicopters speed toward us. The Kingbee CH-34 was in the lead, and directly behind was the Kingsmen slick; the gunships covered each flank. At about one mile out, the CH-34 left the formation and descended to the west. Within moments, enemy antiaircraft guns opened up on the slower helicopter. Without delay the two gunships dropped into their attack formation, one directly behind the other. As the gunships let loose with their rockets and miniguns, the sound of the enemy antiaircraft guns ceased almost immediately.

I discovered later that the Kingbee helicopter's mission was to try to recover their buddies' bodies from the downed CH-34. I never found out if they were successful or not.

Frankie waved to me that the Kingsmen bird was inbound. Having the gunships on station made me feel a lot better. Frankie remained on the radio with Kingsmen Two-five while I helped load another sortie. The Kingsmen aircraft was turned around and loaded in seconds. Two minutes after the aircraft departed, another bird called for instructions.

The next hour went like clockwork. We loaded up eight helicopters arriving in two- to four-minute intervals. Luckily, the gunships continued their onslaught against the enemy gun positions for a good part of the time. Not only were all of the wounded lifted out but over one-third of the force was as well. Unfortunately, because of the lengthy turnaround time and refueling, we had a long wait for the aircraft to return. The waiting was the hard part, especially since the Special Forces advisers were convinced that the NVA were steadily making their way to our location. It was not a matter of if the enemy would attack us; it was a question of when.

While we waited, everyone remained on a high state of alert. Still, I had a chance to talk with a few of the Special Forces advisers. We never discussed anything classified, but I did learn a little about their training and missions. Although they were very informal with one another, the high level of their military bearing and professionalism was quite apparent. It was easy to see why the Yards held the advisers in high esteem. The loyalty and respect seemed mutual.

About an hour or more passed before the choppers finally returned. I decided to keep the loads heavy unless a pilot specifically objected; none did. The enemy antiaircraft guns did not open fire anymore. Perhaps the gunships had wiped them out, or the enemy guns were reluctant to give away their positions to prevent the gunships' wiping them out. In any event, the second group of sorties went off without a hitch.

In less than two hours it would be dusk. A helicopter finally showed up, followed by three more. There was a problem, however, with refueling. We were informed that the other four helicopters would be en route shortly. Since there were only about forty of us remaining, those four choppers would be able to lift us all off the mountain. Everyone's spirits rose as we waited.

Suddenly there was some commotion at the mountaintop to our left. A member of the security force had made his way down the steep slope and was whispering something. The adviser quickly brought his soldiers closer together and repositioned the machine guns.

I waited until he was finished, then approached him. "What's up?"

His expression was stern. "We got trouble. NVA are approaching from the backside of the mountain."

One of the Yards ran up to the adviser, and they conversed momentarily. When the Yard left, the adviser turned to me. "How long do you think it'll be before the choppers arrive?"

I shook my head. "Honestly, I have no idea. I sure hope it's soon, though!"

The adviser's expression did not change. "Okay! When the choppers do arrive, I want these men on the LZ to go first. I'm going to keep the security force in place on top of the mountain for as long as I can. They won't come down onto the LZ until it's time for them to leave or they make contact."

I nodded. "No problem! Sounds good!" Even though I was beginning to get worried, I felt secure knowing that those guys had their shit together.

The adviser had instructed the security force not to fire unless absolutely necessary. So we all knew that once we heard gunfire, we were in big trouble.

Finally a voice came over the radio. "Pathfinder Control! This is Eagle Two-two! Approximately five miles from your location. Request landing instructions. Over."

Frankie and I stared at each other in relief. We were not alone; a few of the Yards close to us smiled.

I grabbed the handset. "Eagle Two-two! This is Pathfinder Control! Winds are calm. Be advised enemy situation has not changed. However, we do have some bad guys closing in on us. Continue approach. Over."

"This is Two-two! Understand! Will be there shortly, partner!"

The adviser held up his hand, and a small group of Yards arose from the brush. Since the pilot of Eagle Two-two had landed on the tiny LZ a few times already, he had the chopper turned around and ready for boarding in no time. The skids barely touched the ground as the little people leaped into the cabin. Within literally seconds, they were whisked away as the helicopter soared skyward.

The second aircraft called for instructions. Once again the chopper turned around without difficulty and was boarded instantly. If the remaining two choppers followed suit, we would all be off the mountain, and out of Laos, in minutes.

Anxiously we waited for the next chopper. Our number totaled twenty-one. Four Americans and seventeen little people. While most of the Yards kept their eyes glued to the mountain, Frankie and I scanned the skies for a chopper.

All of a sudden Frankie pointed. "I see a bird!"

Sure enough, off in the distance a dark speck dotted the

sky. It would not be long before the chopper would be landing. Hopefully the last bird was right behind it.

Suddenly the sound of small-arms fire shattered our optimism.

The adviser pulled me to the side. "Listen, we might run out of time. I want you and your partner to go out on this chopper. Me and the rest of my people will go out on the next one."

I was struck by the offer and the adviser's sincerity, but there was no way. "I really appreciate that, but we couldn't do that even if we wanted to. As Pathfinders, we have to be the last to leave the LZ, no matter what. It's our job!"

I think if the adviser had seen a hint of apprehension in me he would have tried to pursue the matter. He could tell, however, that Frankie and I were not going anywhere.

Frankie shouted that the chopper was inbound and to get the men ready to jump on board. While the adviser got his people together, I ran to help guide the chopper around. Eleven Yards climbed into the cabin. I could hear Frankie instructing the pilot to take off immediately. The aircraft darted out of the depression.

Ten of us were left on the mountain. Four Americans and six Yards, four Yards in the security team plus an RTO and a medic. The Americans consisted of two advisers plus Frankie and me. Since four of us were Americans, the pilot coming to pick us up was going to be carrying out a heavy load.

The gunfire ceased. The four Yards on security tumbled down the slope as they hurried to the LZ. The NVA had gotten too close, so the Yards opened up, hoping to slow the enemy down some. We could hear the NVA yelling to each other from the mountaintop. Fear started to well up inside me. I guess the reality of the situation sneaked up on me. If we didn't get out, we would all be killed or captured. And probably nobody would ever know our fate. Luckily, responsibility always seemed to push fear into a backseat, and my thoughts returned to the mission.

Since, as senior Pathfinder, I had to be the last person

to board the aircraft, I monitored the radio while Frankie, as the next-to-last person, would make sure everyone else got on the chopper okay.

The last chopper called for landing instructions. "Pathfinder Control! This is Kingsmen Two-five! Approximately three miles to the northeast. Request landing instructions. Over."

I felt more secure knowing it was a Kingsmen bird coming in for us. The Kingsmen were pilots from my own unit and were experienced at flying into tight places and situations. Usually they were the pilots tasked to fly missions for the LRPs.

Kingsmen Two-five was Wild Bill Meacham. If anybody could successfully come in to get us out, it would be Captain Meacham. He'd pulled my ass out of the fire on more than one occasion.

"Two-five! Be advised we got bad guys on the mountaintop headed for our location."

Wild Bill's voice always seemed to remain calm no matter what was going down. "Roger! Understand bad guys are closing in. Will continue approach."

Small-arms fire erupted from the mountaintop. I couldn't tell where the bullets were hitting, but I had to let Wild Bill know. "Two-five. Be advised we are receiving small-arms fire. Over."

Wild Bill's reply was monotone; he almost sounded as if he were bored with the whole affair. "Roger. Understand receiving small-arms fire. Over."

The ten of us remained close together, hugging the underbrush on the edge of the LZ. The shooting continued, but none of the rounds were hitting near us. It was obvious that the NVA couldn't see us or hit us from their location. They were shooting blindly or reconning by fire, probably hoping we would return fire and give away our position. But we could hear the rustle of bushes as the NVA attempted to negotiate the steep slope above us.

The senior adviser was crouched next to me, his voice

solemn. "If that helicopter comes in here, there's a good chance that it might get shot down."

I assumed he had a reason for saying that, so I waited for him to continue. "If that happens, we'll need to get to the crew ASAP, if there are any survivors, and then try to E and E [escape and evade] to a safer location. We can request pickup from there."

That soldier was incredible. He always seemed to be one step ahead of a situation. I nodded in agreement, even though the thought of the helicopter getting shot down really bothered me.

I grabbed the handset. "Two-five! Be advised we are still receiving small-arms fire on Lima Zulu. Bad guys are approaching. You may want to abort mission. We are prepared to Echo Echo to a new Papa Zulu. Over."

Wild Bill didn't hesitate in his reply. His gruff voice barked over the handset. "That's a negative! I came all this way and I'm not going back home empty-handed. Do you roger? Over."

"Roger!" I could have kissed the grumpy son of a bitch.

I turned to the adviser. "Get everyone ready! He's coming in!"

Small-arms fire continued to come from the mountaintop, and we heard some shouting. Wild Bill flared into a quick hover, then literally spun the chopper's tail boom around. Before the skids even touched the ground, the door gunner was waving for us to jump on board.

Frankie and I hesitated momentarily to make sure everyone was on the aircraft, then we took off running. I heard noises in the trees on the other side of the LZ. Luckily the bullets were missing the aircraft by a good ten feet.

Frankie and one of the Yards reached out and pulled me into the cabin. I gave a thumbs-up, Wild Bill pulled pitch, and the chopper bolted from the tiny clearing. Some might have called Wild Bill's flying a miracle, others pure skill. I believed it was a mixture of both. I lay back on my rucksack and glanced around the cabin. Everyone was smiling. We were on our way back to Vietnam.

I was trying to get Frankie's attention, but it looked like he was trying to deal one of the Yards out of a necklace or something. Later I stared down at the terrain and recognized the A Shau. Who would have ever dreamed that the A Shau could look good? I felt a twinge of relief that we were out of Laos and heading home.

Wild Bill dropped all of us off at the Special Forces FOB at Phu Bai. The adviser shook our hands and thanked us for a job well done. That was good enough for us. Frankie and I were going to catch a ride back to Camp Eagle with Wild Bill, but we were instructed to wait for the same aircraft that had first brought us to the LZ. The pilot flew us back to our unit and again reiterated that the mission never happened. Frankie and I didn't care. We were glad to have been part of the operation and made it home safely. We both felt pretty good about ourselves.

That night back at the hootch, Frankie and I didn't talk about the mission as we usually did. We were asked a couple of questions, but we avoided mentioning specific details. The guys knew not to bring it up again.

That night as I lay in my cot, I pondered the event. Although it was not the most dangerous mission I had been on, I knew it would be one of the most memorable. Not just because it was in Laos, but because everyone did his part. It was a perfect Pathfinder operation. Besides, as far as I knew, we didn't lose any aircraft or personnel. It didn't get any better than that.

Chapter Sixteen

A day or two after the Laos mission a helicopter went down while participating in an insertion. Its hydraulics failed and the chopper bounced onto the LZ and crashed; all of its crew made it out okay. Another Pathfinder and myself were called out for the aircraft recovery operation. With the help of an infantry platoon that surrounded us providing security, we sling-loaded the wreckage out.

Upon my return to the Pathfinder hootch, I discovered seven new Pathfinders had been assigned to our detachment. They were from the 308th Pathfinder Detachment, 1st Aviation Brigade.

The new members were sitting around on their equipment on one side of the tent while Ron, Joe, and the others sat across from them. I felt a sense of friction as I approached the group. I scanned their uniforms for rank. Most were corporals or privates. I felt a little more at ease; at least none of the new members outranked us.

Ron stood up. "These are the new Pathfinders, Richie. We were just getting acquainted."

Abruptly one of the new members spoke up, his voice somewhat defensive. "We're new as far as just being assigned to this unit, but most of us have been in country for a while."

His words were followed by a momentary silence. The guy seemed apprehensive. Ron introduced me, and I shook each new member's hand. I was sure the same thoughts were going through their heads as mine. How was their coming into the detachment going to affect promotions? Who had the most time in grade? How would upcoming missions be affected? Would we all get along well as a team or would there exist a we/they mentality? The friction continued to increase over the next day or two until a confrontation finally occurred on the third night of their stay, when everyone was sitting around drinking beer, mostly swapping stories. Suddenly one of the new members blurted, "Hey, listen! We didn't ask to come to this unit, so back off!"

A voice yelled back, "Well! You may not have volunteered to come to this detachment, but it sure didn't take you long to sew a Screaming Eagle on your shoulder."

Before long, an argument ensued and others from both sides were quarreling. Finally a corporal from the new group spoke out. His name was Tim Alicoate, and he was clearly respected by his teammates. "Okay! Okay! Let's get everything out on the table and get this shit over with. We've been acting like two dogs sniffing each other out."

Ron agreed. "Hey, y'all! He's right! Everyone listen up!"

The room became silent as Alicoate stood up and spoke. "It's true! We didn't ask to be here, but we're proud to be assigned to such a legendary Airborne division. It's also true that we showed up with the Screaming Eagle already on our shoulder. Who wouldn't? We had the patch sewn on out of respect, and to show you guys that we accept being a part of this unit."

Alicoate paused momentarily. His eyes scanned our group to see if his words had any impact. He didn't have to worry. His short but powerful statement humbled us all.

Slowly Ron rose from his seat. "Let's go around the room and let everyone have their say. Hell! We're one detachment now and we need to start working together as a team."

Each Pathfinder took a turn. Some talked about promotions. The privates discussed how they didn't like taking orders from corporals they didn't know. Most of the new members expressed anxiety at not having one of their sergeants or officers accompany their group. Because of that, they felt they were probably going to get the shit end of the stick all the time.

The discussion lasted about an hour, and when it was finished, we all had a much better understanding of each other. In just a few weeks we were totally integrated and working as one detachment. Luckily the new members proved to be highly competent Pathfinders. I never dreamed that two separate detachments could merge and get along so well.

About a week after the guys from the 308th arrived, we received a new officer, a captain who was assigned as our commander. He replaced Lieutenant Wilberding, who then became the executive officer, i.e., second-in-command. I think Wilberding had mixed feelings. On one hand, he felt as though he was losing a unit that he controlled and somewhat created; on the other, I think he felt a sense of relief at not having total responsibility anymore. I'm sure the loss of command was hard on him, but he never showed it.

Our new commander's name was Capt. James Chase. Chase was of average height with black hair and dark eyes that were set back, making him look somewhat mysterious. He was slim but well built, and walked very erect and confident. We didn't know what unit he was with before coming to us, but it was rumored that he had previously served a tour in Vietnam as an NCO with Special Forces before receiving a commission.

Captain Chase was quite different from Lieutenant Wilberding, and although Chase was easier to talk with and more lenient in many ways, he was not as predictable as Wilberding. Chase also tended to favor men who agreed with him. Overall I considered our detachment fortunate to have him as our new commander. Because he was a captain, we hoped he would have more clout with the upper echelon.

Within a couple of days after his arrival, Captain Chase called every man into his tent so he could get to know them personally and learn more about their professional skills and goals.

When it was my turn, I walked in and saluted sharply. "Sir, Corporal Burns, reporting as ordered."

Captain Chase gestured to a folding metal chair located about two paces from the front of the table he was sitting behind.

"Have a seat, Burns! The reason for this meeting is to get to know each other a little better and to also find out from you if you think there are any problems within the detachment. I'm going to tell you up front, though, I don't like to hear about a problem unless it is accompanied by a solution. Is that clear?"

I nodded. "Yes sir!"

Captain Chase leaned forward in his chair and stared directly into my eyes. "Tell me a little about yourself."

I told Chase about my past experience and some of my goals. He then discussed some of his future policies and ideas for the detachment. I thought the meeting went very well. As it came to a close, I was waiting to be dismissed when Chase rose from his chair, walked around to the front of the table, and sat on its edge. His hand clutched some papers.

"Before you leave, Burns, I want to talk to you about your request to attend MACV Recondo School."

His comment took me by surprise. I had forgotten about the school request, which I had submitted only a week or so earlier. I would have mentioned it in our discussion, but I had not heard anything to date regarding its disposition. I glanced at the papers Chase was holding and wondered if they had something to do with my request.

Chase's demeanor became a bit more formal. "I'd like to know your reasons for wanting to attend Recondo School!"

Bewildered, I glanced up at the captain. "Well . . . sir! If I'm lucky enough to be selected, I hope to better myself as a soldier and also sharpen my combat skills."

I was going to stop there, but I could tell that the captain wanted to hear more than just a pat answer.

I cleared my throat. "Well! You know, sir! I want to see if I can make it. Everyone knows that MACV Recondo School is run by Special Forces and is considered one of the toughest and most realistic courses in the army. Hell! It's the only school the army has ever had where that in order to graduate, you have to actually perform a long-range patrol mission against the enemy."

Chase just stared at me for a moment, then passed the papers to me. "These are your orders to attend Recondo School, with a reporting date of thirty-one July."

I leaped from my chair. "Damn, sir. Are you kidding me? Airborne!" I was ecstatic. I felt like a little kid who just got the Christmas gift of his dreams. I stared at the orders in disbelief.

Chase didn't share my happiness. "Listen. Do you think you're ready for it . . . on such short notice? Recondo School is tough. The course has a high attrition rate."

Something strange was going on. I had the feeling that the captain was trying to discourage me from going. He continued. "What I mean is . . . I can probably get your class date delayed to a later time. You know! Give yourself a little more time to prepare."

There was no way I was going to delay my class date. The MACV Recondo badge was the most coveted patch there was. Besides, one thing the army taught me was to seize an opportunity when it arose, because the chances of its ever coming around again were slim.

I didn't want to get into a pissing contest at my first meeting with the new commander, but I just couldn't give up the opportunity to experience Recondo School. "I really appreciate your concern, sir, but I'll take my chances. I'm as ready as I'm ever going to be. If I flunk out, well, at least I tried!"

Captain Chase didn't appear angry. Instead he moved closer, his voice sounding more like that of a big brother. "Hell, Burns! All right! I'll be honest with you. There is a big operation coming up. I can't tell you anything about it, but it's going to be massive. I'm going to need every man I've got, especially a Pathfinder with your experience."

One didn't have to be a rocket scientist to figure out what the big mission was going to be. The division had been preparing for it for months. We were going to invade the A Shau.

I was caught in one hell of a bind. My new commander was asking me to turn down a school because he needed me. If I didn't, he was sure to think I was disloyal. Damn! I just couldn't honor his request, though. I knew the army. If I didn't go to Recondo School now, I probably would never have the opportunity again and would regret it the rest of my life. Besides, no one was indispensable. If I got killed this very night, Chase and the detachment would certainly manage to go into the A Shau without me.

"I'm sorry, sir! Honest! But I want to go to Recondo School."

Captain Chase appeared more frustrated than angry. "You know I could have these orders canceled by saying you are mission essential."

I tried not to display any emotion. "Yes, sir!"

"If you go, you'll miss out on receiving a few awards. I can promise you at least one medal for participating in such a significant operation."

The captain just didn't understand how important Recondo School was for me. The only award that would mean more to me personally than the MACV Recondo Badge was probably the Medal of Honor, and I wasn't going to receive that in this lifetime. Besides, I had been promised awards before from the units I supported and never received anything.

I tried not to appear nervous as I answered. "I'm really sorry, sir. Recondo School means more to me than any medals. I hope you won't stop me from going."

Chase frowned as he handed me my orders. There was a hint of disgust in his voice. "Here! It's your loss. While you're away at some school, your buddies are going to be making history."

He waved his hand. "You're dismissed."

"Thank you, sir! Airborne!" I saluted sharply and hurriedly fled from the tent before he could change his mind.

I walked back to the Pathfinder hootch elated. I was really going to Recondo School. I knew I was the first Pathfinder in the 101st to attend. I wondered if I was the first Pathfinder ever.

Recondo School was run by 5th Special Forces Group and located at their home base in Nha Trang. The course was three grueling weeks long and its primary purpose was to teach the art of conducting and leading long-range patrols behind enemy lines. Graduates eventually became LRP team leaders. I would have requested the school earlier, but I had been under the impression that a soldier had to be assigned to a LRP company to attend Recondo School. When I was attached to the Tiger Force, however, I saw a sergeant wearing the Recondo badge on his bush hat. He informed me that a soldier from any elite reconnaissance unit could apply as long as he had four months of combat under his belt and six months remaining in country, in addition to meeting the academic and physical criteria for selection. Since Pathfinders were considered elite reconnaissance soldiers, I had filled out the application. I couldn't believe my luck.

I glanced down at the orders and read the reporting date, 31 July 1968. Holy shit! I had less than five days to get ready. I stormed into the Pathfinder hootch and held the orders above my head. "I just got my orders for MACV Recondo School!"

Ron and Buz jumped up from their footlockers. A huge smile spread across Ron's face. "Richie! You did it! Damn! I am definitely going to put in for it, too."

Buz slapped me on the back. "Way to go! I'm envious as hell."

Ron and Buz had wanted to attend Recondo School, but they decided to let me pave the way, since it was my idea, and see what happened. Besides, our detachment was so small, we could never release more than one Pathfinder at a time to attend a school. Lieutenant Wilberding gave me the next few days off to scrounge required items on the school's packing list. I didn't get much sleep the night before I left. All I could think about was Recondo School. I hoped I would be wearing the Recondo badge upon my return to the detachment.

The air force loadmaster signaled that we would be landing at Nha Trang Air Base in a few minutes. I gazed out the window of the C-130 transport and was struck by the beauty of the crystal blue waters and white sandy beaches stretching along the coast of the South China Sea. I knew Nha Trang was a coastal city, but I never expected anything this beautiful. The scene was truly magnificent.

Hastening to the other side of the plane, to the opposite window, I saw a massive mountain range extending from the southern tip of Nha Trang to its northern end. Thick, lush vegetation covered the mountains. Although the mountains didn't appear to be as treacherous or thickly vegetated as the A Shau, there was no doubt they were just as deadly; jet fighters were dropping bombs along the top of the highest mountain in the range. White billows of smoke rose from the jungle floor. The incongruity and stark contrast of the view stuck in my mind: a beautiful coastal city that resembled a peaceful resort, and a battle raging atop the mountains overlooking it.

A fellow 101st member pointed out the window next to mine. "What do you make of that shit?"

I shrugged. "I don't know, but at least we're going to feel right at home."

I learned later that the mountain range was called the Grand Summit, and that an NVA regiment or greater had been sighted and was being engaged by various Special Forces units and forces from the South Korean army.

The crew chief signaled for everyone to take their seats; a moment later the aircraft's wheels touched down on the runway. I walked across the tarmac to the Nha Trang air terminal. Once inside, I searched for an information desk. My eyes locked onto a small group of American soldiers milling about in one of the corners. It was easy to tell they were fellow Recondo students; most wore cammies or tigers and each had his individual weapon and equipment.

I strolled over and introduced myself. They said that two instructors of the Recondo cadre were waiting behind the terminal to transport us to the Recondo compound as soon as one more plane arrived with students. The plane landed about thirty minutes later, and the cadre led us to a three-quarter-ton truck. It was close to noon; the heat was brutal. Luckily, the truck was minus its canvas top, allowing the wind to blow on us.

Only moments had passed when one of the guys shouted, "Check it out!"

To our front, spanning the road, was a large, wooden archway. In the center of the archway was the Recondo badge alongside the Special Forces patch. To the left were the words "Recondo School," and to the right was something written in Vietnamese. My heart pounded with excitement as the truck passed under the arched gateway and into the compound. This was it!

As I jumped off the truck and glanced around, I saw that the compound was exceptionally clean. Even though the ground was basically dirt and gravel, it was neat and clear of litter. All the structures in the compound were Quonset huts: an aid station; a TOC; a supply building; a main classroom; headquarters office; and a row of student barracks. The coveted Recondo badge was visible on most of the structures and was painted in two colors, white and black or olive drab and black. It was shaped like an arrowhead pointing down. In its center was a black "V" and above it the word "Recondo," short for reconnaissance commando.

I stared at the badge. I even knew what it represented if an instructor quizzed me. The arrowhead symbolized woodlore, while the "V" signified the wearer's ability to move against the enemy by air-drop transport, day or night. I vowed that I would leave the school with the MACV Recondo badge sewn on my right shirt pocket or die trying.

The cadre led us to the headquarters building to turn in copies of our orders and receive bunk assignments. I tried to sleep but couldn't. Instead, I experienced another sleepless night; I was just too eager and excited. The next day was one of in-processing, filling out paperwork, and drawing specialized equipment along with tiger fatigues and hats. I was thankful that we had been instructed to bring along our own individual weapons; if I were fortunate enough to make it to the last week of school, I wanted a weapon I knew and trusted while on my graduation patrol.

The first day of school and every day after began with physical training, starting at 0400 hours. PT included a series of strenuous exercises for about thirty minutes, followed by a run and, on occasion, a game referred to as "Australian football." This was nothing more than a free-for-all with no rules in which we all got to beat the hell out of each other.

For the run, each student carried his weapon along with his LBE consisting of his knife, strobe light, ammunition, and so on. Each of us also carried a rucksack with a forty-pound sandbag stuffed inside. The instructors weighed each rucksack before the run and then after the run to ensure that the weight was still at forty pounds. If any sand was missing or if a student didn't complete the run in the prescribed time, he was immediately dropped from the course. The distance of each run increased daily. We were running eight miles a day by the end of the second week.

The first few days of PT were tough for me, especially in the intense heat and humidity. What's more, most of us had not participated in any formal PT or distance running for ages, and our bodies were pretty much trashed from the continuous combat missions we had conducted prior to our arrival.

After PT that first day, we ate a quick breakfast and were then seated inside the main classroom for an orientation. As we took our seats, an instructor read roll call. Our class totaled about sixty-five students, including allied forces. American soldiers came from a variety of army units, along with some Marines from the 3d Marine Division's Force Recon and a few air force Para-Rescue. The foreign students came from the Royal Thai Army and the Republic of Korea.

Our mumbling was silenced by a Special Forces sergeant first class. His steps echoed throughout the hall as he walked across stage. He was an imposing, professional-looking soldier. Once positioned at the center of the stage, he placed his hands on his hips and introduced himself. "Good morning, gentlemen. My name is Sergeant First Class Roberts!"

His eyes scanned the room for a moment, then he continued. "I want to welcome you to Recondo School. Before I begin, however, I want you to know that we have a high attrition rate at this school. So I want you to take a minute to look at the student seated to your right and then to your left."

The instructor paused for a brief moment while we all glanced at each other with puzzled looks. "I hope you took a good look at the man seated on each side of you, because chances are either one or two of you are not going to be here upon graduation day. However, if you are tough enough and you want it bad enough, then you will be here that day. You will prove that you are the best that your country has because you will be Recondo."

If he said that to scare me, it worked. He was right, too. Recondo School had an exceptionally high dropout rate. Quickly I glanced again at the two guys on each side of me. I suddenly felt sorry for them; I'd be damned if I was going to be the one to drop out.

The Special Forces instructor went on to explain the history of the school, the school's policies, the training, and what was expected of us. He also stated that upon graduation, each student would receive an individual Recondo number that would be recorded in his official military record and remain on file with Special Forces and the Department of the Army for the rest of his time in the military.

The sergeant paused at the end of his speech and stared at us somberly. It appeared as if he were looking directly at me. He then said something simple but extremely profound. "Remember one thing, gentlemen. When you're spying on the enemy, whether you are two feet away from him or two miles, do not worry, you are all right, because he doesn't really know where you are located." Little did I know at the time how important and useful that statement would be to me on more than one occasion in the future.

The Recondo instructor turned to walk off the stage but stopped abruptly as if he had forgotten something. "One other thing. For those of you who are fortunate enough to graduate from this school, remember, no matter what happens to you after you leave here, no matter wherever life takes you, you can always be proud that you are Recondo!"

As the sergeant left the stage, we all shouted in unison, "Recondo!"

During the next two weeks, the Recondo School schedule took us through map reading, aerial photo analysis, emergency medical aid, radio communications, principles of intelligence, NVA/VC weapons, immediate action drills, sabotage, extraction techniques, rappelling, call for and adjustment of artillery fire, small boat training, booby traps, and, of course, beaucoup patrolling techniques.

Although the length of classes varied, the amount of training time each day didn't. We trained from before sunup to well after dark every day. Not only were the days long and physically demanding, but the training was intensely realistic. All the exercises were conducted with live fire, including calling in aerial artillery, team immediate-action drills, and the "quick kill" course.

Ironically, my student roster number was ten. Normally, that would not mean anything, but the Vietnamese referred to an American soldier that they didn't like as "you number-ten GI." If they considered you a good guy, you were a "number-one GI." Since my roster number was ten, at most stations the instructor would say, "Who here is number ten?" I would sound off and then be the first one selected for whatever task or event, like rappelling or calling for fire. It was all in good fun and it worked out well for me. Not only did going first build up my confidence, I also got the task over with right away.

Even the medical training was realistic. Like everything else in Recondo School, once a student received training on a task, he had to successfully demonstrate that he could actually perform it. After receiving instruction on how to draw blood and the proper method of administering an IV, we were paired off. My partner was a stocky Marine from Force Recon. First, we had to show that we could inject each other with an IV of intravenous serum albumin blood volume expander. We each did it successfully on the first try. Next we were handed a syringe and told to draw blood from one another. Feeling confident, I volunteered to go first.

My partner had plenty of bulging veins to choose from, so I selected one on the inside of his forearm. I swabbed the spot with alcohol and waited for the instructor to tell me to proceed. There was some commotion across the room and the instructor waved his hand. "Go ahead and continue. I'm going to see if someone's having a problem over there."

Lightly but firmly, I jabbed the tip of the needle into

my partner's vein. I couldn't draw blood, however, and realized I had gone clear through it. After wiggling the needle around for a few seconds, I removed it. I swore under my breath. "Damn!"

The stocky Marine whispered, "What's the matter?"

I smiled. "Oh nothing! Gonna have to try again. No problem!"

He clenched his free hand into a fist as if he were in pain. I looked up and noticed sweat beading on his forehead and trickling down the sides of his face. "You okay?"

The Marine had a low, gravelly voice and spoke with a New York City accent. "I'm fine, dammit! I just hate needles. Let's get it over with!"

Since I'd collapsed that first vein, I picked a new one and tried again. This time when I stuck in the needle, the vein kind of rolled to the side; I'd missed it entirely. The Marine became real nervous and was breathing heavily. He grunted, "Listen, man! I can't take any more of this shit. Do it right and get it over with!"

I didn't know what to say. I could tell, as hard-core as he was, that he was deathly afraid of needles. I felt bad about it. The instructor returned and peered over my shoulder. "There a problem here?"

I was about to explain that I had bungled it a couple of times, but the Marine spoke up. He tried to appear nonchalant. "No problem at all, Sergeant!"

I appreciated what the Marine said, but I knew we hadn't fooled the instructor. Besides, anyone could see the two puncture wounds I had already made. I held the vein in place with the two fingers of my free hand and placed the needle firmly against the skin. I had a gut feeling that if I didn't draw blood on this stick I could be dropped from the course.

I stared up at the Marine. He looked like he was about to blow up. He barked, "Just do it!"

The hell with it! I jabbed the needle into his arm and, luckily, drew blood. As the Marine let out a sigh of relief, the instructor leaned on my shoulder and whispered, "I was going to say that this is your lucky day, but your partner still has his turn on you."

I glanced over at the Marine. He didn't appear quite as nervous. He grinned slightly as he stared at the syringe he was holding. The next day most everyone brandished large, colorful hematomas on their arms, including myself and a stocky Marine.

One of the most thrilling moments in Recondo School was flying at two thousand feet while suspended by a rope under a helicopter in an extraction device called the Maguire rig. The Maguire rig was a simple contraption made of rope and webbing that formed three loops at the end to be used as seats. Hence, up to three men could be lifted from the jungle floor without a helicopter having to land. Of the three men in the loops, the left and right man each had a wrist strap which would, hopefully, hold them in case they slipped from or got shot out of the seat. The middle man, however, simply locked his arms and legs with the two outside men. (Luckily, I got the left seat and didn't have to be the middle man.) When all three were ready to go, the pilot would lift the chopper, taking up the slack on the rope and making it taut. As they lifted off the ground, the two outside men extended their free (outside) arm straight out to the side, which helped keep the rig stable so it would not spin.

The Recondo School compound was located right next to the perimeter, which was lined with defensive walls, machine gun emplacements, concertina wire, and minefields. Throughout my stay at the school, the battle on the Grand Summit continued to rage about four kilometers away. Consequently, enemy mortar rounds hit around and inside the perimeter at least once a day. The school had an 81mm mortar pit positioned near the main classroom that was used for counterfire. It was the weirdest feeling; there we were, attending a school, and we could be wounded or killed at any moment. Of course, the Special Forces instructors didn't let a little thing like a major battle or enemy incoming mortar rounds distract us from class work.

The Recondo instructors were by far the most professional soldiers I had come across during my time in the army. They maintained a high military bearing, they never shouted or belittled a student, and they led by example. Each Recondo instructor had to be a sergeant first class or above with at least one prior tour in Vietnam and a prior assignment to a Special Operations project dealing mainly with reconnaissance. Many had run recon with the supersecret Military Assistance Command, Vietnam, Studies and Observations Group (MACV-SOG). I was so impressed by their bearing and abilities that I vowed that if I stayed in the army, it would be as a Special Forces NCO.

In addition to the American instructors, the school cadre also had Australian warrant officers from the Australian Training Team in Vietnam (ATTV) and the Special Air Service (SAS). They participated in student patrols as well.

During our second week we conducted small-boat training in the South China Sea. After long, grueling hours of small-craft infiltration and capsizing drills, we were flown about ten miles out to sea to Hon Tre Island, a tiny speck of land jutting out of the water. It was a mile in length and covered with dense jungle and jagged rocks. It was there that we put into practice everything we had learned.

The training at Hon Tre proved extensive and the nights sleepless as patrolling remained the primary theme. Sometimes I slept as I walked, but I still managed to function. Verbal communication was replaced by hand signals. Talking by students was kept to a bare minimum, except for emergencies. For me, not being able to talk was like being a fish out of water. However, I ended up becoming skilled at using just hand signals. It wasn't long before each student became proficient at selecting rendezvous sites, identifying booby traps, and performing the duties of the different Long Range Patrol team positions. We also received training on enemy weapons and the placement and removal of mines.

Each of us had to successfully navigate a jungle lane called the "quick kill" course. As we maneuvered through the vegetation, silhouetted targets popped up from the surrounding brush. We had to dispatch them rapidly by firing accurate shots from the hip without even thinking. This was called the "quick kill" method, and I could see why. Everyone did surprisingly well. We also practiced cover and concealment, noise and light security, and sound and smell recognition. And we established OPs and LPs.

Finally, the last day of our second week of training arrived. We completed a final written examination and were given the rest of the day off to take care of personal business before beginning patrol week.

It was midmorning and I went back to the classroom to see if I could grab an extra copy of a handout I thought would be worthwhile to bring back to the detachment. I stepped inside the hut and waited a few moments for my eyes to adjust to the dimness. I took one of the handouts from the stack and, as I turned to leave, I noticed a figure sitting alone in the corner. It looked like one of the Korean students. He was bent over with his hands in his face. He appeared distraught. I thought that perhaps he had received some bad news, like the death of a buddy in his unit or family member back home.

Cautiously I walked toward him. "Hey! You okay?"

He removed his hands from his face. It was An Su, a Korean sergeant I had befriended. He stood up and bowed. "Burns! Hello!"

I returned the bow. An Su wiped the tears from his face. He was embarrassed that I had found him crying. "Today, I told I fail school!"

His statement took me completely by surprise. I couldn't believe An Su was being dropped from the course; he and his fellow Koreans were harder than woodpecker lips. "I'm sorry to hear that, An Su. Did they tell you why?"

He kept his head down to avoid eye contact. "I fail test."

I suddenly felt real uncomfortable. It brought home the reality that no one was safe from failing the school, regardless of how far along he was in the course.

He began pacing the floor. "I try to do good on test, but I not understand English well."

It must have been difficult to comprehend the instruction in a language other than your own, especially at the tempo we had to maintain. I felt badly for him, but I didn't know what to say. The words stumbled from my mouth as I tried to offer some encouragement. "Maybe, though . . . you can come back later . . . you know . . . and try again."

He stopped pacing. He was angry. He grabbed the sergeant stripes on his sleeve and acted like he was ripping them off. "I not be sergeant no more!"

It was not at all shameful to fail a school like MACV Recondo. Most soldiers were welcomed back to their units with open arms for at least trying. Damn! A guy felt bad enough as it was, but busting him in rank was downright merciless.

An Su reached into his pocket, pulled out his wallet, and pointed to the photo of his girlfriend. He had shown it to me before; he was very proud of her.

I pointed to the picture. "I know. That's your fiancée. She sure is pretty!"

His eyes filled with tears again. "Yes! She beautiful girl. But we no can marry now."

I was puzzled. "What are you talking about? She won't care if you failed some school. She'll be happy if you just come home from the war in one piece."

His voice cracked. "I shame her! I shame my family! I shame me!"

This guy had to be kidding me! He was going to lose

his stripes and his fiancée just because he flunked out of Recondo School? Hell! I couldn't believe it.

"I'm sorry, An Su, really."

He lowered his head. "Yes. I know. Thank you."

He sat back down. "You go now."

I knew there was nothing else I could do or say. "I hope everything works out okay for you somehow."

He bowed. "You good soldier, Burns. You will make Recondo."

I shook his hand and quietly left the classroom. I felt sorry for An Su. Besides being a damn good soldier, he was the nicest and most outgoing of the Korean students. I saw a lot of good soldiers get dropped from the course, however. Even one of the guys who sat beside me on the first day. Although I felt sorry for every one of them, I was glad it wasn't me.

The next morning an air of excitement filled the classroom as we waited for the instructors to enter. This was it! Our third week of training, the final test, our graduation patrol. The normal rustling about of papers and chairs ceased as the Recondo instructors filed onto the platform. The senior instructor stepped to the forefront and bellowed, "Good morning, gentlemen!"

We sounded off enthusiastically, "Good morning, Sergeant!"

He placed his hands on his hips. "Welcome to your third and final week of training, most appropriately named 'You Bet Your Life!' "

I glanced around the classroom and noticed I wasn't the only one pondering his words. He was right! We were literally going to bet our lives that we were competent in the tasks and skills we had been taught. This week, we would conduct an actual combat patrol into known enemy territory with just six men and be graded on our individual performance. Even if we proved successful, that did not mean some of us wouldn't be wounded or killed. In fact, a few of the school buildings were named after

Recondo students who had been killed on graduation patrols in the past.

I turned my attention back to the sergeant. "In a few moments you will be broken down into five-man teams and assigned an instructor. Once that is accomplished, your instructor will brief your team on its mission. You will then develop your operational plan and draw all the equipment you will need to conduct the operation. Are there any questions?"

Are there any questions? Probably a million of them, but nobody raised a hand; everyone was too excited. The sergeant didn't seem a bit surprised by the lack of response. It was probably the same with every class.

He continued, "Since there are no questions, report to the back of the room when your name is called. Good luck!"

When feasible, the school attempted to combine teams with students from the same parent unit. When my name was called, I was pleased to learn that, of the five students on my team, three of us were from the 101st Airborne Division. (We'd started the course with five members, but two didn't make it.)

Our team instructor was a tall Special Forces senior NCO who was somewhat slender and stood very erect. I noticed he was wearing a 173d Airborne Brigade patch on his right shoulder, which meant he had previously served with that unit as well as Special Forces. He directed the five of us to a shady spot on the side of a building and motioned for us to sit down.

"My name is Sergeant Loring. I'll be your team adviser throughout your patrol."

He paused a moment, then continued. "You will notice that I said adviser and not leader. This is your patrol, not mine. Each of you will rotate among the various team positions. One time you might be point man, the next time you might be tail gunner. Time permitting, I'll try to give as many of you as I can a crack at being TL [team leader]. You will be graded on your performance in each of these positions; therefore, it will behoove each of you to support one another."

Sergeant Loring paused for questions, but nobody said anything. "The only time I might decide to take over the team is if we make contact and the shit hits the fan or some unforeseen event happens. In any case, unless I specifically give the word, you will take commands from whoever is the designated TL at the time. Is that clear?"

We all replied, "Yes, Sergeant!"

"Good!"

Sergeant Loring pulled a map out of his pants cargo pocket, then crouched down in front of us. "I'll give you a more in-depth briefing later on this evening, but basically we'll be reconning a four-klick area . . . here . . . along the Grand Summit." He pointed to the mountain on the map.

He smiled. "You're all aware of the battle that's been going on up there, right?" We couldn't help but laugh as we nodded.

He returned his attention to the map and pointed to the summit. "Our units along with Korean forces have been fighting the NVA for days all around here. They're at the point now where they've essentially drawn a net around the enemy and are tightening it on them. Unfortunately, Charlie's penetrating the weak points and escaping in small groups and even company-size units, mostly at night."

Sergeant Loring moved his finger down the mountainside on the map. "We think they've been using the cover and terrain all along these ridgelines to make their getaway."

He curled the map in his hand and stood up. "Our main mission is to see if we can spot any enemy groups or stragglers and report their location. Then we can have them engaged by friendly ground forces or taken out with air strikes."

Sergeant Loring stopped again momentarily, then

continued. "We'll be on the ground for four days, unless we're compromised. We insert tomorrow afternoon around dusk. Any questions?"

No one responded.

Loring seemed surprised. "No questions at all?"

One of my fellow 101st guys spoke up. "If we do get compromised or for some reason the patrol is cut short, do we still graduate?"

Loring perked up a bit. "Good damn question! When a team is extracted early on, they're usually inserted into another location the next day. Regardless of whether we reinsert or not, as long as you don't screw up, you'll be okay."

One of the other guys was going to say something, but decided against it. Sergeant Loring raised his eyebrows. "If you got a question, now is the time to spit it out. Remember, the only silly question is the one that's not asked."

Our teammate mumbled, "Well . . . what if we get wounded or killed? I mean . . . do we still graduate then, too?"

Even though that question was probably on all our minds at one time or another, we still laughed. Sergeant Loring couldn't hold it in either. He snickered. "I guess there are some silly questions!"

He placed his hand on the student's shoulder. "Tell you what! If you get greased, I'll personally see to it that you're buried with the Recondo badge sewn on your pocket."

Sergeant Loring stepped closer. "I don't want any of you worrying about whether you're going to pass this patrol or not. I'm not going to give anyone low marks for nit-picking bullshit. You've all made it this far, so I know you've got your shit together. You'd have to really fuck up, like screw up on security or get us compromised in some way, for me to drop you from the course at this point in time."

He stared at us momentarily, making sure he had our

attention. "Just keep alert and stick to the basics. Remember what you've been taught. Understood?"

"Yes, Sergeant!" I think every one of us let out a sigh of relief. The job was tough enough without worrying about being graded on minute details or silly mistakes that didn't cause any problems.

Sergeant Loring went on. "You guys should feel honored. There was a lot of discussion at MACV headquarters as to whether or not students should be used for this mission, since the chances of making contact are fairly high. We assured them that Recondo students are trained well enough to accomplish any recon mission. That's the whole purpose of the school."

The rest of the day, we drew all the gear we would need to accomplish the mission, including ammunition and radios. We checked every item to make sure it was working properly, and then divided up all the equipment so each team member carried an equal load. While we were doing this, Sergeant Loring conducted a flyover of our AO to recon possible LZs and PZs.

Later in the evening, Sergeant Loring laid out the map and briefed us on the more specific aspects of the operation, the selected LZs and PZs, and the route of march. He informed us that since our AO was small, there were only a few clearings suitable as LZs. As a matter of fact, the LZ he suggested we use was so small, it wasn't even on the map. Sergeant Loring assured us that he and the pilot had concluded from the flyover that the clearing was adequately large to land our chopper. There were only two other clearings suitable for use as landing zones. We selected the smaller of the two as our primary PZ and the larger one as our secondary PZ should anything go wrong.

The next morning we did a little PT, which consisted of calisthenics and Australian football. We then ate a good breakfast and rehearsed our patrolling techniques. Throughout our training the cadre had constantly reminded us of the "combative law of physics." "For every action, there must be an immediate and ferocious reaction, or an expedient line of departure." Since a Recondo team consisted of just six men, the odds were that we would be outmanned and outgunned by almost any force we encountered. In order to generate a "ferocious reaction" and an "expedient line of departure" with such a small force, we practiced immediate-action drills (IAs) and we practiced them for hours.

If the team made contact, regardless of direction, we would go into immediate action. For instance, if the team was hit from the front, the odd-numbered men in line, numbers one, three, and five, would move to the left, each man stepping a little farther to the left than the man in front of him. The even-numbered men, numbers two, four, and six, would move to the right in the same fashion, thus forming a pyramid or cone. The first man in line, the point man, would open fire with his weapon on automatic. Once his ammunition was expended, he would turn into the formation and run. As soon as he passed the second man in line, that man would open fire on automatic, then turn and run. As he passed the third man, the third man would open fire, and so on. When it came to the fifth man, he would throw a grenade; the sixth man, the tail gunner, would take out any targets of opportunity in his sights. That procedure not only directed a continuous stream of bullets on the enemy, but also led the enemy to believe he had encountered a much larger force than just six men. Hell, when we practiced with live fire, it sounded like we were an entire company.

If we were hit from the rear, the immediate-action procedure was performed in the exact same manner, just reversed. The procedure was a little different if hit from either side, but just as simple and effective.

It didn't take long for our fatigues to become soaked with sweat as Sergeant Loring yelled, "To the front!" followed by "To the left!" As soon as we conducted one drill, he would initiate another. In no time, however, our team was moving as one entity. God, it was hot! We practiced in the dirt field in front of the billets with no shade whatsoever, yelling *bang . . . bang* until I was hoarse. I couldn't remember when I had been so thirsty.

Finally Sergeant Loring shouted, "Okay, that's enough! Careful how much water you drink or you'll get sick. Fall out at fourteen hundred hours for inspection, ready to go."

First, we all ran for the water, then we headed for the coolness of the hootch to relax for a few hours. I flopped down on my bunk to take a nap, but was too wound up to sleep. In about six hours we would be inserting. I couldn't believe I had actually made it this far in Recondo School. I only hoped I wouldn't screw up on the patrol. I thought that would be worse than getting wounded. 1400 hours came upon us quickly.

Sergeant Loring spoke rather gently, his demeanor friendly. "Okay, fall in! Make one line right here in front of me!"

He looked us over. "Anybody carrying insect repellent, cigarettes, or any other no-no items?"

Some of us said, "No!" while others just shook their heads. Although the mosquitoes were always bad at night in the jungle, insect repellent and cigarette smoke could be smelled by the enemy. The gooks didn't use repellent, and a cigarette could be seen a long way off, especially at night. Use of any items like those could get us compromised, maybe even killed.

Sergeant Loring stepped in front of the first man. He checked to make sure the soldier's equipment was attached correctly, that he had applied camouflage properly on his face, and ensured that the man's weapon was clean and serviceable. He went on down the line performing the same inspection on each of us. He also scrutinized our overall appearance to see if we had anything shiny, no matter how little the object. He then made each one of us jump up and down a few times to ensure that nothing clanked or made even the slightest noise. Those who wore dog tags had already taped them together as well.

As we were taught, each team member carried each item in the exact same place on his person as the next man. For instance, morphine was carried in the left top shirt pocket. Strobe lights and knives were taped on the left strap of the LBE. Maps were stowed in the left pant cargo pocket. Three men carried claymore mines taped to the top of their rucksack frames, while the remaining three carried serum albumin IVs also taped to the top of the rucksack.

This methodology increased one's chances of survival significantly. Since each member knew where every piece of equipment was located, we didn't have to waste time fumbling around trying to find an item in the heat of a firefight or in the dark of night. It also proved useful when switching equipment with one another or retrieving items from wounded or dead teammates.

After the inspection we waited in front of a small hootch that the school used to display captured enemy weapons. We posed for some photos in front of the weapons. There was also a bulletin board showing pictures of dead American soldiers who'd initially been captured by the enemy. Many showed signs of torture. The enemy had a well-known and documented reputation of carrying out heinous war crimes.

The pictures had a definite impact on me. I swore that I would try my best not to be compromised while on patrol. Actually, I think the instructors displayed the pictures as a scare tactic. It worked!

One of my teammates stood beside me. "Damn! That shit is horrible!"

My anxiety level even increased a bit just viewing the pictures. "I know! I don't think anything terrifies me more than being captured."

He then asked the question that I think every soldier

ponders at some time. "How long do you think you would last if you were tortured?"

Although just the thought of being captured horrified me, I decided to make light of it. I chuckled. "Hell! As soon as they started talking about pulling out my fingernails, I'd be talking my head off."

About thirty minutes before takeoff we proceeded to the launch site. Two other student teams showed up behind us. Although there were a few recognition smiles and thumbs-ups, nobody spoke much. We test-fired our weapons and conducted commo checks. I volunteered to hump one of the radios for a while. It made my rucksack heavier, but, except for the instructor, I had by far the most experience at calling in gunships, adjusting artillery fire, and, of course, bringing in helicopters.

Sergeant Loring assigned us our team positions. When it was my turn, he put his finger to my chest. "You're point man!"

Holy shit! Point man meant that I would be the first man in line as we patrolled the jungle. My job was to search and listen for any signs of the enemy and also to look for booby traps. Additionally, I would be the first one to pave the way through wait-a-minute vines and other obstacles.

It wasn't long before we heard the *whup . . . whup . . . whup* of choppers approaching. There were five in all. They were part of the 281st Assault Helicopter Company. Flanking them were two UH-1B gunships. We also had an O-E1 Bird Dog plane that would act as an FAC (forward air controller) for on-call jet air strikes.

The choppers landed and all three teams ran to their designated helicopters. As usual, my heart was pounding and my mouth was dry. Although there were five choppers, two would remain empty because we would be making false insertions.

The false-insertion technique was used to conceal the actual location and hopefully even the insertion of a team into the area. As it came time for a particular team to insert onto its LZ, the chopper transporting them would take the position of last in the flight. All the choppers would fly over the LZ except the last bird, which would hastily touch down and quickly spit out six camouflaged figures. The pilot would then immediately hurry to catch up with the flight. Since all the choppers overflew the LZ and the last bird was missing for just moments, it gave the illusion of a routine overflight, thus deceiving the enemy.

The choppers whined as they ascended. I could feel the coolness of the wind touch my face. The scene of the men surrounding me was always the same when inserting into an LZ. Everyone was quiet, each person lost in his own thoughts. Mixed with my anxiety was a deep sense of pride. I felt honored to be a part of a group of young men who willingly faced danger and hardship head-on. I wondered if the World War II vets had felt the same way when parachuting into Normandy or riding landing craft onto the beaches in amphibious assaults on Japanese-held islands.

I glanced out the cabin and saw the last bird spiral down into a small brown patch. In no time it was back in the formation. The crew chief gave us a thumbs-up, signifying that the team got in undetected. We were next. Our chopper crept to the back of the formation. Sergeant Loring made a gesture with his hand to his mouth, reminding us that, for the next four days, there would be no talking, just hand signals. If talking became necessary for some reason, it would be in a whisper. He then motioned for us to sit in the door. We scooted toward the openings. Three of us sat on one side of the bird and three on the other.

This was it! In just a few moments we would be on the ground. I said a short prayer. The bird flared into a quick hover a few feet off the ground. As soon as one man jumped from the aircraft, we would all follow, even if we discovered it was the wrong LZ or was covered with enemy. We were one, like fingers on a hand. Where one team member went, we all went, even if it meant certain death.

My last thought before leaping to the ground was that if I could just keep my shit together for the next four days, I would be a Recondo.

Chapter Seventeen

The six of us bolted off the LZ and into the tree line about thirty feet away. If anything bad was going to happen, I prayed it would happen before the helicopters got too far away to assist us. As the sound of the chopper faded in the distance, a feeling of intense loneliness overcame me. We lay low for a few moments, weapons at the ready, scanning the area for any sign of the enemy. We were nestled together in a clump of dense foliage on a small plateau on the side of a mountain. The rest of the jungle and surrounding vegetation was not exceptionally thick. Most of the trees were short in height and somewhat sparse. This type of terrain would make it easy for us to maneuver. Unfortunately, it would make it easier for the enemy to detect us as well.

The student team leader quickly checked to make sure he had everybody, then pointed in the direction he wanted us to move. The instructor nodded his approval. I took up my position as point man and headed out. We walked in single file, each team member just a few paces behind the man to his front.

I started out very slowly at first, proceeding with caution. Since talking was not allowed, I glanced back at the team leader every so often to see if he had any instructions for me. The Recondo instructor motioned for me to speed up the pace; he wanted to distance the team from the LZ as quickly as possible. If the enemy had discovered our insertion, they would be crawling all over the LZ soon. We had gone about 150 meters in approximately thirty minutes when I received the signal to halt. The team leader wanted us to lay low for a while and just watch and listen to find out if any enemy were in the area or following us. We formed a circle and sat down, each man facing out. This way we covered a 360-degree perimeter. For the next hour or so we remained completely still and silently listened, watched, and sniffed the air.

It's amazing how acute your senses can become when you really concentrate on using them, especially when your life is at stake. I tried to relax and let my senses take over. As a calmness fell over me, I heard a multitude of strange noises being made by the wind, the insects, and animals. The sounds we were intently listening for, however, were those that were man-made, like a metallic click of a weapon or the *snap* of a breaking twig.

Darkness was setting in. It was time to vacate our position and move one last time. The location the student team leader selected was just a short distance away, but it offered us much better cover and concealment. Upon arrival, the student radio operator reported our situation and location to the school headquarters. The three of us carrying claymore mines crept out about thirty meters to our fronts and each set his mine in place. I inserted the blasting cap into the well of my claymore and ran the wire back to my position. I then hooked up the wire to the claymore's detonator, fondly referred to as the "clacker," and locked the safety mechanism in place. If we did get attacked during the night, the claymores would destroy anyone or anything in their path.

We again formed a circle facing outward. Since there was no immediate threat, the team leader decided to have two men remain awake at all times while the other four slept, rotating shifts every two hours. I was dog-tired physically but wide awake mentally, so I volunteered for the first watch.

I loosened the straps on my rucksack and slid my torso down slightly, resting my head against the rucksack frame. After laying my weapon across my lap, I set the claymore's clacker by my side. As my fellow teammates dozed off, I rehearsed in my mind the different scenarios that could occur and what action I would take if anything happened.

It wasn't long before darkness crept over us. Earlier, I had memorized the exact spot of each bush and shrub to my front. I didn't stare at any particular object very long. Instead, I scanned the area slowly, relying on my peripheral vision to pick up any movement. Instinctively my mind evaluated even the slightest noise. On more than one occasion I had to hold my imagination in check. After what seemed an eternity, I cautiously awakened the next watch. Once I was convinced he was fully alert, I went to sleep.

It was 0200 hours, my turn for watch again. All I could make out was the outline of my teammate's face as I attempted to clear the cobwebs from my mind. I touched him back to let him know I was alert. He touched me once more and again I returned it. I didn't blame him for wanting to make sure I was fully conscious; sleeping on watch was an unforgivable mistake. Besides the possibility of getting everyone killed, it meant automatic dismissal from the course.

The two hours passed by uneventfully. I tried to stay alert as my mind drifted to home at least a thousand times. There was only about an hour of darkness left as the watch came to an end. Since neither of us could sleep, my fellow teammate and I agreed not to wake up the final watch. There was no sense having four of us awake. Once rays of light began filtering through the trees, we woke up the rest of the team.

I retrieved my claymore and checked my equipment. Since we still had a few minutes before moving out, I pulled a spaghetti LRP ration out of my cargo pocket and gobbled down about a third of it. After tucking the rest of the meal back into my pocket, I took a long pull of water from my canteen.

On patrol, we ate one freeze-dried LRP ration a day. The only drawback was that water had to be added to it. In an effort to save as much water as possible for drinking, we'd prepare our first day's packet in the rear before departing on a mission.

Our reconnaissance plan for the day was to patrol upward, almost to the top of the mountain we were on, and then traverse its crest. Once on the other side of the mountain, we would find a defensive position to RON. Other than an occasional wait-a-minute vine, the going was relatively easy. Still walking point, I checked for booby traps and watched and listened for any signs or sounds of movement. The man behind me, commonly referred to as the compass man, ensured that I didn't veer off course. He also kept a watchful eye in the trees above for snipers. Depending on the terrain, we took a five- or ten-minute break every hour.

By noon we were about a hundred meters from the top of the mountain and encountering huge stands of bushes that had enormous sharp thorns protruding from their branches. My hands were getting torn up, so I halted the team momentarily and slipped on a pair of work gloves.

I continued on, and a few moments later my boot laces and pants became entangled in some low-lying wait-a-minute vines. As I struggled to get free, I lost my balance and grabbed onto a large bush that had big red flowers. Suddenly my forearms were on fire. An instant later I felt a burning sensation on my neck, the side of my face, and my shoulders. I glanced back at my compass man for assistance. He was grasping at his neck, and I watched in amazement as a multitude of insects lunged through the air to land on him. Shit! Those were not red flowers at all, they were hordes of red ants!

In no time they had attacked the entire team. The brazen demons even leaped from one team member onto the next. The ants were huge, and each bite felt like the touch of a burning cigarette. They were the most tenacious, aggressive little creatures I had ever seen.

About twenty meters off to my left I noticed a small clearing. Without waiting for orders, I hurried over to it. If the enemy spotted us, so be it; at least we could shoot at them. The team followed right behind me. Once at the clearing, we threw off our rucksacks and stripped off our shirts. By this time the ants were all over me, even up my crotch.

The three of us at the front of the file had the most ants on us. While our other three teammates provided security, we shook out our shirts and pulled the ants off each other. It took us a good ten minutes to rid ourselves of them. I thought the Recondo instructor would be angry with me, perhaps even give me a bad grade as point man. Instead he tried not to laugh. He had seen it all before and viewed the mishap as one of the hazards of patrolling in the jungle. We quickly regained our composure as a team and proceeded on.

Around midafternoon we arrived at the crest of the mountain and halted momentarily to gaze out over the horizon. Offering us a moment's reprieve, a cool breeze cut its way through the stifling heat. The scene before us was magnificent. To our left was the ocean. The water was clear and blue with snowcapped waves rippling onto a white, sandy beach. The view looked like something out of a travel advertisement. But staring at the cool, blue water just made me all the more thirsty. I reached for my canteen and downed a hefty swallow. I looked back at my fellow team members; each was lost in his own thoughts. Finally the Recondo instructor signaled us to continue on.

We patrolled along the mountain's crest, steadily making our way to the other side. About midway across we heard a rifle shot off to the east. It sounded like it was about a kilometer away. The lone shot was immediately followed by two shots in succession. Those shots came from somewhere to the west. I halted the patrol and everyone dropped to one knee. I glanced back at the instructor for guidance. The instructor motioned for everyone on the team to slowly gather around him.

He whispered softly, "They know we're in the area. They might be signaling that we've been spotted, but I don't think so. More than likely, they're not sure of our exact location, just that we're on the ground. They're using the small-arms fire as a signal to bracket us."

Somewhere in my mind I recalled the American Indian using either the same or a similar method of communicating by firing their rifles as signals to decrease the search area and eventually close in on the enemy. I couldn't remember if I'd heard it in a lecture or read it somewhere. Hell, I probably saw it on a TV western.

The instructor continued. "In any event, Charlie is onto us. This is a good learning opportunity to practice what you have been taught. Remember to stick to the basics and exercise the three Ds of counterintelligence."

The three Ds of counterintelligence had been hammered into our heads a hundred times throughout the course: Deny, Detect, and Deceive the enemy. The less the enemy knows about you, the easier he is to defeat.

He motioned for me to move out. "Point man! Keep sharp!"

I nodded and proceeded cautiously. Wow! I thought about how lucky we were that Charlie was presenting us with such a learning opportunity. If we got a chance, we would thank him by calling in an air strike on his ass.

When we arrived at the opposite side of the mountain, we reconned the entire upper portion of the slope. By the time we finished, dusk was setting in, so we hid in some thickets behind a fallen tree. Our second night proved as uneventful as the first except for an occasional ant bite. We continued to be bitten by ants throughout the mission.

In the morning, as we prepared to move out, the instructor held up his notebook for each of us to examine.

It contained new position assignments. I was designated team leader. I had mixed feelings. On one hand, I looked forward to the challenge. On the other, I worried that I might make a mistake, especially if we ran into trouble.

The side of the mountain we were on was not very steep. Although its slope was more gradual, the jungle appeared to be more dense. We would descend the slope into the valley, then proceed up the side of the next mountain directly across from us. I signaled the point man to move out.

Although the sun was shining, it remained dark and shadowy underneath the jungle's canopy. The humidity was a killer. Sweat continually poured down the sides of my face and its salt stung my eyes. A musty odor filled my nostrils. My lungs felt like they were breathing in air that was wet. Rays of sunlight beamed down through small holes in the thick layers of vegetation overhead, and hundreds of insects danced in the light.

As team leader, my place was in the center of the file, and I stared at the teammates to my front. I marveled at how steadily and vigilantly each man traveled, weapon at the ready, senses heightened. Damn, they looked menacing. I realized that I looked like that as well. I felt powerful, like a predator. We moved and thought as one.

By late morning we had made our way to the bottom of the mountainside where the ground leveled off. Suddenly the point man halted the patrol. He had discovered a vacant enemy base camp, a series of foxholes and fighting positions. I signaled the team to spread out and provide security while the instructor and I searched the area. Cautiously we checked for booby traps, weapons, and anything of intelligence value such as documents or equipment.

Every reconnaissance man memorized and utilized the key word SALUTE. SALUTE stood for finding out the enemy's Size, Activity, Location, Unit, Time, and Equipment.

The size of the holes and the way they were arranged led

us to believe that the enemy unit was a battalion-size, infantry-type unit of maybe 250 to 300 men. They probably carried standard infantry weapons—rifles, some machine guns, and small mortars—and conducted patrols around the area. The instructor estimated that they had vacated the location three days ago. Once we were sure that no enemy were in our immediate vicinity, he pulled a camera and a tiny slide ruler from his rucksack.

The instructor had me lay the ruler beside, in, and along the various holes and fighting positions while he took pictures. Once we got the film back to the rear, intelligence would develop it. Then, since the ruler was a known length, they could use mathematics to accurately measure the size and depth of the holes and fighting positions to determine if we were right or exactly what type unit had occupied the camp. This intelligence would be analyzed and matched with information found by the other Recondo and LRP teams, and information from other sources, to form an overall view of the enemy situation. After we finished, I motioned for the team to head out, and we moved to a concealed position about a hundred meters on the other side of the base camp. We took a break, plotted the location, and radioed the information back to headquarters.

It was midafternoon when we reached the side of the next mountain we would patrol up. The terrain in front of us was unbelievable. I had never seen anything like it before anywhere, let alone in Vietnam. The side of the mountain was covered with colossal white boulders. Some of them were the size of cars. The equipment we were carrying combined with the intense heat was going to make the climb a rough one. Just as we started our trek, the point man halted the patrol. He had discovered a cave. The width of the entrance was about that of a normal doorway and around four feet in height.

The instructor whispered to me, "What's your next move, team leader?"

I tried not to show my anxiety. Damn! It was tough enough making these decisions without being graded on them as well.

I attempted to make my expression a serious one. "I'm going to have the team recon the immediate area for any signs of the enemy."

The Recondo instructor grinned slightly. "Anything else?"

Damn! I knew what he was alluding to. He wanted me to say that one of us would go inside the cave and investigate. Unfortunately, I had always been taught to lead by example, so if I made that decision, I would be the one going inside.

I whispered, "Well! Once we finish checking out the outside area, I'll decide if we need to check out the inside."

The instructor appeared satisfied for the moment.

We found no sign that the enemy had been in the vicinity of the cave. As I pondered my decision, one of my teammates pointed to the ground right at the cave's entrance. There, embedded in the sand, was a large animal footprint. It was not fresh, but it was there nevertheless.

The Recondo instructor stared at me with that "What are you going to do" look on his face.

My anxiety heightened as I tried to think of reasons not to go into the cave. A lump got caught in my throat as I whispered, "Sergeant! Do you know what kind of animal it is?"

The instructor shook his head slightly. "Negative! But I can tell you what it's not. It's not a tiger or an elephant."

His comment sure as hell did not make me feel better. The footprint was huge. One of my teammates added, "I think it's a bear!"

A bear in Vietnam? I looked back to the instructor, hoping he would discard such a ridiculous notion. Instead he replied, "Could be. Could be a damn gorilla, too!"

A gorilla! There was no way in hell I was going into that cave. My mind raced to find some rational reason to save my ass.

I put on my best command face. "Well! There's no sign that Charlie's been here. Also, we don't know what kind of animal made that footprint, but whatever it is, it's big. I'd go inside and recon. But if it's a bear or something and it's hibernating or just hiding out, hell, I might have to waste it, and firing a weapon would only give away our position."

I paused to see if the instructor was going to say something. He didn't, so I continued. "As the team leader, I can't afford to compromise the mission or the team."

The instructor just raised his eyebrows a bit. "Okay! You're the team leader."

I felt like a thousand pounds was lifted off my shoulders. I quickly motioned for the team to move out. The last thing I needed was for the instructor to change his mind or to bump into a big gorilla thrashing through the jungle, pounding on his chest.

The going was tough climbing over all those boulders. Although the boulders provided us with plenty of cover, we had little concealment. If the enemy was going to spot us, this would be the place. Although we wanted to get up the slope as quickly as possible, we had to be careful of our footing. By late afternoon we'd made it to the mountain's crest.

As we crossed over the crest to the other side of the mountain, we heard shots fired, but this time they were different. A single shot was fired from one direction, followed by two shots from another direction, and then two more shots fired from a third direction. All of the shots were less than five hundred meters from us.

The instructor didn't whisper this time, he just spoke softly. "I think they know our location. They probably spotted us climbing the boulders. We've probably been compromised."

He waited for a reaction from us. Instead we all remained quiet. He continued, "Since we don't know for sure, we'll continue with the mission. Any questions?"

We just shook our heads.

The instructor pulled out his notebook. "Burns, you're no longer team leader. You did a good job."

He pointed to the tail gunner, the last man in the file, who covers the team's rear. "You two switch places."

I was so glad to have passed what I considered to be the toughest position. I took my place at the rear of the file. The instructor named a new point man as well and we moved out.

Usually the unit that occupies the high ground has the advantage in a firefight. Therefore, I was surprised when the instructor ordered us to head down into a valley. Maybe the instructor figured Charlie knew our tactics and wouldn't think we would head downhill.

Although we remained cautious, we traveled faster than usual even though the jungle was thick. At least it was easier moving downhill. Finally the terrain leveled out as we made the valley floor. Nightfall came quickly, but we were still pushing on. I was dog-tired and just about walking in my sleep. I don't know if I was hallucinating, but the ground looked as if it were covered with bright pearls and diamonds. It was beautiful.

At last the instructor selected a spot for us to RON. We crawled into some thick bushes and put our backs together so we faced outward, covering a 360-degree circle. The instructor pointed to those of us carrying claymores, then signaled to us *not* to put them out. It was too dark and everybody was beat. That was fine with me. I didn't want to leave the safety of the team for anything.

Everyone was so tired, we decided to have two guys stay awake while four slept, as we had been doing all along. I got the third watch, so I slouched down on my rucksack and nodded off to sleep.

It was around 0100 hours when I was awakened for watch. The other teammate on watch was two guys over, observing the other side. I had been awake thirty minutes when I heard the rustling of leaves. The sound was off in the distance to my left. It was probably an animal, so, instead of waking up everyone, I decided to wait a bit.

A few moments later I heard the sound again. This time it was more pronounced. I wanted to wake up the instructor, but I was afraid he would think I was just scared and give me a low grade. I *was* scared. My eyes searched the jungle frantically, but I couldn't see anything. Besides, it was pitch black.

It wasn't long before I heard the noise again. It seemed to be louder, which meant it was closer than before. I reached over and touched the other teammate on watch. He could make out my silhouette, so I placed my hand to my ear. He nodded. He heard it too! To hell with it. If I got a low grade, so be it. I nudged the instructor softly.

He awoke instantly. I signaled that I'd heard something, so he listened for a minute or so, then whispered, "Monkeys!"

I smiled. Man, was glad I woke him up. He didn't appear to be pissed off and I found out it was only monkeys out there. I felt so relieved. The noise continued as the time passed and the rustle of leaves grew louder. Periodically I thought I heard the breaking of a twig. By the sound of the noise, the monkeys were headed our way. I wanted to awaken the instructor again, but I didn't want to be embarrassed. My eyes continued to scan in the direction of the noises.

I don't know how much time had elapsed, but I thought I spotted something moving slowly in our direction. I strained my eyes as hard as I could to make out the intruder. The moonlight or shadows hit just right because I saw a silhouette. The figure was about twenty meters away, moving slowly in our direction.

Shit! If it was a monkey, it was wearing a hat and carrying a weapon! Maybe I was hallucinating and just seeing things. I pulled my eyes from the figure for a moment, then let them return. Damn, it was still there. Not only was the lone figure there, but now I saw a few more behind him. I tried not to panic. It had to be Charlie. No other LRP teams or friendlies were in our area.

I tried not to startle my teammate as I grabbed at his shirt. As soon as he looked at me, I placed two fingers to my eyes, signaling that I'd spotted the enemy. He appeared stunned for just a moment, then started to wake up the guys closest to him. I awoke the man next to me and then the instructor. The instructor seemed annoyed until I again placed two fingers to my eyes. I could tell right away that he believed me. He immediately signaled all of us to be quiet and lay low.

The enemy soldiers were only about ten meters away by then. At least everyone was awake and alert. I placed my weapon so that it was pointed in the direction of the enemy. I then grabbed a grenade, loosened the pin, and placed it at my right side.

At least I wasn't scared anymore. I was far beyond scared; I was terrified. Why the hell did I want to come here and be a Recondo anyway? I must have been out of my mind. I started bargaining with God. I promised him that if he got me out of this one, I would go to church every Sunday for the rest of my life.

I thought about my family at home and how they would feel when they received the news that I'd been killed or captured. No! I was not going to be captured! I would go down fighting, taking as many of the sons a bitches with me as I could.

The gooks were about five meters from us. I could count about ten of them, and it sounded like there were more behind them. Slowly I picked up the grenade and placed it on my lap. I gently slid my hand along my receiver and rested my finger on the trigger. The selector switch was on semi instead of auto, but I didn't want to change it, since Charlie was so close he would probably hear the click. I would flip the switch to rock and roll as soon as the shit hit the fan.

My mouth was superdry. I would have given anything for a swallow of water. Sweat beaded the sides of my face. I had a big lump in my throat, but I dared not clear it. The first gook was about two meters from me now. My heart was pounding out of my chest so hard I just knew he could hear it. Mentally I tried as hard as I could to slow my heart rate, but I couldn't. It was only a matter of time before its pounding would give me away.

My mind was racing frantically. Should I let him walk by and wait for a few of the others to get into my kill zone? I could blow the claymore and then open up. The claymore! Shit! We hadn't put the claymores out! All we had to take on these guys were six weapons and some grenades. We were in a world of shit.

The first gook walked by me just three meters to my front. The gooks continued to walk past us for a long time. There were so many of them it must have been a company of about eighty or more. It was nerve-racking. I felt like I was coming out of my skin. On more than one occasion I just wanted to open fire and end all of the damn suspense. I could not believe that none of them heard my heart pounding. It was all *I* could hear.

At one point throughout the ordeal, one of the enemy soldiers stepped by me at less than a meter away. I remembered what the senior Recondo instructor said the first day of school. "Whether the enemy is two feet from you or two miles from you, you are okay because he doesn't know your location." That statement was the only thing that gave me the confidence to hang in there and not open fire.

At first I didn't know how much time elapsed before they were gone. Later, I discovered that what had seemed like a lifetime had only been two hours. I couldn't believe we got by without making contact. None of us slept the rest of the night.

It was the morning of the fourth day. There was no way we could communicate everything that had happened the night before with just hand signals, so we whispered. Somebody made a point about how lucky we were that we didn't have the claymores out. It was true. If we had put the claymores out, one of the gooks would have eventually tripped over at least one of the claymores' wires, thus initiating a firefight, and we were incredibly outnumbered.

One of my fellow 101st teammates summed up what we all felt. "Damn," he said. "I felt as nervous as a whore in church, sitting in the front pew with a fifty-dollar customer outside." That about said it all.

Nobody delayed in preparing to move out. We wanted to distance ourselves from the gooks as fast and as far as possible. The instructor was sure they were NVA regulars. They were searching for us last night and we doubted they would give up looking for us anytime soon.

The instructor decided it was time to make it to our PZ for extraction. If all went well, we would be there by early afternoon. The instructor let the student team leader run the show, but he made it clear that he would take over at a moment's notice. I still remained in the position of tail gunner as we moved out.

We were traveling fast but still trying to maintain caution and stealth. Around noontime we heard shots being fired. Charlie had either spotted us or was bracketing our location again.

I was steadily guarding the rear of our file as we patrolled through the jungle. I was so into the job that I fell behind at times and had to catch up. I listened intently for any kind of noise out of the ordinary. We had made it up the gentle slope of one mountain and were crossing a

saddle connecting to the next. The terrain was relatively
flat with just a slight incline; however, the jungle was
thick. Near the far point on the opposite side of the saddle was the PZ. Around midafternoon and about a kilometer away from the PZ, I heard what appeared to be a
metallic sound. Could it have been the bolt of a rifle?
The noise did not come from very far away. Damn! Charlie was on our trail. I signaled the team leader and instructor. The instructor took control of the team.

The instructor told the point man to pick up the pace.
We would sacrifice stealth for speed. We needed to make it
to the PZ for extraction before the enemy caught up with
us. The heat and humidity were unbearable. I was gulping
down a swallow of water every fifteen minutes or so.

The instructor halted the team momentarily to check
his map. He figured we were about thirty minutes from
the PZ if we remained at the pace we were traveling. We
radioed our location and our probable time of arrival at
the PZ for extraction. The instructor also requested an
air force 0-1 Bird Dog plane to be on-site during the extraction to mark targets for jet fighters and to control the
air strikes if needed.

We continued moving, pushing our way through the
thick vegetation. When the PZ was approximately ten
minutes away, we halted for a brief moment to catch our
breath. I kept my eyes glued to the rear. Just as we prepared to move, I heard a branch break and what sounded
like a weapon or equipment rattling. I wasn't the only
one who heard it.

It would have been a perfect opportunity for us to lay
an ambush for them. We could have quickly set out the
claymores and hidden in brush. More important, we had
the element of surprise. Part of me wanted to stay there
and waste a bunch of them. I'm sure I was not alone in
that thought. That was not our job, however. Our job
was to bring back intelligence and the film we had shot.
This is difficult to do when you are dead. Besides, we did

not know how many NVA were chasing us. Hell, it could have been the whole company.

Even though he was whispering, the instructor's tone of voice sounded serious. "Everyone stay alert. For all we know they might try to flank us. This time we're not stopping until we make it to the LZ."

His expression had a cold look to it I had never seen before. He stared at us for a moment to make sure we understood. "Okay! Point man, move out!"

We continued to travel quickly but not carelessly. If the enemy had split his force to outflank us or somehow get in front of us, we could walk into an ambush and would not likely survive. I rehearsed IA (immediate-action) drills in my mind and what I'd do if we were hit from the front, the rear, or either side.

We arrived at the PZ about five minutes early. We radioed the school that we needed to be extracted immediately. They said the birds were on the way. We selected a cluster of bushes on the edge of the PZ for concealment, but it offered little cover. There wasn't time to put out the claymores, so we got down low, aimed our weapons in the direction of the enemy, and waited for the choppers. We had nowhere else to go. I felt just a slight twinge of what Custer must have been thinking at his last stand.

While we waited, the instructor pulled a small, bright orange panel out of the top of his rucksack, handed it to the point man, and indicated to the PZ. "Run out there about twenty meters and lie down. When I give you the signal, place the panel on your chest and start popping it." Popping a panel meant opening and closing it so that from the sky it looked like blinking orange.

The point man took off in a flash. We heard the enemy soldiers coming now but could not see them. They had to be close. In no time they would be all over us. An instant later we heard the *whopwhopwhop* of the helicopters. They sounded like they were about a mile out. The instructor signaled the point man to start popping the panel. High above us I got a glimpse of the Bird Dog flying overhead.

I scanned the area to my front, keeping my rifle aimed and close to my face. I kept my weapon on semiautomatic. As tail gunner, my job was to cover the retreat of the rest of the team and take out any targets of opportunity. I knew I would be pulling the trigger any minute.

At last we saw a lone chopper soaring across the LZ. The instructor pointed to two team members and shouted, "You and you, go join the point man. When the bird lands, the three of you get on it and be ready to help the rest of us."

One of the men replied quickly, "Should we pop smoke?"

"Negative!"

The two scrambled off at a dead run. The commo man, the instructor, and I stayed in the tree line, providing security.

We watched the point man stand up holding the panel over his head. The chopper flared into a hover in front of him. The instructor tapped us on the shoulders. "Time to *di di* [run]!"

The three of us headed across the clearing to the bird. Our teammates were on board, waving at us to come on. If I was going to get shot, it was going to be now. I felt like I was in one of those dreams where you're running from or to something and your legs would not move fast enough. To make matters worse, we could now hear yelling coming from the jungle.

I turned around quickly and opened fire. To hell with it. Just because I couldn't see them didn't mean I couldn't hit them. Besides, it might keep their heads down. The instructor and commo man followed suit. When we got a few feet from the bird and out of his line of fire, the door gunner opened up.

Hands reached out from everywhere to grab us. As I was being lifted into the chopper, I heard explosions and gunfire all around us. I scrambled around and glanced outside the cabin. Two gunships had accompanied the slick onto the PZ and were blasting the tree line. I felt our chopper lurch upward and gazed back at the PZ just in time to observe the gunships make a second gun run across the smoke-filled clearing.

I sat on the cabin floor and struggled to catch my breath. My heart and head were pounding. I looked around at my fellow teammates. They were all sucking wind as well. Each face was a mixture of dirt, sweat, and camouflage paint.

The whole scene was contrasted by the Special Forces major sitting directly across from me. I hadn't noticed him until then. He looked like he had just walked off the parade field. The guy was sharp, well built, and somewhat stocky. His pressed set of cammies had a number of skill badges embroidered right onto his shirt, including his name, which read "Lunday". His green beret sat perfectly on his head and lay sharply over his right ear. He appeared to be enjoying the hell out of himself.

With a broad smile he tapped me on the knee and shouted, "You made it!"

I broke out in a big grin. I had made it! I made it out of there alive.

The major leaned closer to me and gave me a thumbs-up. "You graduated!"

I then realized that he wasn't talking about me making it out of the PZ. He meant that I had made Recondo. A sense of accomplishment fell over me, but the major appeared to be more happy for me than I was.

I laughed and rendered a thumbs-up in return.

I found out later that the major was in charge of the instructors and soon to be commandant of the school. When he found out that choppers were extracting a team in trouble, he wanted to observe the operation firsthand, so he jumped on the bird.

The Special Forces major and I swapped stories on the flight back to the Recondo compound. In our wildest dreams, neither he nor I would ever have imagined that, thirty-one years later, his nephew would marry my daughter, neither of whom had been born yet.

When our chopper landed at the compound, a number of our fellow students were on hand to welcome us. To our surprise, our team had spent the most time on the ground during "You Bet Your Life." One team had to be extracted early because they couldn't stop a sick team member's coughing. Another team was extracted on its very first day because it had run into a wasps' nest. The poor guys had welts all over them. The rest of the teams were extracted because of various compromises by the enemy.

The reason everyone was on hand to welcome us was that the school traditionally put on a small graduation party once all the teams were present. The instructors led us right from the helipad to the mess hall. In front were two large, metal, stateside trash cans full of ice, beer, and sodas. Next to them was a fifty-five-gallon fuel drum, cut in half and converted into a barbecue, on which lay some of the biggest, juiciest steaks I had ever seen. Special Forces lived dangerously but they sure lived comfortably. Again, I promised myself that if I remained in the army, which I thought unlikely, it would be with Special Forces.

The next morning we ate a hearty breakfast, then held a graduation ceremony. One of the Marines earned the honor graduate title for having achieved the highest overall score. He was presented with the prestigious Recondo graduation knife with his class and name engraved on it. Each of us was personally handed his Recondo certificate along with a set of orders authorizing us to wear the patch on our right shirt pocket. After receiving my certificate, I returned to my seat and glanced down at it. It was colorfully done with the map of Vietnam in the center and the Recondo badge superimposed over the map, symbolizing that Recondos could strike anywhere in the country. Each certificate was individually inscribed with the Recondo's name, rank, unit, date of graduation, and Recondo number. For some reason, it wasn't until I looked at my Recondo number that I realized I had really made it. I was Recondo. A feeling of pride swept over me. Maybe I'd paved the way for other Pathfinders to follow.

As the formalities came to an end, Major Lunday stood center stage and addressed the class. "Gentlemen, I do not want to stand here and repeat everything that has already been said. I would like to say, however, that each and every one of you performed remarkably well while on your graduation patrols and, as a result of your efforts, brought back some very important information. Like the completion of a puzzle, each team returned with their particular piece that, when connected to other pieces, provided the commanders with an accurate assessment of the enemy situation."

The major stopped momentarily, then continued. "As a matter of fact, your teams did so well, it looks like Recondo students will be utilized to augment and assist other units, not just those in the Nha Trang area, who may need long-range intelligence capability in the future."

Immediately following graduation, everyone lined up at the tailor shop to have Recondo patches sewn on shirt pockets. That night we partied hard at the compound's club and said our good-byes to fellow students and instructors. I had no trouble going to sleep that night. I did take a few moments to recall my experiences during the past few weeks, however. Recondo School was everything I'd hoped it would be. The next morning the three of us from the 101st gathered our gear and caught a flight back to Hue/Phu Bai.

It was early afternoon by the time I made it back to the unit area. As I walked to the Pathfinder hootch, Torch came running up to greet me, then ran back to the hootch to let everyone know I was coming. As I stormed into the hootch, everyone looked at my face, then shifted their eyes to my right shirt pocket. I received a hero's welcome. Ron and Buz drooled at the sight of my Recondo patch and wanted to know everything. A few hours later I was told to report to Captain Chase.

I walked into the captain's hootch and saluted. "Corporal Burns reporting as ordered, sir!"

Chase returned the salute. "Welcome back, Burns."

His eyes glanced up at my pocket. "I see you made it. Congratulations!"

I smiled. "Thank you, sir!"

Chase had an earnest expression on his face. "You missed one hell of an operation while you were gone. Your fellow Pathfinders performed exceptionally well. As a matter of fact, they earned a few medals."

He paused and stared at me. I knew he was searching my face for some kind of reaction. "Your buddy Reynolds is being awarded an Air Medal with V."

That was great! Ron didn't even tell me. I smiled. "That's great, sir! All of the guys deserve more than they will ever get while they're over here."

Chase appeared to be disappointed by my response. His demeanor became a little more abrupt, too. I also noticed that his grip tightened on the pen he was holding. "I've got to tell you, Burns. It's too bad you were in school during this time. You missed all the excitement."

"Yes, sir! I'm sure I did." I tried hard not to grin as I waited to be dismissed.

"Is that all, sir?"

Captain Chase seemed to be disgusted with me, as usual. "Yeah! That's all!"

I saluted, did an about-face, and stepped out of his hootch. As I strolled back to the Pathfinder hootch, I chuckled to myself. You got to be shitting me, sir. *I* missed all the excitement? Hell, I experienced enough damn excitement to last me a lifetime.

Chapter Eighteen

After leaving Captain Chase, I walked back to the Pathfinder hootch and the guys told me a lot had occurred since I had been away. They said we now had a colonel for a group commander. His name was Ted Crozier. Ironically, he had been an Airborne infantry officer at one point in his career and even commanded a Pathfinder unit. We all hoped his past experience would work in our favor. We also received a new group sergeant major and some other high-ranking NCOs. Unfortunately, they were all legs. We didn't think that would be to our advantage at all.

The division had changed names three times in my short absence. It went from the 101st Airborne Division to the 101st Air Cavalry to the 101st Airmobile and finally ended up as the 101st Airborne Division (Airmobile). Some unit's poor lower-ranking enlisted men had to repaint the 101st tab above the patch each time it changed. Rumor had it that General Westmoreland wanted to keep the Airborne tab even though the division was no longer a jump unit. We wondered how the changes would affect our detachment. It didn't take long to find out. The first problem arose that very day.

Lieutenant Wilberding stormed into the hootch. "We've got to do something with Torch!"

Everyone was taken aback by his outburst. Mitch spoke up. "What about Torch, sir?"

Upon hearing his name, Torch strolled out to the center of the tent, wagging his curly tail. Wilberding glanced down at him fondly. "Word has it that headquarters at group wants all the sections to get rid of pets and the like."

Poor Wilberding; everyone jumped on him at once. "Torch isn't a pet, dammit! He's a member of this unit! . . . Torch is an American! . . . Bullshit, sir! We're not giving up Torch!"

Lieutenant Wilberding put out his hands. "Okay! Okay! At ease now! No one's getting rid of Torch. I just talked with the captain. He wants Torch taken out of the immediate area for about a week or so while he squares it away with the new group commander. Captain Chase knows how much Torch means to the unit."

Everyone settled down, including me. I was almost in a panic. I had to give Captain Chase credit; even though he didn't like me and he had a few quirks, he cared about his men. He was not the kind of commander who handed out punishments for minor offenses, and he treated every one of us as a soldier. Moreover, you could stand toe-to-toe with him in a heated argument and he didn't hold it against you. We could have done a lot worse.

The only place we could take Torch was to one of the firebases around the A Shau. They were all dangerous places, but Bastogne was the largest firebase that we had Pathfinders on, and they occupied a bunker there. We decided that Bastogne would be the best place for Torch to lay low for a week. Lieutenant Wilberding said that Joe Bolick had been at Bastogne for some time and needed to be replaced. He also wanted three Pathfinders on Bastogne instead of two. Ron and I were selected as the ones to take Torch out there. Wilberding told us to be prepared to depart for Bastogne the next afternoon.

That night most of the detachment members sat around the Pathfinder hootch drinking beer. Buz wanted to hear all about Recondo School; he couldn't get enough.

"What do you think, Richie? You really believe I could pass the course if I got selected?"

"There is no doubt in my mind, Buz. You just got to want it bad enough—and you want it bad."

Buz was excited. "You're damn right I do. I was mentioning about applying for it, but Sergeant Guerra and Lieutenant Wilberding would never approve it. Actually, they hinted that I could probably get to go to Recondo School if I extended my tour for six months and transferred to the LRPs."

Nothing Buz said surprised me. Neither Sergeant Guerra nor Wilberding was fond of Buz and probably thought that would be an easy way to get rid of him.

I wondered how badly Buz really wanted it. "Let me ask you something? Would you really extend and transfer to the LRPs if that's what it took to attend the course?"

Buz didn't hesitate for an instant in his reply. "In a heartbeat."

I jumped up from my seat. "Well, shit! Let's go over there and talk to some of the guys. A few of the LRPs know that I went to the school and told me to stop by when I got back. The timing is perfect."

Buz and I bought a case of beer from behind the bar and I scrounged up a bottle of Mateus rosé wine. When we entered the LRPs' club, we got more than a few stares from some of the newly assigned LRPs who didn't know us, and they wondered who those guys were wearing black baseball hats. Moreover, I had the Recondo badge on my shirt. Of course, bearing the particular gifts in hand, we were welcomed with open arms.

Kenn Miller spoke first. "Hey, Pathfinder! I see you made it."

I pointed to my Recondo badge. "Damn straight!"

Miller smiled. "It looks good, man. Congratulations."

"Thanks. I brought something along with us."

Miller reached for a corkscrew to open the wine. "Great! Let's get wasted."

I introduced Buz to the LRPs. He ended up hitting it off with an LRP team leader named Ralph Timmons. Timmons said that if Buz could get reassigned to the LRPs, Timmons would accept Buz on his team.

Later, during one of our conversations, I asked, "Hey! How's it going with that new captain you guys got before I left?"

Instantly everyone stopped talking, then someone muttered, "The son of a bitch stepped on a mine."

I was really surprised. I'd never heard of a LRP captain actually going out on a mission on the ground with one of the teams. Maybe the guy was not all that bad.

Another LRP quickly clarified it for me. "Yeah! Right in his own fucking tent."

I couldn't believe it. "Are you shitting me? What was it, a toe popper?" (A toe popper was a small, plastic anti-personnel mine designed to cause just such damage, but to the enemy.)

Miller spoke up. "Almost blew his damn foot off. The CID have been crawling all over us for weeks. Nobody knows who did it. If anyone does, they're sure as hell not going to say anything."

As the party continued, I was discussing Recondo School with some of the LRPs who had not yet attended. Of course, I informed them that when their time came to attend the course, it would probably be a breeze for them, since I went through the last hard class Recondo School would ever have. For some reason, the four or five guys poured their beers all over me. After that, we left the club and went to one of the LRP hootches, where Buz and I ended up spending the night. One of our hosts passed out on the floor, so I slept in his cot.

The next morning the sun was bearing down so brightly that Buz and I could hardly see as we headed back toward the Pathfinder hootch. Every soldier we strolled past gave us a wide-eyed stare and wide passage because my fatigues reeked of stale beer. The rancid odor hung in the air around me.

Once I got back to the hootch, my fellow Pathfinders threatened to throw me out unless I got rid of the fatigues immediately. I stripped them off quickly and shoved them into a waterproof bag. I would wash them when I had some time. Later in the day, Ron and I packed our gear and other supplies together and with Torch headed for the helipad.

I was afraid Torch would step out of the helicopter, so I held on to him tightly as we flew to Bastogne. I could tell he loved the cool breeze flowing through the cabin. His nose was going a mile a minute with all the different smells. At Bastogne, Ron and I replaced Joe Bolick, who needed a well-deserved break, and linked up with Larry Foracker.

Bastogne was larger and had more units on it than the last time I was there. The Pathfinder bunker was still on the top of the hill beside the VIP pad and across from the TOC. A 105 artillery battery was located about twenty meters from the Pathfinder bunker. Bastogne also had a 155 artillery battery and a 175 artillery battery in place. That was a lot of firepower and men. The 175 artillery guns were huge and could shoot a round about thirty kilometers into the A Shau. An artillery battery consisted of three guns plus the soldiers to man them along with an FDC (fire direction control) that plotted where the guns would shoot their rounds, kept track of areas where there were friendlies, and so on.

The main mission of the artillery batteries was to support the infantry companies patrolling the jungle when they made contact with the enemy. Three companies patrolled outside the firebase while one company remained on Bastogne to provide perimeter security. The companies rotated perimeter security every so often. Bastogne also had a POL (aircraft refueling point), communications personnel, engineers, and other supporting units.

Since Bastogne had so many units and had become so visible to Charles, enemy mortar attacks had become more than common, sometimes daily. Considering the number of attacks, casualties had remained minimal; we all knew it was just a matter of time before our luck would change. We were there only a few days when the inevitable happened.

Larry was on the top of the bunker controlling aircraft. It was in the middle of the afternoon, so Ron, Torch, and I were down inside the bunker out of the heat. We heard Larry yell, "Incoming!" followed by the sound of mortar rounds exploding nearby.

Larry warned all the aircraft in the area, then leaped down into the entrance just as the attack ceased. "We've got wounded. I'm calling for a dustoff."

Torch didn't like mortar attacks and knew enough to stay inside the bunker. Ron and I ran out to help the injured. Five men were wounded in all, two seriously. It seemed as if we were just starting to apply first aid when Larry yelled, "The dustoff is inbound! Get them to the VIP pad, now!"

Ron assisted the three who could walk to the VIP pad while I shouted for others to help me carry the two who couldn't. The two men we carried were in tremendous pain, but we had to move them to get them on the chopper. When we reached the pad, one of the men was having trouble breathing; he had been hit in the face. I attempted to clear his airway, but it was blocked. He was gasping for air.

I barked, "Anyone here a medic?"

No one answered.

Someone standing over me muttered, "He's going to need a tracheotomy!"

I shouted, "Anyone want to do it?"

The wounded man was choking to death. I grabbed the ballpoint pen from my shirt, undid it quickly, and threw all the parts to the side but the bottom tube. "I need a knife! Anyone got a knife?"

Someone handed me a pocketknife. I was taught in infantry training to run my index finger down a man's Adam's apple until I found the "V," then make a hole and insert the tube. Since the throat was blocked, he could breathe air into his lungs through the pen's tube.

I prayed out loud, "Please God, don't let me screw this up!"

Someone uttered, "You can do it!"

Just as I placed the tip of the knife on the man's skin, Ron grabbed my shoulder and cried out, "Chopper's here!" I was so intent on what I was doing, I did not even hear it arrive. What a relief!

Ron and I grabbed the soldier and placed him on the chopper first. As the others loaded the remaining wounded, I waved at the medic on board and pointed to the dying man's throat. He acknowledged that he understood the injury. Just as the chopper lifted skyward, more mortar rounds came crashing in.

This time they exploded about twenty meters from us, walking right across the artillery battery while the men manning the guns were returning counterbattery fire. We watched helplessly as the rounds landed right inside the artillery parapets where the men were firing the guns. Many were hurled to the ground, shrapnel tearing through their bodies. Amid the screams and moans, a second volley of explosions came crashing in. This time the rounds were advancing directly toward the Pathfinder bunker and Ron and me.

Larry yelled, "Get down! They're coming right at us!"

Larry leaped from the top of the bunker just as it took a direct hit. Had he stayed in place he would have been dead. Ron and I hastily flattened to the ground beside each other. I heard a loud *boom* as one round hit about ten feet on one side of us and another loud *boom* as another round hit about ten feet on the other side of us. Miraculously, we both stood up unscathed.

"Dustoff inbound!" Larry screamed from the bunker.

Ron popped smoke on the VIP pad, then we raced over to the wounded, who were already being assisted by their comrades. I counted quickly. We had one dead and six wounded, a full chopper load. The man I helped carry to the pad was screaming in agony. Shrapnel had torn through his legs and scrotum. We loaded the wounded on first, then the dead. The accuracy of the enemy mortars left no doubt they had an FO sighting in on us. I prayed the chopper would take off before another volley came in. Luckily, the enemy mortars had ceased for the day.

Torch never bothered any of the units at Bastogne or begged for food from them, and he always stayed at the Pathfinder bunker. If he did accompany me or another Pathfinder around the firebase, he remained right by our side at all times and obeyed every command. The only time Torch was ever alone was when he had to relieve himself. Even then, he went near the perimeter where nobody ventured. Needless to say, it didn't take long for Torch to earn the respect and affection of most of the soldiers at Bastogne.

Torch had experienced enemy rocket and mortar attacks in the past, both at Bien Hoa and Camp Eagle. Just like his fellow soldiers, whenever he heard an explosion or someone yelled, *Incoming*, he ran to the nearest bunker for cover.

Ron, Torch, and I had been on Bastogne about six days controlling aircraft and coordinating artillery fire and other missions with the TOC when another intense enemy mortar barrage came in. The deadly rounds exploded about midway down the hill while I was on top of the bunker controlling aircraft. A chopper was unloading supplies on the main helipad and a Chinook was refueling at the POL point, close to where the mortars were exploding.

I grabbed the radio handset. "All aircraft on Bastogne be advised we are under a mortar attack. You are clear for immediate takeoff. I repeat, take off immediately. Over."

The chopper wasted no time bolting straight up about thirty feet in the air, then darting across the treetops like it was shot out of a cannon. The Chinook, however, remained on the ground. Its ramp was still down and the crew chief was standing outside the bird supervising the refueling. Surely the Chinook's crew knew of the mortar attack. The way the aircraft was situated, however, perhaps they could not see all the ruckus. In any event, if a second barrage of mortar rounds came in and just one of them hit a fuel bladder, the whole POL point including the Chinook would blow sky-high.

Just as I grabbed the handset to warn them again, a second volley of enemy rounds exploded along the hillside. It was then that I spotted Torch. I had thought he was safe inside the bunker. The little guy must have gone to relieve himself and got cut off making his way back to the bunker. He looked frightened and confused. I could tell that he wanted to run toward us to safety, but the mortar rounds were exploding between his location and our bunker.

I called out to Ron and Larry and told them of Torch's predicament. The three of us watched helplessly as Torch tried to figure out what to do. There were some bunkers located at the bottom of the hill behind him and we heard a few soldiers calling to him. I guess Torch realized he couldn't make it to our location so he ran toward the bottom of the hill to those bunkers for safety.

As Torch headed for the bottom of the hill, a third volley of enemy rounds came in. To our horror, the rounds exploded all around Torch as he was running. It looked like one of the deadly projectiles exploded right on him.

It was obvious the NVA was attempting to hit the POL point along with the Chinook. I barked into the handset, "Chinook at POL. Take off immediately! Do you copy? Over!"

The pilot's voice blared over the handset. "Roger, we're departing at this time!"

Soldiers' ponchos, empty sandbags, sheets of plastic, and everything else that wasn't tied down blew across the helipad as the big Chinook pulled pitch and soared right across the firebase at full throttle. The giant helicopter still had its ramp down as it streaked across our bunker. Larry, Ron, and I immediately went to find Torch.

To our dismay we could not find Torch anywhere, not

even parts of his body. We spent the rest of the day querying every soldier on the firebase. Many of them had seen the mortar rounds explode around Torch, but nobody saw what happened to him when the attack was over. We had to assume that Torch was either dead or had fled into the jungle, perhaps wounded.

I was never ashamed to cry over a comrade getting killed or embarassed by seeing someone else cry over a buddy. I think a soldier who dies fighting for his country and protecting his buddies deserves to be cried for, probably more than anyone else. Most of the time I mourned the loss of a buddy alone, but you can imagine how sorrowful the three of us were that night at having lost Torch. In the short eight months of his life that pup had stolen every Pathfinder's heart. Moreover, I always felt Torch was my dog since I had found him. It would be a sad time for the detachment when the word reached them that Torch was missing in action and presumed dead. We radioed the news to the detachment the next morning.

A couple of days after we lost Torch, the monsoon rains poured down with such intensity that our bunker filled with water and collapsed on us during the night. The three of us were damn lucky to crawl out of the rubble with our lives. We erected a poncho hootch for the next few days while the engineers repaired our bunker. They did a great job, too. Our new bunker had almost twice as much room as the old one and the inside stayed relatively dry. Most of the time. Unfortunately, a communications staff sergeant and a specialist showed up for temporary assignment at Bastogne with no place to stay, and we had to share our bunker with them. Their job was to monitor radio traffic and provide communications support to the various units. It proved to be a nightmare for us.

The specialist was a great guy named Florres. Florres chipped in with daily chores and was respectful. The staff sergeant, however, was plain lazy. Moreover, he tried to order us around and even attempted to have us pull his radio watch for him. Fortunately, we were not in his chain of command and had our own jobs to do. We politely told him to go to hell.

A few days later we experienced déjà vu. Larry was controlling aircraft while Ron and I were inside the bunker along with the staff sergeant and Florres. Suddenly Larry yelled, "Incoming!" The same artillery battery closest to us again took direct hits, this time on the very first volley.

Ron and I ran to assist the wounded to the helipad while Larry radioed for a dustoff. We had five or six casualties. One of them was the artillery battery commander who had just taken command a few days prior. His torso and legs were peppered with shrapnel.

The commander was older than most captains. He gnawed on a cigar and attempted to wriggle free as Ron and I carried him to the pad. "What about my men? I don't want to leave the wounded behind!"

As I struggled to hold on to his legs, I uttered, "Your men will be okay, sir. You will all be going out on the same chopper."

My statement seemed to calm him, making our task of carrying him easier. He grumbled, "Dammit! I can't believe it happened to me again. I got hit the last time I was over here and had to go back to the States. I finally get another combat command and the sons a bitches screw me up again."

As we placed the captain on the pad, he shouted to his men who were already manning the guns and returning counterfire. "That's it! Give them hell! Kill every one of those rotten bastards!"

Larry yelled that the chopper was one mile out, so I popped smoke. Just as the chopper landed, another volley of mortars came crashing in. Again the same artillery battery took direct hits. The NVA definitely had an FO sighting them in. We loaded the wounded quickly, then I ran in front of the chopper and signaled for it to take off. I quickly dropped to my knees as the chopper darted away, skimming the top of my head. Larry radioed for another dustoff. Six or seven more men were wounded, so Ron and I ran to the bunker to get Florres and the staff sergeant to help us carry them to the pad. Even though they were not Pathfinders, they would give us a hand.

As we stormed through the entrance, Ron cried out, "Richie and I need help! We got more wounded to get out."

Florres motioned toward us, but the staff sergeant grabbed him. "You're not going anywhere, Florres. You keep your ass right here."

Florres stared at the sergeant in astonishment. "But there's wounded men out there, Sergeant. We got to go and help them."

The sergeant snapped back, "This ain't our battle. If we go out there, we can get killed."

Florres pleaded, "No sweat, Sergeant. I'll go while you stay here. I won't be long."

The sergeant became furious. "Dammit, Florres. I'm giving you an order to stay right here. You go out there and I'll have your ass court-martialed. Is that clear, Specialist?"

The sergeant then pointed at Ron and me. "That goes for you two as well. Understand?"

I couldn't believe what I was hearing. I replied bluntly, "You don't have any authority over us."

The sergeant shouted at me, "I'm a damn staff sergeant in the United States Army and I'm ordering you two to sit your young asses down and keep your mouths shut or I'll have the both of you court-martialed for insubordination!"

I tried to suppress my anger as I spoke. "I respect your rank, but I'd be court-martialed if I didn't go and get out the wounded. I'm a Pathfinder. That's my job."

Before the sergeant could respond, Ron barked, "We don't have time for this. C'mon, Richie! Let's go!"

The sergeant shouted, "You two just want to go and play hero and try to get some damn medals. I'm an NCO and—"

Ron cut him off. "*We're* NCOs and you're nothing but a damn coward. We don't give a damn about any medals; there's wounded men out there who need our help."

As we turned to leave, the sergeant stepped toward Ron and reached out to grab him. I had never seen Ron angry before. His face turned red, he clenched his fist, and I could see the veins protruding from his neck. "You lay a hand on me, you cowardly son of a bitch, and I'll kick your ass."

The sergeant stopped in his tracks as fear swept over his face. Ron reached down, grabbed his M-16 rifle, and chambered a round. He pointed the weapon at the sergeant. "I ought to kill you right here."

I couldn't believe what I was seeing. Ron looked as though he were really going to shoot the guy. He even had me scared. Slowly I stepped forward and placed my hand on the weapon, pushing it downward. "C'mon, buddy. The asshole's not worth it. He's the one who has to live with himself."

Ron hesitated momentarily, then put the weapon to the side. I snickered. "Holy shit! Remind me never to piss you off, okay?" Ron smiled and together we rushed out.

Larry was still on top of the bunker and shouted down at us. "Hey! What the hell took you guys so long? I got two dustoffs inbound. You got to get all the wounded to the pad right away!"

Although some of the injured were still being carried to the pad by their buddies, we had enough wounded already at the pad to fill the first dustoff. The chopper was in sight, so I popped smoke while Ron guided the bird in. A familiar face showed up to help us load the wounded on the helicopter. It was Florres. He looked at Ron and me and shrugged. "Screw him. What's he gonna do? Send me to Vietnam?"

Just as the chopper lifted off, Larry yelled, "Another dustoff inbound. Pop smoke!"

Ron and I looked at each other and realized neither of us had any smoke grenades left. Florres stayed with the wounded while Ron and I ran to the bunker to get some more.

The chopper was in sight, so Ron yelled to Larry, "Just throw me a smoke."

Larry threw the smoke grenade and Ron caught it and handed it to me. "Here, Richie. You pop it and I'll guide the bird in like before."

Just as I grabbed the grenade from Ron and turned to head back to the pad, an explosion encompassed me. I was thrown to the ground like a rag doll. I tried to get up amid the gray smoke and dirt, but could not regain my balance. My legs just didn't seem to work. My ears were ringing, my vision was blurred, and I felt a burning sensation in the back of my neck. I attempted to push up with my hands, but gravel was embedded in both palms.

Finally I made it to one knee and stood up. A gruff voice behind me bellowed, "Are you all right?"

I turned around and saw it was Colonel Beckwith. He was brushing himself off as he walked toward me. The mortars must have barely missed him as well.

I could see the concern on his face. "I'm okay, sir." I gave him a thumbs-up.

He just smiled, shook his head, and walked back toward the TOC.

Suddenly I remembered Ron. He was standing right beside me when the explosion occurred. I prayed he wasn't dead. The force of the explosion had blown me down the side of the hill, so I couldn't see him. I turned around just in time to see Ron stand up.

He glanced over at me. "You okay?"

"Yeah. You?"

Ron patted his shirt with his hands and nodded. "I can't believe we're not dead. That mortar round hit right on us."

Just then Larry's voice boomed, "Damn! That was close!"

Ron and I looked up at Larry, on top of the bunker. Right below him our water cans were covered with holes and water was streaming out of them, just like on some TV western after the gunfight. The sandbag in front of Larry had been ripped wide open. The bunker had taken a direct hit. Luckily, when the engineers repaired our bunker, they constructed a wall out of sandbags about two feet high along the top. That little wall saved Larry's life.

Just then we heard a helicopter. The second dustoff was only seconds away from landing. There wasn't time to guide him in. I ran to the pad and popped smoke. The chopper landed a moment later and Florres and I loaded the remaining wounded.

Suddenly another barrage of mortars came crashing in. The first round hit about twenty meters from the chopper. The second round came closer, the third even closer. The enemy was walking the rounds toward the aircraft. The door gunner's eyes got about as big as plates.

As soon as we placed the last of the injured on the chopper, the door gunner screamed into his headset for the pilot to go. Just as the helicopter lurched forward, an enemy mortar round hit right between Florres and me. Instead of exploding, however, the round bounced across the pad and slid into the perimeter.

Florres stared at me in disbelief. "Did you see that shit?"

I laughed. "Let's get the hell out of here!" The two of us ran to the bunker for cover. It was truly a miracle that the mortar round did not explode. Florres and I were standing only two feet from each other when it hit right between us. There is no way we would have survived.

About an hour or so later, after everything calmed down, Larry, Ron, and I were sitting on top of the bunker. Florres and the sergeant were down inside, probably discussing Florres's future. An NCO from the TOC came by.

He called up to us. "You guys okay?"

Ron, Larry, and I glanced at the NCO with puzzled expressions. Ron answered, "Yeah, Sergeant. We're okay."

The NCO pulled out a small notebook and pen from his upper shirt pocket. "I'm going to need your names, service numbers, and unit."

The three of us hesitated to reply, thinking that it might be something bad. The NCO sensed our reluctance and continued. "The old man [referring to Colonel Beckwith] witnessed what you guys did during the mortar attacks and is putting you in for awards."

The three of us were taken by surprise. Being recommended for an award was one thing, but being put in for an award by Colonel Beckwith was an honor.

After we gave the NCO the information and also Florres's name, Larry asked, "What kind of awards do you think we'll get?"

The NCO replied nonchalantly. "Probably Bronze Stars with Vs." A Bronze Star with "V" meant it was for valor.

The three of us were pretty excited about it. The NCO then asked if any of us were wounded. Ron and I had blood all over the front of our fatigues from carrying the wounded, but the NCO pointed to the blood on the back of our collars and hands and Larry's arms.

I spoke up first. "I don't know if it's shrapnel that hit me in the neck or gravel."

Ron and Larry said the same thing. The NCO had concern in his voice. "If you guys go to the battalion medics and get treated you'll probably receive Purple Hearts."

In all honesty I was contemplating it when Ron replied; he was real irritated. "You got to be kidding. There's no way we'd accept Purple Hearts after seeing the wounds those other guys got. They're the ones the Purple Hearts are for." Ron was right, and Larry and I agreed. Not only would we be embarrassed, but the guys back at the detachment would never let us live it down.

The sergeant and Florres completed their job at Bastogne and left. From the time Ron threatened the sergeant with his rifle, he never bothered any of us again, including Florres. He just kept to himself and minded his own business.

Buz Harding came out to Bastogne to replace me. I stayed a couple of days, then returned to Camp Eagle. Ironically, right around the time Torch was missing, Captain Chase had gone to the new colonel to request that the Pathfinders be allowed to keep Torch, since he was a full-fledged member of our detachment. Chase did such a good job discussing the matter that the colonel agreed. His triumph only added to our sadness.

I was back at the unit only a day or so when we were told that a crew chief from another aviation unit wanted to see us. A few of us went outside the tent to see what he wanted. To our complete surprise and joy, he was holding Torch in his arms.

"Is this your dog?"

We went running to him and I grabbed Torch from him. Torch barked and wagged his tail. He was overjoyed to see us. The crew chief was relieved. "Man, I've been trying to run down his owners for days. We're stationed up north. It was just by luck that we ran into one of your pilots who said he thought he belonged to the 101st Pathfinders, so we flew down here to check it out."

I shook the crew chief's hand. "I can't thank you enough. We thought he was dead. Where did you find him?"

"I'm a crew chief for a Chinook. We were refueling at Bastogne about a week ago and came under a mortar attack. Just as we were taking off, your dog ran onto the ramp and right into our aircraft. We couldn't believe it. We knew his owners had to be American to be on Bastogne and figured someone was missing him. I got to tell you. We almost wish we hadn't found you guys. He's a great dog, but we could tell he was unhappy."

I couldn't believe it, either. His Chinook was the one I'd instructed to take off that had the ramp still down. When the mortars were exploding around Torch, he probably saw the Chinook as the only place for cover and ran inside.

We all thanked the crew chief again. He couldn't wait to get back to his crew and tell them the whole story. We spoiled Torch the rest of the day. That night, however, after a few beers, someone suggested we bust Torch from corporal to private first class for going AWOL under fire.

The vote was almost unanimous until someone said, "Let me ask you all something. Wouldn't every one of you jump on a helicopter if you were under a mortar attack and had the chance?"

We thought about it and recanted. We decided that instead of busting Torch, we should promote him to sergeant for being so smart as soon as he had the time in grade.

Ron, Larry, and I never did receive any awards for our actions at Bastogne. We knew Colonel Beckwith was true to his word. We could only assume that the recommendations were lost somewhere between his unit and ours.

The first week of September, the monsoon rains were so bad that most aircraft did not fly except for emergencies, and that was risky. There were no missions going on, so most Pathfinder detachment members stayed in the rear at Camp Eagle except for those out on the firebases. Even the enemy was hindered by the weather and hunkered down somewhere in the jungle.

Around the sixth of September, we were told that a typhoon named Bess was going to hit us either that night or the following day with winds blowing from 120 to 150 miles an hour. Since we did not receive much warning, we hurriedly secured the tents and huts as best we could while the aircraft crews tried to tie down the choppers.

Around noon Lieutenant Wilberding came to the hootch. "I need two volunteers."

I said, "What's up, sir?"

Wilberding explained. "An infantry company from the 1st/327 is stranded out in the A Shau and needs to be extracted."

A Pathfinder named Kip Nelson chimed in. "How does anybody expect us to do that when no aircraft are flying?"

Wilberding looked at Kip excitedly, like he was the bearer of good news. "Luckily, two chopper crews have volunteered to fly the mission."

Kip bowed his head and snickered. "Oh, that's great, sir." Everybody laughed.

Four or five of us piped up to volunteer. Wilberding wasted no time with his decision. "Burns, you and Nelson get ready to leave within the hour."

Once Wilberding left, Kip turned to me and said jokingly, "Why don't I listen to my parents? They told me not to volunteer for anything."

I decided to bite. "Well, why did you volunteer?"

Kip had a surprised expression on his face. "Hell! I didn't think I'd really be picked."

I just laughed and shook my head. Kip missed his calling in life. He should have been a stand-up comedian. I never once saw him down or angry. Even when something bad happened, he would come up with some kind of joke or funny remark. He was a little taller than me, heavyset, with a round, smooth face. He had a great sense of humor and wit and the facial expressions to go with them.

Kip and I quickly packed our gear. As we headed to the helipad to board the chopper, I became a little frightened. The winds were already blowing about fifty miles an hour and the rain was the worst I had seen it. Moreover, the fog was thick, making visibility poor. We were in for one hell of a ride.

There were two helicopters and we boarded the lead one. As I sat on the floor and the pilots started the engines, I kind of wished I hadn't been picked, either.

Chapter Nineteen

As our helicopter lifted for takeoff, the rain blasted through the cabin with such ferocity that we were forced to close the doors. Once airborne, we felt as if the aircraft was flying sideways. I had never flown in an aircraft with the wind thrashing it around so violently. Feeling that at any moment we were going to crash, I held on to anything that was bolted to the cabin.

I didn't have any doubts about the mission's success until we passed the foothills and began heading toward the A Shau. Thick layers of fog covered the mountains like ghostly black clouds. Many a helicopter had crashed into the side of a mountain in Vietnam in weather conditions a lot less adverse than this. For the sake of the infantry company stranded down there, I hoped we could pull it off. It was going to be rough. If the mission did fail, it would not be because of a lack of audacity or skill from the flight crews.

My heart pounded up into my throat as the chopper descended into the eerie mist. The pilots carefully maneuvered through the fog until we were flying low-level along a river. After a few minutes the helicopter banked right, along a branch of the river that eventually converged into a small, water-filled clearing. Suddenly the pilot brought the helicopter to a wobbly hover. The aircraft swayed and bounced for a minute or so until its skids settled on the ground but beneath the water.

Kip and I slid the door open and leaped from the bird. The water was about a foot deep as we hurriedly jogged through it. The second chopper did not have enough room to land. I felt sorry for that pilot as he struggled to keep the aircraft stable in the powerful winds. Kip and I made our way to the edge of the clearing that was located right at the bottom of a mountain. We were greeted by two soldiers, both covered with mud.

One of them shouted in my ear to be heard above the blades of the helicopters and the storm. "We're here to take you to the CO."

I shouted back. "How far away is he?"

The soldier pointed toward the side of the mountain. "Just a short ways up the side of this hill. It's real muddy and slippery, though."

My eyes scanned the clearing. "Do you have any men that are ready to get on these choppers right now?"

The soldier shook his head. "No!"

I turned and looked at Kip. He knew exactly what I was thinking and turned his back to me so I could have access to the radio in his rucksack. To save time and fuel, it would have been helpful if the unit had troops ready to hop on the two birds we came in on.

I grabbed the handset. "Eagle Lead. This is Pathfinder Control, over."

"This is Eagle Lead."

"Roger, Eagle Lead. We do not have any sorties ready at present. How long can you wait? Over."

"This is Eagle Lead. If you can get them here in zero five mikes [five minutes], we'll take them home. We can't wait any longer than that. Over."

"Roger, Eagle Lead. I copy."

"This is Eagle Lead. We're having a difficult time keeping the aircraft steady. We're going to make a go-around. Have them ready to board in zero five."

"This is Pathfinder Control. Roger."

I told Kip, "We've got to get two sorties ready to load up ASAP."

The two soldiers led us up the side of the mountain. But it was not easy; there was so much mud that for every step we took forward, if felt like we slid two back. Luckily the CO was close by. Most of his troops, however, were scattered on the slopes above us.

I tried desperately to catch my breath. "How's it going, sir?"

The CO smiled. He was genuinely happy to see us. "The Pathfinders! All right! Maybe we'll get out of this hellhole after all!"

We could hear the choppers inbound. Kip got on the radio while I spoke with the CO.

"Sir, we've got to get two chopper loads to the clearing ASAP or we'll miss a chance to get some of your men out of here right away."

I thought the CO might question me and waste valuable time. Instead he acted immediately. He shouted to six or seven troops nearby, "You men grab your shit right now and make it down to the LZ to board those choppers. Hurry it up!"

Grabbing their rucksacks and weapons and making their way down the hill, the men didn't waste any time. Actually, most of them fell on their butts and slid half the way to the bottom. I counted seven.

Kip was communicating with the pilots and turned to me. "They said they'll take eight pax each."

I notified the CO. "The choppers will take sixteen in all, sir. Eight on each bird. We need nine more men."

The CO looked above us and pointed to the men closest to him. "You, you, and you . . . you two . . . you four. Get moving ASAP if you want to go home."

There was an actual mud chute or gutter above us and it went almost all the way to the bottom of the mountain. Kip and I burst out laughing as four or five of the soldiers sat in it and soared by us like an amusement park ride.

Kip got on the radio and pleaded with the pilots to wait a few moments longer. Of course, if they didn't, we would understand; they could not afford to run out of fuel.

I watched the lead bird come in and land in the clearing. Once it took off, the second bird came in. Finally Kip stepped toward me. "Two sorties on their way back to Eagle."

The CO, his radio operator, Kip, and I stood in a circle. Kip had on cammies with a bush hat and I had on tiger fatigues. The brim of his hat was folded in the front like a "V," and it was raining so hard that the water was streaming off his hat in front of his face. With that stand-up comic look and a calm voice, he stared at the CO and said, "Where's the park ranger?"

It was such a stupid statement that the four of us just laughed. Leave it to Kip to bring some humor to a stressful situation. The CO was a captain who appeared to be in his mid-twenties and was squared away. He was very personal, but professional. He clearly had the respect of his men. Although they jumped when he told them to do something, he treated them with dignity.

Besides being completely soaked and covered in mud, his men looked haggard and weary. I was curious. "How long have you guys been out here, sir?"

The CO shook his head. "Well, we were patrolling a different area of the A Shau for about three weeks and all set to go back home to Camp Eagle. Of course, the morale was high as we waited for the choppers to pick us up. Just as we boarded the choppers, I received new orders. They needed us to assist another company and act as a blocking force. Instead of going home, the choppers dropped us off on the opposite side of this mountain. It was tough on the men and their morale dropped. I didn't feel too great about it, either. We've been here about a week. We should have been extracted a day or so ago, but the weather's been too bad. I guess they were waiting for it to clear up, but now that a typhoon is coming we've got to get the hell out of here."

After listening to the captain's story, Kip and I were more determined than ever to get these poor guys home.

While the helicopters were gone, we identified the next

group of soldiers to leave and made sure they were already waiting at the LZ so they could board the choppers immediately upon arrival. Kip and I passed the time talking with the commander and two other soldiers, his RTO and his FO—the forward artillery observer who was attached to his company from the artillery. He said the two men never left his side.

The FO was a specialist who had been with the CO and the unit for about eight months and been wounded three times while serving with it, once badly enough to be medevacked to Japan. After healing, however, he asked to be returned to the same company. That said a lot about the unit and its commander.

Two or three hours passed as the choppers shuttled the company back to Camp Eagle. They crammed more guys on board in an effort to beat the clock. The turn-around time was about forty minutes, longer if the aircraft had to refuel. The weather continued to deteriorate until the small clearing that we used as an LZ was waist-high in water because the river was overflowing. By the time we had only two more lifts to go, I seriously wondered if we would get out. I didn't say anything, but I could tell that Kip was thinking the same thing. The CO, his RTO, the FO, Kip, and I would be the last ones to leave.

Suddenly the pilot's voice came over the radio. "Pathfinder Control. This is Eagle Lead. Over."

I pulled the handset out of the plastic bag I kept it in to keep it dry. "This is Pathfinder Control. Over."

"Roger! We're about three miles out from the southeast. Over."

"This is Pathfinder Control. Roger. Will pop smoke when you are inbound."

There was no sense for the pilot to request landing instructions. What was I going to tell him? Winds fifty miles an hour, gusting to seventy-five? Visibility fifty feet and dropping?

The force of the wind had the rain thrashing us horizontally. Some of the smaller trees were bending in half and jungle plants with enormous leaves were taking a brutal beating as they whipped around in circles from the gale. A huge, dark gray cloud hung in the air about fifty feet above us. It was only a matter of time before it would encompass us completely. Once that happened there would be no way the helicopters could fly in or attempt to land.

We could hear the choppers approaching but could not see them. The best thing Kip and I could try was to guide the pilots in by their sound, if we had to, until they could descend below the cloud cover and see us. I shouted for one of the soldiers at the bottom of the hill to pop smoke. The smoke grenade emitted swirls of violet smoke that were quickly blasted away by the wind into wisps of nothingness.

Whopwhopwhop . . . the distinctive sound of the choppers' blades grew louder. They were not far from us at all. I prayed that their blades would not hit the side of a hill. As Kip and I fixed our eyes in the direction of the sound, we saw the first aircraft cut through the dense fog. The scene looked eerie, like a horror movie. The only thing missing was a graveyard with Count Dracula.

As the first chopper hovered over the clearing, the second helicopter appeared. Gradually the first chopper descended. Since the water was waist-high, the chopper did not touch down but lowered its skids into the water.

We watched the soldiers struggle through the water to get to the chopper, their rucksacks and weapons weighing them down. They had a rougher time trying to climb on board. Once the first chopper was loaded, the second one hovered down. Incredibly, the pilots kept the birds stable during the whole process. A silence fell over the eleven of us who remained behind.

Two men provided security while the rest of us stood around in a circle. I was so wet, the skin on my hands was wrinkled. The temperature had dropped as well and we were cold.

Finally the FO spoke. "Damn, I hope we get out of here!"

The RTO tried to crack a joke. "What's the matter, man? You afraid of a typhoon?"

The FO scoffed. "I ain't afraid of no typhoon. I don't want to be here tonight when Charlie comes looking to see what was going on and there's just us."

I had been so busy, I hadn't thought much about the enemy. I decided to query the CO. "The NVA are pretty much hunkered down with this weather, too, don't you think, sir?"

The CO seemed to welcome the conversation. "Yeah, they're not coming out in this. We did spot an NVA patrol in this area two days ago, but they disappeared before we could make contact. There must be at least a company of them close by."

As much as I did not want to think about it, the FO was right. Charlie would definitely check out what the choppers had been doing at our location. If they detected the few of us, they would attack us with their entire unit. If we didn't make it out on the next load, we would be in big trouble from the typhoon, the enemy, or both.

It seemed like forever before Eagle Lead's voice came over the radio. "Pathfinder Control. This is Eagle Lead. Over."

As Kip grabbed the handset, everyone expressed relief. "Eagle Lead. This is Pathfinder Control. Over."

"Roger. This is Eagle Lead. We're about four miles out. How is the visibility at your location? Over."

What the pilot really wanted to know was if the visibility had gotten worse; it had. "This is Pathfinder Control. Visibility is approximately three zero feet, over."

The pilot wanted to make sure he'd heard Kip right. "Understand three zero feet. Over."

Kip sighed. "That's a roger. Over."

There was a moment of silence before the pilot replied. "Roger."

The eleven of us slid our way down the hill. Once at the bottom, the first two men stepped into the water on the LZ. To our surprise, it was almost at chest level. The two men quickly trudged back out of the water, and we all remained on the edge of the clearing where it was only knee-deep. I turned on my strobe light and silently prayed that the chopper would make it in and get us out of there. It wasn't long before we heard the helicopters' approach. They sounded very close, probably a half mile away.

The pilot's voice crackled over the radio. "Pathfinder Control. This is Eagle Lead on final."

"Roger, Eagle Lead. We can hear you approaching. Over."

Kip and I stared into the fog, hoping to see a chopper emerge. Instead we heard both aircraft fly over us.

Kip alerted them immediately. "Eagle Lead. Be advised we just heard you pass our location. Over."

I was monitoring my radio as well in case Kip's went down. I could detect frustration in the pilot's voice. "Roger. We're having a rough time of it. It's like flying in soup. Will attempt another approach. Over."

The sound of the choppers faded, then became loud again. "This is Eagle Lead on final. Over."

Whopwhopwhop . . . Kip and I had heard enough helicopters in our day and estimated the birds to be a hundred feet from us. We could tell they were going to overfly our position.

Kip got on the horn. "Eagle Lead. We will advise when you are directly overhead. Over."

Eagle Lead knew the drill. "Roger."

I placed three fingers in front of Kip's face, folding them in succession: three . . . two . . . one . . . the pilot was directly over us. Kip bellowed, "Now!"

"Roger. I think I have your location. Will make another go-around. Over."

Kip and I discussed the situation and decided that we would tell the pilots to abort the mission if the next attempt was unsuccessful. There were just too many hazards for the aircraft. Besides crashing into a mountain, they could also experience a midair collision that would be fatal for both helicopter crews. I informed the CO and his men of our decision. They understood.

Whopwhopwhop . . . the choppers were approaching again. "Pathfinder Control. This is Eagle Lead on quarter-mile final."

"Roger."

The noise was straight to our front. I kept the strobe light high above my head and just stared into the fog. All of a sudden the fog began swirling and a large, dark object loomed toward us. It was Eagle Lead. The crew chief and door gunner were hanging all the way outside the bird to help guide the pilots in. I planned for six men of our group to go out on the first bird and the remaining five of us on the second. I signaled the men to get on the chopper.

The six men struggled and stumbled as they trudged through the wind, rain, and chest-high water. Even with the crew helping to get them on board, many of the men slipped on the skids or floor of the cabin, falling back into the water. Finally, when all six had boarded, Kip gave the okay for the chopper to depart.

The second bird dropped slowly into the LZ. It had been hovering in the fog all this time. It must have been hell on the pilots as they fought to keep the aircraft stable in the high wind and low visibility. The remaining five of us headed toward the bird. The FO was first in line, followed by the RTO, the CO, Kip, and then myself.

I felt a tingling sensation run up and down my spine. I touched Kip on the shoulder. "All we need is one gook with an AK and we're all history."

Kip chuckled. "Yeah! We're sitting ducks . . . and I feel like a duck right now."

It looked like we were walking into a little tornado as the chopper's blades whipped up the wind and water. The water rippled around us, and I could hardly see as the rain pelted at my eyes. I just put my head down and tried to place one foot in front of the other.

Kip glanced back at me. "This is why they call it rotor wash."

I just shook my head.

I squinted my eyes and could see that the first two men had already gotten on board. The CO was next. The two men inside and the door gunner clutched at the CO's fatigues and equipment, yanking him aboard. Kip was next. Just as Kip tried to climb up, the chopper swayed and dipped. The pilot was having a difficult time keeping the aircraft stable since everyone in it was on one side of the cabin. Quickly the crew chief had two men move to the other side to counterbalance the load.

Kip tried to climb on again. I pushed him from behind with all my might, but the chopper was wobbling fiercely. To make matters worse, the water had risen higher than our chests. The only way Kip was going to make it up and inside the aircraft was to take off his rucksack. He fumbled with his rucksack straps and loosened them enough to get it off his back. The crew chief grabbed the ruck while I took hold of his rifle. After a brief struggle, Kip was on board and I handed him his weapon.

The visibility kept decreasing. Hastily I slipped off my ruck and passed it up to someone in the aircraft. I then slung my weapon over my shoulder, stepped on the skid, and reached up to the cabin. Someone grabbed my right hand, but just as I was grappling to get on board, I slipped. I fell back into the water and my rifle fell off my shoulder. Luckily my hand caught the sling before the weapon vanished into the water.

Kip stuck his hand out. "Give me your weapon, Richie!"

Reluctantly I passed my rifle to Kip. Then I tried to climb on board again as hands reached out to grab me, but the chopper jerked and I fell back into the water a second time. I looked into the faces of the men above me

and thought I saw fear in their expressions. A sense of
frustration and panic swept over me. God! What if the
pilot had to leave because of lack of fuel or safety of the
aircraft and men? I would be left all alone in the A
Shau . . . with no weapon or equipment . . . and an enemy unit nearby. No way in hell!

My frustration quickly turned to anger as I waited for
the chopper to dip down on my side. When it did, I
leaped up onto the skid with all my might and thrust my
arms out for anything I could get my hands on. I managed to grab onto a fatigue shirt and someone seized me
by the collar. Someone else grabbed me under the arm.
Once my body was halfway in the cabin, I was hastily
yanked on board. Immediately the crew chief informed
the pilot that everyone was accounted for and the chopper hovered upward through the fog.

The flight was extremely rocky. At times it sounded as
if the chopper's blades were going to be torn from the
aircraft. All of us were soaking wet and the temperature
had dropped considerably. Some of the guys were shiver-
ing, even though the doors were closed. Everyone appeared to be happy and relieved except the RTO. The
flight was scaring the hell out of him. I smiled and gave
him a "thumbs-up." He returned the gesture, grinning
halfheartedly. He had a right to be anxious. We were not
yet out of danger. The winds had picked up considerably,
and it would not have surprised me if the pilots had been
forced to land or even to crash. I kept my thoughts to
myself.

Luckily the visibility at Camp Eagle was better than in
the mountains and we arrived safely at the aviation helipad. The company commander and his men gathered
around us. He was genuinely pleased.

"If either of you ever decides to transfer to a line
company, I'd take you in a heartbeat."

Kip and I responded with our usual "Thanks, but no
thanks." We considered the offer quite a compliment,
however.

The RTO stepped forward to shake our hands; he was jubilant. "Man, you guys did great! I gotta tell ya, though, the flight back here scared the ever-lovin' dogshit outta me."

Everyone chuckled as he continued. "Damn! I was so worried, I didn't know whether to shit or go blind . . . so I just closed one eye and farted."

Everyone lost it. I had to give it to those country boys; they could come up with the weirdest sayings to make a guy laugh.

Kip laughed the hardest. Tears rolled down his cheeks. "That was great!" There was no doubt in my mind that I would be hearing Kip repeating that line mixed in with his own material.

Kip and I stayed to help the flight crews tie down and secure the choppers, then made our way to the Pathfinder hootch and dry clothes.

The typhoon came blasting in later that night and continued through the next day with winds gusting up to one hundred miles per hour. Once it was over, everything was soaked. A number of Quonset huts had their roofs blown off and some of the tents collapsed. Unfortunately, many of the choppers were damaged, with some even turned over. Once the sunshine broke through, it took a couple of days to dry out clothes and equipment. However, almost everything returned to normal in short order.

We pulled a few missions here and there, but for the most part the rest of September was relatively uneventful for the detachment. Sometime in October, two Pathfinders were requested to support Special Forces out of Phu Bai. The operation was to take place the next day. Tim Alicoate and I were picked for the mission.

Tim was one of the most proficient Pathfinders I had ever known. Some people just have a knack for certain things: Tim was cut out to be a Pathfinder. I guess he was great at it because he loved it.

Tim was a few years older than me and had served an enlistment in the navy prior to joining the army. He had a sense of humor similar to Kip's. Tim always attempted to make the best of a bad situation. Although we were the same rank, I am sure that, being nineteen years old, my youth and immaturity showed at times. Even so, Tim always treated me as an equal. Since Tim loved to drink beer, his call sign was Poptop.

We were informed that we would be leaving on a chopper at first light to set up an LZ for an estimated company-size unit. It was supposed to be a training exercise conducted by Special Forces advisers and little people.

As we left the briefing, Tim smirked. "A training exercise my ass."

I knew what Tim meant. In the briefing, we asked for the location and were told it had not yet been coordinated. Calling the movement a training mission and not providing us the coordinates was just the Special Forces' way of maintaining security. I wondered if I'd be crossing into Laos again. At least this time there didn't appear to be a sense of urgency.

The next morning Tim and I conducted commo checks with our radios, then headed for the helipad. The sun was just beginning to rise over the horizon. A lone chopper was revving up while its crew members performed their various preflight checks. Tim and I walked over to talk to the aircraft commander.

Tim spoke first. "How's it going, sir?"

The AC seemed a bit anxious but courteous. "Morning! We'll be leaving in about zero five."

Tim shrugged his shoulders. "Are we going to have gunships or a chase bird escorting us?"

The AC tried to appear indifferent. "No! We'll be going solo on this one."

I felt like we were pulling teeth here and decided to intervene. "Where exactly is the LZ that we're going into located at, sir?"

The AC let down his guard a little. "The LZ is actually

an old, abandoned French airstrip. I've flown over it a few times before. It should be more than adequate for the mission."

Tim decided to try his hand at dentistry and pull a few teeth. "Where is the LZ located at, sir? Is it far?"

I could hear a hint of resignation in the AC's voice. "It's near the A Shau . . . there will be a long turnaround time."

Tim and I test-fired our weapons into a fifty-five-gallon drum filled with sand, then boarded the chopper. Sometimes you can learn more from what is not said instead of what is said. We both concluded that the LZ was probably located on the far side of the A Shau, since the AC had stressed that there would be a long turnaround time. His reluctance to be specific confirmed to us that this was not a training mission, but more than likely a Mike Force that was either flying or walking into Laos.

Tim and I just wanted information regarding our part of the operation and didn't really care about anything else. We understood the need for secrecy and didn't care if the operation was in Laos or not. Unlike a map, there was no black line on the ground to mark the borders of the neighboring countries, so we wouldn't know if we were across the border anyway.

Our flight flew us past Firebase Birmingham, then Bastogne and over the A Shau. Even though I had flown over it more times than I could count, the A Shau's majestic mountains and deep valleys, curtained with beautiful but vicious jungle, still fascinated and overwhelmed me. My imagination wandered. If I had X-ray vision, I thought, I bet I would see thousands of NVA hiding under that thick vegetation.

I glanced over at Tim, who was lost in his own thoughts. I was glad he was accompanying me on the mission. Besides being a skilled Pathfinder, Tim was someone you could count on no matter what happened. I had bet my life on him in the past and he had never let me down.

Our chopper continued its flight over the A Shau. After a long while, we felt the helicopter descend. Tim tapped me on the boot, then pointed outside. About a mile or two off to our front sat the old airstrip. It was nestled on a plateau surrounded by mountains. The French probably built it to land small, fixed-wing aircraft. The aged and tattered landing strip might have been operational in its day, but like everything else in the jungle that sits long enough, the vegetation had reclaimed much of it. Our chopper touched down at the far end of the strip, and Tim and I jumped out. We crouched and remained in place until the helicopter left, then scrambled to the edge of the wood line.

We lay low and listened for sounds that might be human. After a few minutes, each of us conducted a commo check with the chopper before it flew out of range. Our PRC-25 radios were good for only five to eight miles and we were a hell of a lot farther away from Phu Bai than that. Once we finished our commo checks, we reconned the LZ for hazardous obstacles and to determine the best avenue of approach for the choppers. Tim and I figured we had an hour or so before the helicopters arrived, so we took our time. Besides, for all we knew, the place could have been mined or had enemy trail watchers observing it.

I examined the surroundings for a few moments, then looked at Tim. "What do you think?"

Tim pointed to a few tall trees on the eastern edge of the strip. "I think the birds can clear those trees without any problem."

I grunted. "No! I mean, what do you think about here?"

"Oh! I think we're alone, way out in the middle of nowhere, with our asses hanging out."

Quickly my eyes scanned the edge of the wood line. "I hope we're alone."

Being his usual self, Tim's response was optimistic. "Hell! We'll be out of here in no time, Richie!"

"Yeah! I guess you're right." I knew Tim well, however, and noticed the concern on his face.

The most dangerous time for a Pathfinder team was that time spent on the ground waiting for the initial force to arrive. Just about any size enemy force can overrun the team because there are only the two men in it. Moreover, if enemy soldiers are in the vicinity, they will see the helicopter land and investigate. Unfortunately, the Pathfinders must remain at the location to guide in the arriving force, no matter what.

I took a few azimuths with my compass while Tim continued to look for obstacles on the ground and at the approach. Once we finished, we settled among some trees in the wood line near where we would be landing the first chopper of the flight.

The sun began to beat down, the humidity started to go up, and the insects commenced to eat us alive. I grabbed a John Wayne bar from my ruck and peeled off part of the wrapper. "You want some?"

Tim's face grimaced. "Nah! It's too early in the morning for chocolate."

A moment later, Tim licked his parched lips. "I could sure use a cold one about now, though."

That was Poptop. I nodded my head. "I could go for a six-pack."

Tim's eyes got big. "Hell, Richie! Let's buy a damn case when we get back and split it."

I chuckled. "It's a deal!"

About two hours passed and there was still no sign of the aircraft. A few times we tried to contact the birds on the radio, hoping they were en route, but we heard nothing. I hated that part of a mission.

"Damn! When the hell are they coming?" I whispered to Tim.

Tim tried to act nonchalant. "You know the army, hurry up and wait."

A horrible thought crossed my mind. "You don't

think the mission was canceled and they forgot about us, do you?"

Tim scoffed, "Nah!"

He contemplated for a moment or two, then muttered, "If they did . . . with all the damn gook divisions between here and Camp Eagle . . . we'll probably end up being captured."

I frowned. That thought was scary. I had hoped Tim would say something to lift my spirits.

Tim looked over at me again. "You know the first thing the NVA will ask us, don't you?"

I could think of a lot of things. "What?"

Tim squinted and spoke with an Oriental accent. "Do you speak Nipponese?"

His comment and facial expression were so ridiculous, I had to laugh. The Americans had just as many slang names for the enemy as the enemy had for us. They were referred to as gooks, slopes, dinks, and nips. I visualized the silly scene in my mind and laughed again.

The time continued to pass and it was midmorning; I was beginning to worry. If there were any gooks in the area when the chopper dropped us off, they were probably investigating the LZ. What if we were forgotten?

Tim tried to reassure me and himself. "We'll wait twenty-four hours, then E and E back to Eagle. We're going to be picked up, so I'm just speaking hypothetically."

"Sounds good! We could probably make it to Bastogne." I tried to sound convincing. "We'll just follow the sounds of the artillery if we get close to it."

Tim chuckled. "Wouldn't it be the shits if we made it all the way to Bastogne . . . humping for days . . . with no food . . . dodging hundreds of enemy soldiers . . . and one of our own guys blows us away when we try to enter the firebase?"

I laughed. Even though it sounded funny, it could really happen. Suddenly a voice came over the radio.

"Poptop! This is Kingsmen Lead, about five miles to

the southeast with a flight of five. Request landing instructions. Over."

Before the operation we'd decided to use Tim's call sign instead of Pathfinder Control. That way, if any gooks were listening in, they wouldn't know who the hell Poptop was. Moreover, a lot of pilots in the division knew Tim by his call sign.

Tim snatched the handset. "Roger, Kingsmen Lead. This is Poptop. Land two two zero degrees. Winds out of the southwest at five, gusting to eight. Enemy situation negative at this time. Recommend staggered right formation. Be advised of some tall trees on your final approach into the Lima Zulu. Call one mile final. Over."

"This is Kingsmen Lead. Roger."

Tim's smile reached across his entire face. "I told you they'd be coming . . . that they were just late."

I hit him on the shoulder. "What do you mean? I'm the one who told you! I knew they wouldn't forget about us."

Tim smirked. "Bullshit!"

After a few moments the pilot came back over the radio. "Poptop! This is Kingsmen Lead. One mile final."

"Roger! Enemy situation still negative. You are clear to land. Over."

While Tim stayed on the radio, I ran out to the LZ to guide in the flight. Earlier it had been requested that we not use smoke unless necessary. I placed myself in front of where I wanted the first helicopter to land and raised my arms, signaling "guide in on me."

As I stood there, all alone, totally exposed, in the middle of the clearing, I wondered if an enemy sniper had me in his crosshairs, but I didn't have time to contemplate the thought as Kingsmen Lead flared to a hover in front of me. I signaled the aircraft to touch down and watched as the little people and their advisers bounded from the choppers.

I could tell by their conduct and interactions with

their leaders that they were seasoned troops who had spent time together with their Special Forces advisers. They were armed to the teeth and ready for a fight.

It took a few hours for the birds to fly back and forth from the LZ to Phu Bai. When the last flight landed, Tim ran toward the lead bird and signaled for me to hop on board. I entered the aircraft from the right side while Tim jumped on from the left. A moment later our chopper along with the rest of the flight was headed back to Camp Eagle.

Later that night Tim and I were true to our deal; we split a case of beer. Mitch, Frankie Farino, and a few others were sitting around as well.

One of them called to us. "Hey! I heard you guys had a long wait today, out in the middle of nowhere."

Nonchalantly, Tim replied, "Yeah! But it was no sweat . . . just a training exercise."

I decided to play along. "Shit! We were so damned bored, we were hoping for something to happen just to kick some ass. Right, Poptop?"

Tim took a big swallow of beer, then said in his best Oriental accent, "Do you speak Nipponese?"

Chapter Twenty

To everyone's surprise, President Johnson had stopped all bombing along the DMZ a month back, and this policy was to continue indefinitely. Consequently, thousands of enemy soldiers were infiltrating into the south from Laos right across our area of operation. We read in *Stars and Stripes* that Johnson had halted all bombing because of pressure from antiwar groups protesting the killing of Vietnamese civilians. The only people being killed along the DMZ by American bombs, however, were North Vietnamese soldiers attempting to infiltrate south. After the bombing halt, the only people being killed were American soldiers who had to fight the increased numbers of North Vietnamese soldiers.

Although I was only nineteen years old, I felt that the new policy just didn't make sense. It seemed to us that the president and the American people back home cared more about the lives of enemy soldiers than they did about us. One of the new guys in the detachment received a large envelope sent to him from his home state, California. Inside was a photo showing a group of young people our age smiling while waving Viet Cong and NVA flags. We were angry and confused—how could they do that to us? To their brothers, sons, husbands, nephews, uncles, cousins, and next-door neighbors? We compared our situation to World War II. Our country would have lost many more American lives if bombing had been halted along the Normandy beachhead or on Iwo Jima. Moreover, those battles might not have ended as victories.

I not only felt uneasy about the way the news media portrayed us in Vietnam, I felt unsure that our government and our own people supported us.

It was early November and I had about one month left in my tour, about ten months left in the army, when Ron, Joe Bolick, Tim Alicoate, and I were all promoted to sergeant. Tim and I were even on the same promotion orders. Ron and I also put in our request to be reassigned to the LRPs. We would receive a thirty-day free leave and then begin a six-month tour of duty with the LRP company.

We received about twenty new members within the detachment, including four lieutenants. The detachment was broken down into four sections with a lieutenant in charge of each. Units consistently change in the army, sometimes for the better and sometimes for the worse. Although I didn't know in which direction our detachment was headed, I felt that it was no longer the same detachment I had known and it was time for me to move on. I volunteered to go on missions just to stay out of the rear until my tour was up.

Two weeks later, in mid-November, a newly created firebase called Brick began receiving a lot of enemy assaults. Because of the bombing halt, intelligence estimated two more NVA regiments were operating in Brick's area.

Firebase Brick was about the size of a very small parking lot, and it was situated on a small mound about forty feet high. Lush, green elephant grass stretched out for about a hundred meters on Brick's three sides, then merged into thick jungle. The backside of Brick was mostly brush and small trees for about thirty meters before turning into jungle as well. From it, we could see treetops for literally miles.

Although Ron, Larry, and I had only about three weeks left in country, we volunteered to go to Brick to recon it and eventually bring in artillery guns and control aircraft. Ron, Larry, and I selected a large hole on the perimeter to set up operations. Even though Brick was defensible against an enemy ground attack, it was an easy target for mortars. Consequently we were mortared a minimum of twice a day. On at least three occasions enemy mortar rounds exploded right on the edge of our hole, the shrapnel missing us by inches. The situation became more nerve-racking for us since we had just a few weeks left before going home.

On the perimeter of the backside of Brick was a tree that had a trunk around ten feet in diameter. I had never seen anything like it. One of the men struck it with an ax and the ax just bounced right off. I got Ron to take a look at it and see if he knew what kind of wood it was. It was late afternoon and a storm was approaching.

Ron ran his hand along the tree bark, which was real smooth. "It sure is hard wood. I can tell one thing, Richie. We don't have trees this big in Arkansas."

I snickered. "Yeah! We don't have trees this big in Boston, either. What kind of wood do you think it is?"

Ron laughed. "Hell! It's real red looking. My best guess is that it's mahogany."

I nodded in agreement. Mahogany sounded good.

Just as we were pondering the situation, a huge bolt of lighting streaked across the sky above us.

Ron was suddenly nervous. "There's a storm brewing, and we ain't exactly standing in a safe spot."

I was puzzled. "What do you mean?"

Ron appeared surprised. "Didn't you just see that lightning?"

I shrugged. "So what?"

Ron shook his head. "We might not have these kind of trees in Arkansas, but we do have this kind of lightning . . . if it strikes here, you'll be a damn crispy critter."

More lightning cracked across the sky. At first I thought Ron was kidding, but I could tell by his expression that he was really concerned.

I tried to make light of it. "Listen, I've walked in plenty of storms and even a hurricane once and I've never been struck by lightning."

Ron's tone was serious. "Being from the city, you probably had buildings around you. We're at the highest point around here. At least there's no metal nearby."

I would have said something earlier, but I didn't think it was important. I pointed to the stake behind him. "What about that engineer stake?"

Ron turned to look. About two feet away from him was a metal engineer stake sticking straight up out of the ground. "Shit! We've got to get out of here . . . and now!"

Before Ron could say anything else or move, a thunderous *crash* slammed both of us to the ground. Lightning had struck the engineer stake right beside us.

Both Ron and I remained still for a moment, stunned. As we rose to our feet we noticed that the top of the engineer stake had actually melted and the earth was scorched in a line, right between our feet, from the metal stake to the big tree trunk.

Quickly, Ron stomped out the leftover sparks on the ground with his foot. To my surprise, smoke was coming off his back where his shirt was damp from sweat. My shirt was smoking as well. Lightning screeched across the sky, again striking nearby.

That was all I needed to see. I shouted to Ron, "Let's get out of here!"

We took off at a dead run. I could have won the Olympic one-hundred-meter race. At first Ron was beside me, but he ended up lagging behind, he was laughing so hard. Once I was safely back in the hole, it dawned on me how ironic it would have been to safely make it through a year in Vietnam, only to get killed in the end by nature. I swore to take lightning seriously from then on.

Ron, Larry, and I had been at Brick just a few days when Ron was called back to the rear. The next day two LRPs arrived on Brick to set up a radio relay. Two of their company's LRP teams were going to be inserted a few kilometers away. Instead of the usual six-man configuration, the two teams would be going in "heavy" with twelve men each. In addition to reconnaissance, they would be conducting ambushes and, if possible, a prisoner snatch.

The site where Larry and I set up was a good spot for communications, so we invited the LRPs to set up near us. Besides, our hole was big enough for four people to jump into during mortar attacks. Since LRP teams often operated at a distance beyond their PRC-25 radio capability, it was necessary to have a relay team that could receive and transmit communications between the team on the ground and their commander in the rear. One of the LRPs was S. Sgt. Lawrence Bowman; the other LRP was a radio operator (RTO). Larry and I enjoyed their company, and Bowman and I talked on many occasions for hours.

Since Larry and I had two radios, we kept one on the aircraft frequency and the other on the LRP frequency to listen in. That way, if the LRP teams needed any aircraft support or some kind of special situation developed, we would be on top of it.

During a team insertion one of the LRPs broke both ankles leaping from the chopper. The following day the team leader requested a dustoff to medevac the injured LRP. The chopper arrived on station but the vegetation was too thick for the aircraft to land, so the chopper lowered a basket down through the jungle canopy. The LRP's teammates secured him in the basket and the dustoff hoisted him up from the jungle floor. Since the medevac was only a few kilometers from our location, we called him straight into Brick. Larry visually guided the bird to a spot in the elephant grass close to the perimeter. Immediately the relay team RTO raced to the helicopter and helped his injured comrade out of the basket and inside the chopper. A few minutes later the LRP was on his way to the hospital.

As we watched the relay team RTO assist his buddy, Bowman grunted. "I got a bad feeling about this."

Clearly, having the medevac hover above the team in the field wouldn't help conceal them from the enemy.

"You think they might end up being compromised?"

He shook his head. "I don't know . . . maybe they should request extraction. Then again, Charlie might think that the whole team left. I'd opt to *di di*. Why take the chance?"

Bowman paused for a moment, then continued. "Ah, hell! It ain't my call!"

I listened on my radio as Captain Eklund, the LRP commander, spoke to the relay team. "Linwood Nine. This is Linwood Six. Over."

"Linwood Six, this is Nine. Over."

The relay team informed Eklund that the injured man had been safely medevacked.

"This is Six. Keep me posted. Out!"

My curiosity got the best of me. I queried Sergeant Bowman. "Who's the team leader?"

"Contreros," he muttered.

I knew of Contreros and had even met him before, but I did not know him personally. "Maybe he'll think it over and request extraction."

Bowman murmured, "Not Contreros! The guy's either crazy or medal-hungry or both."

The relay team RTO returned from helping the injured LRP while Bowman and I heated up some coffee in my canteen cup. I had just started to sip it when I heard an explosion in the distance. It sounded like a claymore. The explosion was followed by gunfire. The rifles had the distinct sound of M-16s. It was the LRP team. Bowman and his RTO anxiously waited by their radio to find out what was going on.

Finally the LRP team radioed that they had initiated an ambush, killing some NVA soldiers, including three enemy nurses. They also had a wounded POW and a number of documents for intelligence to examine. The gooks were obviously part of a medical unit. Fortunately none of the LRPs were injured. Unfortunately, one of the gooks escaped the ambush and, although wounded, hightailed it through the jungle.

Bowman put down the radio handset. A big smile spread across his face. "Airborne, goddammit! Good job!"

Bowman immediately reported the news to Captain Eklund. Even over the horn it was easy to tell that Eklund was pleased about the captured soldier. His enthusiasm was short-lived, however, when the team reported that the wounded POW was also a nurse and had died moments after the ambush.

Eklund contacted the relay team. "Linwood Nine. This is Linwood Six. Over."

Bowman grabbed the handset. "This is Linwood Nine."

"This is Six. Inform Two-three that a reaction force is en route to their location to develop the situation and that their team will be extracted and inserted at a new location. Over."

Bowman relayed the message and Contreros acknowledged.

About thirty minutes had passed and Sergeant Bowman was becoming worried. He was standing beside me while his RTO listened on the radio. "Damn! They need to get those guys out of there ASAP."

I could tell Bowman was battling with himself. He grabbed the handset. "Linwood Six. This is Linwood Nine. Over."

"This is Six."

"This is Nine. How's the reaction force and extraction coming along? Over."

Eklund responded abruptly. "It's in the works!"

Although Staff Sergeant Bowman was a large man with a hardened face and gruff voice, he was very personable. When he was serious, however, you listened. Just then he was serious. "I don't know if it's the CO or higher, but someone is fucking up. It's taking entirely too long to get those guys out of there."

Bowman grew impatient and grabbed the handset. "Linwood Two-three. This is Linwood Nine. Over."

Bowman had a distressed look on his face. "Damn! Gooks have jammed the frequency!"

I was surprised. "Are you sure?"

Bowman passed me the handset. "Listen for yourself."

I had heard stories about the enemy jamming radio frequencies but never experienced it. I heard a couple of voices speaking an oriental language, but it didn't sound like Vietnamese to me. I was no expert, but I had spent a month with the South Vietnamese, and the language I was hearing sounded more like Chinese to me.

Bowman nodded. "What do you think?"

"It sounds oriental, but I don't think it's Vietnamese."

Bowman grabbed the handset and listened again. "Damn, Burns! I think you're right! I don't think it is Vietnamese."

Bowman turned the knob of his radio to the alternate frequency and waited about five minutes. When he returned to the primary frequency the foreign-language transmissions had ceased. Unfortunately, a much more serious problem was about to occur.

Captain Eklund called over the radio. "Linwood Nine. This is Six. Over."

Bowman let out a sigh of relief. "This is Nine."

"This is Six. Advise Two-three that there will not be a reaction force or an extraction at their location. Do you copy? Over."

Bowman's expression was one of disbelief. "This is Nine. Understand there will not be a reaction force or extraction. Over."

There was a slight pause before Eklund came back. When he did, his voice sounded resigned. "That's affirmative!"

Bowman pressed Eklund for details. He was not going to relay the bad news to Two-three without a damn good explanation. Eklund informed Bowman that division headquarters had committed all of its helicopters to a major operation that day, so no aircraft were available to bring in the reaction force or take the team out. Reluctantly, Bowman relayed the bad news to the team.

After Bowman relayed the message, he handed the handset to his RTO and then hung his head. "Damn! Those guys have been on the ground too long. They're in deep shit! You can bet your ass the NVA are going to try to get payback. I'd like to shoot the stupid son of a bitch that pulled those choppers from the team."

It wasn't long before Captain Eklund arrived on the scene in a small observation helicopter. Eklund could then communicate with the team directly, since he was within radio range. Just as Eklund's chopper circled the area, we heard the *crack* of small-arms fire.

Bowman was pissed. "I knew it, dammit! That's a fucking AK!"

A few moments later all hell broke loose as the sounds of the enemy's AKs and the Americans' M-16s echoed together. Larry remained on the Pathfinder frequency to control and assist aircraft coming on the scene. I kept our other Pathfinder radio on the LRP frequency to keep Larry apprised of their situation and to assist the LRPs in any way I could.

Contreros radioed that he had a man wounded and requested a dustoff. Eklund said he would try to get a medevac on station ASAP. I handed Bowman a list of the various medical evacuation units in case he needed it if Eklund was unsuccessful.

Larry informed me that a light fire team of Cobras had radioed that they were inbound to support the team. Immediately I notified the artillery battery and mortars not to fire so as to clear the way for the gunships to fly over Brick. Another loud crescendo of small-arms fire could be heard just as the two Cobras arrived on the scene. For a while the Cobras just circled the area and did not engage the enemy. Something was wrong. Perhaps they didn't have the team's exact location. After a few minutes, however, the Cobras began gun runs.

Each Cobra dropped into a steep dive, blasting the area with rockets. As they turned around for another attack they let loose with their miniguns, each gun firing six thousand rounds a minute. Even from six kilometers away we could see branches and leaves showering off the trees like rain.

While we watched in awe, Larry shouted, "Dustoff is inbound!"

I searched the skies and, sure enough, a slick was soaring in fast from the northeast. I called back to Larry. "Roger! I got him in sight. If the Cobras remain on station, recommend they fly a holding pattern to the east so the dustoff can get in and out safely."

Larry grabbed the handset. "Already on top of it."

The medevac hovered over the team's position. Since the jungle was too thick for the dustoff to land, it lowered a jungle penetrator to evacuate the wounded LRP. But that was taking entirely too long, and I was amazed that the chopper was not shot out of the sky.

The relay RTO clenched his fist. "I know they've got to strap him in, but what the hell is taking them so long to get him out?"

"The penetrator is probably getting caught up in the trees. I'll tell you one thing, those dustoff crews got balls," Larry replied.

Finally the medevac lifted straight up until the penetrator cleared the treetops, then it sped away. As soon as the medevac cleared the area, the Cobras went back to work. Approximately ten minutes later the Cobras along with Eklund's chopper returned to Camp Eagle to refuel. It must have got lonely out there for the members of Team Two-three.

With the aircraft out of the area, Contreros requested artillery support. Luckily for the besieged LRP team, a 105 artillery battery with its three guns had just been placed on Brick. Larry gave the all-clear to the artillery that no aircraft were in the area. A moment later the three guns opened up. I had never seen artillerymen so galvanized or motivated as those guys. It was a unique mission for them. Like the rest of us on Brick, they'd watched helplessly as the LRPs fought for their lives. Suddenly they had a chance to help out. Furthermore, for the most part artillerymen never get to see their rounds explode. Since we were only six kilometers away and on a hilltop, they could watch each round impact into the jungle.

About an hour or so elapsed before Eklund returned. This time he was on board a slick accompanied by four Cobras.

Bowman and his RTO cheered up. Bowman's voice sounded optimistic. "Damn! They just might make it the hell out of there."

Although we could still hear sporadic sounds of small-arms fire, the situation did look encouraging. If the Cobras could keep the NVA at bay long enough for the team to make it to the LZ, they just might be able to get out on Eklund's chopper.

Suddenly there was an enormous explosion right at the spot where the LRP team was located. The blast sent a huge cloud of dark gray smoke and brown dirt billowing upward. All of the leaves were torn from their branches and flew skyward like pieces of confetti.

Dumbfounded, I turned to Bowman. "What the hell was that?"

Bowman was flabbergasted. "I don't know. I've never seen anything like it."

For a moment the four of us just stood there numb until Bowman grabbed the handset in an effort to contact the team. "Linwood Two-three. This is Linwood Nine. Over."

He repeated the transmission several times. Finally a voice sputtered, "They're dead! They're all dead!"

Bowman tried to get more out of the LRP, but it was evident he was in shock. Finally the LRP came back. "This is Two-three. I need help."

Bowman's voice remained calm. "How many others with you are alive?"

The LRP's words were slurred. "I think . . . I'm alone. There's just bodies all around."

The LRP's voice cracked. "They're coming again!"

Bowman responded immediately. "Find cover!"

"There's . . . just bodies . . ."

Sergeant Bowman could not make out what the LRP was saying. He kept the tone of his voice relaxed and unruffled. "Which team member are you?"

The LRP sounded frightened. "They're coming again. I need help."

Although Sergeant Bowman looked as if he were dying inside, he remained calm and started giving advice. "Listen! Check to see if anyone's alive. Use your weapon and find cover. Use the others for cover. Stack their bodies and get behind them. . . . Do you understand?"

He glanced up at me. "Shit! I don't even know if he heard me."

Suddenly Bowman's radio battery went dead. While he fumbled to replace it, he had his RTO turn on their spare radio. Unbelievably, that radio went down as well. We could hear shooting.

Tears welled up in Bowman's eyes. "I lost contact. We got to do something. We got to get them some help."

My radio was already on the LRP frequency. I passed it to Bowman. "Here. Take my radio. I don't need it."

Bowman handed the radio to his RTO and told him to keep trying to contact the LRP. He turned his attention back to me. "We've got to do something, Burns. We've got to go in there and get him and any others out."

I felt helpless. "We'll do something. Do you know who the guy is?"

Bowman relaxed a bit. "I think it's one of the new guys. If it is, he doesn't have any experience."

Bowman started pacing. He was close to crying. "Dammit! We've got to do something ASAP! Those guys need help now. We've got to get a reaction force together."

Bowman was right, and every second counted.

His eyes scanned the firebase. "Do you think you can round up a reaction force . . . maybe from the infantry?"

My adrenaline started pumping. "I can try. We're going to need a chopper."

I turned to Larry. "Larry, we've got to get hold of a chopper that will come in here and then fly us to the LRP team's location."

Larry nodded. "I'll get one in here somehow."

As I turned my attention back to Bowman, I heard Larry's voice. "Any aircraft in the vicinity of Brick. This is an emergency. Please respond. Over."

Larry would keep trying to get us a helicopter, but it was going to be tough. Not many choppers landed at Brick because it was such a small firebase with few men and units.

An infantry platoon guarded Brick's perimeter. I decided to try them first. I ran to the perimeter and found a small group of four or five infantrymen playing cards.

"Hey, guys! Who's in charge here?"

They looked up at me like I was from another world and didn't like the fact that I had interrupted their card game.

I was becoming angry. "It's an emergency! Who's in charge of you guys?"

One of them spoke up. "The LT is crashed, but our sergeant is right over there."

He pointed to two soldiers standing a few yards away. "The one on the left."

I spotted the two soldiers and raced up to the one on the left. He was a buck sergeant like myself. "I'm Sergeant Burns. Are you in charge of the infantry platoon?"

The sergeant paused momentarily. He had a wearied look about him. "Yeah! I'm the acting platoon sergeant until we get one in. What do you need?"

I explained to him that there was a LRP team in trouble and asked him if he could spare some men to use as a reaction force. I told him the men would receive a more detailed briefing once we had everybody together.

It was a tall order and he paused momentarily to think it over. "I can't order my men to do something like that."

Even though I had anticipated the answer, I was disappointed and I am sure my expression showed it. He spoke again. "I'll go, though. I can ask for a few volunteers but can't promise anything."

I was elated. If he could get enough men to go with him, all we needed was a chopper. "Airborne! We'll meet you at my location ASAP. Make sure you bring plenty of ammo."

Since I didn't know how many soldiers the sergeant would bring with him, I continued to visit all the units, asking for help. Once I was finished I raced back to see if Larry had had any luck getting hold of a chopper. I didn't know how much time had elapsed, but the Cobras were steadily firing up the area around the LRP team and I saw a dustoff hover over their position for quite some time.

Larry had already anticipated my question. "I got hold of two choppers so far but neither of them could drop what they were doing. I'll keep trying."

Bowman was eager for information. "How did you do, Burns? How many men did you get?"

"At least five."

Bowman was devastated. "Is that all?"

I tried to be optimistic. "Well! We might have more, it depends how many guys the infantry platoon sergeant brings along."

I queried Bowman about the LRP team's situation and discovered that more of them were alive. Damn, we had to get in there fast.

Only a few minutes had gone by when the infantry sergeant showed up with two other men. Bowman thanked them for volunteering, briefed them on the situation, and had them hang loose while we waited for a chopper. A while later the other four men I had rounded up arrived. Bowman's mouth fell open.

As the four men approached, it was quite evident that they were not combat arms. They just had that REMF look about them. I was sure Bowman was wondering if they even knew how to fire their weapons.

He grimaced. "Are these the rest of the men?"

I shook my head. "That's all I could get. Two of them are commo and have brought along radios that we'll need. I don't know what MOSs the other two are."

Bowman muttered, "At least they volunteered. They're good fucking soldiers in my eyes."

While Bowman briefed the four REMFs, a lieutenant came rushing up to the infantry sergeant. The two went off to the side, then the lieutenant walked up to me. "My men won't be part of your operation!"

He paused to see if I had anything to say, then continued. "I heard what's going on and I know you need them, but I just can't authorize their participation. Their duty is guarding this firebase."

I didn't comment. I didn't know what to say other than, "Yes, sir!"

The lieutenant turned to leave, stopped for a moment, then turned back around. As he faced me, his eyes looked to the ground as if he felt ashamed. "I'm sorry, Sergeant. Really. If there was any way I could help those guys out, I would. I would go myself."

"I understand, sir."

I did understand somewhat. Larry wanted to be part of the reaction force as well, but one of us had to stay behind and control air traffic. The lives of the flight crews depended on us. There was no way both of us could go.

Bowman was through briefing the four REMFs and walked toward me. I started to tell him what happened, but he stuck out his hand. "I know! I heard!"

He went over and sat by his RTO to keep abreast of the situation. I sat with Larry, waiting for a chopper.

Suddenly off to the south, about five miles out, a lone Huey was flying toward our location.

Larry jumped up, grabbing the handset. "Unidentified aircraft in the vicinity of Brick. This is Brick Control, over."

The pilot's voice crackled over the radio. "Roger. This is Eagle One-one-five. Over."

It was a 101st helicopter. He was hauling some supplies to one of the units. Larry informed him of the situation and what we wanted him to do. At first the pilot wavered. He wasn't landing at Brick, and the unit he was committed to needed the supplies. It wasn't long, however, before the chopper was inbound to pick up our "reaction force."

Sergeant Bowman leaped for joy. He had gone over each man's position with us, so when we hit the ground at the scene we would all be on the same sheet of music. We rehearsed our movement while waiting for the chopper. Sergeant Bowman would be in command, with me second. He would be point while I picked up the rear. Our biggest concern was that the LRP team might take us for gooks and fire on us.

The six of us stood in line waiting for the chopper. Bowman was thrilled. I was apprehensive. The four REMFs were scared shitless. Just as the chopper approached on final, he banked left and flew away from the firebase.

Bowman went ballistic. "What the fuck is going on? Why isn't he picking us up?"

Larry put up his hand, gesturing Bowman to wait while he listened on the radio. Finally Larry shouted to us, "A reaction force is already on the way. The LRP commander doesn't want you guys bumping into each other and fucking up the works."

Bowman calmed down a little but was still upset. "I don't see any choppers. Where the hell is the reaction force?"

Larry shrugged. "Should be here any minute. The reaction force is made up of guys from your LRP company."

Bowman looked as if a giant weight had fallen off his shoulders. His RTO smiled and gave a thumbs-up.

Later on we found out that the gooks had detonated one of their huge claymore mines into the team. Regrettably, almost half the LRP team was killed. The others were all seriously wounded. Luckily they were hard-core and fought like hell. They earned the respect of everybody in the division. They damn sure had mine.

I had only seven days left in country when I returned from Brick to the detachment. It was midafternoon, and I went straight to the hootch to see Ron. When I walked inside, Ron was sitting near his cot, writing a letter. He had recently acquired a monkey, and the mischievous creature was sitting on Ron's shoulder.

As I approached Ron the little monkey jumped up on me, grabbed the pen from my pocket, and retreated to a corner to examine his newfound treasure.

I pointed to the monkey. "He's a cute little guy. Maybe we can teach him to steal stuff for us."

Ron smiled. "Yeah! The only problem is that the little shit will steal anything. I have to keep most of my stuff locked in my footlocker."

Ron knew me better than anyone and he could tell from my face that something was bothering me. "What's going on, Richie?"

I cleared the lump from my throat and looked him straight in the eye. "I don't know how else to tell you this but straight up. I'm not going to extend. I'm going to go home."

Instead of being angry, Ron stood up and slapped me on the back. "That's okay, Pumpkin Pie. I understand, really. If I didn't want Recondo School so bad, I'd probably go home, too. Besides, after being here I just don't think I would be able to put up with all the Stateside bullshit."

Ron glanced at me with that Andy Taylor look. "What made you change your mind?"

I pondered the question a moment. I wanted to be as honest as I could with both Ron and myself. "I guess the LRP team getting all shot up was like an omen. Hell! I don't know! Maybe I'm just plain scared. What I do know is that I've had enough."

I smiled. "I'll probably regret the decision my first damn day in a stateside unit."

Ron turned and picked up a letter from the field table. "You'll probably regret it the minute you step off the plane. My mother says there are antiwar protesters everywhere and returning soldiers have been called baby killers and rapists. Some guys even get spit on."

Ron placed the letter from his family down beside the one he was writing. There was a tone of frustration in his voice. "My family just doesn't understand, especially my two sisters. They think I'm foolish or crazy for extending. They just don't understand the importance of what we're doing and that I'm a soldier. Besides, someone's got to help the Vietnamese defend their freedom!"

Ron ripped up the letter he was writing and decided to start over. He grabbed another piece of paper. "Trouble is, they're listening to all these antiwar pukes who have no idea what the hell is really going on over here, either."

Ron shook his head. "Can you believe my sisters are even thinking of joining in the protests? How can they go against me when I'm over here risking my life?"

Ron was becoming upset, and I could tell he was hurt. "Ron, your sisters just want you home. They're afraid for you and they probably feel helpless. In their mind, they probably think that if they join in the protests, they can stop the war and get you home."

He calmed down a bit. "But they don't understand how important it is to me."

I tried to be positive. "Of course they don't understand. How can they? How can anyone understand what it's like to be here unless they experience it firsthand? It's impossible; you said yourself so many times."

Ron sighed. "Yeah! I guess you're right. My sisters wouldn't do anything against me intentionally."

I decided to leave Ron alone to write his letter. "I'll tell you what. Let me go and pack my stuff, then we'll get some chow. After that we'll drink a few beers."

Ron grinned. "Sounds good. Come back and get me on the way to chow."

As I headed toward my bunk I felt relieved that I'd told Ron the truth and gotten it off my chest. I also felt sad, though. In a few days I would be going on leave and wouldn't see Ron for at least nine months or more.

Just about the whole detachment got together that night. A few beers ended up being one hell of a party. Although everyone had a good time, an underlying sadness filled the room. Those of us who had originally come to Vietnam with the detachment would all be leaving in the next few days. Not only would we miss each other, we would also miss Tim Alicoate and the rest of the guys from the 308th Pathfinders who had merged with us earlier in the year.

One member I would surely miss above all others. Regrettably, he would not be going back to the States with us. It was Torch. I watched the little guy make his rounds entertaining each group of guys. He had no idea that in a day or two he would never see me or many of the others again.

Tim Alicoate read my mind and sat next to me. "Don't worry, Richie, we'll take good care of him."

I nodded. "Yeah! I know you guys will. I just wonder what's going to happen to Torch when the Pathfinders eventually leave."

I took a big swallow of beer and tried not to think about it. Someone walked up behind me and placed his hand on my shoulder. It was Frank Procella. Frank had joined the detachment with Tim and the others from the 308th.

Frank was a black guy who stood a little over six feet tall and had a slender build. He was an extremely intelligent man with a kind face and a friendly demeanor. Frank was finishing his last year of college when he decided to join the army and go to Vietnam. Frank felt that the best way to find out the truth about the war was to experience it firsthand. He could have opted for some cushy job away from the fighting. Instead, Frank volunteered for the Airborne, then Pathfinders.

Frank was an excellent Pathfinder and could handle any situation, regardless of how complicated or dangerous. Morever, he would literally give you the shirt off his back. He was one of the finest human beings I had the pleasure of knowing, and we were damn lucky to have him in the unit.

As I turned to look at Frank, he smiled. "You don't have to worry about Torch, Richie. I'm taking him home with me."

If anyone else had told me that, I would have thought it was a bad joke. I knew Frank, however, and could see that he was telling the truth.

I was bewildered. "What do you mean you're taking Torch home with you, Frank? I don't understand."

Frank smiled like he'd been caught with his hand in the cookie jar. "I'm going to bring Torch to stay at my father's cattle ranch in California when I DEROS in April. He'll make a good ranch dog."

I turned and glanced at Tim and some of the others. I could tell that Frank had already told them.

I was still leery. "What about Scout Dogs? They're actual members of the army and not allowed to go home!"

Frank's smile grew wider. "Torch doesn't fall in that category. There is a lot of paperwork, red tape, and of course a large fee, but it can be done."

Tim chimed in. "You know Frank, Richie. He's already researched it. If Frank says it can be done, it can be done."

I could not describe to anyone the elation and relief I felt at that particular moment. If everything worked out,

Torch would be safe in California in four months' time. Silently I prayed that Frank would pull it off.

The next few days flew by, and before long it was time to say farewell to everyone. I had an incredibly tough time saying good-bye to Torch. It was almost as if he could understand what was happening. I knew that no matter how long I lived, I would never forget him. My sadness was lessened considerably knowing that Frank would try his best to get Torch back to the U.S.

It was not easy saying good-bye to any of the guys, but some of the farewells were especially difficult, guys like Joe Bolick, Mitch, Larry, Tim (Poptop) Alicoate, Frankie Farino, Buz Harding, Frank Procella, and most of all Ron. At least Ron and I would be linking up in September, to possibly join the merchant marine. All of those guys were like my family, even Lieutenant Wilberding and Captain Chase. In a way, some of them were even closer than family.

Those guys knew me better than anyone, and each one of them taught me something. Their friendships and experiences also left me with memories that I knew would never compare to anything else in life. As I said my good-byes, we all said it was only until we met again. We all knew, however, that it wasn't true. Maybe saying that we would meet again made our departures easier. In reality, this would be the last time we would ever see each other.

As I shook Ron's hand, tears welled in my eyes. I tried desperately not to let my voice quiver. "I'll see you in September."

Ron's eyes watered as well. "Roger that, Pumpkin Pie. Be careful landing all those student pilots."

I chuckled. "You be careful LRPing around. Hell! If I know you, you'll end up honor graduate at Recondo School and a LRP team leader before you know it."

Ron sensed my concern. "I'm doing the right thing; it's what I want."

We hugged each other and I walked away. I didn't look back.

My orders had me reporting to Bien Hoa and flying out of Vietnam on the sixth of December with a thirty-day leave at home. My stateside assignment was to Fort Rucker, Alabama, home of the Army Aviation School. I was assigned to the 53d Aviation Battalion, Company E, 30th Infantry (LRP)/5th Infantry Detachment (Airborne Pathfinder). For my remaining nine months in the army I would be supporting and landing student helicopter pilots.

I caught a flight on an air force C-130 from Hue/Phu Bai to Bien Hoa. At Bien Hoa, I stayed a couple of days for out-processing. Since almost everyone in the division had deployed to Vietnam at the same time a year earlier, we were all leaving for home at the same time with the exception of those who had been seriously wounded or killed. Unfortunately, we had over fifteen hundred men killed. The number of wounded was far greater. Although it was gratifying to see a few old faces I knew in other units, it was disturbing to note how many more were absent. Those who were present seemed to have aged considerably in just one year.

The day before departure we were given a silver 101st Airborne Division unit coin for combat service with the division. The souvenir meant a lot to me and I have cherished it always.

Ultimately, the time arrived to board our plane, commonly referred to as the "freedom bird." Everyone remained solemn as we stood in a single file waiting for the airman to escort us to the aircraft. More than one story had circulated about soldiers walking to the aircraft their last few minutes in Vietnam only to be killed by incoming enemy mortar fire. Although I was sure the story was bullshit, it did cause me a twinge of anxiety. Finally an enlisted airman waved us toward the plane.

My eyes squinted as I walked out of the shade and onto the tarmac. It was midmorning and the sun was beating down as relentless as always. Beads of sweat were already forming on my forehead. It was hard to believe that in a few moments my nostrils would breathe in air free of the pungent smells of war and the other wretched odors of Vietnam.

I glanced back for one last look and noticed a group of new guys off to my left. They were nervously standing around in their brand-new fatigues and shiny clean faces. I wondered how many of them would be killed or wounded in the upcoming year. They were probably wondering the same thing. My eyes turned back to the front and gazed past our airplane and across the runway. Two jet fighters revved their engines, waiting for authorization to take off and help some unit in trouble.

As I stepped up onto the metal stairs to board the plane, the soldier in front of me whispered, "Look! A round eye! Damn, what a sight!"

I gazed up. Sure enough, there was an American flight attendant, welcoming soldiers inside the aircraft. It sure was nice to see an American girl. She looked so wholesome and clean. The whole scene looked so out of place. Suddenly, going home felt like going to another planet. We all stumbled, fumbled, and mumbled to our seats, all the while gaping with our mouths hanging open at the round-eyed American women.

Finally the pilot's voice blared over the intercom. "Gentlemen! Please fasten your seat belts. In a moment we'll be taxiing to the runway for takeoff."

Not only did everyone quit talking, everyone quit moving. My body was as rigid as stone. I held my breath. The engines grew louder as the plane raced down the runway. I am sure it was only a few seconds, but it seemed like many minutes. Suddenly we heard the distinct *thump* as the aircraft's wheels left the ground and lifted the plane into the air.

Everyone on board screamed in unison. I heard my own voice yell with the rest. We did it! We were heading home. We had survived our time in Vietnam. It was not a dream; it was for real.

I settled back in the seat and my mind drifted into an ocean of thoughts. I remembered the flight to Vietnam from Fort Campbell and recalled how frightened I was on the first combat assault that Joe Bolick and I went in on. I remembered the fighting at Bien Hoa during Tet, with the NVA running across the airstrip and the enormous mushroom cloud that sprouted when the ammo dump exploded. God, it seemed so long ago, but the memories were as clear as if they had just happened.

I tried to get some sleep but just couldn't as my mind raced, reliving flying as door gunner during the Battle for Song Be City, flying out to the A Shau in the little bubble helicopter, and the mission on top of the mountain in Laos supporting Special Forces. I thought back to when we first arrived at Camp Eagle and it was just the Pathfinders and LRPs securing the entire division area and the time I was attached to the Tiger Force.

I knew that I would never forget the lessons I'd learned at Recondo School or while serving with the South Vietnamese Airborne. The names Bastogne, Vehgel, and Brick would be forever engraved on my brain, as would be the faces of the men I served with, especially those who had died. I felt an extreme sense of honor and pride at having served with such men.

I don't know how much time had elapsed as I reminisced on the past year. I was finally feeling sleepy. I felt good, proud of myself. It would feel so great to get home, serve my final nine months in the army, and get back into civilian life.

Little did I know that a year and a half later, I would be back in Vietnam again.

Glossary

Ammo: Ammunition

AO: Area of operation

ARVN: Army of the Republic of Vietnam

ASAP: As soon as possible

Beaucoup: French word for many, commonly used by the Vietnamese

Berm: A built-up area surrounding a fortification, such as a rise in the ground or a dirt parapet

B-52: Long-range bomber capable of dropping tons of five-hundred-pound bombs

CA: Combat assault

Cammies: Camouflage fatigues

Charlie: Enemy soldier

C&C ship: Command and control helicopter

Cherry: A person who has completed only the five required jumps in jump school

CID: Criminal investigation division

Claymore: M18A1 antipersonnel mine composed of C-4 explosive propelling seven hundred steel balls outward in a sixty-degree arc and lethal at fifty meters

Clerks and jerks: Rear-echelon personnel

CO: Commander

Commo: Abbreviation for communication

Conex: A large, steel shipping container measuring approximately six feet by eight feet and six feet in height

CP: Command post

DEROS: Date of Estimated Return from Overseas

Dinks: Enemy soldiers

DMZ: Demilitarized zone. The area separating North and South Vietnam

Dustoff: Call sign for medical evacuation helicopter

E&E: Escape and evasion

FAC: Forward air controller. Pilot of a small, fixed-wing plane that marks the target for and controls air strikes

Fire in the hole: A traditional warning shouted before an explosive device is detonated

FO: Forward observer

Fourth Point of Contact: The fourth point of contact when performing a parachute landing fall is the buttocks

Frag: Hand grenade

FSB: Fire support base

Gooks: Enemy soldiers

Grunt: Infantryman

Horn: Radio handset

I Corps: The northernmost of the four separate military zones in South Vietnam.

John Wayne bar: A round, chocolate-covered coconut bar found in a C ration

KIA: Killed in action

Klick: A term used by soldiers meaning a thousand meters in distance; a kilometer

LBE: Load-bearing equipment

Leg: Nonairborne personnel

Little people: Used fondly when referring to oriental allies such as South Vietnamese, Cambodians, or Montagnards

LRP ration: An experimental lightweight food packet consisting of a dehydrated meal

LT: Lieutenant; pronounced "ell-tee" in dialogue

LZ: Landing zone

Making contact: Engaging the enemy

Medevac: Medical Evacuation Helicopter

Montagnards: The tribal hill people of Vietnam

MOS: Military Occupational Specialty

NCO: Noncommissioned Officer

NVA: North Vietnamese Army

OJT: On-the-job training

OP: Observation post

PLF: Parachute landing fall

PZ: Pickup zone

R&R: Rest and relaxation

Recon: Reconnaissance

REMF: Rear-echelon motherfucker

Roger: Term used in radio communications: "I have received and understood all of your last transmission"

RON: Remain overnight

RTO: Radio Operator

Ruck: Abbreviated version of rucksack

Sapper: A specially trained enemy soldier who has the mission of sneaking into areas and destroying targets

Sitrep: Situation report

Slick: Helicopter

Sortie: One aircraft making one takeoff and one landing

Starlight Scope: An image intensifier that uses reflective light from the moon and stars, enabling one to "see" at night. The scope could be easily mounted to the M-16 rifle

Steel Pot: Helmet

Strobe Light: A small, high-intensity marking light

Tail Boom: The long rear portion of the helicopter

TO&E: Table of organization and equipment

292 Antenna: A large antenna used by the military to increase the range of tactical radio sets

VC: Viet Cong

Victor Charlie: phonetic call sign for VC (Viet Cong)

VS-17 Panel: A brightly colored panel used by troops on the ground to signal their position to friendly aircraft

Wait-a-minute vines: A densely growing vine covered with thorns that made walking through them quite difficult

Wasted: Killed

WIA: Wounded in action

Wilco: Term used in radio communications: "will comply"

Index

397

Reconnaissance deep behind enemy lines
was all in a night's work...

WAR PAINT
The 1st Infantry Division's LRP/Ranger Company in Fierce Combat in Vietnam

by Bill Goshen

The eyes and ears of the Big Red One, America's
most famous infantry division, had teeth too—
the Long Range Patrol. Bill Goshen tells it like it
was because he was there, a member of one of
these elite hunter/killer units that spread fear in
the hearts of the VC and NVA.

Published by Ballantine Books.
Available at a bookstore near you.

Look for Gary Linderer's two books on LRRPs, LRPs and Rangers in gut-chilling, extreme combat far behind enemy lines. When every mission may well have been their last, these brave men went willingly into harm's way with only their skill, sense of duty, personal weapons and each other between themselves and death.

Phantom Warriors Book I and Book II: LRRPs, LRPs, and Rangers in Vietnam

---

by Gary A. Linderer

Published by Ballantine Books.
Available at a bookstore near you.

*The only day-to-day account of this
elite combat unit in Vietnam*

Diary of an Airborne Ranger
A LRRP's Year in the Combat Zone

by Frank Johnson

When nineteen-year-old Frank Johnson arrived in
Vietnam in 1969, he volunteered for the elite L
Company Rangers of the 101st Airborne Division,
a long range reconnaissance patrol (LRRP) unit.
He kept a secret diary, a practice forbidden by the
military to protect the security of the LRRP operations. Now, more than three decades later, those
hastily written pages offer a rare look at the daily
operations of one of the most courageous units that
waged war in Vietnam. Johnson's account is
unique in the annals of Vietnam literature. It is a
timeless testimony to the heroism of the LRRPs
who dared to risk it all.

Published by Ballantine Books.
Available at a bookstore near you.

Forged in blood and courage, sacrifice and survival, in a jungle war none of the soldiers who experienced it will ever forget, this is a true story you won't want to miss.

Rites of Passage: Odyssey of a Grunt

by Robert Peterson

Robert Peterson arrived in Vietnam in the fall of 1966, a young American ready to serve his country and seize his destiny. What happened in that jungle war would change his life forever. Peterson vividly relives the tense patrols in the Viet Cong-infested Central Highlands, the fierce ambushes and enemy charges. From this deadly hell he reveals the special brotherhood formed between these brave young men.

Published by Ballantine Books.
Available at a bookstore near you.